Donors, Democracy and Development in Africa

Mark Simpson

Donors, Democracy and Development in Africa

Western Aid and Political Repression

palgrave
macmillan

Mark Simpson
School of Advanced Study
University of London
London, UK

ISBN 978-3-031-74916-2 ISBN 978-3-031-74917-9 (eBook)
https://doi.org/10.1007/978-3-031-74917-9

This Palgrave Macmillan imprint is published by the registered company Springer Nature Switzerland AG.
The registered company address is: Gewerbestrasse 11, 6330 Cham, Switzerland

To Natalie Inês, Nicholas Tiago and Ellie for demonstrating civic virtue every day in their work; to Ponia for showing me the fruits of both perseverance and patience; and to Allison for everything of value we share.

Preface

The origins of this book lie in efforts before, during and since the COVID pandemic to make sense of the relentless global rise of authoritarianism. Aspects of democratic regression were emerging in age-old democracies in the West, and more noticeably so in some of the newer democratic systems of former Eastern bloc states which had appeared to have become robust liberal polities. Some developing countries, which had undergone transitions from repressive rule even before those in Eastern Europe, also displayed symptoms of backsliding. These authoritarian governments adopted similar methods to undermine checks and balances and resist constraints on the exercise of power, hobbling political oppositions and restricting the efforts of independent media and organised civil society groups to scrutinise the decision-making of executive branches.

To what extent were the countries of Sub-Saharan Africa (SSA) part of this regression? Did the governments of those African democracies which emerged in the aftermath of the Cold War also use the health emergency to strengthen their hold on power, and what was happening there to political freedoms and civil and human rights? An additional (and for this author more pressing question) was what was occurring in those African states characterised by truncated transitions, i.e. ones where the trappings of multi-party democracy had been put in place, buttressed by constitutions containing provisions that catered for political transitions and respect for civil and human rights, but which to all intents and purposes had remained for decades under the de facto and repressive rule of single parties, and often the same leaders. Had they experienced further regression as part of the global wave of democratic backsliding?

Underlying such interrogations was a concern to examine what role international aid had played, and continued to play, in either assisting or impeding political liberalisation. As someone who had lived through democratic transitions in several African and non-African countries, working in both international development and peacekeeping, the impact of Western aid flows to such authoritarian African regimes was of particular interest. Three such regimes (Uganda, Ethiopia and Rwanda) all benefitted from significant amounts of Western aid over decades, ranking close to the top by volume and relative economic importance of aid received, and repeatedly lauded by Western donor agencies as model aid recipients. For this reason, they were ideal case studies to analyse links between the inflow of external resources and the state of their political governance.

The pandemic had barely abated before what was already characterised as a New Cold War took a turn for the worse with Russia's invasion of Ukraine in February 2022. Heightened tensions between the West and Moscow (in conjunction with deteriorating relations between the West and Beijing), introduced new dynamics into the interactions between Western countries and Uganda, Ethiopia and Rwanda. Efforts by the West to isolate Russia economically and politically were accompanied by initiatives to secure African support for condemnatory resolutions in international bodies.

There was a strong sense of déjà vu. As was the case throughout the Cold War, and despite initial indications of enthusiasm in the early post-Cold War years for the employment of aid in support of democratisation in SSA as a key American foreign policy objective for the region, this goal appears to have again taken a back seat to Washington's other core interests. Coupled with deals recently struck between London and Paris and Rwanda which triggered new and substantial flows of development assistance to Kigali, and with continued Western aid being disbursed to Uganda and Ethiopia, elements of continuity rapidly overtook what for a brief moment during the pandemic had seemed to be signs of rupture. Such ties continue to help these regimes remain in power. Needless to say, the implications of the latter are of particular concern to those brave political opposition figures, democracy and human rights activists, and members of the independent media, who continue to demand change from inside those countries.

What started out as a solitary exercise in interrogating the news gradually took on the form of a manuscript, given shape by exchanges in academic and media settings on events in these three countries, and when questions were raised as to why they continued to be successful aid recipients. Such exchanges had a number of consequences. Firstly, it became clear there was a broad interest in these countries and the contentious issues they raised. This led to the idea of analysing these regimes in a way that balanced the demands of academia with the interests of a wider readership. A light touch has been adopted in relation to existing academic literature and theories, despite the constant temptation to go down the manifold 'rabbit holes' which appeared along the way. Secondly, the kinds of 'why' and 'what' questions posed required analysis that is situated within the recent history of individual countries, including the history of their relations with the West, and the adoption of various disciplinary lenses to enable comparisons and find meaningful common denominators. Such considerations have informed the approach taken.

If the result of this effort is that it helps a Western readership to better appreciate the nature of the ruling parties in the three African countries, the role their aid relations with Western donors have played in their development, and on that basis to pressure for reforms, then the book will have met a key objective. If it helps the citizens of those African countries fighting for change to deepen their understanding of both the positive and negative impacts of Western development assistance on their well-being, then the recompense will be even greater.

London, UK — Mark Simpson

Acknowledgements

As with all such undertakings, I have accumulated debts in the course of researching and writing this book to many persons who may not even be aware of their contributions. I have continued to stay in touch with colleagues and friends from an extended stint in Zimbabwe between 2005 and 2010, a period during which one of the great political, economic and social collapses in post-independence Africa occurred. This experience informed how issues raised in this book have been framed and analysed. Dr Godfrey Kanyenze's research into the devastating effects of Zimbabwe's protracted authoritarian rule on the welfare of the country's citizens continues to inspire, as do Dr Daniel Ndlela's efforts to highlight the role of inherited inequalities in the development process. Professor Tony Hawkins continues to expose the economic falsehoods pedalled by the ruling party in Zimbabwe. I have gained much over the years from exchanges on financial economics with Professor Daniel Makina of the University of South Africa and with Dr Dale Doré who from his current Nordic fastness continues to fight the good fight for his African homeland. All my Zimbabwean former colleagues have each in their way reminded me of what can happen when regime survival considerations trump all others. Over many years I have also had the privilege of having Professor Roger Norton of Texas A&M University as a work colleague and friend. He and I have regularly exchanged ideas on a wide range of development issues, though I have no doubt that the profit from such discussions disproportionately accrued to me. Jason Calder, a former colleague from the Carter Center, continues to work on conflict resolution, election observation and development issues and has shared useful insights from his work. Exchanges and get-togethers with Gaurang Naik, Tony Fernandes and Raj Chandaria echoed in many ways those of our BSc (Econ) studies at the London School of Economics, helping take the edge off some of the frustrations of COVID restrictions and serving as a reminder of the continued importance of *rerum cognoscere causas*. Professor John Calabrese of the American University in Washington, D.C., introduced refreshing amounts of levity into our communications during the dark days of the pandemic and subsequent assaults on American democracy. Professor Spyros Economides was a shining example of fortitude in adversity and thereby indirectly helped me to persevere. The Institute of Commonwealth Studies at Senate House has continued to provide a most welcoming environment for research, and I am grateful to its Director Professor Kingsley Abbot, and my Institute colleagues, for opportunities to share my own research findings and to benefit from those of others. Isobel Cowper-Coles at Palgrave Macmillan helped steer this book with consummate professionalism to its final destination. Finally, and as always, Dr Allison Beattie not only did much heavy lifting on the text, but more importantly served as a constant reminder that there was a place for effective altruism in the business of international development.

Contents

About the Author

Mark Simpson is currently a senior research fellow at the Institute of Commonwealth Studies in the University of London's School of Advanced Study. He has worked for the United Nations Development Programme in Mozambique, Zimbabwe and Botswana, the United Nations Department of Peacekeeping Operations in Angola and East Timor, and the Carter Center. More recently, as part of a European Union programme, he was the Principal Advisor to the late Prime Minister of the Kingdom of Eswatini. He is the co-author with Professor Tony Hawkins of *The Primacy of Regime Survival: State Fragility and Economic Destruction in Zimbabwe* (Palgrave Macmillan 2018).

Abbreviations

AAI	African American Institute (US)
AAPO	All Amhara People's Organization
ACOTA	Africa Contingency Operations Training and Assistance
ADP	Amhara Democratic Party
AGOA	Africa Growth and Opportunity Act
ADF	Allied Democratic Forces
ANDM	Amhara National Democratic Movement
APRRP	African Peacekeeping Rapid Response Partnership
AU	Africa Union
BJP	*Bharatiya Janata Party*
BPSTA	British Peace Support Team Africa
BWI	Bretton Woods Institution
CA	Constituent Assembly (Ethiopia)
CAA	Citizenship Amendment Act (India)
CC	Constitutional Conference (Ethiopia)
CCI	Council of Constitutional Inquiry (Ethiopia)
CDR	Coalition for the Defence of the Republic (Rwanda)
CHRI	Commonwealth Human Rights Initiative
CHOGM	Commonwealth Heads of Government Meeting
COVID-19	Coronavirus disease of 2019
CR	Council of Representatives (Ethiopia)
CSO	Civil Society Organisation
CUD	Coalition for Unity and Democracy
DAC	Development Assistance Committee of the OECD
DANIDA	Danish International Development Agency
DFID	Department for International Development (UK)
DoC	Drivers of Change

DOD	Department of Defence (US)
DP	Democratic Party (Uganda)
DRC	Democratic Republic of Congo
EOM	Election Observation Mission
EPDM/ANDM	Ethiopian People's Democratic Movement/Amhara National Democratic Movement
EPLF	Eritrean People's Liberation Front
EPRDF	*Ethiopian People's Revolutionary Democratic Front*
EPRP	*Ethiopian People's Revolutionary Party*
ESDL	Ethiopian Somali Democratic League
EU	European Union
EU EOM	European Union Election Observation Mission
EUFM	EU Follow-up Mission (to Uganda)
FCO	Foreign and Commonwealth Office (UK)
FDI	Foreign Direct Investment
FDRE	Federal Democratic Republic of Ethiopia
FIS	*Front Islamique du Salut*
FRELIMO	Liberation Front of Mozambique
FRONASA	Front for National Salvation (Uganda)
GBS	General Budget Support
GDP	Gross Domestic Product
GNI	Gross National Income
HRW	Human Rights Watch
IDA	International Development Association
IMET	International Military Education and Training Programme (US)
IMF	International Monetary Fund
INGOs	International Non-Governmental Organisations
IPEP	International Panel of Eminent Persons
ICU	Islamic Courts Union
LRA	Lord's Resistance Army
MCA	Millennium Challenge Account
MCC	Millennium Challenge Corporation
MCP	Malawi Congress Party
MDGs	Millennium Development Goals
MDR	*Mouvement Démocratique Républicain*
MDRP	Multi-Country Demobilization and Reintegration Program
MEISON	All-Ethiopia Socialist Movement
MEP	Member of the European Parliament
MINUSCA	United Nations Multidimensional Integrated Stabilization Mission in the Central African Republic

MINUSMA	United Nations Multidimensional Integrated Stabilization Mission in Mali
MINUSTAH	United Nations Stabilization Mission in Haiti
MLLT	Marxist-Leninist League of Tigray
MLSTP	Movement for the Liberation of São Tomé and Príncipe (MLSTP)
MMD	Movement for Multi-party Democracy (Zambia)
MOD	Ministry of Defence (UK)
MPD	Movement for Democracy (Cape Verde)
MPLA	Popular Movement for the Liberation of Angola
MRCD	*Mouvement Rwandais pour le Changement Démocratique* (Rwandan Movement for Democratic Change)
MRNDD	*Mouvement républicain national pour la démocratie et le développement* (National Republican Movement for Democracy and Development)
NATO	North Atlantic Treaty Organization
NDI	National Democratic Institute (US)
NEC	National Enterprise Corporation (Uganda)
NEC	National Electoral Commission
NFPO	National Consultative Forum of Political Organisations (Rwanda)
NGOs	Non-governmental Organisations
NRA	National Resistance Army
NRM	National Resistance Movement (Uganda)
OAU	Organization of African Unity
ODA	Official Development Assistance
OECD	Organisation for Economic Co-operation and Development
OLF	Oromo Liberation Front
ONLF	Ogaden National Liberation Front
OPDO	Oromo Peoples Democratic Organization
PARMEHUTU	*Parti du Mouvement de l'Émancipation Hutu* (Hutu Emancipation Movement Party)
PDRE	People's Democratic Republic of Ethiopia
PFM	Public Financial Management
PKK	Kurdish Workers' Party
PDR	Party for Democracy and Renewal (Rwanda)
PMAC	Provisional Military Administration Council (Ethiopia)
PP	Prosperity Party (Ethiopia)
PRC	People's Republic of China
PRSPs	Poverty Reduction Strategy Papers
R2P	Responsibility to Protect
RANU	Rwandan Alliance for National Unity

RDB	Rwanda Development Board
RENAMO	Mozambican National Resistance
RIB	Rwanda Investigation Bureau
RNC	Rwandan National Congress
RPA	Rwandan Patriotic Army
RPF	Rwanda Patriotic Front
SAP	Structural Adjustment Programmes
SDGs	Sustainable Development Goals
SEPDM	Southern Ethiopian People's Democratic Movement
SIDA	Swedish International Development Cooperation Agency
SSA	Sub-Saharan Africa
SSR	Security Sector Reform
TLF	Tigray Liberation Front
TFG	Transitional Federal Government (Somalia)
TNA	Transitional National Assembly (Rwanda)
TPLF	Tigray People's Liberation Front
UEDF	United Ethiopian Democratic Forces
UN	United Nations
UNAMID	United Nations-African Union Mission in Darfur
UNAMIR	United Nations Assistance Mission for Rwanda
UNAR	*Union Nationale Rwandaise* (Rwandese National Union)
UNDP	United Nations Development Programme
UNGA	United Nations General Assembly
UNIP	United National Independence Party (Zambia)
UNITA	National Union for the Total Independence of Angola
UNLF	Uganda National Liberation Front
UNMISS	United Nations Mission in South Sudan
UPC	United People's Congress (Uganda)
UPDF	Uganda Peoples' Defence Forces
UPM	Uganda Patriotic Movement
USAID	United States Agency for International Development
V-Dem	Varieties of Democracy Institute (Sweden)
WHO	World Health Organization
WPE	Workers' Party of Ethiopia
WTO	World Trade Organization

CHAPTER 1

Contexts Controversies and Commonalities

This book focuses on three important and widely studied regimes in Sub-Saharan Africa, namely Uganda, Ethiopia and Rwanda. In order to contribute to extant research on the role of Western aid in the maintenance of authoritarian governance in Africa, a good place to start is to situate the provision of Western aid to these specific countries within the wider context of Western development assistance to Sub-Saharan Africa as a whole since the end of the Cold War, and the significance of such external resources to the peoples and governments of the region. Another important initial step is to place these interactions between Western and African governments within ongoing scholarly debates about the effects of aid on an extensive range of variables in beneficiary countries.

Both comparative and multi-disciplinary approaches have been adopted in analysing changes in Western donor policy, as well as events in the three African countries. The former approach helps identify any significant differences and similarities in the development of the three countries and the role of Western aid in shaping those trajectories. The latter, through the adoption of perspectives from a range of disciplines, enables a comprehensive and nuanced understanding of those factors contributing to both change and continuity.

M. Simpson, *Donors, Democracy and Development in Africa*,
https://doi.org/10.1007/978-3-031-74917-9_1

All three countries have occupied prominent positions in the development policies of the Western donor community towards Africa for many years. The extended timeframe of interactions between them, and the availability of information covering this prolonged period, warrants the adoption of a historical approach to the study of relations between the parties, to changes within donor countries and most importantly to the historical evolution of the governing regimes in those African countries, focusing on those factors which had an effect on the governance styles they adopted. The update provided in this book on the current state of these donor-recipient interactions can only be properly understood against the backdrop of the earlier elements of change and continuity which characterised both the aid relationships and the authoritarian features of all three African regimes.

The Place of Aid in the West's Relations with Africa

Following Africa's decolonisation, and during and since the end of the Cold War, development assistance has been a prominent and enduring feature of the interactions between Western governments and those of Sub-Saharan Africa (SSA). Western resources aimed at promoting development in the region have been disbursed by the bilateral agencies of donor countries and their regional institutions such as the European Union (EU), through multilateral institutions such as the World Bank, the International Monetary Fund and UN agencies whose major funders are Western governments, as well as a wide range of Western non-state actors. The West has also sought to assist development in SSA through trade liberalisation schemes which grant African economies preferential access to Western markets, such as the various arrangements between Africa and the EU and the US The stated objectives of these schemes are to improve Africa's integration into the global economy, increase the export revenues of African countries and assist with their economic structural transition to higher productivity and more skill-intensive activities which are meant to lead to rising incomes and living standards.

SSA's greater development needs have meant that for decades the region has been at the centre of the attention of Western development actors, and this has translated into the high levels of resources disbursed for the region such that it became the world's most 'aid-intensive region'; between 1990 and 2020, net annual Official Development Assistance (ODA) to SSA increased from US$17.8 billion to nearly US$67 billion

(World Bank 2024). One consequence of the magnitude of such North-South flows is that levels of 'aid dependency' amongst African recipients has been significantly greater than other regions of the developing world. Since 1960 ODA has consistently represented a higher percentage of the Gross Domestic Product (GDP) of the SSA region than, for example, the South Asia region and has accounted for a greater share of national budgets and government expenditure. In the case of Gross National Income (GNI) per capita, in 2022 the SSA region's average stood at 49 per cent, as compared to South Asia's 8 per cent (World Bank 2024). Therefore, given the volumes of aid received by SSA countries compared to other parts of the developing world, such assistance has played a greater role in providing African beneficiary governments with the necessary resources to implement their political, social and economic governance plans.

Western decisions on the allocation of development aid (who gets what, why, when and how), and the ways African beneficiaries manage the resources received and what results are achieved, have loomed larger in national decision-making on both sides of the relationship than in the case of Western ties with other parts of the developing world. The significance of Western development assistance to countries in SSA, and the pressures on donor agencies to show positive results for their outlays, has meant that if specific African countries were identified as the best locations for donors to invest resources based on the prospect of solid rates of return, there was a strong compulsion to identify winners and to grant them preferential treatment. At the same time, given the importance of such external resources to recipient governments, the scope for tensions in such privileged relations was also greater than in situations of lower levels of aid dependency. The interests of donors in supporting those countries to achieve specific goals, and that of recipient governments in ensuring their own priorities remained paramount (and which may or may not have coincided with those of Western agencies), meant mutually acceptable compromises had to be regularly negotiated.

Since Western aid has been critical to the political economies over which those privileged African governments preside, they have had to perfect their 'aid diplomacy' skills.[1] Their strategic goal has been to safeguard their position at the centre of the positive attention they receive from Western donors, and thereby guarantee the disbursement of additional aid. They have done so by ensuring the progress they report to their benefactors is considered to both validate the initial Western decisions to grant them aid and most importantly that such progress is seen by their Western backers to outweigh any identifiable shortfalls in other areas. On the donor side, what kinds of progress they had agreed with their beneficiaries were important meant their aid relationship with these African governments was gradually circumscribed to an increasingly restricted set of acceptable performance criteria.

Aid and Its Discontents: Variants of the Debates

In parallel with the growth of the Western development enterprise, a number of critical voices have questioned the positive role of aid in development. One pioneering aid sceptic was P.T. Bauer (1972), who by the early 1970s was already raising doubts that aid helped (and according to some champions of aid that it was absolutely essential) to trigger growth and reduce poverty. At the risk of oversimplification, the debate between Western advocates of aid such as Sachs (2005) who have argued that a key requirement for the elimination of extreme poverty is a major increase in aid and contemporary aid sceptics such as Easterly (2001), Moyo (2010) and Deaton (2013) has been largely dominated by economists, and with extensive recourse to econometrics. Both sides use increasingly longer time periods, better data and models with modified specifications to gather evidence to buttress their respective positions. The focus of this debate, one which continues to be mired in controversies, has largely been on the specific area of economic growth and the extent to which aid has either positive or negative effects on this key aspect of development.[2]

The majority of aid sceptics (best viewed as aid critics) nevertheless accept that certain kinds of aid have been effective in terms of meeting their objectives. Examples of this include humanitarian assistance, or those resources targeted at public goods such as some forms of health provision, with widespread vaccination and other types of infectious disease control programmes having led to major improvements in the welfare of populations in developing countries. Rather than the complete abolition of aid flows, some critics have made the case for specific reforms to existing aid systems to improve their effectiveness. For example, Easterly has argued that one of the main problems with aid is that it does not reach its intended target, namely the poorest. He has proposed a range of remedial measures to address the problem, foremost amongst which the need for independent evaluations of aid agencies and the resources they provide in order to better establish what works and what does not, and thereby strengthen accountability (Easterly 2007).

Given that the central concern of aid sceptic economists has been on what they see as its questionable role in fostering economic growth, some argue (such as Moyo in the case of Africa) that development assistance has become an 'aid curse' and had a strongly counter-productive impact on growth. Amongst other harmful effects, critics suggest that development assistance has encouraged wasteful rent-seeking behaviour, facilitated corruption, distorted domestic politics by weakening transparency and domestic accountability of aid recipient governments as they come to view donor partners as their most important constituency and insulated recipient governments from internal pressures to remedy harmful economic policies. In sum, they see aid as having weakened the incentives for aid-dependent states to use the resources at their disposal judiciously to expand, diversify and modernise their economies, invest in productive infrastructure, support market development and encourage entrepreneurship and an export orientation. More generally, they suggest that aid has reduced the pressures on governments to establish and sustain social contracts based on the provision of public goods and implementation of sound economic and social policies in exchange for citizen compliance with obligations such as the payment of taxes. Aid replaces the need for tax collection, thereby weakening pressures for better accountability.

Another variant of the aid debate is concerned with its effects on the political governance of recipient countries. This to some extent overlaps with the focus of those economists associated with aid scepticism, as scholars such as Easterly and Deaton have also drawn attention to the role of aid in supporting autocratic rulers. Those who have engaged most extensively in this debate have sought to establish causality between aid flows and specific outcomes such as democratic transitions, the consolidation of authoritarian regimes and the status of political and civil rights in aid-recipient countries. While extensive quantitative work has been undertaken, often using regression analysis, to generate empirical evidence on the impact of aid on levels of democracy, it may be said that in the round such efforts remain largely inconclusive. Some findings suggest a small positive correlation between aid and levels of democracy (Kersting and Kilby 2014). Others, however, find no evidence to support the argument that aid promotes democracy (Knack 2004). Part of the reason for such inconclusiveness lies in the lack of definitional clarity regarding both democracy and aid, with the result that any conclusions based on data sets only reflect how these concepts are defined. Such problems are revisited in a recent and comprehensive review of existing literature and evidence on the impact of overall aid on democracy, and which analyses the specific impact of democracy promotion aid. It is significant that in terms of the latter—that is, assistance targeted at core democratic processes and institutions such as elections, political parties, media and pro-democracy civil society organisations—the research was able to establish positive effects for such aid on democratic outcomes (Gisselquist et al. 2021).

More fine-grained evidence on the relationship between aid and democracy has been generated by country case studies, including several focused on African states, such as those in the edited collection of Hagmann and Reyntjens (Hagmann and Reyntjens 2016). This examines the multiple ways Western aid has helped sustain and reinforce the authoritarian systems of specific aid recipients, identifying examples of what is characterised as 'collusion' between donors and de facto single-party African regimes. At the forefront of concerns driving such research is the need to understand why and how—notwithstanding repeated statements by Western capitals on the importance attached to democracy and human rights in their aid programmes—such assistance to repressive governments has taken place (the motivations of both donors and authoritarian aid beneficiaries being central to the research), and what the effects of such support has been on political freedoms and civil and human rights in specific countries. This research has helped fill what has been until recently a glaring gap in the literature on aid and its effects and raised a number of issues that merit further examination.

The Importance of Historical Perspectives

Uganda, Ethiopia and Rwanda have for decades occupied centre stage in Western donor policies and programmes in Africa and benefitted disproportionately in the scale of development assistance they have been granted. They are particularly worthy of study because of what at first sight is a puzzling and glaring disconnect between the levels of Western largesse they have enjoyed for many years, and the fact they have invariably performed poorly in terms of the political freedoms and civil rights of their citizens. According to the annual reports produced by Freedom House (possibly the most widely referenced Western source on global trends in the enjoyment of such rights),[3] and using 2000 as a baseline year, all three countries have been repeatedly ranked as either 'Not Free', or at best 'Partly Free'.

In addition, there is the remarkable durability of their authoritarian systems, and the extended periods in office of their leaders (in particular Kagame in Rwanda and Museveni in Uganda). While in the early post-Cold War years the latter were seen by the West as the foremost representatives of the continent's reformist 'new leaders', ones committed to turning a new page for their countries, the fact that both have been in power for decades (and nearly four decades in the case of Museveni) means that any 'novelty' initially associated with them has long expired. They have so successfully clung to power they have come to resemble Cold War-era African strongmen such as Mobutu, rather than, as the West had originally hoped, protagonists of the liberalisation of their political and economic systems, and for establishing the necessary conditions for peaceful democratic political transitions.

The history of aid relations between these countries and their donors during and since the end of the Cold War, and more recently in the context of the West's ongoing 'War on Terror', has been characterised by change but more importantly remarkable continuity. In Chap. 3, these features are situated in the broad historical record of the West's interactions with Africa during the Cold War. The chapter assesses the role of aid and the relative importance attached to the promotion of democracy in Western foreign policies during the competition between the superpowers, particularly the positions taken by the key Western players in Africa, namely the US, the UK and France. Such analysis serves as a baseline for evaluating more recent Western commitments to promote liberal values through development assistance, and again serves to highlight strong elements of continuity.

It is useful to revisit the international context in which these three African countries, and their respective regimes, were first embraced by the West. The early 1990s constituted a moment of euphoric Western triumphalism. Official pronouncements from many Western capitals, and in particular Washington, regarding the post-Cold War world they saw taking shape were characterised by remarkable self-confidence in the superiority and universal validity of Western liberal political and economic thought and praxis. At the same time, there was growing awareness and concern, both in Western capitals and in SSA, of the problems accumulated by the latter during the Cold War, and which included its dire economic performance, its regression in key welfare indicators and the existence of widespread armed conflict.

As examined in Chap. 4, the early to mid-1990s was when the 'new leaders' of Ethiopia, Uganda and Rwanda first came to be viewed positively in Western capitals. They appeared to share the West's political, economic and social values, as well as a common understanding with Western development agencies as to what constituted both development and development progress. As a result of gradual improvements in the situation in SSA in the run-up to the new millennium, interactions between Western capitals and the leaders of three African countries came to be seen as exemplary. Thereafter, these regimes sought to ensure they were always seen to be part of the prevailing Western *zeitgeist* and that donors continued to believe that both sides did indeed partake a common language and a shared set of values and goals.

At the same time, in the 1990s there were always Western voices urging caution in dealing with the 'new leaders', and who questioned the grounds for such 'Afro-optimism'. Despite such warnings, most Western capitals believed trusting partnerships had been established with the three regimes, with one consequence being that they became 'donor darlings' in terms of the Western development assistance provided. If at any given moment in time changing Western geo-strategic interests impacted on the specific kinds of aid provided, and questions were raised at to what was happening in terms of political freedoms and civil and human rights in their countries, one constant has been the continuous disbursement of large amounts of aid over extended periods, and their low levels of volatility.

A historical prism has also been adopted to examine the key characteristics of these regimes, without which neither their governance styles nor their longevity can be properly understood. Chapter 5 explores some of the legacies of their pasts, and how these ruling parties, born out of the liberation movements which had engaged in armed struggles in Uganda, Rwanda and Ethiopia, reflected the turbulent histories of their countries. In all three cases authoritarianism had been a prominent feature of colonial rule (Uganda and Rwanda), and the imperial era (Ethiopia), and was also central to the workings of the post-colonial and post-imperial governments against which these movements had taken up arms (single-party systems or military dictatorships).

Historically, all three countries suffered from high levels of inter-ethnic tension and political instability. There was also a pervasive recourse to the use of violence against opponents, both by those in power to retain it and by those seeking to gain it. In addition, the fact these ruling parties had emerged from armed insurgencies (and it could be argued that they have never fully emancipated themselves from their military past) had a number of enduring consequences. Amongst these were a continued preference for top-down, centralised and secretive decision-making, the value attributed to unquestioning obedience to directives from the centre, the laying down of single unquestionable party lines, a deep aversion to any form of dissent and disregard of the need for accountability, the prominent role played by security forces within national life and above all an intense pre-occupation with security and stability, with both of the latter over time becoming synonymous with regime maintenance. As highlighted in this chapter, such intolerance of pluralism can also be traced to the historical influence of the ideologies they were exposed to, most particularly (though to varying degrees) Marxism-Leninism, and the practices of communist states and those countries engaged in advancing forms of African Socialism. These proved to be sources of inspiration in terms of how these movements not only viewed their earlier struggles but also shaped their subsequent plans for their countries once in power, and which together reduced the possibility they would go on to establish liberal systems of political and economic governance.

A historical perspective is also required in examining the evolution of what it is argued constitutes a fundamental enabling factor for the consolidation of authoritarian rule in these three African countries, namely the international development architecture which emerged after the end of the Cold War. In the run-up to the turn of the century, an international development system took shape. As Chap. 6 details, successive international summits and compacts on development, the frameworks which emerged from these events and specific areas they focused on (as well as their silences on others), the priority targets set, the aid disbursement modalities adopted, and the rules and roles donors and aid recipients were expected to respect and adopt, all converged and led to the downgrading of democracy promotion in the aid policies of most Western donors, and the reduction of strict and time-bound political conditionalities attached to their aid.

In addition, a historical approach is essential in order to understand the ideas and concepts of development which arose post-Cold War, and which constituted a fundamental factor in the various ways the ties between Western donors and these countries evolved. The Western donor insistence that their beneficiaries should show 'ambition' in terms of their national aspirations was a key contributor to the establishment of a conducive environment for authoritarian regime entrenchment. From the point of view of Western donors, even better if those regimes drew inspiration (which they did, though selectively) from the experiences of the Asian developmental states referenced in Chap. 8. Such Western advocacy ignored the fact that such Asian growth successes were attractive to these African regimes not only because of the rapid development they had achieved, but because they had successfully maintained their authoritarian political systems. Chapter 9 explores how these African regimes used their ambitious developmental aspirations, both domestically and externally, to justify their governance styles. In this context, the various methods they adopted to cope with Western pressures on the need for decentralisation and greater popular participation in decision-making at local level are examined (Western interests in these being based on the expectation they would result in improved development outcomes). Donor-recipient dynamics around these specific issues illustrate not only how they were able to maintain a tight grip on domestic political and economic processes at all levels, but also their skills in managing Western concerns whilst simultaneously ensuring their core interests were safeguarded.

Both donors and recipient countries also agreed that for beneficiaries to receive privileged treatment, they needed to be meeting (or at least be seen to be trying to meet) standards of 'good governance'. Depending on the context, this took the form of a normative concept, a development goal, a reform agenda and a framework to assess progress. Notions of 'good governance', explored in Chap. 6, played a powerful role in Western aid policy and programmes, with development progress coming to be measured on the basis of apolitical technical criteria centred on economic and social welfare gains.

Following 9/11, as Western countries engaged in the 'War on Terror' their priorities shifted. Chapter 10 reviews the ideas which emerged on the transnational threats posed by fragile and failed states, the nexus established between security (both that of Western countries and that of aid recipients) and development and its policy implications which drove the ensuing rapid securitisation of Western aid, and its negative effects on political and civil rights. Though calls for political reform never entirely disappeared from the West's interactions with post-Cold War Africa—with Washington in particular continuing to invest in democracy promotion activities—political and civil and human rights conditionalities attached to Western development assistance were gradually diluted, with aid being withheld (and always temporarily), only in the most egregious cases of political repression and human rights abuses.

The Utility of Comparative Approaches, Multi-disciplinarity and Data Analysis

There are strong similarities in how all three African regimes set about defending their policy space against Western donor interference, and in their reactions to shifts in Western development priorities, to domestic developments in their own countries and to events in their respective regions and at a global level. By adopting a focused comparative approach based on a common set of variables, and insights from development economics, international relations, security studies, political science and law, amongst others, this analysis helps show how these regimes have adapted to, and profited from, such changes in order to preserve their hold on power.

As a contribution to existing literature on the subject, this analysis examines and links various data sets, enabling a nuanced and contextualised understanding of the evolving donor-recipient relationship over an extended period of time. The data sets used include various ODA flows by donor and recipient, economic development data, and others such as security assistance trackers. Key indicators used were drawn from composite development frameworks such as the MDGs and SDGs. Taken together, the evidence generated explains the shifts that have occurred in total volumes of Western ODA flows to these countries, variations in their composition and adjustments to disbursement modalities. The analysis also traces the relative importance attached by Western donors to changing definitions of what constitutes development progress, the principles governing partnership arrangements, and the ways these three aid-recipient countries have adjusted to, and profited from, such changes.

Chapters 7 and 8 track regime consolidation processes in the three African countries. The first focuses on how these regimes embarked on the closure of political space, how this objective reflected a deep and long-standing hostility towards any genuine form of multi-democracy and their abhorrence of dissent and strong sense of entitlement to rule in perpetuity. Across all their regimes, similar methods were used to deal with political opposition and critical voices from the media and organised civil society, and these also bear a strong resemblance to those of other authoritarian governments referenced in Chap. 2. They constructed political systems which advantaged incumbents, merging ruling party and state institutions which were meant, at least in constitutional terms, to reflect the separate characters and functions of governments and the public sector. Civil services came to be dominated by loyal ruling party cadres, with membership and demonstrations of loyalty to the ruling party unstated preconditions for professional advancement in state institutions. They reduced their legislatures to rubber-stamping entities, introduced repressive legislation to silence critical voices, revised constitutions to extend the mandates of incumbents and regularly applied targeted and punishing violence to ensure maintenance of the political status quo.

To secure advantageous outcomes, elections in Uganda, Rwanda and Ethiopia have been marked by extensive ruling party interference in the work of electoral constituency demarcation commissions and the decision-making processes of electoral supervisory bodies. As numerous election observer missions reported, these ruling parties have employed patronage for electoral purposes, ignored distinctions between ruling party personnel and state employees and public assets, engaged in the stuffing of ballot boxes and voter intimidation and when necessary excluded foreign election observer missions judged likely to be critical. Not only does the manipulation of electoral processes by these African incumbents share common features, but they also appear in the playbooks of other regimes around the world explored in detail by Cheeseman and Klaas (Cheeseman and Klaas 2018).

Comparative and multi-disciplinary approaches have been applied to the themes explored in Chap. 8, which examines how regime preservation imperatives played out in efforts to resist Western blandishments to liberalise their economies. Recognising the threats to their rule which might emanate from independent sources of economic power, they have used their powers of incumbency to restrict economic competition. This has enabled them to dispense preferential access to market opportunities, to grant appointments to state-operated enterprises as sinecures for regime supporters and to build their own business empires. Not only have the latter expanded the support base of these ruling parties, but the revenue flows generated fall outside the remit of public financial management systems and play critical roles as sources of party finance during elections.

Chapter 11 takes forward the comparative analysis, examining the various ways these regimes responded to the opportunities presented by the West's 'War on Terror', and how they marketed themselves as allies to the West. To strengthen their security apparatus as essential regime props in what were already highly militarised societies, they have shown not only dexterity in terms of their fluency in 'development speak', but their historical origins as armed insurgents facilitated their adoption of 'security speak'. In the new post-9/11 environment, they enhanced their capacity to deal with both external and domestic threats made possible through the significant amounts of Western security assistance they were granted, while their participation in those peace-keeping operations considered to be of importance to Western national security helped shield them from external opprobrium for their behaviour on other fronts. As detailed in this chapter, such capacity has also been used by Rwanda and Uganda to secure additional sources of revenue, through their plundering of the riches of the neighbouring Democratic Republic of Congo, such activities being comprehensively detailed in numerous UN and NGO reports.

Dissimulation, Hybridity and Donor Responses

In analysing these regimes through historical, comparative and multidisciplinary lenses, what catches the observer's eye is their dissimulation and presentation skills. They have sought to project the institutions over which they preside as embodiments of Western 'best practice', and 'gamed' their relations with Western donors by telling the latter exactly what they wanted to hear. This is a cross-cutting theme in the book. Since Western development aid is treated by these regimes as both a constraint which needs to be skilfully managed and an essential regime prop to be exploited, they have displayed tremendous abilities in presenting a sufficiently acceptable public face to Western interlocutors such that any pressure to reform never became unmanageable, and the tap of development assistance remained open. This has required a delicate balancing act, juggling the reality of widespread internal repression while at the same time reassuring Western capitals they continued to subscribe to the same democratic values as their benefactors. When necessary, reminding Western donors of their commitments to respect 'national ownership' of development processes, or declaring their Western benefactors were displaying signs of neo-colonial arrogance, or diversifying the cast of their external supporters, often had the desired effect in terms of reducing external pressures to reform. An overview of some of the stratagems adopted is presented in Chap. 12 and helps answer the 'why' and 'how' questions concerning their relations with Western donors.

The ambiguous 'hybrid' nature of these regimes (a concept analysed in Chap. 5), ones displaying features of both adherence to liberal democratic principles and authoritarian practices, posed a number of problems for Western donors. If their partner regimes appeared to be neither undertaking significant moves towards strengthening political and civil rights in their countries nor relentlessly pushing their countries backwards to those bloody dictatorships they had removed from office, the question is whether they had reached a state of equilibrium, and if so deviations from the Western democratic template should not therefore be seen as temporary. Signs of political and economic liberalisation might indicate genuine reforms are being undertaken, and that the intended end point is a robust liberal multi-party democracy. However, they can also be window-dressing, a means to buy time until appropriate solutions to demands for political reform (be these domestic or external) are devised. The aim of dissimulation by these regimes is therefore to stabilise the situation prior to further entrenchment of an authoritarian political status quo. This in turn poses an additional question for Western donors, namely that if the authoritarian nature of the regimes they are engaging with is clear, and appears to be enduring, whether they should continue to support them.

Much post-Cold War Western donor bilateral agency analysis of the political economy dynamics of countries they were operating in has often been deficient (and also weak in the those produced by multilateral lenders, and practically non-existent in the case of the family of UN agencies), failing to identify many crucial variables influencing the behaviour of authoritarian aid-recipient governments. Such shortcomings included a shallow understanding of the ramifications of regime survival imperatives and both formal and informal decision-making processes, the role corruption plays in the co-optation of elites, the composition of political opposition groups, the media, CSOs, as well as the links between their security sectors, legislative bodies, judiciaries and private sector economic agents, amongst others, and of the ties between these actors and ruling parties.

This situation largely prevailed in Western donor agencies until the potential for more nuanced policy-relevant analysis arose in the mid-2000s, through pioneering work undertaken by the UK's Department for International Development (DFID) and its Driver of Change (DoC) approach.[4] This new instrument in the development toolkit aimed to identify linkages between economic, social and political factors in shaping the operational environment of partner countries, and the chances of success for realising development objectives given these variables. The DoC approach was based on the premise that politics, political processes and regime interests were fundamental in determining development outcomes, and that improved understanding of such factors would enable the improved design and implementation of development interventions.

However, despite such tools, donor agencies continue to devote little time and effort into understanding and addressing the more uncomfortable question of how their own activities, and most particularly the significant resources they inject into beneficiary countries (particularly given the problem of 'aid fungibility'), impact on local power dynamics, by either strengthening or weakening the position of authoritarian partner governments and the prospects for democratisation. In the search for a better understanding of power relations and other structural and institutional factors enabling or impeding progress, analysis, such as that conducted through DoC, has been conducted as if donor agencies were actors extraneous to the political economies of aid-recipient countries, their activities disconnected from how power and authority is exercised, how aid is employed by beneficiary governments and specifically the role their resources play in regime maintenance.

To such blind spots might be added an operational assumption of many Western development staff, namely that the local institutions they interact and negotiate with, such as ministries and their civil service staff, are to a large extent replicas of their own state institutions. Post-colonial state structures in Africa were formally constituted along the lines of the modern Western state, and this contributed to the belief amongst donor agency personnel that such institutions operate in accordance with certain basic and familiar principles, such as that civil services are staffed by personnel appointed largely on the basis of their qualifications and professional competence, that they operate according to 'rational-bureaucratic-legal' principles rather than to patrimonial considerations and that the holders of political power do not believe they have a legitimate claim on the public assets they control. However, Chabal and Daloz in an earlier path-breaking work on the nature of the post-colonial African state:

> The reality of the exercise of power on the continent points to a necessary caution when it comes to assessing the degree to which such formal bodies do amount to a modern (Weberian) state. Is the official proclamation of the rule of law, for instance, not often deceptive? (Chabal and Daloz 1999, p. 5)

The challenges presented by development complexity, added to factors analysed in Chap. 12 such as 'sunk costs' considerations, the emphasis on the need to spend funds given global aid commitments, coupled with the specific expertise of most staff working in Western governmental development programmes (largely economic and social sectors), all militate against any serious questioning of the possible negative effects of donor support. When assisted by the willingness of these regimes to resort to data manipulation to show progress which they can attribute to their policies, and which donors can connect to their injections of aid, it becomes easier for Western donors to adopt a more comfortable default position. Political economy analysis in policy and programme design is limited, development work is circumscribed to technical tasks and progress reports are circumscribed to a reduced number of apolitical issues which constitute the evidence base for aid allocation decisions.

COVID-19 and the Second Cold War: Revelations and Inflection Points

One of the key objectives of this book is to update the history of relations between Western donors and these African regimes. How they have evolved over the last four years, ones which have seen major disruptive events of global significance, provides material and another opportunity to identify elements of change, continuity and rupture, and to assess the likely short- to medium-term effects of these developments.

What happened in all three countries during the recent COVID-19 pandemic (examined against the backdrop of global democratic backsliding in Chap. 2) was a watershed in terms of its impact on relations between Western donors and the regimes in Kampala, Addis Ababa and Kigali, though for different reasons and with distinct implications for democracy in the three countries. Prior to COVID-19 these regimes had been able to explain away their repressive policies and actions, and market their authoritarian political and economic systems as ones better aligned to national realities than those promoted by the West, and more capable of delivering on global development targets. However, during the pandemic their concurrent heavy-handed and violent repression of dissent was exposed as never before, and their violations of political, civil and human rights were of such magnitude that they were difficult to downplay. Images of the bloodied bodies of civilians, and the savage methods used by the security forces to quell protests during Uganda's 2021 elections, were transmitted around the world. Even more gruesome reports and footage of the war in the Tigray region of Ethiopia, and its horrific humanitarian consequences, were widely circulated. This quickly put paid to the idea that the earlier granting of the Nobel Peace Prize to Abiy Ahmed, partly based on his commitments to strengthen democracy and respect for civil and human rights, had been an informed one. As the most recent successor to one of the original 'new leaders', and who in Western eyes had displayed promising signs of 'novelty', despite Abiy Ahmed's efforts to rebrand the ruling party he was now seen to have quickly reverted to the repressive tactics favoured by his predecessors. In the case of Kagame, COVID-19-era accounts of his more subtle methods of repression, ones which included targeted assassinations[5] and the rendition of opponents, also severely tarnished the reputation of one of the West's 'donor darlings' (though many of those who follow events in Rwanda argue that such a reassessment was long overdue).

With the West distracted by more pressing concerns, and despite what appears to be their current ability to ride out Western criticism, it is likely that future efforts by these three regimes to present the political and economic governance systems over which they preside as anything other than anti-democratic and repressive will be met with much greater scepticism. Given the evidence now available to the general public and decision-makers in the West on the nature of these regimes, any attempts by Western executives to deepen ties with the governments of these countries will likely be subjected to intense scrutiny by the legislative and judicial branches of Western governments, as well as the media and organised civil society lobbies. This has already been the case in the context of UK government's policy of deporting its illegal migrants to Rwanda, with numerous questions being raised around the morality of partnering with Rwanda on the scheme.

At the same time, however, other forces are at work, with contrary effects. The heightened tensions in the context of a New Cold War between the West and Russia, and between the West and China, have meant a frenzied search by the major powers for allies is currently underway. After indications in the early days of the Biden administration that democracy promotion would again be treated as a priority American foreign policy objective, the renewed geo-strategic competition with Moscow following the invasion of Ukraine has meant the West's building of alliances, even with regimes known to be oppressive, seems to have taken precedence over any concerns regarding their domestic policies, reducing the likelihood of any meaningful Western pressure will be placed on these regimes to liberalise their political systems

There are already some disturbing similarities between aspects of the current relations between Western countries and the Ugandan, Ethiopian and Rwandan regimes, on the one hand (outlined in Chap. 13), and, on the other, the West's relations with Africa during the Cold War and the West's War on Terror. For the time being, Western licence again seems to have been granted to the three regimes to proceed with the entrenchment of their authoritarian political and economic systems of governance, processes in which Western development assistance continues to play a crucial facilitating role. Therefore, if there is a single overarching framing question which informs this book, it is that posed by Angus Deaton, and which retains its contemporary relevance and still requires an answer: "Why can't the donors withhold aid if the president … uses aid flows to bolster his own political position?" (Deaton 2013, p. 299).

Notes

1. For a comprehensive and engaging study of how African governments have sought to engage with their donor partners, see the edited volume by Whitfield (2009).
2. For examples of such research, which come down on the side of the positive effects of aid on growth, see Clemens et al. (2012) and Arndt et al. (2016). For a landmark study which concluded it was difficult to find any robust positive impact in the aid-growth relationship, see Raghuram and Subramanian (2005).
3. The overall scores and classification of countries by Freedom House are based on their aggregate scores on a total of ten political rights indicators covering areas such as electoral processes and extent of political pluralism and participation, and fifteen civil liberties indicators which are used to report on dimensions such as freedom of expression and association, and the rule of law. On the methodology and individual country scores and classification, see Freedom House: https://freedomhouse.org/.
4. For an early DFID statement on its rationale for the adoption of DoC, see DFID (2004).
5. For a recent exposé of the inner and murderous workings of the Kagame regime, see Wrong (2021).

References

Arndt, Channing, Sam Jones and Finn Tarp. 2016. "What Is the Aggregate Economic Rate of Return to Foreign Aid", *World Bank Economic Review*, Oxford University Press, Vol 30, Issue 3, October 2016.

Bauer, PT (1972). *Dissent on Development.* Harvard University Press, 1972.

Chabal, Patrick and Daloz, Jean-Pascal. 1999. *Africa works: disorder as political instrument.*, Oxford: James Currey and Bloomington, Indiana: Indiana University Press, 1999.

Cheeseman, Nic and Brian Klaas. 2018. *How to Rig an Election*, Yale University Press, 2018.

Clemens, Michael A. Steven Radelet, Rikhil Bhavnani, and Samuel Bazzi. 2012. "Counting Chickens When They Hatch: Timing and the Effects of Aid on Growth." *Economic Journal*, Oxford Academic, Vol 122, Issue 561, 2012.

Deaton, Angus. 2013. *The Great Escape: Health, Wealth and the Origins of Inequality*, Princeton University Press, 2013.

Department for International Development. 2004. "Drivers of Change". Public Information Note, London: DFID, September 2004.

Easterly, William. 2001. *The Elusive Quest for Growth: Economists' Adventures and Misadventures in the Tropics*, Cambridge: MIT Press, 2001.

Easterly, William. 2007. *The White Man's Burden: Why the West's Efforts to Aid The Rest Have Done So Much Ill And So Little Good*, Oxford University Press, 2007.

Gisselquist, Rachel M. et al. 2021."Does aid support democracy? A systematic review of the literature". WIDER Working Paper 2021/14, Helsinki: United Nations University World Institute for Development Economics Research, January 2021.

Hagmann, Tobias and Filip Reyntjens (eds). 2016. *Aid and Authoritarianism in Africa: Development without Democracy*, London: Zed Books, 2016.

Kersting, Erasmus and Christopher Kilby. 2014. "Aid and Democracy Redux", *European Economic Review*, Vol 67, Elsevier, April 2014.

Knack, Stephen. 2004. "Does Foreign Aid Promote Democracy", *International Studies Quarterly*, Vol 48 No 1, Oxford University Press, March 2004.

Moyo, Dambiso. 2010. *Dead Aid: How Aid Is Not Working and How There Is a Better Way for Africa*. Penguin, 2010

Raghuram, G. Rajan and Arvind Subramanian. 2005. "Aid and Growth: What Does the Cross-Country Evidence Really Show?". IMF Working Paper WP/05/127, Washington D.C.: International Monetary Fund, June 2005.

Sachs, Jeffrey. 2005. *The End of Poverty: Economic Possibilities for Our Time.* Penguin Press, 2005.

Whitfield, Lindsay. 2009. *The Politics of Aid: African Strategies for Dealing with Donors.* Oxford University Press.

World Development Indicators. 2024. *The World Bank*, Data Bank.

Wrong, Michela. 2021. *Do Not Disturb: The Story of a Political Murder and an African Regime Gone Bad*, London: Fourth Estate, 2021.

CHAPTER 2

COVID-19 and Political Repression

Authoritarianism revamped

Over the course of 2020–2022, as governments around the world dealt with the COVID-19 pandemic and its devastating health, economic and social consequences, those of an authoritarian bent took the opportunities presented by the crisis to entrench their rule. Declarations of states of emergency allowed many authoritarian leaders to weaken institutional checks and balances and circumvent democratic oversight of their decisions. New restrictions on civil and political liberties were introduced which enabled such governments to further suppress opposition political groups. Elections were postponed on epidemiological grounds, public gatherings and demonstrations were outlawed, and security forces granted increased licence to quell protests with increasing recourse to intimidatory violence against expressions of dissent. By applying measures further restricting what was often already limited space for open and robust party-political competition, free and fair elections, the operations of independent media and the monitoring of human rights by civil society organisations, these regimes demonstrated both their inventiveness and resilience as they set about strengthening their hold on power and maintain the political status quo.[1] One of the starkest and most prominent features of democratic regression during COVID was the return of the men in uniform to the political stage.

M. Simpson, *Donors, Democracy and Development in Africa*,
https://doi.org/10.1007/978-3-031-74917-9_2

Military coups and the suspension of democracy and constitutional rule—ubiquitous in Latin America and Africa during the 1960s–1980s, but which had fallen out of favour as a form of regime change with the end of the Cold War—reappeared during the pandemic. Myanmar saw its gains in terms of the consolidation of democracy reversed in February 2021 when the armed forces declared the results of the 2020 general elections, won by Suu Kyi's National League for Democracy, invalid and went on to impose a state of emergency and martial law. In Mali, the civilian government of President Keita was overthrown in August 2020 by the country's armed forces, with power then being held by a military National Committee for the Salvation of the People. In September 2021, Guinean soldiers arrested President Alpha Condé, dissolved the government and suspended the constitution. In January 2022 the military in Burkina Faso overthrew President Roch Kaboré, suspended the constitution and concentrated power in the hands of its Patriotic Movement for Safeguarding and Restoration, while in Niger a coup in July 2023 also replaced the democratically elected civilian president with a military junta. In Sudan, a military coup failed in September 2021, led by military forces and civilian elements loyal to deposed former President Omar al-Bashir, which had sought to overthrow the country's transitional Sovereignty Council of Sudan which included both civilians and military elements. However, another attempt in October 2021, led by Lieutenant-General Abdel Fattah al-Burhan who had chaired the Sovereignty Council, was successful. A state of emergency was declared and the Council was dissolved, with al-Burhan assuming power as de facto head of state.

Global Democratic Backsliding

Such widespread setbacks in terms of democracy did not, however, emerge only with the onset of the COVID-19 health emergency. Pandemic-era democratic regressions were part and parcel of an ongoing and broader process of 'democratic backsliding', one well underway before COVID. In many countries, essential components of democracy, such as the rule of law, the separation of powers and in particular the independence of the judiciary, freedom of speech and assembly and the regular holding of free and fair multi-party elections, were already being weakened before the virus became a global health concern in December 2019.

Defined as the "substantial de-facto decline of core institutional requirements for electoral democracy" (Luhrmann and Lindberg 2019, p. 1096), this ongoing wave of autocratisation reversed gains made during an earlier

'Third Wave of Democratisation', one characterised by a surge in transitions to democracy in a wide range of countries during the last quarter of the twentieth century.[2] The current reversal of such democratic gains began at least a decade before the COVID-19 pandemic, further weakening any residual early post-Cold War optimism regarding the prospects for the gradual universalization of liberal democratic principles as the dominant form of government.[3] In its 2021 global report on the state of political and civil rights, Freedom House noted its survey results showed the "15th consecutive year of decline in global freedom" (Freedom House 2021a), with reversals in every region of the world. Another think tank, the Varieties of Democracy (V-Dem) Institute in Sweden (host to the world's largest database on the status of democracy in over 200 countries), observed in its 2021 Democracy Report that the "level of democracy enjoyed by the average global citizen in 2020 is down to levels last found in 1990" (V-Dem Institute 2021, p. 6). The V-Dem report also noted that between 2010 and 2020, the percentage of the world's population living in autocracies had increased from 48 per cent to 68 per cent (V-Dem Institute 2021, p. 7). As an American think tank observed, "what's novel about the pandemic isn't the authoritarian response. What's different is the scale and speed with which it is happening all over the world at the same time" (National Endowment for Democracy 2020).

Even before the outbreak of the pandemic, apparently well-established democracies were already under pressure from the forces of autocratisation. EU member states such as Hungary, under the leadership of Prime Minister Victor Orbán and his Fidesz party since 2010, had embarked on building what Orbán himself proudly described in 2014 as an 'illiberal state' (Mahony 2014). Using his party's supermajority in parliament to shape the political playing field to its advantage, he regularly invoked the examples of countries such as China, Russia and Turkey, whose leaders strongly rejected liberal norms, as worthy of emulation (Eddy 2014). Fidesz loyalists gradually took over key state institutions, from the Constitutional Court and the Public Prosecutor's Office to the State Audit Office and the National Bank.[4] The country's divergence from the EU's values and norms opened up a growing chasm between Brussels and Budapest, with the EU Parliament regularly condemning policies seen to infringe on judicial independence, freedom of expression, the rights of minorities such as the Roma and the treatment of refugees.

In March 2020 the Hungarian Parliament voted to grant Prime Minister Orbán the right to rule by decree indefinitely and to take any measures judged necessary to deal with the COVID pandemic without parliamentary oversight. The criminal code was amended to make it an offence to spread 'fake news' during a pandemic (a familiar instrument in the toolkit of authoritarian governments), a catch-all which allowed the government to block the circulation of any information it viewed as anti-government under the guise of ensuring the effectiveness of its pandemic response (Beauchamp. 2020). The opportunist element in this further centralisation of power in the hands of the Prime Minister was clear, given that at the time of the March 2020 parliamentary vote the number of COVID-19 cases in Hungary was negligible.[5]

Poland, governed by the Law and Justice Party since 2015, also came under heavy criticism from EU institutions and member states for its policies. These included efforts to undermine the independence of the judiciary through legislation which effectively granted the ruling party the right to appoint judges known to be sympathetic to its policies. Further encroachments on judicial independence took the form of what became known as the 'Muzzle Law', which empowered a disciplinary body (established by the Law and Justice Party government), to effectively punish judges who questioned the ruling party's judicial reform programme. The weakening of judicial independence led concerned observers to opine that "Poland can now be considered the first EU Member State to no longer have an independent judicial branch following sustained attacks deliberately targeting Polish courts, judges and prosecutors" (Pech et al. 2021, p. 3).

Arguably the most prominent of post-Cold War democratic backsliders (at least in terms of its global repercussions) was the US during the presidency of Donald Trump. His election campaign, based on an anti-establishment, populist and demagogic platform, had used demonising rhetoric, depicting opposition figures such as the Democratic Party's presidential candidate, Hillary Clinton, as enemies of the US and part of a corrupt elite which had lost touch with 'the people' which Trump claimed to understand and represent. He would go on to question his electoral defeat, sought to have the results overturned and then encouraged his supporters to storm the Capitol in January 2021 to disrupt the formal certification of results and prevent the transfer of power. As two analysts had presciently observed in 2018 on the international impact of the US' democratic backsliding under Trump, "Both existing and potential autocrats are likely to be emboldened with Trump in the White House" (Levitsky and Ziblatt 2019, pp. 206–207).

And autocrats around the world were, in fact, heartened by such developments. Moscow in particular derived immense propaganda mileage from the invasion of the Capitol, with Putin's supporters arguing that not only American democracy was dysfunctional but Washington no longer held the moral high ground in terms of democratic practice and should therefore no longer preach to others on their shortcomings in political governance (Maynes 2021). The opportunity for authoritarian regimes to gloat over America's political malaise was also not missed in Africa. The Zimbabwean head of state, Emmerson Mnangagwa—who had overthrown his predecessor Robert Mugabe in a military coup in November 2017, but had been unable to remove his country from the US list of countries under sanctions for its government's continued violations of human rights and democratic freedoms—commented, "Yesterday's events showed that the US has no moral right to punish another country under the guise of upholding democracy" (Vinga 2021).

President Erdoğan, who has dominated Turkish politics since 2003 and driven an ongoing process of autocratisation, used the pandemic to speed up the introduction of new repressive measures to add to those introduced following a failed military coup d'état in July 2016.[6] Following this attempted coup, a state of emergency had been introduced and renewed at regular intervals for two years, while a massive purge took place of those suspected of being opposed to Erdoğan's Islamist agenda. Tens of thousands were imprisoned, others were dismissed from their public sector jobs including members of the judiciary, while civil society groups were closed and media freedom severely circumscribed.[7] During the pandemic, charges of terrorism on the grounds of links to the failed 2016 coup plotters, or the outlawed Kurdish Workers' Party (PKK), were frequently brought against political opponents. A large number of mayors, elected for the opposition People's Democratic Party, were removed from office in the course of 2020 and replaced with Ankara's appointees (Yackley 2020). Protests organised by opposition parties and civil society organisations were routinely banned, while the country's official media regulator regularly censured the content of broadcasts by outlets critical of the government.

As Western countries turned inwards during the pandemic to focus on the health emergency, Putin and his United Russia party took the opportunity to extend Moscow's control over the Crimea and the Eastern Ukrainian territories seized from Ukraine during the war of 2014. Moscow also persevered with efforts to destabilise the EU and NATO member

Baltic states of Lithuania, Latvia and Estonia, employing cyber-warfare against their financial systems and public institutions.[8] In addition, Russia conducted large-scale military exercises in the neighbourhood, and the latter would take on an increasingly menacing form, with Russian forces again invading Ukraine in February 2022.

Putin's government also continued to quash internal dissent by jailing political opponents (most notably the prominent anti-Putin opposition figure Alexei Navalny, arrested in February 2021 and sentenced to a custodial term in a labour penal colony where he eventually died) and restricting the operations of civil society organisations and the free media. During the pandemic it used new legislation on the spreading of 'misinformation' to harass civil society activists, human rights defenders and journalists, with the already constrained space for protest shrinking further after the outbreak of the war with Ukraine due to additional clampdowns on protests and the media (Human Rights Watch 2021).

There were also diminishing prospects for any political transition in Russia, as Putin employed yet another favoured tool of authoritarian leaders to consolidate his rule. A referendum in June 2020 saw the public voting in favour of a set of constitutional amendments proposed by Putin, which were then signed into law in April 2021. One of these amendments granted Putin the right to run for two additional six-year terms in office.

During the pandemic, Xi Jinping's China persevered with its strategy of projecting its military presence in the South China Sea. Beijing kept up its assertions of sovereignty over large swathes of the Sea and islands claimed by its neighbours, to the growing concern of South and South East Asian countries as well as the US and Australia (Tangen 2020). Beijing continued to tighten restrictions on its Uyghur population in an effort to contain separatist tendencies in Xinjiang, including the establishment of detention camps in Xinjiang which the government claimed were used for 're-education' and 'vocational training' purposes.[9]

Beijing also pressed ahead with undermining those residual freedoms enjoyed by the population of Hong Kong to ensure a compliant, if not completely subservient, pro-Beijing government in that territory. The introduction of Hong Kong's National Security Law in June 2020, which brought the territory's security legislation into line with the mainland's, further reduced the city's autonomy.[10] The Law was then used to hobble the pro-democracy movement in Hong Kong.

In the case of rising powers in the developing world which had previously enjoyed a track record of free and fair elections, and in which the separation of powers and democratic values and norms appeared to be firmly embedded, leaders with strongly authoritarian tendencies also seized the opportunities presented by the public health emergency to entrench their rule. India, long touted as the world's largest democracy, had already embarked, under the rule of Narendra Modi and his Bharatiya Janata Party (BJP) following election victories in 2014 and 2019, on a pre-pandemic path of growing autocratisation and deviation from democratic norms. In pursuit of its Hindu-supremacist agenda, the government's pre-pandemic measures included the highly controversial Citizenship Amendment Act (CAA) of December 2019. In a country with a long tradition of secularism, this instituted a religious test for citizenship and therefore political rights, with the legislation providing a pathway to Indian citizenship for large numbers of migrants from various neighbouring countries and confessional backgrounds while specifically denying this to Muslims from those same countries.[11] The result was to disenfranchise sections of the country's Muslim population seen as likely to vote for opposition parties rather than Modi's BJP. As observed by Jaffrelot, one of the foremost scholars on contemporary India, Modi and the BJP had succeeded in establishing an 'ethnic democracy', destroying the country's secularist traditions by casting Muslims and other minority groups such as Christians as alien implants and non-members of a Hindu-dominant body polity (Jaffrelot 2021).

During the pandemic, India experienced other forms of deterioration in its democratic credentials. On March 24, 2020, the government suddenly imposed, with little advance notice and minimal consultation with local governments (but with a surfeit of force being employed by the police to ensure compliance), what became by population size the world's largest COVID-19 lockdown. Given only hours advance notice before the lockdown came into effect, millions of migrant workers lost their livelihoods overnight, and a massive exodus of workers and their families from the cities to their rural homes followed in what became India's largest population movement since Partition and one with dire humanitarian consequences.[12] The outlawing, on epidemiological grounds, of large-scale gatherings and protests largely put paid to ongoing protests against both the CAA and the government's pandemic responses.

In Brazil, growing autocratisation was evident soon after the election of Jair Bolsonaro as President in January 2019 on a far-right, nationalist and populist platform similar to those which had brought others such as Trump, Orbán, Modi and Erdoğan into power. During his election campaign, Bolsonaro had cast himself as an anti-establishment political outsider, determined to save Brazil from what he depicted as a creeping left-wing takeover of the country. Putting himself forward as a 'strong man' who would forcefully tackle Brazil's problem of spiralling violent crime, Bolsonaro engaged in rewriting the history of the role of the armed forces in the 1964 military coup, an event he depicted as a heroic intervention that saved the country from communism. Once in office he filled key government posts with both serving and retired military personnel, and in March 2019, on the 55th anniversary of the 1964 coup, he encouraged the country's armed forces to officially celebrate the occasion (Brooks 2019).

His willingness to ignore the mandates of the country's other branches of government soon became evident. When in March 2020, in the context of disagreements over the Federal Budget, he found himself thwarted by the Legislative and Judicial branches, he called out his supporters in Brasilia to protest against Congress and the Federal Supreme Court, with some of those present calling on Bolsonaro to close down both branches of government and for the armed forces to intervene (*Folha de São Paulo* 2020). Other actions during the pandemic garnered him both international notoriety and plenty of derision. Like Trump, who also became famous for his championing of a range of unproven COVID cures, Bolsonaro went on to publicly champion unscientific quick fixes against COVID-19 such as the use of an anti-malarial drug and railed against the need to use masks and practise social distancing. What became an official anti-scientific public disinformation campaign run from Brasilia led to the failure of the central government to develop the appropriate and timely policy measures to deal effectively with the pandemic. The result of such official disinformation was that Brazil had amongst the world's highest COVID-19 death tolls.

The Pandemic and the West's Favoured African Regimes

In Uganda, Ethiopia and Rwanda, several disturbing events took place during the pandemic. Notwithstanding the increasing number of voices, both inside and outside those countries, warning that all was not as portrayed by the governments in Kampala, Addis Ababa and Kigali, it was arguably only their behaviour during COVID-19 that finally led, if somewhat belatedly, to some serious questioning by Western decision-makers about the status of political freedoms and civil and human rights in those countries. As evidence of their transgressions mounted, a clearer and more disconcerting picture emerged of the extent to which regime survival imperatives, and a willingness to use violence to maintain the status quo, dominated government thinking in Kampala, Kigali and Addis Ababa. As the West's relations with its formerly close African friends became more acrimonious, the latter responded to Western criticisms with vituperative language, the rapid process of mutual estrangement contrasting sharply with the cosy ties of previous years.

In January 2021 general elections were held in Uganda, and the incumbent, President Yoweri Museveni, in power since 1986, was eventually declared the winner of the presidential race, with his party, the National Resistance Movement (NRM), also securing a large majority in the National Assembly. That Museveni had been able to run for office in 2021 was a result of successive constitutional amendments introduced by his ruling party. In 2005 a two-term limit on the presidential term of office was scrapped which had enabled Museveni to run again in the 2006 elections, the same amendment allowing for the reintroduction of multi-party elections after decades of what the NRM had termed its 'no party democracy'. In December 2017 yet another amendment was introduced, this one removing the age limit cap which would have prevented Museveni from running for his sixth term in 2021. Born in 1944, Museveni's advanced age, together with these constitutional amendments, meant Uganda was effectively being gifted a President for Life.

During the 2021 election campaign, Museveni faced an unprecedentedly strong challenge from the political opposition, and the state apparatus set up under his rule responded brutally to the threat of regime change, encouraged by Museveni's threatening election campaign discourse which included his characterisation of opposition figures and supporters as public enemies. After being nominated in November 2020 as the ruling NRM's presidential candidate, he warned his opponents that "we shall deal with you. Whoever tries will regret. Nobody should be intimidated by these crooks. I am already president and want to come back...Nobody has more guns than us".[13]

Images flashed around the world of his security forces arresting the main opposition figure, Bobi Wine, before polling day and then employing lethal force against Wine's supporters (Burke and Okikor 2020). The crackdown continued after Museveni's inauguration, with hundreds of opposition activists being detained in round-ups, and accusations of torture in police stations and prisons, all serving to reveal in the starkest possible terms the repressive nature of the Kampala regime (Burke and Okikor 2021).

Copious evidence was also gathered on electoral irregularities before, during and after polling day.[14] A litany of human rights abuses and electoral irregularities was compiled and disseminated by Ugandan activists and shared with Western diplomatic missions and international think tanks. An expert on Uganda at the International Crisis Group, a Western NGO focused on the prevention and resolution of conflicts, concluded that "even by the low standards of recent Ugandan elections, the 2021 election cycle stood out for the brazenness of official attempts to intimidate the opposition and the ferocity of the police response to protests" (Mutiga 2021).

Western countries, which had long supported Museveni, could not but react to the patently poor quality of the election process and its accompanying violence. Before polling day Washington withdrew its election observer mission, its embassy in Kampala expressing frustration at the denial of accreditation of a large number of its observers which meant "it was not possible for the United States to meaningfully observe the conduct of Uganda's elections at polling stations across the country" (U.S. Embassy Kampala 2021). In April 2021 the American government introduced visa restrictions on those held "responsible for, or complicit in, undermining the democratic process in Uganda, including during the country's January 2021 general elections and the campaign period which preceded it" (U.S. Department of State 2021a). Announcing these restrictions, US Secretary of State Antony Blinken affirmed that the Ugandan government's actions "represent a continued downward trajectory for the country's democracy and human rights" and characterised the electoral process as "neither free nor fair". The Parliament of the EU, the largest provider of aid to Uganda, passed a resolution in February 2021 criticising the election process, declaring it to have been neither "democratic nor transparent". Furthermore, the resolution also called for EU sanctions "against individuals and organisations responsible for human rights violations" (EU Parliament 2021).

In Ethiopia, Prime Minister Abiy Ahmed, in power since April 2018, had inherited a full in-tray of problems from his predecessors, but had initially enjoyed strong Western approval ratings. Like his predecessor, Meles Zenawi, he was seen as another African 'new leader' who would spearhead rapid political liberalisation. Therefore, under his administration, Ethiopia initially continued to benefit from a constant flow of substantial Western development aid. In October 2019, a high-water mark in the West's approval of Abiy Ahmed's reformist plans was reached when he received the Nobel Peace Prize, primarily for his work in resolving a long-standing territorial dispute with Eritrea which had led to an extremely bloody war between the two countries. References were also made to his commitment to pursue policies on the domestic front which promised a new dawn in terms of respect for civil and political rights after the repressive policies pursued by previous governments. He oversaw the release of a large number of political prisoners, relaxed media restrictions, legalised outlawed opposition groups and lifted an existing state of emergency. In addition to his efforts to bring an end to the conflict with Eritrea, the Nobel Committee's announcement of the award to Abiy Ahmed cited his "important reforms that give many citizens hope for a better life and better future" (Norwegian Nobel Committee 2019).

However, by November 2020 Abiy Ahmed was presiding over a country where, once again, civil war had broken out, the latest conflict pitting the armed forces of the central government and soldiers from their former foe, Eritrea, against the forces of the ruling party of the regional government of Tigray, namely the Tigray People's Liberation Front (TPLF), the dominant partner in the Ethiopian People's Revolutionary Democratic Front (EPRDF), governments of Meles Zenawi and his successor Hailemariam Desalegn.[15] The conflict was one with strong ethnic overtones and with disturbing eliminationist rhetoric being employed by Abiy Ahmed.[16] Pictures of military operations in Ethiopia's highlands were accompanied by images of devastated towns and refugees flooding across international borders, and numerous reports of the massacre of civilians and mass rape (Amnesty International 2021).

With the advantage of hindsight, it is now clear that much had been overlooked by Western capitals in terms of the new Ethiopian leader's background and his attitudes to dissent and political pluralism. Eager to anoint another 'new leader' in Africa, the West ignored the fact that Abiy Ahmed had served as a Minister in EPRDF governments and for a period was its Third Chairman. He was therefore very much a product of the EPRDF's style of political governance. After taking over as Prime Minister in April 2018, he continued to rule as leader of the EPRDF until he established his own Prosperity Party (PP) in late 2019, which united most of those political parties which had previously come together in the

TPLF-dominated EPRDF. In addition, he had gained military experience as a fighter in the coalition of rebel forces which had seized power in 1991 and gone on to serve in the new Ethiopian army. His exposure to the use of force to achieve political objectives, the internalisation of military practices such as top-down decision-making, the need for secrecy and demands for unquestioning loyalty to leaders, all influenced his authoritarian style of governance which increasingly bore a disturbing resemblance to that of his predecessors. In their search for an African success story, Western donor countries seemed to have been easily dazzled by his early statements of intent and the liberalising measures he implemented, failing to recognise the strongly authoritarian and repressive elements of his approach to governance until it was too late.

With the war in Tigray quickly spreading to other parts of the country, and the threat of neighbouring states besides Eritrea being sucked into the conflict, the idea, so fondly promoted by both Addis Ababa and the West, of Ethiopia as a post-Cold War island of stability in a turbulent Horn of Africa, lay in tatters. Most dismaying of all was the fact that by mid-2021 international humanitarian agencies were reporting that the country, which had once aspired to achieve middle-income status by 2025, was instead again facing a problem with which it had historically been associated, namely a famine of biblical proportions (*UN News* 2021).

Washington expressed its strong displeasure at these developments, announcing visa restrictions on those it held responsible for the conflict. On May 23, 2021, US Secretary of State Antony Blinken announced the US had decided to "impose wide-ranging restrictions on economic and security assistance to Ethiopia" (U.S. Department of State 2021b). The inclusion of Washington's security assistance programme in the package of sanctions might reasonably be seen as a recognition that American assets and training, previously provided to Ethiopia to enhance the country's international peacekeeping and anti-terrorism capabilities, were now being used for purposes of internal repression.

As the conflict dragged on and its humanitarian consequences became increasingly serious, Washington increased the pressure on Addis Ababa. By early November 2021 and following failed attempts by senior American officials to secure agreements from Addis Ababa to allow humanitarian assistance into Tigray, there was talk the State Department was working on a declaration that the Ethiopian government's actions against Tigrayans constituted genocide. In line with the provisions of the 1948 Geneva Convention on the Prevention and Punishment of the Crime of Genocide, this raised the possibility that the US might seek UN approval for a multilateral intervention in Ethiopia (Finnegan 2021). And while Washington sought to be even-handed in terms of assigning responsibility for the country's descent into chaos, blaming Eritrean, Ethiopian and Tigrayan authorities and forces, responsibility for the humanitarian crisis was mostly assigned to Addis Ababa, the US Special Envoy for the Horn of Africa referencing "an intentional effort by the authorities to deprive Ethiopians who are suffering from receiving lifesaving assistance" (United States Institute of Peace).

Washington also ratcheted up the pressure on the government through economic means. In early November 2021 it announced the suspension of Ethiopia from the benefits of its African Growth and Opportunity Act (AGOA), under which Addis Ababa had enjoyed duty-free access to American markets for a range of its exports. In a letter to Congress, President Biden cited its "gross violations of internationally recognized human rights", adding the decision was the result of that government's failure to "address United States concerns about their non-compliance with the AGOA eligibility criteria" (White House, November 2, 2021a).

Further indications of Ethiopia's fall from grace in the eyes of its long-standing Western supporters came in the form of an April 2021 report by the International Development Committee of the UK's House of Commons. At a time when Ethiopia was still the largest recipient of UK bilateral aid, amongst the Committee's recommendations was that "the UK Government should bear in mind its obligations to take appropriate action in line with the UN Genocide Convention should the Ethiopian Government fail to take the actions it needs to protect its people" (House of Commons International Development Committee 2021).

In the case of Rwanda, it was the arrest in August 2020 of an opposition figure, Paul Rusesabagina, that was judged particularly newsworthy by the Western media. This was partly due to the fact that Rusesabagina claimed he had been forcibly abducted in Dubai and taken to Kigali whilst en route to visit neighbouring Burundi, in an operation planned by the country's Rwanda Investigation Bureau (RIB). Western media coverage also reflected his high profile given the role he had played in saving the lives of many ethnic Tutsis during the 1994 genocide, as depicted in the Oscar-nominated 2004 film *Hotel Rwanda*. The fact he had been awarded the US Presidential Medal of Freedom in 2005 by President George W. Bush for his "remarkable courage and compassion in the face of genocidal terror" also ensured the incident flashed across the radar screens in Washington and other Western capitals (White House November 9, 2005).

Rusesabagina had become increasingly vocal and critical of the rule of Paul Kagame and his Rwandan Patriotic Front (RPF) and had sought refuge in the US. He took on the role of president of an exile opposition movement, the MRCD (*Mouvement Rwandais pour le Changement Démocratique*, or Rwandan Movement for Democratic Change). After his arrest, he faced several charges ranging from murder to terrorism (*BBC News* September 14, 2020). He was eventually found guilty of being part of a group held to be responsible for 'terrorist attacks' and sentenced to twenty-five years in prison (*Al Jazeera* 2021a).

The Rusesabagina case shone a powerful spotlight on the ability of the Kagame regime to silence its critics, with often deadly results for those targeted. His abduction sparked greater international interest in the workings of the regime, and in its leader who had been even more prominent on the international stage than his Ethiopian or Ugandan counterparts, and a permanent fixture at international events such as the Davos World Economic Forum and G-7 meetings.

Yet even before Rusesabagina's arrest, some Western analysts had already sought to draw attention to the methods employed by the repressive state apparatus constructed by the RPF after it took power in 1994. They had also revisited aspects of Rwanda's recent history deemed to be settled matters, casting doubt on many details of the official narrative constructed by the RPF. This storyline was one which had emphasised the squeaky-clean redemptive role the RPF had played before, during and after the 1994 genocide and had been accepted by decision-makers in the West, thus helping them justify the massive support they provided to Kigali. Amongst those aspects of Rwanda's recent history revisited was that of massacres of Hutus carried out by the RPF, both during and after its march on Kigali in 1994, with journalists and scholars reviving claims that a 'parallel' or 'double' genocide, or at the very least serious war crimes, had been committed by the RPF.[17]

The Rusesabagina affair was now linked to an extensive catalogue of incidents of political repression which identified Kigali's preferred and deadly modus operandi for dealing with its political opponents, wherever they might be. Amongst other prominent cases was the January 2014 assassination, in South Africa, of the former head of Rwanda's intelligence services, which South African authorities subsequently attributed to

Rwandan-based operatives (Maphanga 2021). Colonel Karegeya was known to have fallen out with Kagame and had served a prison sentence for insubordination. Moving to South Africa, he had set up the opposition Rwandan National Congress (RNC), following which he was sentenced, *in absentia*, to a twenty-year prison term on charges which included undermining state security (*BBC News* March 26, 2014).

The Rusesabagina and Karegeya affairs (just two amongst many such cases) demonstrated the Kagame regime's determination, and capacity, to conduct extra-territorial punitive operations to silence any dissidents it believed constituted threats to its continued rule. During the pandemic, Freedom House released a report on 'transnational repression' around the world, i.e. the efforts of governments to silence dissidents amongst their exile communities and concluded that in the case of Rwanda "authorities take an extremely broad view of what constitutes dissent...The Rwandan government is among the most prolific transnational repression actors worldwide" (Freedom House 2021b, p. 22).

Subtler methods of intimidation to deal with political opponents were also noted with increasing frequency. So, for example, the case of Diane Shiwa Rwigara was widely covered in the Western press. A prominent critic of Kagame who had planned to run against him as an independent candidate in the August 2017 presidential elections, her attempts to do so were stymied in July 2017 when she was disqualified by the country's electoral commission on technical grounds related to her alleged failure to collect enough supporting signatures and her supposed forgery of those she had obtained (*Voice of America* July 7, 2017). Rwigara continued to suffer harassment by the state even after Kagame's victory in 2017, with police raiding her home in order to collect evidence of alleged tax evasion. She was subsequently arrested and imprisoned on charges that included inciting insurrection against the government, before being released on bail in October 2018 (*Al Jazeera* 2018a).

Kagame was declared the victor of the August 2017 elections, with an astonishing 98 per cent of votes cast. His securing of yet another term had only been possible by his having taken a leaf from the regime-preservation manual of his former mentor Yoweri Museveni, securing through an earlier 2015 referendum (with 99 per cent of Yes votes), the approval of a constitutional amendment allowing him to stand, at the end of his second mandate in 2017, for yet another seven-year term. The amendment also meant that after this additional seven-year term he would then be entitled to run for two more five-year terms, and if successful, this would carry him through to 2034.

In the face of a clear pattern of state-sponsored political repression which had become increasingly difficult to ignore, in February 2021 the EU Parliament passed a strongly worded resolution on Rwanda. As a major donor, which had provided billions of euros in aid to Rwanda since 1994, the condemnatory tone of the resolution would not but have been noted in the corridors of power in Kigali. Over and above criticisms of Rusesabagina's arrest in "uncertain circumstances", and violation of his rights while detained, the EU Parliament accused Kigali of having "arrested, detained and prosecuted critics and government opponents in politically motivated trials in Rwanda, and repeatedly threatened others outside the country". The resolution also called on Rwanda to ensure "the independence of the judiciary" and to "open up its political sphere and improve its human rights record" (European Parliament 2021a).

A change in attitudes towards the Kagame regime was also evident in the US. In a rare show of bipartisan consensus at the tail end of the Trump administration, in December 2020 a group of Democrat and Republican senators and representatives sent a letter to Kagame. They not only called for Rusesabagina's release and return to the US, but also expressed "grave concern with the manner in which your government transferred Mr. Rusesabagina from the United Arab Emirates to Rwanda and then immediately placed him in solitary confinement and charged him with multiple crimes, including terrorism", adding that the American government was "monitoring his condition closely" (United States Congress, Human Rights Commission 2021).

By January 2021, American criticisms of Kigali were being voiced in international fora. On the occasion of the UN's Human Rights Council's Universal Periodic Review of Rwanda, the US Mission issued a statement; amongst its recommendations were that Rwanda "promote the right to freedom of expression by ending detentions and harassment of members of the media and civil society for their reporting", and called on the Kigali government to "independently and transparently investigate credible allegations of unlawful or arbitrary arrests and detention, killings, and enforced disappearances of human rights defenders, political opponents, and journalists" (U.S. Embassy Rwanda 2021). Other Western delegations issued similar statements; Canada called for "independent investigations into all alleged cases of enforced disappearance", Denmark expressed "concern about allegations of arbitrary detention and torture in detention facilities", and Norway stated that it "remained concerned about the interpretation and implementation of legislation in relation to the freedoms of expression, assembly and association, and the protection of human rights defenders", while the UK delegation expressed its concerns about Rwanda's "restrictions to media freedom and civil and political rights" (United Nations General Assembly Human Rights Council 2021, pp. 5–8).

Further signs of Kagame's growing toxicity in the eyes of Western leaders included the non-inclusion of Rwanda in a pandemic-era virtual tour of Africa conducted by Antony Blinken on April 27, 2021, during which the US Secretary of State engaged with the Presidents of Nigeria and Kenya (U.S. Department of State 2021c). That same month Kagame was also notably absent from a Biden White House-hosted virtual summit on climate change attended by forty world leaders, including five other African presidents (White House March 26, 2021b).

COVID-19 as Regime Consolidation Opportunity in Uganda, Ethiopia and Rwanda

The three regimes in Uganda, Ethiopia and Rwanda used the COVID-19 pandemic to weaken their respective oppositions and consolidate their rule, violate democratic norms and standards and introduce measures for their own benefit. Invoking the importance of preserving life, they took advantage of the public health emergency to speed up an ongoing process of restrictions on the media, further constrained the right to freedom of assembly, sanctioned the abusive enforcement by security forces of emergency measures and, when necessary, simply postponed elections.

In Uganda, Museveni chose not to invoke the constitutional provision conferring upon the President the right to declare a state of emergency, as the relevant Article 110 did not cover disease as a valid ground for such a declaration. Over the course of early 2020 he instead issued a series of directives of questionable legal validity restricting various rights and freedoms, which were eventually turned into Ministry of Health statutory instruments. Furthermore, by adopting this approach rather than declaring a state of emergency, he was able to avoid parliamentary scrutiny of his "self-assigned 'exceptional powers'" (Avocats Sans Frontières 2020).

During Uganda's 2020 election campaign, such restrictions were used to benefit the ruling party and the President. Curfews and limitations on public gatherings were imposed by the Electoral Commission on public health grounds and enforced by police (Electoral Commission, Republic of Uganda 2020). This in effect meant an end to election campaigns, but such restrictions were limited to the country's populous urban areas and certain districts known to be strongholds of opposition parties. Invoking public health considerations, the Electoral Commission's Chairperson also announced a ban on citizens witnessing the vote counting at polling stations, previously a permitted activity (*Independent* (Kampala) 2021). Together with a ban on social media which came into effect forty-eight hours before polling day, this severely constrained the ability of CSOs and journalists to monitor election abuses.

In Ethiopia, in March 2020 the country's National Electoral Board announced that parliamentary and presidential elections scheduled for August 2020 (and significantly given what subsequently took place in the Tigray region, also the elections for Regional State Councils) would be postponed due to COVID-19. A few days later the Council of Ministers, and then Parliament, approved a five-month state of emergency which granted Abiy Ahmed's government extensive powers to combat the virus, amongst which a ban on gatherings of more than four people.

Given the looming expiry in October 2020 of the terms of both the government and the parliament, and to resolve a constitutional crisis brought about by the postponement of the elections, the country's Council of Constitutional Inquiry (CCI) deliberated on the constitutionality of the options presented by Parliament. Amongst the CCI's recommendations, subsequently approved by the country's Upper Chamber in Parliament, were that the terms of Abiy Ahmed's federal government, led by his new ruling PP, and the terms of members of both chambers of parliament and the regional councils should be extended until elections could be held. Elections would only be postponed for as long as COVID was judged a threat to public health, and the same principle would apply to extensions of the State of Emergency (*Addis Standard* June 10, 2020a).

Given the experience of opposition political forces with previous states of emergency which had been used to deal with anti-government protests, such as those declared in 2005 by Meles Zenawi, and in 2016 and 2018 by Prime Minister Hailemariam Desalegn and which had resulted in mass arrests of opposition supporters and the closure of critical media outlets, the opposition interpreted these measures as an attempt by Abiy Ahmed to use the pandemic to extend his term in office. Criticisms were levelled at the lack of consultations with other political parties prior to the postponement of the elections, with the government using its large majority in Parliament to push through its decision, and for it not having considered establishing a coalition government until elections could be held. In June 2020 two ethnic-based political parties, the Oromo Liberation Front (OLF) and the Oromo Federalist Congress (OFC), issued a joint statement in which they declared the postponement of the elections and extension of the government's term of office to be "an illegal and illegitimate act that not only violates the constitution but also endangers the peace and stability of the country", while another ethnic-based party, the Ogaden National Liberation Front (ONLF), warned the country was "entering a more dangerous political phase which can only be described as a sudden and profound halt in the democratization process" (*Addis Standard* June 11, 2020b). Such concerns proved prophetic; by November 2020 federal forces were battling those of the Tigrayan regional government led by the TPLF which accused Abiy Ahmed and his government of ruling illegitimately. The regional government ignored the proscription on elections, holding its own regional poll in September 2020 which Addis Ababa declared illegal.

In March 2020 a new law on 'hate speech' and 'disinformation' was introduced and justified on public health grounds (Federal Negarit Gazette March 23, 2020). Given the vagueness of the definitions used, the law not only raised the possibility that it might be used to restrict freedom of expression, but also increased the likelihood it would be employed against political opponents or anyone who expressed opinions contrary to those of the government.

With the war in Tigray raging, Addis Ababa went ahead with the postponed general elections in June 2021. These were staggered in two phases (June and September 2021). The outcome was a landslide for Abiy Ahmed and his party. In the June elections the PP won 410 seats out of a total of 436 seats up for grabs in the House of Peoples' Representatives. It then went on to run uncontested in the separate September ballot held in the Somali state, taking all 23 parliamentary seats. On October 4, 2021, Abiy Ahmed was confirmed by the House of Representatives as Prime Minister for another five-year term.

While the consensus was that these elections were freer and fairer than previous ones, with marked improvements in the performance of the national electoral body, there were nevertheless numerous reports of the harassment of opposition leaders and supporters and the unequal playing field faced by the opposition. An American election observer mission concluded that while

> the overall electoral process leading to the June 21 elections...showed marked improvements over past elections...the electoral environment fell short of key standards concerning human and civil liberties, electoral campaigning, adequate security for all parties, and overall peace and security. (International Republican Institute and National Democratic Institute 2021, p. 2)

And on June 25, 2021, the US Secretary of State issued a press statement judging it to have been "an electoral process that was not free and fair for all Ethiopians" (U.S. Department of State 2021d).

In the case of Rwanda, the government was widely congratulated for its timely adoption of precautionary measures to deal with the virus, such as its promotion of hand washing and social distancing even before the first reported case of COVID in the country was confirmed in mid-March 2020. While a state of emergency was not declared, the country was subjected to the continent's first and strictest lockdown, and presidential statements and Cabinet resolutions were used to introduce a de facto special legal regime of powers and rules which allowed existing laws to be circumvented. In addition to the arrest of government critic Rusesabagina, the public health emergency also saw the harassment and arrest of journalists, in particular those who reported abuses committed by both police and soldiers during their enforcement of the lockdown restrictions (Civicus 2020). The pandemic was also used to justify the increased tracking and surveillance of citizens by the police, though couched in terms of the need to target those seen to have violated lockdown regulations (*KT Press* July 24, 2020).

Washington's Summit for Democracy and Notable Absences

Confronted by the reality of democratic regression around the world, and the damage done under the Trump administration to the credibility of the US as the self-ascribed global champion of the democratic cause, the new Biden administration launched an initiative to recover lost ground. The Summit on Democracy, held in Washington in December 2021, was cast by the US State Department as an event aimed at the development of concrete actions to secure "global democratic renewal" in the face of the "serious challenges from within and outside their borders" faced by democracies (U.S. Department of State, The Summit for Democracy 2021e).

Some of the groundwork for the Washington event, and which helped clarify the new administration's policy towards SSA, was laid by Antony Blinken's tour of African states in November 2021. On the one hand, the trip was clearly an attempt to repair the damage inflicted on US-Africa relations under the Trump administration, most notably the former President's widely publicised comments on African states as 'shithole countries', which unsurprisingly caused serious offence in African circles.[18] At the same time, it was also meant to signal that the US was back on the world stage following Trump's isolationist policies, that it had interests in Africa and was willing to play a constructive role there and, in particular, that Washington was willing to work with African countries to support their democratisation efforts (U.S. Department of State 2021f). It would not have gone unnoticed in Addis Ababa, Kampala and Kigali that whereas in the past their countries would normally have been considered almost mandatory stops during a tour by a US Secretary of State, on this occasion Blinken steered clear of them all, limiting his visits to Nigeria, Kenya and Senegal.

The December 2021 Washington virtual summit brought together over 100 heads of state and governments and representatives of multilateral organisations, civil society, the private sector, organised labour, journalists and human rights activists. It culminated in a series of commitments by participating governments to engage in a joint crusade for democratic renewal based on three themes, namely "strengthening democracy and defending against authoritarianism", "fighting corruption" and "promoting respect for human rights" (White House Summit for Democracy Summary of Proceedings December 23, 2021c).

Given recent developments in Uganda, Rwanda and Ethiopia, which had already resulted in American criticism of their governments, it was significant that prior to the event the US State Department set out its view that the challenges facing democracy around the world had taken the form of "the rise of leaders who are undermining democratic norms and institutions" and that the repressive activities carried out by authoritarian leaders ranged from "targeting journalists and human rights defenders to meddling in elections" (U.S. Department of State, The Summit for Democracy 2021e). Such words of censure might have easily been understood by the governments in Addis Ababa, Kampala and Kigali as criticisms directed at themselves.

It was a good indication of the rift which had opened up between Washington and its former privileged African allies that the criteria adopted by the Department of State for inviting specific countries was that these constituted "a regionally diverse set of well-established and younger democracies whose progress and commitments will advance a more just and peaceful world". The absence of the leaders of Uganda, Ethiopia and Rwanda meant they were clearly no longer considered members of this select group of states. Their exclusion stood in sharp contrast to the praise they had previously been showered with when they were seen to be leading their countries towards the shiny uplands of democracy and economic freedom.

The Spurned Favourites React and Wait

Faced with such Western ostracism, the three regimes reacted differently to the cold shoulders from various Western capitals. All depicted the estrangement as the result of either Western misunderstandings of their policies or the product of Western arrogance and lack of respect for their sovereignty and sought to remind their benefactors of their importance as friends of the West.

Abiy Ahmed (when it was clear he would not be on the invitation list for the Washington summit) wrote an open letter to Biden on September 17, 2021. He argued that threats of sanctions and other punitive measures reflected Washington's failure to understand that the war against the TPLF was part of the wider global war on terror, with his enemy having been "recently designated as 'terrorist' by our House of Representatives", the military actions undertaken therefore constituting "rule of law" operations. He reminded the American President that "Ethiopia has remained the US's staunch ally in fighting the terrorism threat of Al Shabab in the Horn" (Abiy Ahmed Ali 2021).

Museveni's exclusion from the December 2021 summit drew defiant responses from Kampala. The Minister of State for Foreign Affairs claimed the snub reflected ignorance of Uganda's importance as a regional player and that "Be it in democracy, be it in trade, be it in security, you cannot ignore us. You cannot do anything in the region without Uganda". He also stated that Washington's criticisms of the government reflected its ignorance of local conditions and arrogance, as "they don't appreciate the structures and how systems in many parts of the world operate, and they simply believe because they are a world power, they can get their way hence the many mistakes they've made" (*Daily Monitor* November 28, 2021).

In contrast, Rwanda's public reactions to growing Western criticism were muted, though its restraint did not imply inaction. There were oblique allusions to Kigali's resentment at the interference of outside powers in its internal affairs, and what it saw as Washington's attempt to determine the global standards for good democratic practice. So, for example, at a World Policy Conference on Global Governance in Abu Dhabi in October 2021, Kagame argued that there was a juxtaposition between "a country and nation that is trying to express itself the way they think is best for them and also another side where those who think they are powerful want to shape those values and interests or what you should do" (World Policy Conference 2021).

But at the same time Kigali engaged in some extremely adroit diplomacy to reduce the scope for Washington, London, and other European capitals to apply pressure on it to reform. Throughout 2022, Kigali sought to re-establish its *bona fides* with the US and UK, while simultaneously reducing its dependence on them by strengthening relations with other powers. Its efforts to restore its value as a partner in the eyes of London included volunteering to act as a 'holding pen' for part of the UK's caseload of failed asylum seekers in the framework of the 'UK-Rwanda Migration and Economic Development Partnership', an attempt by the Conservative government to deliver on one of its main election promises, namely to reduce illegal migration into the UK.[19] Kigali also took the opportunity presented by American efforts to rally support in the UN for a condemnation of Russia's invasion of Ukraine to align with Washington, with Rwanda one of only twenty-eight African countries voting in favour of the UN General Assembly (UNGA) resolution of March 2, 2022, which denounced Moscow's actions. The payback was quick, with Blinken then including Rwanda as one of the three African countries he visited in August 2022.

Kigali also sought to secure the goodwill of other African states. These efforts included its intervention to support the Mozambican government in its ongoing struggle against the Islamist insurgency in the northern province of Cabo Delgado. Following their deployment in July 2021, Rwandan forces quickly regained ground previously lost to the jihadists. Not only did the operation lead to expressions of gratitude from

Mozambique and other countries in Southern Africa, but Rwanda was also able to remind Western countries of its continued value as a player in global anti-terrorism efforts.

Its operation in Mozambique also helped diversify its Western support base. Post-genocide Rwanda's relations with France had been marked by longstanding suspicion and deep hostility; Kigali had regularly accused Paris of bearing a major responsibility for the 1994 genocide because not only President Mitterrand had failed to intervene at the time (and in the view of the RPF France had possessed the means to do so), but the French had actively supported the then Hutu government.[20] In a clear indication of the RPF's intention to distance itself from the previous regime's strong ties with Paris and the wider Francophonie, Kigali had joined the Commonwealth in 2009, despite serious concerns expressed at the time regarding the country's human rights record.[21]

Yet in a remarkable turnaround, Kagame visited Paris in May 2021 to attend a meeting on post-pandemic funding for African countries. Later that same month President Macron visited Rwanda. In the course of his trip, Macron helped lay to rest the contentious issue of French responsibility for the genocide by accepting the findings of a report by a French commission on the issue of France's role, which concluded that it had not been complicit, but rather simply blind to the preparations underway to commit genocide. While he stopped short of issuing a formal apology for France's role in the genocide, he nevertheless took the opportunity to state that "France did not understand that, in seeking to obstruct a regional or civil war, in reality it remained alongside a genocidal regime…I am here to recognise the scale of our responsibilities" (Ministère de l'Europe et des Affaires Étrangères May 27, 2021).

This appeared to satisfy Kagame, enabling the resetting of relations between the two countries, the process facilitated by Macron's announcement of a new and substantial injection of French development assistance for Rwanda (*Africanews* 2021). The diplomatic thaw between Paris and Kigali was a major diplomatic success for the Rwandan government. Not only did it secure new and significant inflows of aid, but it had successfully established its position as an important strategic ally of a major European power to compensate for its deteriorating relations with Washington. Furthermore, it is important to note that the major Western foreign investment project in Mozambique in the offshore gas fields of Cabo Delgado was led by France's energy giant Total, which had been forced to shut down its operations following a major Al Shabaab attack on the town of Palma in March 2021 (*France 24* April 3, 2021). Rwandan military operations in Mozambique therefore appeared directly linked to the need to provide security to Total's gas operations, amidst speculation that "France, seeking to protect its corporate interests militarily as it had done elsewhere in Africa, could be bankrolling Rwandan troops to protect the gas concessions" (*Christian Science Monitor* 2021). And as noted by Rwandan dissidents, at a time when there were growing criticisms from other Western countries, Paris chose to remain silent on the political repression and human rights abuses under Kagame (*Al Jazeera* 2021b).

For all three regimes, threats to the significant support they received from some Western donor countries might have been a disappointing development, but not necessarily a matter of grave concern. Above all, they understood that for a variety of reasons the turbulence introduced into these relations during the pandemic was unlikely to be long-lasting. Foremost amongst grounds for such optimism was their firm grasp of the low importance attached by Western powers to the democratization of their countries during the Cold War and that declarations of the primacy of this principle in terms of Western engagement with African states had never been absolute but rather always contingent on the pursuit of other Western interests. For them, the key lesson was that it was possible to ride out what seemed to be just another bout of Western sanctimonious proselytising and opprobrium and wait until conditions changed and their value as allies was again recognised.

Notes

1. For an excellent overview of the trend, see Gebrekidam, Selam (2020). "For Autocrats, and Others, Coronavirus Is a Chance to Grab Even More Power". *New York Times*, March 30, 2020.
2. The idea of successive global waves of democratisation was popularised by Samuel Huntington in his 1991 work *The Third Wave: Democratization in the Late Twentieth Century* (University of Oklahoma Press, 1991). According to the Huntingtonian historical schema, the first wave occurred between the early nineteenth and early twentieth centuries with the expansion of the (predominantly male) suffrage in the US, the UK, Italy, France, and the British Empire's white dominions such as Canada and Australia. The second wave took place after the Second World War, with many democracies being established in the new states which emerged from decolonisation. The third wave began with the democratic transition in Portugal in 1974 and Spain's the following year and continued in the

1980s with shifts from military rule to constitutional democracies in Brazil, Argentina, Uruguay and Chile. This was followed by several transitions in East Asia, such as the Philippines and Taiwan which adopted multi-party democratic systems of government, the democratic transitions in the Soviet Union, in Moscow's former Eastern Bloc allies, and then in Sub-Saharan Africa.

3. Liberal democracy may be defined as a form of representative democracy based on universal suffrage and regular, free and fair competitive elections between multiple freely formed political parties. In such systems the separation of powers between different branches of government (executive, legislative and judicial) is defined in constitutions. The latter place limits on the powers of governments through a system of checks and balances, contain provisions for the rule of law, and protect a set of political and civil rights such as the right to vote and run for public office and freedom of thought, expression and association.
4. On the changing of Hungary's constitutional order and placement of Fidesz party loyalists in key positions in the state apparatus, see Bánkuti et al. (2012).
5. According to WHO data, on March 30, 2020, there were only 325 confirmed cases.
6. Various theories abound as to the forces behind the failed coup, ranging from secularist elements concerned with Erdoğan's Islamist agenda to Islamist elements which had fallen out with him.
7. A referendum was held in April 2017 on proposed constitutional amendments, which Erdoğan and his ruling party narrowly won. These included the abolition of the post of Prime Minister and the introduction of a strong Executive Presidency, the incumbent exercising the roles of both Head of State and Head of Government, and enjoying increased powers regarding judicial appointments.
8. The first Baltic country subjected to Russian cyber warfare was Estonia in 2007, the attack effectively shutting down the country's banking system and government Internet. See McGuinness (2017). Lithuania's National Threat Assessment claimed the country's decision-makers and public institutions were being subjected to continuous Russian cyber attacks in 2020 (State Security Department of the Republic of Lithuania 2021).
9. Comprehensive data on various aspects of the Chinese government's repression of the Uyghurs has been collected and analysed by the Australian Strategic Policy Institute.
10. Like the security legislation of other authoritarian regimes, the definition of 'national security' and what actions might be considered to 'endanger' it were so broad as to permit any action to be considered a threat to national security.

11. The amendment catered for Hindus, Sikhs, Parsis, Jains and Buddhists who had migrated from Afghanistan, Bangladesh and Pakistan and who were seen by the Indian government as persecuted minorities in their countries of origin.
12. Subsequent investigations revealed that prior to the announcement of the March 2020 lockdown, Modi had failed to inform, let alone consult, key ministries and state governments. This meant the authorities were ill-prepared to provide the necessary assistance to both those on the move and those who remained in cities, and lost their livelihoods (BBC News 2020).
13. The quote is from a widely circulated report compiled by Bruce I. Afran, Bobi Wine's US-based attorney. See Afran (2021).
14. Irregularities included pre-marked ballots for Museveni, ballot stuffing and destruction of ballot papers containing votes for the opposition, the banning of campaigning in strongly pro-opposition areas, reports of police and army personnel at polling stations intimidating voters to cast their votes for Museveni and NRM candidates, the prohibition on citizens witnessing the counting process, and the denial of permits to both domestic and international election observers. See Afran (2021).
15. The EPRDF was a coalition of ethnic-based parties established in 1989, namely the Tigray People's Liberation Front (TPLF) which was very much the senior partner and led by Meles Zenawi, the Ethiopian Peoples' Democratic Movement Party (EPDM) which later became the Amhara Democratic Party (ADP), and the Oromo People's Democratic Organization (OPDO). In 1992 the Southern Ethiopian People's Democratic Movement (SEPDM) joined the EPRDF. Abiy Ahmed was an OPDO member of parliament, and later its Chairman. In March 2018 he became Chairman of the EPRDF, and in April 2018 Ethiopia's Prime Minister.
16. On July 18, 2021, the Prime Minister's Office released a statement in which Abiy Ahmed characterised his Tigrayan opponents as "the cancer of Ethiopia", stating that it was necessary to remove the "invasive weed". See, Collins (2021).
17. On this point, and for a comprehensive account of the RPF's subsequent violations of human rights in both Rwanda and the neighbouring Democratic Republic of Congo, see Rever (2018).
18. Trump's comments were made during a discussion with White House staff and members of Congress in January 2018 on immigration legislation. There was strong criticism of his use of language by a range of African sources, including the African Union which stated that it was "frankly alarmed". See: *Al Jazeera* (2018b).

19. This highly controversial programme, announced in April 2022, was championed by the UK's Home Secretary, Priti Patel. It provided for the removal to Rwanda of illegal migrants and those asylum-seekers judged to have arrived in the UK after travelling through third countries considered safe, and in which they had not claimed asylum. Upon arrival in Rwanda, they would be entitled to claim asylum in that country. A five-year memorandum of understanding between the UK and Rwanda was signed, with a sweetener of £140 million being paid to Rwanda to set up the scheme, with additional amounts to be paid to Rwanda to cover in country costs for each individual migrant and asylum seeker.
20. In fact, strained relations between the RPF and Paris preceded the 1994 genocide. France had provided the Hutu-dominated government in Kigali with extensive military support to repulse an RPF offensive from its bases in Uganda in 1990. Kagame repeatedly accused France of aiding the 1994 genocide, in particular through its *Opération Turquoise*. This UN-mandated operation, composed overwhelmingly of French troops, was launched when the mass murder of Tutsis had already largely been completed. It was meant to provide security and protection in safe zones to displaced persons and other civilians judged to be in danger from the fighting. By the end of June 1994, such groups were predominantly composed of Hutus. Given evidence that killings of Tutsis by Hutus continued in the supposed safe zones established by the French operation, *Turquoise* would subsequently be seen by Kigali as an attempt, in the face of the RPF's advances, to save the genocidal Hutu *Interahamwe* and remnants of the former government. See Republic of Rwanda (2020).
21. The Commonwealth Human Rights Initiative (CHRI), an international NGO focused on monitoring compliance of members of the Commonwealth with international human rights instruments, produced an extensive report on Rwanda prior to its admission to the organization. Amongst its conclusions were that in terms of democracy and the protection of human rights, "the government of Rwanda is not sufficiently committed to these values", that there was a "climate of fear within civil society", that in terms of freedom of expression "the government had a record of shutting down independent media outlets and newspapers and harassing journalists", while Rwanda's judiciary has "systemic weaknesses". It noted that while Kigali had managed to convince the outside world that it respected the provisions of the country's constitution in the areas of democracy and human rights, the truth was that it "uses the constitution opportunistically as a façade, which hides the exclusionary and repressive nature of the regime" (Commonwealth Human Rights Initiative 2009, pp. 8–9).

References

Abiy Ahmed Ali. 2021. "An Open Letter to President Joseph R. Biden Jr". Published on the website X (formerly Twitter) on September 17, 2021. Accessed on May 1, 2024. https://twitter.com/AbiyAhmedAli/status/1438869469464567808/photo/1

Addis Standard. 2020a. "News Alert: HoF approves CCI's Recommendation to Extend both Houses, State Councils Term Limit: Constitutional Expert raises Questions". June 10, 2020, Addis Ababa. https://addisstandard.com/news-alert-hof-approves-ccis-recommendation-to-extend-both-houses-state-councils-term-limit-constitutional-expert-raises-concern/

Addis Standard. 2020b. "News: OLF, OFC and ONLF oppose HOF's "Unilateral Decision" to extend incumbent's term limit, call for inclusive dialogue", Addis Ababa, June 11, 2020.

Afran, Bruce. 2021. "Report on Governmental Abuse, Violations and Misconduct in Advance of the January 14, 2021 Presidential Election and its Aftermath". Princeton, New Jersey. February 4, 2021.

Al Jazeera. 2018a. "Rwandan opposition activist Diane Rwigara released on bail", October 5, 2018. https://www.aljazeera.com/news/2018/10/5/rwandan-opposition-activist-diane-rwigara-released-on-bail

Al Jazeera. 2018b. "Trump's 'shithole' remarks spur international anger", January 12, 2018. Accessed May 1, 2024. https://www.aljazeera.com/news/2018/1/12/trumps-shithole-remarks-spur-international-anger

Al Jazeera. 2021a. "'Hotel Rwanda' hero given 25-year sentence in terrorism case", September 20, 2021. https://www.aljazeera.com/news/2021/9/20/rwanda-court-finds-hotel-rwanda-hero-guilty-in-terrorism-case

Al Jazeera. 2021b. "Macron 'Silent' on Kagame Abuses: Rwanda Opposition Leaders", May 25, 2021. Accessed on May 1, 2024. https://www.aljazeera.com/news/2021/5/25/macron-silent-on-kagame-abuses-rwanda-opposition

Amnesty International. 2021. "Ethiopia: Eritrean troops' massacre of hundreds of Axum civilians may amount to crimes against humanity". February 26, 2021. https://www.amnesty.org/en/latest/news/2021/02/ethiopia-eritrean-troops-massacre-of-hundreds-of-axum-civilians-may-amount-to-crime-against-humanity/

Australian Strategic Policy Institute "Xinjiang Data Project", https://xjdp.aspi.org.au/

Avocats Sans Frontières. 2020. "Uganda's de facto state of emergency to address the Covid-19 pandemic". June 11, 2020. Accessed May 1 2024. https://asf.be/ugandas-de-facto-state-of-emergency-to-address-the-covid-19-pandemic/

Bánkuti, Miklós et al., 2012. "Hungary's Illiberal Turn: Disabling the Constitution", *Journal of Democracy*, Vol.23, No.3, July 2012, Johns Hopkins University Press

BBC News. 2020. "Paul Rusesabagina: Hotel Rwanda hero charged with terrorism", September 14, 2020. https://www.bbc.co.uk/news/world-africa-54147759

Beauchamp, Zack. 2020. "Hungary's 'coronavirus coup' explained", *Vox* April 15, 2020. https://www.vox.com/policy-and-politics/2020/4/15/21193960/coronavirus-covid-19-hungary-orban-trump-populism

Brooks, Brad. 2019. "Brazil Military Takes up Coup Commemoration at Bolsonaro's Behest". *Reuters*, March 31, 2019. https://www.reuters.com/article/us-brazil-politics-idUSKCN1RC09J

Burke, Jason and Samuel Okikor. 2020. "Bobi Wine Protests: Death Toll Rises in Uganda's Worst Unrest in Years', *Guardian* (UK Edition) November 19, 2020. https://www.theguardian.com/world/2020/nov/19/bobi-wine-protests-death-toll-rises-in-ugandas-worst-unrest-in-years.

Burke, Jason and Samuel Okikor. 2021. "'It was a Torture Chamber': Ugandans Abducted in Vicious Crackdown", *Guardian* (UK Edition), April 22, 2021. https://www.theguardian.com/world/2021/apr/22/torture-abducted-uganda-crackdown-museveni. Accessed May 4 2024.

Chambraud, Tancrede and AFP. 2021. "France and Rwanda strengthen relations, increase cooperation". *Africanews.com,* May 27, 2021. https://www.africanews.com/2021/05/27/france-and-rwanda-strengthen-relations-increase-cooperation// Accessed May 4 2024.

Civicus. 2020. "Multiple journalists arrested throughout Covid-19 lockdown period" September 9, 2020. https://monitor.civicus.org/updates/2020/09/09/multiple-journalists-arrested-throughout-covid-19-lockdown-period/ Accessed May 1 2024.

Collins, Tom. 2021. "Genocide fears after Ethiopian PM vows to crush 'weeds' of Tigray". *Times (London),* July 19, 2021. https://www.thetimes.co.uk/article/abiys-pledge-to-crush-weeds-of-tigray-raises-fears-of-genocide-in-ethiopia-sx0xkqb2v. Accessed May 2 2024.

Commonwealth Human Rights Initiative. 2009. "Rwanda's Application for Membership of the Commonwealth – Report and Recommendations of the Commonwealth Human Rights Initiative". New Delhi, 2009.

Daily Monitor. 2021. "US sidesteps strategic ally Uganda on democracy summit", November 28, 2021. Accessed May 1, 2024. https://www.monitor.co.ug/uganda/news/national/us-sidesteps-stragetic-ally-uganda-on-democracy-summit-3633900?view=htmlamp

Eddy, Kester. 2014. "EU urged to monitor Hungary as Orban hits at 'liberal democracy". Financial Times, July 30, 2014. https://www.ft.com/content/0574f7f2-17f3-11e4-b842-00144feabdc0

European Parliament. 2021a. European Parliament resolution of 11 February 2021 on Rwanda, the case of Paul Rusesabagina (2021/2543 (RSP)). https://www.europarl.europa.eu/doceo/document/TA-9-2021-0055_EN.html

European Parliament. 2021b. European Parliament Resolution of 11 February 2021 on the Political Situation in Uganda (2021/2545 (RSP)). https://www.europarl.europa.eu/doceo/document/TA-9-2021-0057_EN.pdf

Federal Negarit Gazette. 2020. "Hate Speech and Disinformation Prevention and Suppression Proclamation". Proclamation No.1185/2020, Addis Ababa, March 23rd, 2020.

Finnegan, Conor. 2021. "After ending Ethiopia's Trade Status, US Weighs Sanctions, Genocide Designation over Tigray War". *ABC News,* November 3, 2021. https://abcnews.go.com/Politics/ending-ethiopias-trade-status-us-weighs-sanctions-genocide/story?id=80928248.

Folha de São Paulo. 2020. "Com Apoio de Bolsonaro, Manifestantes Ignoram Coronavírus e Fazem Atos Pró-Governo", 15 Março 2020, São Paulo.

France 24. 2021. "France's Total closes Gas Plant after Mozambique Jihadist Attacks" April 3, 2021. Accessed on May 1, 2024. https://www.france24.com/en/africa/20210403-france-s-total-closes-gas-plant-after-mozambique-jihadist-attacks .

Freedom House. 2021a. *Freedom in the World 2021: Democracy under Siege*, Washington DC

Freedom House. 2021b. "*Out of Sight, Not Out of Reach – The Global Scope and Scale of Transnational Repression*", February 2021, Washington D.C.

Gatehouse, Gabriel. 2014. "Patrick Keregeya: Mysterious death of a Rwandan exile". *BBC News,* March 26, 2014, https://www.bbc.co.uk/news/world-africa-26752838

House of Commons International Development Committee. 2021. "*The humanitarian situation in Tigray*", April 30 2021, London.

Human Rights Watch. 2021. World Report 2021, New York: Russia Chapter, 2021.

Huntington, Samuel. 1991. *The Third Wave: Democratization in the Late Twentieth Century* Oklahoma, University of Oklahoma Press, 1991.

Independent (Kampala). 2021. "Byabakama: Voters will not be allowed to witness vote counting". Kampala, January 6, 2021.

International Republican Institute and National Democratic Institute. 2021. "Ethiopia June 21, 2021 National Elections Report". August 5, 2021, Washington D.C.

Jaffrelot, Christophe. 2021. *Modi's India: Hindu Nationalism and the Rise of Ethnic Democracy*, Princeton University Press.

KTPress. 2020. "COVID-19: Police Outlines Tough Measures Against Errant Violators", July 24, 2020. Accessed May 1, 2024. https://www.ktpress.rw/2020/07/covid-19-police-outlines-tough-measures-against-errant-violators/

Lawal, Shola. 2021. "Rwanda keeps the Peace in Mozambique. Why?", *Christian Science Monitor*, December 20, 2021. Accessed on May 1, 2024. https://www.csmonitor.com/World/Africa/2021/1220/Rwanda-keeps-the-peace-in-Mozambique.-Why

Levitsky, Steven and Daniel Ziblatt. 2019. *How Democracies Die – What History Reveals About Our Future*, London: Penguin Books

Luhrmann, Anna and Staffan I. Lindberg. 2019. "A Third Wave of Autocratization is Here: What is New About It?" *Democratization* Vol 26 No 7, 2019.

Mahony, Honor. 2014. "Orban wants to build 'illiberal' state" EU Observer. 28 July 2014. https://euobserver.com/eu-political/125128

Maphanga, Canny. 2021. "Process of applying for extradition of alleged assassins of former Rwandan Intelligence Head is complete -NPA" *News24*, 24 April 2021. https://www.news24.com/news24/southafrica/news/process-of-applying-for-extradition-of-alleged-assassins-of-former-rwandan-intelligence-head-is-complete-npa-20210424

Maynes, Charles. 2021. "As US reels from Capitol Violence, Moscow Enjoys the Show", *Voice of America*, January 07, 2021

McGuinness, Damien. 2017. "How a Cyber Attack Transformed Estonia", *BBC News*, 27 April 2017. https://www.bbc.co.uk/news/39655415

Ministère de l'Europe et des Affaires Étrangères. 2021. "Rwanda – Speech by President Emmanuel Macron at the Kigali Genocide Memorial" Kigali, May 27, 2021. https://www.diplomatie.gouv.fr/en/country-files/rwanda/news/article/rwanda-speech-by-president-emmanuel-macron-at-the-kigali-genocide-memorial

Mutiga, Murithi. 2021. "Uganda's Museveni Clings to Power – But Trouble Lies Ahead", *Q&A/AFRICA*, 19 January 2021. Crisis Group. https://www.crisisgroup.org/africa/horn-africa/uganda/ugandas-museveni-clings-power-trouble-lies-ahead

National Endowment for Democracy. 2020. "Pandemic of power grabs: Autocrats' opportunities in disaster", *Democracy Digest*, April 23, 2020, Washington D.C. https://www.demdigest.org/what-does-pandemic-democracy-look-like/).

Norwegian Nobel Committee. 2019. "Announcement". 11 October 2019, Oslo. https://www.nobelprize.org/prizes/peace/2019/press-release/

Pech, Laurent et al. 2021. Poland's Rule of Law Breakdown: A Five-Year Assessment of EU's (In)Action, *Hague Journal on the Rule of Law* 13, Issue 1, April 2021, Springer

Republic of Rwanda. 2020. "Turquoise: military operation to the rescue of the genocidal government and its army". *National Commission for the Fight against Genocide*, June 22, 2020. Accessed May 1, 2024. https://www.rba.co.rw/post/Turquoise-Military-operation-to-the-rescue-of-the-genocidal-government-and-its-army#google_vignette

Rever, Judi. 2018. *In Praise of Blood: The Crimes of the Rwandan Patriotic Front.* Canada: Random House, 2018.

Selam, Gebrekidam. 2020. "For Autocrats, and Others, Coronavirus Is a Chance to Grab Even More Power." *New York Times,* March 30, 2020.

State Security Department of the Republic of Lithuania. 2021. National Threat Assessment Vilnius, 2021.

Tangen, Ole. 2020. "Is China taking advantage of COVID-19 to pursue South China Sea ambitions?" *Deutsche Welle*, May 26,2020. https://www.dw.com/en/is-china-taking-advantage-of-covid-19-to-pursue-south-china-sea-ambitions/a-53573918

The Electoral Commission. 2020. "Suspension of General Election Campaign Meetings in Specified Areas of the Country". Press Statement, December 26, 2020, Republic of Uganda.

U.S. Department of State. 2021d. "Building a Stronger Democracy in Ethiopia" Press Statement, June 25, 2021. https://www.state.gov/building-a-stronger-democracy-in-ethiopia/#:~:text=Democracy%20flourishes%20when%20institutions%20of,to%20vote%20on%20June%2021

U.S. Department of State. 2021a. "Imposing Visa Restrictions on Ugandans for Undermining the Democratic Process", Press Statement, Antony Blinken, Secretary of State, April 16, 2021. https://ug.usembassy.gov/statement-by-u-s-ambassador-natalie-e-brown-on-cancellation-of-u-s-diplomatic-observer-mission-of-ugandas-elections/

U.S. Department of State. 2021c. "Secretary Blinken's Virtual Travel to Africa". Press Statement, April 26, 2021. https://www.state.gov/secretary-blinkens-virtual-travel-to-africa/

U.S. Department of State. 2021e. "The Summit for Democracy: Further Information", Washington D.C. Accessed May 1, 2024. https://www.state.gov/further-information-the-summit-for-democracy/

U.S. Department of State. 2021f. "The United States and Africa: Building a 21st Century Partnership". Speech given by Antony Blinken, Secretary of State, Economic Community of West African States, Abuja, Nigeria, November 19, 2021. https://www.state.gov/the-united-states-and-africa-building-a-21st-century-partnership/ Accessed May 1, 2024.

U.S. Department of State. 2021b. "United States' Actions To Press for the Resolution of the Crisis in the Tigray Region of Ethiopia", Press Statement, Antony J. Blinken, Secretary of State, May 23, 2021. https://www.state.gov/united-states-actions-to-press-for-the-resolution-of-the-crisis-in-the-tigray-region-of-ethiopia/

U.S. Embassy Kampala. 2021. "Statement by U.S. Ambassador Natalie E. Brown on Cancellation of U.S. Diplomatic Observer Mission of Uganda's Elections". January 13, 2021. https://ug.usembassy.gov/statement-by-u-s-ambassador-natalie-e-brown-on-cancellation-of-u-s-diplomatic-observer-mission-of-ugandas-elections/

U.S. Embassy Rwanda. 2021. "U.S. Statement at Universal Periodic Review of Rwanda". January 25, 2021, Geneva. https://rw.usembassy.gov/u-s-statement-at-the-universal-periodic-review-of-rwanda/

UN News. 2021. "UN agencies scale-up response to address looming 'famine' catastrophe in Tigray", June 10, 2021. https://news.un.org/en/story/2021/06/1093722

United Nations General Assembly Human Rights Council. 2021. *Report of the Working Group on the Universal Periodic Review – Rwanda*, Forty-seventh session, June 21–July 9, 2021. A/HRC/47/14. https://undocs.org/A/HRC/47/14

United States Congress, Human Rights Commission. 2021. "Members of Congress Release Letter Calling for Return of Paul Rusesabagina on Humanitarian Grounds", Press Release, February 16, 2021. https://humanrightscommission.house.gov/news/press-releases/tlhrc-co-chairs-call-humanitarian-release-paul-rusesabagina

United States Institute of Peace. 2021. "*Taking Stock of U.S. Policy on Ethiopia: A Conversation with Ambassador Jeffrey Feltman*". November 2, 2021. https://www.usip.org/?site_keywords=feltman%20ethiopia

V-Dem Institute, *Autocratization Turns Viral*, Democracy Report 2021, University of Gothenburg, Sweden.

Vinga, Alois, 2021, "Under-Sanctions Mnangagwa Flags US For Washington Violence", *New Zimbabwe,* January 7, 2021.

Voice of America. 2017. "Three Rwandan Presidential Candidates Disqualified Amid Criticism", July 07, 2017. https://www.voanews.com/africa/three-rwandan-presidential-candidates-disqualified-amid-criticism

White House. 2005. "*Citations for the Recipients of the 2005 Presidential Medal of Freedom*", November 9, 2005. https://georgewbush-whitehouse.archives.gov/news/releases/2005/11/20051109-10.html

White House. 2021a. "*A Message to the Congress on the Termination of the Designation of the Federal Democratic Republic of Ethiopia (Ethiopia), the Republic of Guinea (Guinea), and the Republic of Mali (Mali) as beneficiary sub-Saharan African countries under the African Growth and Opportunity Act (AGOA)*", November 02, 2021. https://www.whitehouse.gov/briefing-room/statements-releases/2021/11/02/a-message-to-the-congress-on-the-termination-of-the-designation-of-the-federal-democratic-republic-of-ethiopia-ethiopia-the-republic-of-guinea-guinea-and-the-republic-of-mali-mali-as-beneficia/.

White House. 2021b. "President Biden Invites 40 World Leaders to Leaders Summit on Climate". March 26, 2021. Accessed May 1, 2024. https://www.whitehouse.gov/briefing-room/statements-releases/2021/03/26/president-biden-invites-40-world-leaders-to-leaders-summit-on-climate/

White House. 2021c. "Summit for Democracy Summary of Proceedings", December 23, 2021. Accessed May 1, 2024. https://www.whitehouse.gov/briefing-room/statements-releases/2021/12/23/summit-for-democracy-summary-of-proceedings/

World Policy Conference. 2021. "Conversation with President Kagame", Transcript. Abu Dhabi, 1 October 2021. Accessed on May 1, 2024. https://www.paulkagame.com/world-policy-conference-conversation-with-president-kagame-abu-dhabi-1-october-2021/

Yackley, Ayla Jean, 2020, "Turkey ousts Kurdish opposition's last mayor", *Politico*, September 30, 2020. https://www.politico.eu/article/turkey-ousts-kurdish-oppositions-last-mayor-ayhan-bilgen-in-crackdown/

CHAPTER 3

Elements of Continuity: Promoting Democracy During the Cold War

Political Freedoms and Washington's Cold War Africa Policy

At a White House Conference on Africa in June 1994, President Clinton sought to present his Administration's Africa policy as a clean break with that pursued by Washington during the Cold War. Most salient amongst such shifts was a commitment to give greater priority to the state of democracy in Africa and the promotion of political freedoms:

> For decades we viewed Africa through a cold war prism and through the fight against apartheid. We often, I think, cared in past years more about how African nations voted in the United Nations than whether their own people had the right to vote. We supported leaders on the basis of their anti-Communist or anti-apartheid rhetoric perhaps more than their actions. (U.S. Publishing Office 1994)

That during the Cold War Washington's geo-strategic interests had often trumped the democratic aspirations of African peoples were hardly novel revelations to African democracy activists and human rights defenders. The West had been willing to overlook significant democratic deficits in those states and political movements in the developing world it supported to keep them out of the Soviet orbit and assisted right-wing authoritarian regimes on the basis of their strong anti-communist rhetoric.

M. Simpson, *Donors, Democracy and Development in Africa*,
https://doi.org/10.1007/978-3-031-74917-9_3

The Cold War tension between the realpolitik imperatives of establishing alliances with authoritarian anti-communist military or single-party regimes on the one hand and a declared interest in promoting multi-party democracy on the other was never satisfactorily resolved. The incompatibility of pursuing both these objectives reflected competing views within American foreign policy circles of the risks and benefits of democracy promotion.

One school of thought took a short-term approach in relation to friendly right-wing authoritarian regimes such as the military dictatorships in Latin America, treating them as bulwarks against the spread of communism. Any pressure on such regimes to democratise was seen as potentially destabilising, opening the door to communist takeovers. Another school adopted a longer-term perspective on the requirements for stability, seeing support for right-wing authoritarian regimes presiding over state-sponsored repression, corruption, inequality, and lack of economic and social progress for their populations as itself contributing to the conditions for communist-inspired uprisings. The unsettled question whether to support dictatorships or democratic reforms as the best way to ensure stability in the developing world would continue to rear its head in the post-Cold War era.

Throughout the Cold War, the Western democracies, and the U.S. in particular, had regularly proclaimed that their foreign policies had as key objectives not only the thwarting of Communism, but also the export of 'freedom' defined in terms of market-friendly economic systems and multi-party democracy. Declarations by African political actors of an anti-communist stance, support for market economic principles and of adherence to democratic principles, and the promise of pro-Western voting patterns in the UN, were usually sufficient to gain the favourable attention of Washington and other Western capitals. However, little effort was expended in scrutinising the routine hortatory commitments of their African allies to multi-party democracy, constitutional rule, respect for human rights and the rule of law. Even less attention was paid to the kleptocratic practices of many pro-Western African leaders, simple declarations of an anti-communist stance being usually sufficient for inclusion in the club of friendly pro-Western African states.

U.S. activities in the former Belgian Congo, seen as an ideological and geo-strategic battleground in the Cold War, were emblematic of the overall American approach to Africa. Washington's efforts during the Eisenhower administration to destabilise and then remove the leftist Prime

Minister Patrice Lumumba helped secure the road to power for the staunchly anti-Communist military strongman, Mobutu Sese Seko.[1]

Mobutu was not noted for either his interest in nurturing political pluralism, or deep concern for the welfare of the Zairean population, nor for the transparent management of public resources (both those provided in the form of aid or generated domestically). Throughout the period from the 1960s to the 1980s, the dominant thinking in the U.S. State Department and Pentagon has been appropriately designated the 'Mobutu or Chaos' approach to Zairean affairs, and one applicable to other African countries.[2] According to its assumptions, 'chaos' would be the inevitable result of pushing Mobutu to loosen his monopolistic hold on power, increasing the dangers of territorial dismemberment given the country's susceptibility to secessionist force and the opportunities for communist expansion into the heart of Africa arising from armed conflict and civil unrest and the possibility of an unfriendly successor regime denying Western access to the country's vast mineral wealth.

Mobutu's extended rule from 1965 to 1997 saw the collapse of the country's physical infrastructure and widespread impoverishment of the Zairean people, and his own obscene personal enrichment. According to Transparency International, Mobutu stole an estimated US$ 5 billion during his tenure in office (Transparency International 2004). Such uncomfortable realities were the price the U.S. seemed willing to pay given the extensive covert and overt support it provided Kinshasa. So long as there was some semblance of politico-military stability in Zaire, and Kinshasa adopted a solidly pro-Western foreign policy stance, geo-strategic imperatives during the Cold War meant Mobutu remained a trusted U.S. ally for decades.

The same logic explains Washington's extensive support to armed anticommunist rebel movements, such as to the National Union for the Total Independence of Angola (UNITA) in its struggle against the Soviet and Cuban-backed Marxist Popular Movement for the Liberation of Angola (MPLA). Its leader, Jonas Savimbi, became a darling of right-wing circles in the U.S., and in 1986, President Reagan added Savimbi to the roll call of the America's favoured 'freedom fighters'. He benefitted from significant covert U.S. military assistance during the Reagan years and the administration of his successor George H. W. Bush (Rampe 1989). Despite claims to be fighting for the establishment of a multi-party-political system in Angola, his democratic credentials would remain unquestioned until the end of the Cold War. He then dismally failed the test, rejecting the results of the country's first democratic elections in 1992 which he lost, and returning to the bush and subjecting Angola to yet another round of bloody conflict which only ended when he was killed by government forces in 2002.

It was clear that during the Cold War, the top U.S. foreign policy priority in the developing world, and in Africa specifically, was to overthrow anti-Western revolutionary governments such as the MPLA, support friendly states and dissident movements, and halt, and where possible roll back, the spread of Communism. Such objectives would be pursued even if they meant that the African governments and movements supported by Washington exhibited few of the features of the freedoms the U.S. and its Western allies claimed to be promoting. And as will be shown later, the 'Mobutu or Chaos' thesis has had a long shelf-life in a post-Cold War context and would be applied not only to a post-Mobutu DRC, but to many other African countries.

British Development Assistance and Anglophone Africa's First Strongmen

London's Cold War-era relations with its former British colonies in Africa paid no more than lip service to the principle of multi-party democracy. In the case of Malawi, for example, two years after its independence in 1964 a new constitution transformed the country into a *de jure* one-party state under the Malawi Congress Party (MCP). A party resolution followed making Hastings Banda the MCP's President for Life, with the country's single-party legislature then passing a resolution in 1971 declaring him the country's President for Life. During his long years in office from 1964 to 1994, Banda presided over a highly personalised and increasingly idiosyncratic system of government; all adult citizens were compelled to be members of the ruling MCP, with the authorities imposing a strict set of restrictions on public conduct based on the President's own social mores which included the banning of trousers for women.

On a darker note, the regime also developed an extensive network of informants and enforcers to crush any contestation of Banda's rule, with Malawi earning a dismal reputation in terms of its human rights record. This went hand in hand with the President accumulating significant personal wealth. As was the case in many African countries, the distinction between funds in the national treasury and the private assets of its leader was a purely *pro forma* one. There was widespread corruption amidst deepening poverty, hunger and unemployment, with the majority of Malawi's population dependent on increasingly stagnant small-scale peasant agriculture.

Banda adopted a stridently anti-communist position in foreign affairs. Diplomatic relations were established with Taiwan, and the country did not recognise the People's Republic of China (PRC). It broke ranks with the rest of Africa and exchanged ambassadors with apartheid South Africa, and the country did not become a member of the Frontline States, the coalition of Southern African countries committed to supporting groups fighting against apartheid in South Africa and white minority rule in Rhodesia. It also provided significant support to the anti-communist RENAMO (Mozambican National Resistance) insurgents in neighbouring Mozambique in their struggle against the Marxist FRELIMO (Liberation Front of Mozambique) government.

Under Banda, Malawi's performance in terms of key development indicators was poor, even when compared to the less than stellar track record of SSA as a whole. Its Gross Domestic Product (GDP) per capita (in current US$) declined from US$287 in 1980 to US$169 in 1994, the last year of Banda's rule and only a quarter of the SSA average of US$657 in 1994 (World Bank 2024). Child malnutrition was widespread; by 1992 and towards the end of Banda's rule, the prevalence of stunting for children under five years of age stood at 55.8 per cent.[3]

Despite the government's oppressive domestic politics and poor development outcomes, this did not impact negatively on flows of UK and broader Western development assistance. Malawi received substantial Western aid and became an early Western 'donor darling'. Over the period 1970–1990, annual Official Development Assistance (ODA)[4] disbursements to Malawi from Organisation for Economic Co-operation and Development (OECD) countries increased from US$25.9 million to US$216 million (in current prices). And while the UK's share of total OECD member disbursements fell from 66.8 per cent in 1970 to 23.4 per cent by 1990, the latter figure was still high given there were nineteen other OECD bilateral donor members, a clear indication of London's strong interest in providing development assistance to Malawi (OECD Statistics 2022). The Bretton Woods Institutions (BWIs), dominated by Western donors also contributed significant resources to Malawi under Banda's rule, with the World Bank's annual disbursements rising nearly tenfold from US$9.6 million in 1970 to US$95 million by 1990 (OECD

Statistics 2022). By 1990, Malawi's ODA per capita had reached US$53 (in current prices), compared to the SSA average of US$34.8, and represented nearly 25 per cent of GNI per capita (World Bank 2024).

London's lack of concern for the status of political freedoms (and rule of law, respect for human rights and levels of corruption), in countries benefiting from British aid, also made itself felt in West Africa. Following a brief period of democratically elected civilian rule after Nigeria's Independence in 1960, this was brought to an end by the armed forces in 1966. With the exception of a truncated return to civilian rule between 1979 and 1983, Nigeria was governed by a succession of military governments, the latter themselves subject to being replaced through coups by rival groups in the armed forces.[5] Widespread repression of those opposed to military rule was particularly marked between 1983 and 1985 under the rule of General Buhari, with the introduction of legislation permitting detentions without trial for individuals deemed to threaten the security of the state, the banning of strike action, in addition to draconian press laws which included jail sentences for those judged by military tribunals to have brought the military government into disrepute.

Given the size of the Nigerian economy and population, Western aid never took on the importance it had in countries such as Malawi. It is nevertheless significant that Western ODA to Nigeria continued to flow without interruption throughout the long years of military rule, and notwithstanding increasing levels of corruption which should have raised concerns over the use of donor funds. During the protracted rule of General Ibrahim Babangida (1985–1993), the country underwent what one analyst colourfully described as the "Zaireanization" of the military oligarchy and the "consolidation of avaricious dictatorship" (Lewis 1996, p. 80). Public resources were plundered, and the country became the locus for a range of criminal activities such as drug trafficking and international commercial fraud. However, such poor performance in terms of the management of public finances did not deter London from continuing to channel development assistance to Nigeria, with Lynda Chalker, the UK Minister in charge of DFID's precursor, the Overseas Development Administration (ODA), paying numerous visits to Nigeria under military rule.

In Ghana, the overthrow of civilian governments by the armed forces was also a recurrent feature of the country's politics, but UK development assistance to Ghana was also generous throughout the country's extended periods of military rule. Disbursements during the first military regime from 1972 to 1979 totalled US$45.9 million (in current prices), such transfers taking place uninterruptedly on an annual basis. The next period of military rule from 1981 to 1992 would see even higher annual disbursements totalling US$351 million (OECD databank).

Paris and its African Protégés

Similar patterns of patronage of authoritarian regimes were present in Francophone Africa during the Cold War. Following decolonisation, Paris established an extensive and complex web of relations with its former African colonies known as *Françafrique* (and which included the former Belgian colonies of Zaire, Burundi and Rwanda). Based on close and often extremely opaque personal ties between French and African leaders, these served to protect French interests in Africa. The arrangements were viewed by critics both in France and in Africa as paternalistic, corrupt and responsible for propping up repressive (and in some cases tyrannical) regimes, with France abstaining from attaching any political reform conditionality to its assistance so long as its acolytes defended its commercial and strategic interests.

Substantial military assistance was provided to its favourites, with Paris in exchange securing military bases in several francophone African countries. Military interventions in support of favoured African rulers when challenged by rivals were common and facilitated by the invocation of numerous bilateral military assistance and defence treaties signed after independence between France and its former colonies, while assistance was given to rebels to remove leaders who had stepped out of line and threatened French interests.

Paris also deployed large numbers of French development experts to its former African colonies in the context of *accords de cooperation,* and it became a critical source of loans and grants; France's disbursements of ODA to its former colonies in West and Equatorial Africa, together with the three other francophone African countries of Zaire, Burundi and Rwanda, grew from US$151 million in 1970 (in current prices) to US$2.04 billion by 1990 (OECD Statistics 2022).

Paris ensured those strongmen it relied upon to protect its interests were kept in power and did so irrespective of their domestic track records. For example, in the Ivory Coast, Houphouët-Boigny was successively elected unopposed as President, both he and Hastings Banda competing for the title of longest-ruling African President. And like Banda's Malawi, all citizens were compelled to be members of the ruling party. Throughout his long years as President from 1960 to 1993, Houphouët-Boigny played the role of France's point man in Africa and surrounded himself with French advisors. He also acted as a bulwark against left-leaning governments in Francophone Africa such as Sekou Touré's in Guinea, and later that of Thomas Sankara in Burkina Faso, who sought to lessen their countries' dependence on their former colonial masters.

The strong element of cynicism in France's dealings with its former colonies in Africa reached new heights through its support of the grotesque rule of Jean Bédel Bokassa in the Central African Republic. Bokassa, who seized power in a military coup in 1966, eventually declared himself President for Life and ruled the country until 1976, during which time he also proclaimed himself Emperor of Central Africa. Enjoying close personal relations with President Valerie Giscard d'Estaing, and with his country becoming a key source of uranium for France's nuclear programme, Bokassa presided over a system of brutal personalised rule characterised by the murder of political opponents, the routine use of torture by his security forces, extravagant expenditure on vainglorious projects in imitation of his hero Napoleon Bonaparte and the accumulation of massive personal wealth. In this case, however, his excesses were of such magnitude, and resulted in growing civil unrest, that they became too embarrassing for Paris, and he was eventually removed by a contingent of French soldiers in September 1979.

Betting on Continuity

The West's Cold War track record in pursuing a democratisation agenda in its relations with its favoured African leaders was one that would not be lost on later authoritarian leaders in SSA. While Western capitals had regularly claimed they attached great importance to the promotion of democratic practices, civil liberties and respect for human rights, on numerous occasions they had also shown they were willing to put such objectives on the backburner if there was any risk that the close relations they enjoyed with particular African leaders might be jeopardised, and when larger issues were at stake. Post-Cold War African leaders were therefore able to draw a number of conclusions from this earlier period in the West's relations with Africa.

Firstly, it was clear that the West's main Cold War priority had been to ensure political stability in those SSA countries it saw as its ideological allies, a stability defined in minimalist terms as a lack of civil unrest and armed conflict. For Western countries such stability enabled predictability and continuity in their relations with their preferred African regimes, even if this meant overlooking the repressive measures they regularly employed to prevent regime change. Signalling that one's country enjoyed political stability (and emphasising that this was a rare commodity on the continent), making it clear that such stability was an essential precondition for the maintenance of political alliances with Western countries, and signalling that continued Western aid was essential if such ties were to be sustained were all stratagems profitably employed by African regimes during the Cold War to strengthen their hold on power, and ones which could be successfully used in a post-Cold War context.

Secondly, in those African countries where there were significant Western economic interests, an additional tactic was to raise the possibility of Western companies losing the favoured position they enjoyed in terms of markets and access to raw materials by linking threats faced by these regimes to risks to such Western interests. In a post-Cold War world, and particularly with rise of the PRC as a challenger to Western influence on the continent, a variant of this tactic employed by African governments was to intimate an intention to turn to alternative economic partners.

Thirdly, identifying a strategic threat to the West's security—as with international communism during the Cold War—and then marketing oneself as an important ally in a given Western crusade usually resulted in substantial, and usually unquestioning, Western assistance. Therefore the ability of African regimes to identify post-Cold War threats faced by the West—such as global terrorism in the post-9/11 world, or the challenges posed to Western dominance by China's rise in terms of economic power, diplomatic and military influence and development model, or more recently the return of Russia to the African stage—and to offer to assist Western-led endeavours to counter such threats, put them in a position to receive privileged treatment.

In addition to Western security and geo-political concerns, there was a particularly promising new item on the West's post-Cold War agenda which could be profitably used by African regimes in their dealings with Western capitals. This was the emerging global consensus on the need for a new international struggle for development, and in particular Western commitments to help reverse Africa's economic and social regression. For those African regimes sufficiently perceptive and agile, this would provide them with the opportunity to prove their good intentions regarding development, and to use the reputation they thereby garnered to fend off demands for reform of the authoritarian political systems over which they presided.

Notes

1. For an overview based on declassified documents of the nature and extent of Central Intelligence Agency involvement in the Congo during the period 1960–1968, see Robarge (2014).
2. An excellent insight into the hold of the thesis within U.S. policy circles is provided by Schatzberg (1991).
3. Prevalence of stunting defined as the percentage of children aged 0–59 months whose height for age is more than 2 standard deviations below the median for the international reference population. World Bank. "Prevalence of Stunting, height for age (% of children under 5)". The World Bank Group. Accessed March 1, 2023. https://data.worldbank.org/indicator/SH.STA.STNT.ZS?locations=MW-ZG&view=chart
4. The OECD-DAC defines ODA as flows provided by official state agencies to recipient countries and multilateral institutions with the objective of promoting economic development and welfare, and high levels of concessionality with a grant element of at least 25 per cent in the case of soft loans. Military aid (except for some forms of assistance related to support to counter-terrorism capacity-building and the training of local forces in humanitarian activities such as disaster response) and credits linked to the promotion of the commercial interests of donor countries are excluded from the definition.
5. The first period of military rule ran from 1966 to 1979. It began with the overthrow of the civilian Prime Minister, Tafawa Balewa, with General Aguiyi-Ironsi heading a Federal Military Government of Nigeria. The latter was then toppled by another group within the military, with General Gowon succeeding him, only to be removed in turn in 1975 by General Murtala Mohammed. In 1976 Murtala Mohammed was ejected by General Obasanjo, who oversaw the return to civilian rule in 1979. A second period of military rule began in 1983 with the overthrow of the civilian President Shehu Shagari, the country being ruled by General Muhammadu Buhari until 1985. He was in turn removed by General Ibrahim Babangida who ruled as head of Armed Forces Ruling Council of Nigeria until 1993.

References

Lewis, Peter. 1996 "From Prebendalism to Predation: The Political Economy of Decline in Nigeria". *The Journal of Modern African Studies* 34: No. 1, Cambridge University Press, 1996.

OECD Statistics from the OECD Query Wizard for International Development Statistics: https://data.oecd.org (Accessed March 15 2022).

Rampe, David. 1989. "Bush Pledges Angola Rebel Aid". *The New York Times*, January 12, 1989.

Robarge, David. 2014. "CIA's Covert Operations in the Congo, 1960–1968: Insights from Newly Declassified Documents". *Studies in Intelligence*, 54, No.3 (September 2014), Washington D.C.: Central Intelligence Agency, 2014.

Schatzberg, Michael G. 1991. *Mobutu or Chaos? The United States and Zaire, 1960–1990.* Lanham, Maryland: University Press of America/Foreign Policy Institute. 1991.

Transparency International, *Global Corruption Report 2004.* London: Pluto Press 2004.

World Bank. World Development Indicators, The World Bank Group, Accessed August 2 2024. https://data.worldbank.org/indicator/NY.GNP.PCAP.CD?locations=MW-ZG

CHAPTER 4

Embracing the 'New Leaders'

The Continent's Nadir

For SSA, unremarkable economic growth during the 1970s slowed even further during the 1980s. SSA's GDP per capita in 1970 stood at US$1,384 (in constant 2012 US$) increasing marginally to US$1,515 by 1980; this represented only a 9.4 per cent increase over the entire decade. By 1990, GDP per capita had fallen to US$1,308, i.e., below where it had stood in 1970 (World Bank 2022). One consequence of such a prolonged economic stagnation was its effect on key welfare indicators. Poverty levels reflected this decline in economic growth rates; if in 1970, 48 per cent of the population of SSA were living below the extreme poverty metric of US$1.00 a day, by 1995 this had increased to an estimated 65 per cent (Artadi and Sala-i-Martin 2003, p. 6). Not only had there been a dramatic increase in both the absolute numbers and share of the poor in Africa's total population, but rapid progress in reducing poverty in other parts of the developing world meant global poverty had taken on an increasingly Sub-Saharan African face.

Additional aspects of this sobering situation included the rising external debt of African countries, growing marginalisation of the continent in global trade, continued reliance of most African economies on the export of primary products, widespread decay of the state apparatus in many countries, the collapse of public services, pervasive corruption and the region's numerous civil wars and their attendant humanitarian crises.

M. Simpson, *Donors, Democracy and Development in Africa*,
https://doi.org/10.1007/978-3-031-74917-9_4

These manifestations of malaise made themselves felt against the backdrop of the HIV/AIDs pandemic, which though still in its infancy in the late 1980s was already claiming thousands of lives daily. The 1980s came to be widely seen as a 'lost decade' for African development.

In addition, with the rare exception of multi-party democracies in countries such as Botswana and Mauritius, by the 1980s most African countries were dominated by either civilian single-party systems or the equally ubiquitous form of no-party military rule. Irrespective of their individual ideological colouration, what both regime types shared were strongly centralised, and often highly personalised and authoritarian, forms of governance, an unwillingness to brook dissent exemplified by the banning of opposition political parties, the restrictions placed on civil society organisations and the media, and their regular recourse to force to crush any opposition to the political status quo. Amongst external observers, as well as Africans, such poor performance generated a pervasive sense of gloom regarding the continent's prospects in terms of economic development, democratic governance and human rights, feelings which came to be characterised as 'Afro-pessimism.'

However, in the immediate aftermath of the end of the Cold War, such pessimism gradually gave way to more sanguine views of Africa's prospects. The turnaround was partly a consequence of the winding down of several prolonged wars in Africa, and which had contributed to a widely held image of an entire continent mired in destructive wars, violent death, disease, famines, large numbers of internally displaced persons and refugees, and a region regularly requiring massive injections of international humanitarian assistance. In the West, there were now reasonable grounds for optimism that a basic precondition for development, namely the absence of armed conflict and its attendant destruction, might now be met.

The rapid unravelling of Cold War Eastern bloc support systems, which had propped up self-proclaimed Marxist and other leftist regimes in Africa, meant the latter suddenly found themselves stripped of the significant political, military and economic assistance they had relied on. This compelled ruling parties such as Angola's MPLA and Mozambique's FRELIMO, both formerly Moscow's 'fraternal' allies, to seek accommodations with their respective rebel movements.[1] When accompanied by Western interest in bringing an end to such wars, and specific conflicts had become bruising stalemates in which purely military solutions seemed increasingly unlikely and local protagonists were exhausted by their exertions, many belligerents were forced to the negotiating table.

An additional consequence of the winding down of the global contest between Moscow and Washington was that the geostrategic value of aid-recipient countries, and their capacity to resist external pressures in the form of aid conditionality, was also reduced. Threats of denial of access to their economies, territories and populations, of defections to the opposing bloc, or the withholding of supporting votes in international fora, all tactics previously successfully used by the governments of many developing countries to gain advantage in their relations with one or the other superpower, were no longer critical factors in the foreign policy calculations of Western countries, since for a while there was simply no opposing camp to turn to.

The impact of the downfall of communist regimes in Eastern Europe, the discrediting of Marxist economics and Leninist political models as alternatives to market economics and multi-party democracy, was not restricted to the avowedly Marxist-Leninist regimes in Africa. Other African regimes espousing one or another variant of 'African Socialism',[2] and who eschewed key components of Marxist thought such as the necessity of class conflict as a driver of progress, as well as those which adhered to conservative political and economic philosophies but shared with those on the Left a belief in the benefits of single-party rule, all found their political and economic doctrines being contested.

Signs of a Turnaround

Early post-Cold War progress in terms of the cessation of armed conflicts in SSA included the ending of hostilities in Namibia, leading to its independence in March 1990, and the agreement in 1992 which put a stop to the prolonged civil war in Mozambique which had pitted the Marxist FRELIMO against the rebel South African-backed RENAMO. At the time there seemed to be realistic prospects for a repeat of the same in Angola, while Eritrea's independence in 1993 following a protracted armed struggle against Ethiopia brought an end to another seemingly interminable conflict. Ceasefires, and the subsequent signing of peace agreements in the early 1990s, were also accompanied by processes of political decompression. Namibia, Angola and Mozambique would all go on to adopt liberal constitutions entrenching, *inter alia*, the separation of powers and the holding of multi-party elections.

Africa also witnessed the fall of despots. In May 1991, Halie Mariam Mengistu, widely held to be responsible for the death of hundreds of thousands of Ethiopians during his rule between 1977 and 1991, was overthrown. Across the border in Somalia, Siad Barre, for many years one of Mengistu's regional opponents and whose rule had also been characterised by massive human rights abuses, was overthrown that same year.

In addition to the winding down of several long-running conflicts in SSA, growing numbers of Africans demanded democratic change. People took to the streets to call for political reforms and improved living conditions, mirroring protests taking place at the same time in many Eastern bloc countries. Given the widespread economic malaise in SSA, protests initially focused on 'bread and butter' deprivation issues such as salary arrears and increases in the prices of basic commodities and utilities, with particularly strong anger expressed at the widespread corruption which was seen as a major contributor to the economic problems affecting ordinary citizens.

In the case of Francophone SSA countries, such popular demands came to be channelled through the National Conferences which mushroomed in French-speaking African countries, and which brought together leaders and representatives from all walks of life to discuss the future of their countries. Pioneered in Benin in February 1990, in the course of 1990–1991 National Conferences would be held in Gabon, Congo, Mali, Togo, Niger and Zaire, while organised opposition groups in the Central African Republic, Cameroon, Chad, Burkina Faso, the Ivory Coast and Mauritania demanded such exercises be replicated in their countries.[3]

When measured in terms of the holding of free and fair multi-party democratic elections, the outcomes of these conventions were mixed. Some autocratic leaders such as Mobutu used the initiative of a National Conference, launched in September 1991, to buy time. He manipulated the process, suspending it in January 1992, reconvening it later that year only to dissolve it again in December 1992. Others, such as the leaders of Cameroon and the Ivory Coast, simply refused to allow National Conferences to be held. Nevertheless, their influence was profound and lasting in terms of fostering a democratic political culture in society, even when resisted by governments. As by one observer of National Conferences noted at the time, one effect of open public debate was that "simply by repeating over and over the notion that multi-party democracy is indispensable to good government, a civic loyalty to that idea can be created" (Clark 1994, p. 325).

Political protests spread to countries as different in their governments' ideological leanings as Zambia under the leadership of Kenneth Kaunda

(African Socialist and non-aligned in terms of foreign policy) and Kenya (conservative, strongly pro-Western and anti-communist). What they shared was growing popular resentment directed at single-party regimes, economic hardships and the lack of political and civil rights. Where governments did not make rapid and significant concessions on economic issues to the demonstrators, the tendency was for popular attention to then view the existing political dispensation as the chief constraint to reform, and for demands to escalate accordingly and to include the introduction of multi-party democracy.

At the same time, many African governments found themselves compelled to adopt economic liberalisation policies in exchange for assistance with their crippling foreign debt and their economic problems. Influenced by the advice of the BWIs, the late 1980s and early 1990s saw a widespread acceptance amongst African governments of the need for some form of market-driven economic reform. There was a strengthened focus on economic growth and the private sector; these elements brought together as Structural Adjustment Programmes (SAPs) based on the economic prescriptions of the then dominant 'Washington Consensus', a package of policies which aimed to reverse decades of statist economic policies in the developing world and provide greater scope for the private sector to drive growth.[4]

Amongst the early effects of the widespread discrediting of both heavily statist economic policies and single-party rule, and the collapse of the Soviet Union and concomitant disappearance of Soviet aid, were the multi-party elections held in 1991 in the two former Portuguese colonial island states of Cape Verde and São Tomé and Príncipe. Both countries had been ruled since independence by Marxist liberation movements heading up single-party systems.[5] Not only was the fact they held multi-party elections under new constitutions significant, but just as important was that both ruling parties lost, but nevertheless handed over power to opposition parties.

Another early post-Cold War change took place in Benin. Following a series of strikes by teachers and civil servants in December 1989, the country's leader and army general Mathieu Kérékou—who had seized power in a military coup in 1972, instituted single-party rule and declared Marxism-Leninism to be the state's ideology in 1974—agreed to the establishment of a National Conference. This body went on to declare itself 'sovereign' in that its decisions would have the force of law. It drafted a new constitution which was approved in a popular referendum, and it then took on the role of transitional government until elections were held in March 1991. Kérékou lost to his rival, and peacefully relinquished power.

Zambia followed a similar trajectory. Ruled by Kenneth Kaunda since independence in 1964, he had instituted a single-party system in 1973 under his United National Independence Party (UNIP) and adopted a variant of African Socialism known as Zambian Humanism. As a result of growing popular discontent, which expressed itself in food riots in Lusaka in June 1990, constitutional amendments were introduced in December 1990 which paved the way for multi-party legislative and presidential elections in October 1991. These were won by the main opposition party, the Movement for Multiparty Democracy (MMD), and power was handed over peacefully to its leader Frederik Chiluba, thus putting an end to 28 years of UNIP and Kaunda rule.

By the end of 1991, a wide range of other African countries had committed to holding multi-party elections. These included single party Marxist-Leninist states such as Mozambique, Angola, Guinea-Bissau and Congo, countries such as Tanzania subscribing to the tenets of African Socialism, those headed by conservative pro-Western regimes such as Kenya, and others under military rule at the time such as Nigeria and Lesotho. Though characterised by fits and starts as many incumbents sought to resist change, Africa nevertheless was a major player in the 'Third Wave' of democratisation. In addition, by the mid-1990s, SSA's economic growth rates seemed to have finally turned a corner and moved into positive territory, with the region's annual GDP growth (in constant 2010 US$) rising from −3.5 per cent in 1993 to 2.3 per cent in 1996 (World Bank 2022).

The End of the Cold War and America's New Afro-optimism

Moves towards the adoption of multi-party democracy and liberalising economic reforms meant views that the continent was undergoing both an economic and political turnaround rapidly took hold in many Western capitals. Such progress was seen as proof positive of the universal validity of Western political and economic doctrines and strengthened the belief that political reform along liberal lines could, and should, march hand in hand with the adoption of market-oriented economic policies, and that increasing political pluralism and economic liberalisation were mutually reinforcing.

The template for American support to such developments in Africa was laid down during the George H. W. Bush administration, with officials in the first flush of post-Cold War triumphalism projecting a new world order based on the twin global processes of democratisation and economic liberalization. At the 1990 G7 summit in Houston, the Political Declaration issued by leaders spoke of the "historic advances of democracy we have witnessed over the past year", and underscored the common position of G7 members that "political and economic freedoms are closely linked" (G7 1990a). The summit's Economic Declaration reaffirmed the views expressed in the Political Declaration, arguing that in developing countries there was

> A growing acceptance of the view that growth can be encouraged by a stable macroeconomic framework, sectoral reform to provide more competition, and an opening of markets. Open, democratic and accountable political systems are important ingredients in the effective and equitable operations of market-oriented economies. (G7 1990b)

According to U.S. Secretary of State James Baker III, G7 partners saw the spreading of democracy as the "imperative of our time", and he announced that Western nations would "help secure and promote democracy's advance in all regions of the world" (G7 1990c). And Africa would be an integral component of the new global *zeitgeist*.

Washington's Linking of Development Aid to Democratisation

In November 1990, Herman Cohen, U.S. Assistant Secretary of State for African Affairs, claimed that "Africans, too, have come to realize that development and democracy go hand in hand, and that is one of the primary reasons for the wave of democratic reform that is sweeping the continent today" (U.S. Department of State 1990, p. 271). In the same statement, he also announced that American aid policy would be tailored to support countries "pursuing the mutually reinforcing goals of political liberalization and market-oriented reforms" (U.S. Department of State 1990, p. 272). In December 1990, the United States Agency for International Development (USAID) launched its 'Democracy Initiative'.

Its overall objective was to place democracy "on a comparable footing with progress on economic reforms and the establishment of a market-oriented economy, key factors which are already used as criteria for allocating funds" (USAID 1991 p. 14). Democracy Assistance would thereafter become a major component of USAID's work, and between 1991 and 1999 the agency's annual spend on democracy and governance initiatives grew from US$165 million to US$635 million (Carothers 2009, p. 11).

The Democracy Initiative was also explicit about the application of political conditionality, an example of the early post-Cold War linking of grants and loans to political reforms. Regular USAID assessments of progress on democratisation were to be undertaken, with results used to determine beneficiary countries and levels of disbursements. In other words, American aid would be used to leverage political reforms in developing countries.

Bill Clinton, Africa's Renaissance and the 'New Leaders'

The optimism of the George H.W. Bush White House regarding Africa's prospects was carried over into the first and second Clinton administrations from 1993 to 1997 and 1997 to 2001, respectively. Under Clinton, the U.S. committed to robust engagement globally to enlarge the number of 'market democracies', and some of the flavour of this Clinton era optimism can be seen in the upbeat musings of Africa experts close to the Clinton White House

In 1998 Howard Wolpe, Clinton's Special Envoy to the Great Lakes region, and David Gordon of the Overseas Development Council jointly argued that the positive changes taking place in Africa meant Afro-pessimism had passed its sell-by date. The new reality was that of a continent in which "governments are becoming accountable to citizens; in which economic policies are empowering a growing private sector; in which real progress is being made in addressing difficult but tractable social problems". Furthermore, such developments were being driven by a "new leadership dynamic" spearheading "a 'dual transition' to more open political systems and market economies" (Gordon and Wolpe 1998, p. 50).

Clinton's optimistic views on the continent's prospects had already been on show at a White House Conference on Africa held in June 1994, a first for an American administration. In his address to the Conference, Clinton stated that "Africa matters to the United States. It has to matter to us", adding that as "Africans turn away from the failed experiments of the past, they're also embracing new political freedoms" (U.S. Government Publishing Office 1994, pp. 1150–1151).

During a tour of Africa in 1998, Clinton repeatedly heaped praise on those he characterised as representing a "new generation" of African leaders spearheading a turnaround in the continent's fortunes. He saw such positive developments as an "African Renaissance", borrowing a term strongly championed by the then South African Deputy President Thabo Mbeki.[6] The choice of the specific African leaders seen to embody this new reformist ethos, and which the Clinton administration would come to focus on, had been identified earlier by Secretary of State Madeleine Albright. During her visit to seven African countries in December 1997, amongst which Rwanda, Uganda and Ethiopia, Albright referred to Washington's desire to place relations with Africa on a new footing based on perceived shared values with the continent's 'new leaders'. In her address to the Economic Commission of the Organisation of African Unity (OAU) in Addis Ababa on December 8, 1997, Albright spoke of "Africa's new leaders [who] have brought a new spirit of hope and accomplishment to their countries…[and who know that] the greatest authority any leader can claim is the consent of the governed" (Albright 1997).

Such sanguine views were echoed by other officials. Before Clinton's Africa tour, at a hearing of the U.S. Senate's Subcommittee on African Affairs in March 1998 and significantly entitled 'Democracy in Africa: The New Generation of African Leaders', Susan Rice, the Assistant Secretary of State for African Affairs, spoke of "a new interest in individual freedom and a move away from repressive one-party states". Furthermore, she specified that it was with the continent's new leaders that "we seek a dynamic, long-term partnership for the 21st Century" (U.S. Senate 1998, p. 3). And in the course of the same hearing, the Chairman of the Subcommittee, Senator John Ashcroft, named the African leaders seen by the Clinton administration to be spearheading the turnaround, amongst which Rwanda's Paul Kagame, Yoweri Museveni of Uganda and Meles Zenawi of Ethiopia.

Many of the handpicked African leaders Clinton met during his 1998 tour—and specifically those present at his meeting with Central and East African leaders hosted by Museveni in Entebbe—had, with the exception of the Ugandan President, all come to power after the end of the Cold

War. During his visit to Uganda, Clinton praised his host for "the progress that has been made in these last few years in improving economic conditions, in improving political conditions" (U.S. Government Publishing Office 1998a). In remarks he made following his meeting with leaders in Entebbe on March 25, 1998—designated the 'Entebbe Summit for Peace and Prosperity', and which resulted in a Joint Declaration of Principles signed by the U.S. President and six African leaders—Clinton highlighted the commitments made by the African signatories to "promote democracy and human rights", the fact they had all "emphasized the importance of freely elected, accountable governments", and had committed to work together with the U.S. for "a new economic future where the talents of Africa's people are unleashed" (U.S. Government Publishing Office 1998b).

During his trip, Clinton also referred to an important initiative winding its way through the U.S. legislative process, namely the Africa Growth and Opportunity Act (AGOA), which he would eventually sign into law in May 2000. Cast in the lofty language of a new partnership with Africa, the AGOA aimed to reduce SSA's dependence on aid through the adoption of free market economics and to strengthen SSA's economic integration into world markets by extending duty-free entry into the American market for a range of African exports. In addition to verifiable progress in terms of the establishment of market economies, the granting of access to American markets on beneficial terms would be based on additional eligibility criteria. These included commitments on the part of AGOA beneficiaries to poverty reduction and the provision of health and education, the rule of law, political pluralism, combating corruption, strengthening protection of workers through adherence to core labour standards and improvements in terms of human rights (U.S. Congress 2000).

Parisian Responses and London's Post-Cold War Enthusiasm for Africa

Post-Cold War American confidence in the improved prospects for democracy and market economics in Africa, and the commitment to use development assistance as a tool to encourage progress on these objectives in aid-recipient governments, was soon echoed in other Western capitals. After decades of policy continuity based on the certainties provided by the Manichean zero-sum international Cold War rivalry, European former colonial powers were also forced to adapt to the changes sweeping the continent.

French influence in post-colonial Africa has been a central component of France's claim to continued world power status, enhancing its role as a critical member of both the EU and NATO, and helping justify its permanent seat on the UN's Security Council. Yet the post-Cold War seismic shifts taking place in its African zone of influence, most notably growing popular demands for democratic change, compelled Paris to re-examine its Africa policy. While its primary concern remained that of safeguarding French interests, it was also clear that if these were not to be put at risk Paris had to deal with the unwillingness of many African regimes it supported to reform or face the risk of civil unrest which might result from such intransigence.

By the middle of 1990, it was clear the groundswell of popular demands for political reform in Francophone Africa was not going to abate, and could no longer be ignored. At the June 1990 Franco-African Summit, attended by thirty-five African delegations, President Mitterrand highlighted the link between democratic practice and development, and put his African counterparts on notice that Paris would henceforth apply political conditionality to its assistance:

> France will link its entire contribution effort to efforts made to move in the direction of greater freedom...Aid will be more lukewarm toward regimes that conduct themselves in an authoritarian manner without accepting evolution towards democracy; it will be enthusiastic for those who take the step with courage. (CSIS Africa Notes 1990, p. 2)

Across the Channel, a decision was also taken to apply political conditionality to British aid, along lines similar to those set out in USAID's Democracy Initiative, with elements of both positive conditionality in the form of 'rewards' for the delivery of the desired results, and negative conditionality with aid resources withheld for non-compliance. In June 1990, i.e. the same month as Mitterrand's Franco-African summit speech, UK Foreign Secretary Douglas Hurd announced that "Governments which persist with repressive policies, with corrupt management or with wasteful and discredited economic systems, should not expect us to support this folly with scarce aid resources" (Cumming 2001, p. 176).

Soon after the 'New Labour' government came to power in 1997 under Prime Minister Tony Blair, Foreign Secretary Robin Cook announced the UK would pursue an ethical foreign policy. One of the foreign policy goals was that of "promoting democracy around the world", with Cook announcing the need to "support the demands of other peoples for the democratic rights on which we insist for ourselves" (Cook 1997).

Blair was not far behind Clinton in his fulsome praise of improvements in Africa's fortunes, and often appeared to see himself as the continent's saviour. Commitments were made to tailor the UK's diplomatic, military and international development policies to help Africa overcome its numerous problems, which Blair at the Labour Party Conference of 2001 characterised as "a scar on the conscience of the world" (*Guardian* 2001).

The British Prime Minister's vision of a 'New Deal' for Africa was predicated on the establishment of a different kind of relationship between the West and African countries, one in tune to the new mood music dominant in international development circles. Blair, as Clinton had done earlier, would regularly characterise the new footing upon which he was seeking to place the UK's relations with Africa as a mutually beneficial 'partnership', the latter a term which became ubiquitous in British pronouncements on its development assistance. In exchange for more aid and investment, debt relief, improved market access for African products, and technical assistance to build 'good governance' and physical infrastructure, Africa would commit to "true democracy, no more excuses for dictatorship, abuses of human rights; no tolerance of bad governance" (*Guardian* 2001).

Blair was assisted in this endeavour by Clare Short, the Labour Government's first Secretary of State for International Development from 1997 to 2003. Heading up a new separate Ministry, the Department for International Development (DFID), she enjoyed cabinet status, increased autonomy and a rapidly growing budget and staff complement, all indications of the Labour government's commitment to international development and the willingness of Blair and his Chancellor of the Exchequer Gordon Brown to provide the new department with the requisite funding to meet its ambitious objectives. While in 1997 (the year of DFID's establishment), the UK's ODA spend was £2.1 billion, by 2017 it had increased to nearly £14 billion (UK.GOV 2017a), with DFID responsible for the lion's share of total UK government ODA expenditures (UK.GOV 2017b). This massive increase in its financial resource envelope helped transform DFID into a highly regarded Western bilateral donor agency, both within the community of international development agencies and in aid-recipient countries, and DFID came to be seen as a thought leader on a par with the World Bank in terms of the technical expertise of its cadres.

Short set out to change not only the UK's own development policy, but to shape post-Cold War Western donor praxis. The latter was facilitated by her membership of the Utstein Group of like-minded Western International Development ministers.[7] Under the banner of a 'donor harmonization' drive, this Group set out to reform international aid architecture, and in particular the role of Western bilateral donors and the BWIs, so as to achieve greater coherence in aid policy, improve donor coordination, encourage the adoption of a sharper focus on pro-poor development policies and strengthen national capacity in recipient countries to manage aid flows and development.

By the late 1990s, DFID's focus on poverty reduction had contributed to the adoption of Poverty Reduction Strategy Papers (PRSPs) as the most important programmatic development document governing relations between donors and aid-recipient countries. Containing the national objectives of partner countries in terms of poverty reduction, they clarified which sectors were priorities, how targets were to be achieved, and what kind of external support was needed from donors. Production of PRSPs became the key trigger for the granting of debt relief, and their implementation was required to meet conditions attached to structural adjustment loans from the BWIs.

Poverty reduction became DFID's *raison d'etre*, and its first White Paper set out its commitment to help achieve the UN target of halving the numbers of those living in extreme poverty.[8] A second White Paper in 2000 emphasised the UK government's strong support for the UN's MDGs and the UK government's commitment to meet the UN's target of 0.7 per cent of Gross National Income (GNI) developed countries should spend on ODA (DFID 2000).

Early in her stewardship of DFID, Short laid out the new approach her department would take towards African countries receiving British aid and portrayed this as a step change compared to earlier aid policies which were seen as having been based on an unequal donor-recipient relationship. The innovation was cast in terms of the UK's abandonment of self-interest and its adoption of a principled commitment—or at least one divorced from commercial interests—to support poverty reduction and sustainable development[9] wherever the need was greatest. Responding to a question on her priorities for Africa in a debate in the House of Commons on May 21, 1997, she made it clear that in pursuit of those objectives she aimed "to work in partnership with African Governments – what we need is not donor countries telling other countries what to do, but partnerships…underpinned through support for good governance and human rights" (House of Commons 1997, col 701).

The Labour government went on to develop close relations with some of the same African leaders previously designated by Clinton as worthy of support. Blair invited Meles Zenawi of Ethiopia to become part of his 17-member Commission for Africa (together with Tanzania's Benjamin Mkapa, the only African Heads of Government to join the body), and which aimed to forge a new form of relations between the developed world and Africa to help boost the latter's development. At the 2005 launch of the Commission for Africa report—which Blair went on to promote at the G8 Gleneagles Summit of July 2005—and which Zenawi attended as one of the non-G8 leaders invited, Blair acknowledged the continued existence of conflict and dire poverty on the continent. He nevertheless also painted an upbeat picture of Africa's progress, pointing out that "Democracy has new life. War has given way to peace in many countries. Economies with the right governance and help make progress" (National Archives 2005a). At the end of the summit, he announced various commitments made by developed countries in terms of debt relief, increased aid (specifically to double aid flows to Africa by 2010) and improved trade access for African exports. Blair also referenced the fact that there had been undertakings "from the African side…a firm and strong commitment to good governance, to democracy, to human rights, to respect for the rule of law…In the end it is only vibrant African leadership, capable of giving good governance to its people, that can make the ultimate difference" (National Archives 2005b).

Voices of Scepticism and Calls for Caution

As Clinton, Blair and their lieutenants were enthusiastically engaging with Africa's new leaders, words of caution were being proffered by African experts from the worlds of politics, academia and the media in the West. For example, Senator John Ashcroft (referenced earlier in the context of the US Senate Sub-Committee hearing) urged restraint in terms of U.S. government endorsements of specific African leaders. Referring to Madeline Albright's enthusiasm for what she had characterised as a sea change in the quality of African leadership, Ashcroft warned of the dangers of disappointment and of "declaring success stories before their time". He argued that while those African leaders identified by the Clinton White House as worthy of support had been responsible for overthrowing some of the continent's most brutal regimes, it was also the case that in addition to restrictions on press freedoms, violations of civil liberties and political oppression, "they preside over *de facto* one-party States which do not allow for self-government and have not established mechanisms for the peaceful transfer of power" (United States Senate 1998, p. 2). He also presciently warned of the possibility that "we will wake up in several years and find a new generation of African leaders has become an old generation of African strong men" (United States Senate 1998, p. 3).

In the run-up to Madeline Albright's December 1997 African tour, such concerns had also been expressed by Human Rights Watch (HRW). In a briefing paper sent to Albright before her departure for the continent, it referred specifically to the leaders of Uganda, Rwanda and Ethiopia and was foresighted given the subsequent evolution of their regimes. It warned of the dangers of acclaiming their stewardship of their countries since those leaders regularly claimed that:

> The interests of stability require the restriction of political rights...and advocate political systems characterized by restrictive legal structures that undercut core democratic freedoms, ensuring that opposition parties, civil society and the media cannot effectively challenge the party in power. Despite claims to the contrary, the ideology appears to be a restatement of one-party rule, with the difference that private enterprise is encouraged. (HRW 1997)

Africanists at American think-tanks and academic institutions also urged greater circumspection. At the March 1998 Senate Sub-Committee hearing, George Ayittey, a Ghanaian economist based in the U.S., warned of the dangers of cultivating relations with rebel leaders who, while overthrowing dictators who had employed extensive and extreme violence to run their countries, had themselves come to power through the barrel of a gun, as was the case with Meles Zenawi, Yoweri Museveni and Paul Kagame. Taking issue with the optimistic views of the Clinton White House regarding progress on Africa's democratisation, he enumerated numerous cases of recent setbacks suffered by democratic forces on the continent, the prevalence of continued strong man rule in Africa and expressed concerns about what he saw as the Clinton administration's apparent *de facto* prioritisation of stability over democracy in its Africa policy. Echoing Senator Ashcroft's unease with Washington's cultivation of its newly found African favourites, Ayittey observed that:

> Africa's postcolonial experience with rebel leaders has been ghastly and trenchantly disconcerting…Most of the rebel leaders, who set out to remove tyrants from power, have turned out to be crocodile liberators, who left wanton carnage and human debris in their wake. They preached "democracy" but were themselves closet dictators, exhibiting the same tyrannical tendencies they so loudly denounce in the despots they replaced. (United States Senate 1998, p. 22)

In his opinion, American silence when electoral gerrymandering had taken place meant that Washington on occasion had done "little but wink at manifest cases of [electoral] fraud" (p. 19). He concluded that in sharp contrast to the upbeat messages initially put out in Western capitals regarding their newly rediscovered and apparently unconditional post-Cold War support for democratisation on the continent, the reality was that "Africa's democratization experience in the 1990s has been marked by vapid Western pronouncements, truculent duplicity and scurrilous abandonment. When the going got tough, the West cut and ran" (United States Senate 1998, pp. 21–22).

Exemplifying the lack of clarity in America's policy towards Africa, U.S. Secretary of State Madeline Albright, in her December 1997 address at the headquarters of the OAU during her tour of Africa, had made the uncontroversial point that democracy was "always and everywhere a work in progress". It must, however, have disappointed African democracy activists that while she stated that democracy had certain "universal qualities that transcend institutional choices", such as the "primacy of the will of the people" and respect "for the rule of law", she failed to specify the need for, *inter alia*, regular free and fair multi-party democracy overseen by independent electoral bodies, or the need for a free press and an independent judiciary. And by referencing the importance of democracy "in all its forms – and there are many" (Albright 1997), she provided useful arguments for many of Africa's strongmen, well-versed in how to dress up the political systems over which they presided as ones enabling the free expression of the political preferences of their citizens.

The members of the Senate Sub-Committee heard similar words of caution from Pauline Baker, another eminent African expert. She focused her criticisms on what one human rights expert later characterised as the "irrational exuberance" permeating the Clinton administration's African policy (Rosenblum 2002). She questioned what she saw as the priority granted by the Clinton administration to the market-friendly economic reforms implemented by the new African leaders, warning that "tolerating human rights abuses and calling non-democratic leaders democratic simply because they apply favourable economic policies merely invites another round of disillusionment" (U.S. Senate 1998, p. 31). She noted that positive marks were being given to leaders for the apparent political and security stability they had brought to their countries and argued such approval had been granted at the same time as these leaders had been already begun to deemphasise the importance of democracy. Furthermore, she warned that the result of pursuing such a highly selective and myopic policy, through the embracing of a "new generation of strong men in the name of post-Cold War stability and economic reform", would be "nurturing the kind of crony capitalism in Africa...and encouraging a replay of the pattern of personal rule that has dogged the continent for decades" (U.S. Senate 1998, p. 31).

The American press also took up the theme of the need for caution in America's dealings with the 'new leaders'. *The New York Times*, while pointing out that many of these leaders had embraced market reforms, also highlighted the persistence of authoritarianism, evident, for example, in Museveni's insistence on one-party rule under the guise of a 'uni-party' or 'no-party' democracy in Uganda, and the development of a highly militarised and authoritarian Tutsi-dominated government in post-genocide Rwanda. As a result, the paper opined that the Secretary of State had allowed "some of her hosts to use her presence as an advertisement for American endorsement of their undemocratic regimes" (*New York Times* 1997).

In the aftermath of Clinton's 1998 Africa tour, David Rieff presented a robust case for continued Afro-pessimism, attacking the White House's spin and myopia, and its extremely selective highlighting of developments that were "promising but unrepresentative" (Rieff 1998, p. 14). Clinton era Afro-optimists had committed the fundamental mistake of "an overestimation of the qualities and commitment to democracy of a new generation of African rulers who, however different stylistically they are from their predecessors, are cut very much from the same basic mould - the African 'Big Man'" (Rieff 1998, p. 15). Furthermore, he noted the ability of such leaders, so apparent during Clinton's tour, to adopt language that would resonate appropriately with the West's post-Cold War international development priorities, cautioning that their "talk of free markets and democratic openings should certainly not be taken at face value. Some may be sincere, but it cannot be overstressed that…this is the talk donors now demand" (Rieff 1998, p. 15).

Notes

1. For an overview of the process of Soviet withdrawal from Africa during the Gorbachev era, and the impact of such developments on African regimes with close ties to Moscow, see Webber (1992).
2. While definitions of African Socialism vary considerably, and it lacked the coherence of Marxism-Leninism, the range of projects initiated under the banner of African Socialism nevertheless shared certain features. Amongst these were the belief that African societies were only partially penetrated by capitalist practices and had always been communal, and were therefore immune from the class conflict of the advanced capitalist West. Socialism was indigenous to Africa, while capitalism was rejected because it fed conflictual social relations and undermined the cohesion of traditional African life and the still fragile national unity built up during the independence struggles.
3. For a comprehensive assessment of such events, see Robinson (1994).
4. The Washington Consensus embodied the West's development economics orthodoxy during much of the 1990s. Devised as a response to Latin America's 1980s debt crisis and poor growth rates, its reforms aimed to reverse decades of statist development policies, and included fiscal conservatism, the liberalisation of external trade, interest and exchange rates, deregulation and privatisation. In sum, the policy prescriptions sought to reduce the role of the state in the development process and increase that of markets in the allocation of resources. With minor modifications, the Washington Consensus was subsequently exported from Latin America to Africa during the 1990s. These measures were gradually supplemented by additional reform items seen as essential for sustaining economic growth and providing a greater role for markets and the private sector in the economy, and which focused on the role of public institutions, such as civil service reform and improvements in public financial management systems.
5. In the case of São Tomé and Príncipe, the Movement for the Liberation of São Tomé and Príncipe (MLSTP) had ruled since independence in 1975 as the only legal party in the country, until the adoption of a new constitution approved in a national referendum in August 1990 led to multiparty elections in January 1991. In the case of Cape Verde, in September 1990, the ruling African Party of Cape Verde's Independence (PAICV) abolished the

single party system in place since independence. It lost both the legislative and presidential elections to the main opposition Movement for Democracy (MpD) the following year, with the leader of the MpD taking office in March 1991.

6. Mbeki first began employing it in official discourse in 1996–97, the aspirational concept thereafter featuring regularly in both ruling African National Congress (ANC) and South African government policy statements.
7. Established in 1999, this group of like-minded donors brought together the International Development Ministers of Norway, the Netherlands, the UK and Germany, and who were subsequently joined by the Development Ministers of Sweden and Canada.
8. DFID (1997). White Paper. *Eliminating World Poverty: A Challenge for the 21st Century*, November 1997. Poverty reduction would eventually be enshrined in the UK's International Development Act of 2002 as the central objective for the provision of development assistance.
9. Through recognition of the limits imposed by environmental, economic, and social factors, the principle holds that development should meet the needs of the present generation without compromising the ability of future generations to meet their own needs.

References

Albright, Madeline. 1997 "Secretary of State Madeline Albright's Remarks at the Economic Commission for Africa December 9, 1997, Addis Ababa, Ethiopia" included on the webpage entitled "Africa: Albright Visit 1/2, 12/17/97", hosted by the African Studies Centre, University of Pennsylvania. 1997. Accessed May 1 2024 https://www.africa.upenn.edu/Urgent_Action/apic_111797.html

Artadi, Elsa V. and Xavier Sala-i-Martin. 2003. "The Economic Tragedy of the XXth Century: Growth in Africa" Working Paper No. 9865. National Bureau of Economic Research, Cambridge MA. July 2003. https://doi.org/10.3386/w9865

Carothers, Thomas. 2009. *Revitalizing Democracy Assistance – The Challenge of USAID*, Washington D.C.: Carnegie Endowment for International Peace 2009.

Clark, John F. 1994. "The National Conference as an Instrument of Democratization in Francophone Africa", *Journal of Third World Studies* 11 No.1 (Spring 1994) University of Florida Press.

Cook, Robin. 1997. "Mission Statement for the Foreign and Commonwealth Office", London 1997, http://www.britishpoliticalspeech.org/speech-archive.htm?speech=292 (Accessed July 15, 2018).

CSIS Africa Notes. 1990. "The 1990 Franco-African Summit". No.115, Washington D.C.: Centre for International and Strategic Studies, August 30 1990.

Cumming G. 2001. *Aid to Africa: French and British Policies from the Cold War to the New Millennium*, Aldershot, Ashgate, 2001.

DFID. 1997. *Eliminating World Poverty: A challenge for the 21st Century*, White Paper on International Development, November 1997 Cm 3789.

DFID. 2000. *Eliminating World Poverty: Making Globalisation Work for the Poor*, White Paper on International Development, December 2000. Cm 5006.

G7. 1990a. "Political Declaration: Securing Democracy". 1990 Houston Summit, Houston 10 July 1990. Reproduced on the website of the University of Toronto G7 Research Group: http://www.g7.utoronto.ca/summit/1990houston/political.html (Accessed May 2 2024).

G7. 1990b. "Houston Economic Declaration", 1990 Houston Summit, Houston 11 July 1990. Reproduced on the website of the University of Toronto G7 Research Group: http://www.g7.utoronto.ca/summit/1990houston/declaration.html (Accessed May 2 2024).

G7. 1990c. "Chairman's Statement", 1990 Houston Summit, Houston 10 July 1990. Reproduced on the website of the University of Toronto G7 Research Group: http://www.g7.utoronto.ca/summit/1990houston/chairman.html (Accessed May 2 2024).

Gordon David F and Howard Wolpe. 1998. "The Other Africa: An End to Afro-Pessimism". *World Policy Journal* 15 No.1 (Spring, 1998) Duke University Press.

GOV.UK 2017a "Statistics on International Development: Provisional UK Spend 2017" (Chart C1: UK ODA Levels between 1970 and 2017). https://www.gov.uk/government/statistics/statistics-on-international-development-provisional-uk-aid-spend-2017 (Accessed May 2 2024).

GOV.UK. 2017b. "Statistics on International Development: Provisional UK Spend 2017". Chart 2: UK ODA Contributors Share of Total UK ODA. https://www.gov.uk/government/statistics/statistics-on-international-development-provisional-uk-aid-spend-2017.

Guardian, 2001. Full Text: Tony Blair's Speech (Part One) October 2, 2001. https://www.theguardian.com/politics/2001/oct/02/labourconference.labour6 (Accessed 11th June 2018).

House of Commons Hansard. 1997. "Debates for 21 May 1997" 21 May 1997 : Column 701 https://publications.parliament.uk/pa/cm199798/cmhansrd/vo970521/debtext/70521-18.htm (Accessed May 2 2024)

HRW. 1997. "Human Rights Watch Briefing Paper for United States Secretary of State Madeline Albright". New York and Washington D.C.: Human Rights Watch, December 8, 1997. (https://www.africa.upenn.edu/Urgent_Action/apic_111797.html) (Accessed April 4, 2024)

National Archives. 2005a. "Presidency Press Conference at Gleneagles (8 July 2005)". (webarchive.nationalarchives.gov.uk/20070506094810/http://www.pm.gov.uk/output/Page7891.asp) Accessed May 2, 2024

National Archives. 2005b. "Prime Minister's Remarks at the Launch of the Commission for Africa Report (11 Mar 05)". March 11 2005. webarchive.nationalarchives.gov.uk/20080909054543/http://www.number10.gov.uk/Page7314 (Accessed May 2, 2024).

New York Times. 1997. "Ms. Albright's Awkward African Tour" December 17, 1997. https://www.nytimes.com/1997/12/17/opinion/ms-albright-s-awkward-african-tour.html (Accessed July 2, 2018).

Rieff, David. 1998. "In Defense of Afro-Pessimism". *World Policy Journal* 15 No.4 (Winter, 1998/1999) Duke University Press.

Robinson, Pearl T. 1994. "The National Conference Phenomenon in Francophone Africa", *Comparative Studies in Society and History* 36 No.3 (July 1994) New York: Cambridge University Press, 1994.

Rosenblum, Peter. 2002. "Irrational Exuberance: The Clinton Administration in Africa". *Current History – A Journal of Contemporary World Affairs* 101 Issue 655 pp 195–202, Philadelphia, PA. May 2002.

U.S. Congress. 2000. "Trade and Development Act of 2000 -Subtitle A -Trade Policy for Sub-Saharan Africa, Section 104. Eligibility Requirements". 2000. https://legacy.trade.gov/agoa/eligibility/#:~:text=The%20Act%20authorizes%20the%20President,barriers%20to%20U.S.%20trade%20and (Accessed May 2 2024).

U.S. Department of State. 1990. "Democratic Change in Africa", *Dispatch*, Vol 1, No.12, November 19, 1990.

U.S. Government Publishing Office. 1994. Public Papers of the Presidents of the United States: William J. Clinton (1994, Book I), "Remarks to the White House Conference on Africa". June 27, 1994. pp 1150–1151. https://www.gpo.gov/fdsys/pkg/PPP-1994-book1/pdf/PPP-1994-book1-doc-pg1150.pdf (Accessed May 2, 2024)

U.S. Government Publishing Office. 1998a. Compilation of Presidential Documents, "Remarks at the Kisowera School in Mukono, Uganda. *March 24, 1998*" www.gpo.gov/fdsys/pkg/PPP-1998-book1/pdf/PPP-1998-book1-doc-pg426.pdf (Accessed March 11, 2018).

U.S. Government Publishing Office. 1998b. Compilation of Presidential Documents, "Remarks at the Entebbe Summit for Peace and Prosperity *March 25, 1998*". https://www.govinfo.gov/content/pkg/WCPD-1998-03-30/pdf/WCPD-1998-03-30.pdf (Accessed March 12, 2018).

U.S. Senate. 1998. "Democracy in Africa: The New Generation of African Leaders". Hearing before the Sub-Committee on African Affairs. Committee on Foreign Relations, United States Senate Second Session, March 12, 1998.

https://www.govinfo.gov/content/pkg/CHRG-105shrg48230/html/CHRG-105shrg48230.htm

USAID, 1991. *Policy – Democracy and Governance*, Directorate for Policy, U.S. Agency for International Development, Washington, D.C. November 1991.

Webber, Mark. 1992. "Soviet Policy in Sub-Saharan Africa: The Final Phase", *Journal of Modern African Studies*, 30 No.1 (March 1992), Cambridge University Press.

World Bank. World Development Indicators, The World Bank Group, Accessed February 13 2022 and March 1 2024. https://data.worldbank.org

CHAPTER 5

Bloody Legacies, Regime Hybridity and Donor Rationalisations

Burdens of the Past and Regime Formation

While in the early post-Cold War years Africa's 'new leaders' were being feted by the West as representatives of a wave of political and economic liberalisation sweeping the continent, as noted earlier there was already copious evidence of their willingness to use extreme violence and other illiberal methods to maintain their grip on power. Long before the COVID pandemic which laid bare the highly authoritarian nature of the regimes in Uganda, Rwanda and Ethiopia, their autocratic tendencies were already common knowledge amongst journalists, academics, democracy activists and human rights defenders, who warned Western donors of the dangers of ignoring the signs and of failing to look behind the façade of the formal structures, legislation and official declarations of these regimes. Furthermore, even before their movements had seized power, there were clear indications of the likely authoritarian direction of travel these countries would subsequently take. In other words, the key features of the governance styles these regimes adopted could easily be discerned in how the liberation movements from which they sprang had operated during their rebellions, the influence of the illiberal ideologies they were attracted to and the political histories of their countries.

M. Simpson, *Donors, Democracy and Development in Africa*,
https://doi.org/10.1007/978-3-031-74917-9_5

The Impact of Historical Influences

A rich field of 'rebel-to-ruler' scholarship has examined those factors shaping the transitions of liberation movements into political parties and then governments, and how these influence the governance styles and strategies they went on to adopt for their post-conflict nation-building projects (Fisher 2020, Lyons 2016). Some analysts have specifically focused on the military aspects of their struggles, and how these impacted on the nature of the post-conflict states these movements then established. Particular attention has been paid to the extent to which they have been militarised (i.e. the role played by the armed forces and associated security bodies in economic and political systems), how the values and ethos they expounded have been assimilated by wider society and the various ways this shaped the domestic and foreign policies of these states.[1]

In terms of ideological influences, the emancipatory discourse of these movements during their insurgencies (promises of peace and stability, restoration of law and order after extended periods of arbitrary rule, an end to repression and exploitation and improvements in the living conditions of the destitute masses) always went hand in hand with strongly authoritarian practices. The combination was unsurprising given the varying degrees of influence of Marxist-Leninist thought (the transformative and emancipatory political ideology that has always held most appeal for liberation movements). Leninist organisational principles, as well as Maoist teachings on insurrectionary 'people's war', resonated deeply within the upper echelons of African liberation movements such as the NRM, EPRDF and RPF.

Their impact can be detected, for example, in the adoption by these movements of highly centralised decision-making processes which bear a strong resemblance to the Leninist practice of 'democratic centralism', i.e. a degree of democracy in making collective decisions at higher level, after which lower bodies were then expected to unconditionally follow the diktats of senior figures. The influence of Communist movements around the world also helps explain the personality cults which soon developed around their leaders as 'founding fathers', sources of superior insights into what was required to ensure final victory.

As with many other liberation movements, their armed struggles explain the prominence of senior military figures within their higher decision-making bodies, as well as the emphasis in their propaganda on the extensive experience of their leaders as military commanders. The latter would be marketed as an important qualification for the most senior public posts after eventual victory, including that of national leader.

Great emphasis was placed on the need for unity within the ranks, a prerequisite for military success and final victory. Significant effort was therefore devoted to establishing a single 'correct' political and military line around which all should rally. In the case of the NRM, it appointed 'political commissars', tasked with ensuring those in the movement's armed wing, the National Resistance Army (NRA), were adequately indoctrinated. Exiled Rwandans who joined Museveni's NRA were exposed to the practice of continuous political education, and the RPF would adopt the practice following its founding in 1987. In the case of the EPRDF—and given that of the three movements it was the one in which the influence of Marxist-Leninist thought was most profound, and its leadership most familiar with both Soviet bloc and Chinese practices—political commissars played prominent roles in the TPLF which made up the rump of the EPRDF's military forces. The need to ensure the 'correct line' was followed until final victory, in situations where threats to their movements were constant and multifarious, helps explain the high levels of intolerance displayed towards internal dissent, with differences of opinion quickly labelled as dangerous 'sectarianism', and with summary justice dispensed to those judged to have deviated from the official line.

The impact of various forms of revolutionary leftist thought can also be detected in the hostile attitudes these movements exhibited towards political pluralism in general, and more specifically their strong aversion to the divisiveness they saw as its natural accompaniment. Such influences shaped their understanding of what constituted a democratic political system, and most importantly the relative importance they came to attach to the individual political and civil rights of their future citizens, as against improvements in the economic and social indicators of larger collectivities. Notwithstanding comments they had made during their struggles when engaging with Western interlocutors on the importance they attached to individual liberal political and civil rights, in other contexts these leaders regularly expressed scepticism regarding the relevance of multi-party democracy to African societies.

Amongst other ills, they viewed multi-party systems as one of the root causes of the political chaos which had engulfed many post-independence African states (not least the political instability of Uganda and Rwanda), with the prevalence of ethnic-based parties solidifying and deepening pre-existing inter-ethnic rivalries and contributing to the weak sense of national unity which had afflicted their societies. Multi-party democracy was also seen by them to have facilitated nepotism and corruption; control of the state apparatus, and the opportunities that arose for political leaders to engage in the distribution of public largesse to strengthen their support bases (and for individual enrichment), had been seen by many post-independence political parties in Africa as ends in themselves. Given the underdeveloped nature of their economies, and limited scope for individual economic advancement through private enterprise, this had raised the premium on securing leverage over the distribution of economic benefits through control of the state apparatus. The lack of opportunities for enrichment outside political life also explained the temptation on the part of incumbents to always seek, at any cost, to prolong their terms in office, and to resort to increasingly authoritarian methods to do so.

Marxist-Leninist and African Socialist concepts were also apparent in their understanding of the forces behind socio-economic cleavages, and all three movements came to frame their respective struggles in terms of the need for revolutionary transformation of their societies, with the freeing of citizens from oppression and exploitation as the ultimate objective. In this context, they also saw multi-party democracy as a key explanation for the lack of development on the continent, and specifically in their own countries. The short-term political horizons of governments operating within such systems, the compromises associated with the need to engage in horse-trading, the temptations presented by control of economic policy to seek short-term gains and to engage in patronage, had all militated against the long-term planning required to address the formidable economic, social, legal and institutional constraints on development which their countries faced.

An additional influence on the way these movements subsequently governed concerned the political culture within which they had emerged. The regimes they set out to overthrow were all marked by strong elements of authoritarianism (and in the case of Ethiopia, Marxist-inspired totalitarianism under the Dergue). All three countries had been plagued by widespread internal strife, military coups, and the rule of 'strongmen', long-serving leaders who had centralised decision-making in their own persons with few, if any, constraints on their power. Such figures had often come to power through the barrel of a gun, used force to maintain their positions, and instituted either *de jure* or *de facto* single-party (or more correctly single-person) rule, and displayed high levels of intolerance towards not only organised political opposition but any expression of dissent.

This had often been accompanied by highly dirigiste attitudes towards management of their economies. Directed investment, the prominent role played by state enterprises in production and distribution, (and in extreme cases such as Mengistu's Ethiopia, the application of Marxist-inspired antagonism towards any role at all for markets and private enterprise), had been prominent features of their economies. The widespread use of other economic instruments such as taxes, subsidies and controlled exchange rates to ensure that their economies delivered specific outcomes and benefitted specific groups were, *gross modo*, until the early 1990s characteristic of the dominant approach to economic development in post-independence SSA and applied by successive governments in post-independence Uganda and Rwanda as well as Imperial and then post-Imperial Ethiopia.

A strong economic role for the state in much of post-independence SSA had been justified in terms of a belief that the weakness of indigenous entrepreneurial classes meant only states could bring about the desired development transformation. It also suggested a fear amongst many post-independence governments of the emergence of autonomous centres of economic power not beholden to the political centre. Access to opportunities for wealth creation and employment therefore came to be carefully controlled by those in power, manipulated for political ends and treated as largesse to be distributed to secure support. While strongly criticised by the new leaders in Uganda, Ethiopia and Rwanda, the economic practices of the regimes they overthrew nevertheless exerted a strong influence on the policies they themselves went on to adopt.

Finally, there was the nature of colonial rule in Uganda and Rwanda, and the expansion of the imperial Ethiopian state, which shaped the three liberation movements. They include the ethnic division and rivalry attributable to the 'divide and rule' colonial policies pursued by London and Brussels in Uganda and Rwanda, respectively, in particular how specific ethnic groups and regions were privileged and others side-lined, and in the case of the Ethiopian empire its conquest of those regions and peoples not part of its dominant ethnic core.

Organised violence had constituted an integral part of European colonial and Ethiopian imperial pacification projects and was met by armed resistance from those they sought to subject. These were profoundly formative experiences and led to the extensive militarisation of those societies. Early resistance movements in Uganda and Rwanda had resorted to arms to defend the interests of those they claimed to represent, such as the late nineteenth century struggles of the Bunyoro in Uganda against British encroachments in the run-up to the establishment of a British Protectorate in 1894, and that of the inhabitants of northern Rwanda between 1910 and 1912 to resist incorporation into German East Africa before the territory's transfer, under a League of Nations mandate, to Belgian control at the end of World War 1. In Ethiopia, the late nineteenth century saw armed resistance of various ethnic groups to the expansion of the Ethiopian state under Emperor Menelik II, followed by successive wars conducted by that state in the face of Rome's colonial ambitions. While these earlier armed struggles constituted a source of inspiration which the NRM, EPRDF and RPF would draw upon, they also meant the use of armed force in the pursuit of political objectives had already become largely normalised in those societies.

All these influences both impacted on these movements during their own insurgencies and then shaped the regimes they subsequently established. Given that the strategies and tactics they adopted during their armed struggles had enabled them to defeat their enemies, it was unsurprising that they should have gone on to believe that these could simply be transferred and applied to a new situation in which they held state power. Notwithstanding their declared intentions to become the antitheses of the systems they sought to overthrew, to introduce fundamental changes to the ways their countries had previously, and disastrously, been governed, and to free their peoples from the deadly predations of the past, the baggage the new leaders brought into office profoundly shaped how the new regimes sought to organise their societies.

The NRM and Uganda's Post-independence Instability

From independence from British colonial rule in 1962, until the victory of Museveni's NRM in 1986, Uganda underwent numerous changes in government, most of these unconstitutional and accompanied by the employment of force to overthrow existing governments, with incumbents then using violence to cling to power. The country was afflicted by regular army mutinies, coup d'états, protracted and bloody civil wars, and the widespread abuse of human rights.

Milton Obote led the country to independence, serving as Prime Minister between 1962 and 1966. The country suffered its first military munity in January 1964, an early indication of the prominent role the armed forces would play in the country's politics. Foreshadowing Uganda's later involvement in the affairs of its large and troubled neighbour, the then Zaire, the Uganda military also supported a rebellion in the east of that country in 1964. Idi Amin, then a colonel in the Ugandan army, was accused of profiting illegally from Zairean gold and ivory, with Obote also coming under suspicion and which led to demands for a Parliamentary inquiry. Obote then suspended the constitution, and in March 1966 declared himself President under a new constitution which granted him extensive powers. He banned opposition parties and instituted a one-party state in 1967. Following an assassination attempt in 1969, he declared a state of emergency and gave free rein to the General Service Unit, the country's military intelligence organisation, to quash political opposition.

In what became known as the 'Move to the Left', Obote then used his enhanced powers to implement his socialist policies. The government took over a wide range of enterprises, including plantations, banks, manufacturing plants and mines. The consequences for the economy were disastrous, leading to widespread shortages and growing popular discontent. At the same time, and aware of the importance of exercising control over the armed forces, Obote granted preferential treatment to his ethnic brethren in the allocation of posts within those institutions.

In January 1971, Idi Amin seized power in a military coup, interpreted by some as a corporatist move on the part of the armed forces concerned with defending their economic interests under threat from Obote's socialist policies (Lofchie 1972). Others highlighted the role of inter-ethnic rivalries in the context of rising tensions between Obote and Amin, each relying on different ethnic groups within the armed forces for support, with Amin and his ethnic base moving against Obote and his brethren after he was demoted in 1970 from Commander in Chief of the Armed Forces to Commander in Chief of the Army (Omara-Ottunnu 1987).

Amin appointed himself President for Life and ruled as the country's military dictator until his own overthrow in 1979. He oversaw the collapse of the Ugandan economy following his expulsion of the country's economically dominant Asian community in 1972 and instituted a reign of terror to eliminate his political opponents which led to the death of at least 100,000 people.[2] Under Amin, the security forces were ubiquitous and widely feared and they routinely applied summary justice to those they apprehended.

The country's first civil war, which began in 1972 and lasted until 1979, involved various anti-Amin forces. The country also suffered invasions by neighbouring Tanzania, firstly in 1972 in support of forces led by the overthrown Obote, and then in October 1978 in an operation known as the 1979 Liberation War. The latter brought together fighters from a range of Ugandan exile groups (including guerrillas led by Yoweri Museveni, then operating as the Front for National Salvation (FRONASA)). These exile forces came together to form the Uganda National Liberation Front (UNLF), and with the support of Tanzanian troops eventually ousted Amin.

Elections in 1980 then saw the return of Obote as President—the polls being accompanied by widespread claims by opposition figures of rigging—with Obote reacting with targeted violence against those questioning the results. Rebel forces continued to operate in the south of the country, most notably those led by Museveni which had been renamed the National Resistance Army (NRA), the military wing of his National Resistance Movement (NRM). Headed by Museveni in his role as Chairman of the High Command of the NRA, the NRM would eventually unite various groups under its banner. What became known as the 'Bush War' lasted from 1980 to 1986 and pitted Ugandan government troops against a range of insurgents which included Amin loyalists and NRA forces.

Obote was overthrown in a military coup d'état in July 1985 by factions within the national army. Driven by perceptions that the Acholi, who made up the bulk of both rank-and-file soldiers and officers, were being discriminated against in favour of Obote's kith and kin from his Lango ethnic group, the coup was led by two Acholi generals. They established a Military Council and briefly ruled the country as *de facto* heads of state until Museveni's NRA forces entered Kampala in January 1986.

Several aspects of Uganda's post-independence developments (and specifically its notorious political instability) had a profound influence on the NRM, the positions it adopted and governance systems it went on to implant. Firstly, there was the tenuous sense of national unity which constituted a major obstacle to any efforts to create a broader national consciousness. Uganda was characterised by significant ethnic diversity and major fault lines running along a North-South axis, with predominantly Bantu-speaking groups in the south and Nilotic groups in the north. In terms of political systems, historically the south was characterised by centralised states with complex monarchical political systems such as the kingdom of Buganda, while in the north polities were, broadly speaking, less centralised and based on chiefdoms. To these divisions were added others along confessional ones created by the operations of rival Protestant and Catholic missionaries, as well as between these Christian denominations and an indigenous Muslim population. British colonial policy had contributed to the rivalries which made themselves felt after independence, nurturing elements from the south to fill administrative posts while northerners found avenues for the fulfilment of their ambitions in the colonial army.

Nevertheless, while the impact of the colonial legacy in terms of prospects for nation-building was undoubtedly an onerous one, an eminent Ugandan scholar has argued the primary responsibility for the country's post-independence woes lay squarely at the feet of its leaders:

> Rather than reverse this negative legacy, post-colonial leaders have, for the most part, exacerbated it by fomenting further ethnic division and conflict; adopting an uncompromising approach to issues of national importance; marginalising or seeking to marginalise whole areas and ethnic groups; adopting disastrous economic policies, and further weakening an already weak state apparatus. (Golooba-Mutebi 2008a, p. 2)

To promote national unity and encourage the transfer of particularistic loyalties to a new overarching political entity, the NRM sought to mitigate the effects of such cleavages. It focused on the post-independence role played by the country's political parties, and more specifically what had proven to be the extreme fragility of the country's multi-party democracy and constitutional rule. Given the country's politicians' inability, or lack of interest, in reaching across ethno-regional lines to build broader support, political parties had come to represent specific ethnic groups in society. The NRM linked the country's violent post-independence history to the activities of such ethnically based political parties, and the mobilisation of ethnicity for political ends which had exacerbated existing fault lines. If the NRM's claim to represent a new and superior set of organising principles that would cure Uganda of its past afflictions was to be believed, these realities had to be addressed.

Since multi-party democracy was seen to have led to the ethnicization of politics, political instability, predatory strong man rule and the dysfunctionality of the Ugandan state—and if allowed to exist in the future would continue to do so—and given the movement had declared it was fighting for the restoration of the political rights of Ugandans, this was an issue for which an appropriate solution had to be found. In the NRM's Ten-Point programme, developed while it was still fighting the Obote regime, there were early indications of the policy it would follow regarding multi-party democracy. Adopting socio-economic emancipatory language, the programme made clear that the establishment of a multi-party system should be postponed until more important national goals were met, such as the eradication of poverty, a minimum standard of living being cast as an enabler, if not pre-condition, for the introduction and sustaining of multi-party democracy:

> Democracy in politics…is not possible without a reasonable standard of living for all the people of Uganda. An illiterate, sick, superstitious Ugandan does not really take part in the political life of the country even when there is formal democracy…the NRM after removing Obote must think of democracy in a total context of real emancipation. (National Resistance Movement 1986, p. 4)

External ideologies and personal experiences also informed Museveni's thinking, and the NRM's positions, on the challenges facing Uganda, and how they could be overcome. Museveni had attended the University of Dar-es-Salaam in Tanzania in the mid-1960s, a country undergoing a transformation under the banner of Nyerere's brand of African Socialism, and which included efforts to overcome tribal differences, build national cohesion and create a Pan-Tanzanian identity through the establishment of a single-party state. The ideology also emphasised the promotion of economic equality and the objective of a society freed of what were seen as exploitative capitalist practices. In Dar es Salaam Museveni interacted with national liberation movements from across Africa, many with strong Marxist-Leninist leanings. Most notable amongst these was FRELIMO, its military forces using Tanzanian territory as rear bases to launch operations into Portuguese-controlled Mozambique, and according to one source Museveni took part "in combat and striker camps inside Mozambique territory".[3]

His sojourns in Mozambique enabled Museveni to familiarise himself with the guerrilla strategy and tactics employed by FRELIMO, in particular the establishment of 'liberated zones' in the north of the country in which FRELIMO employed its approach to 'popular participation', and which the NRM would then try and reproduce in Uganda. The Ten-Point Programme made clear the NRM's own experience in the bush, in particular the ways in which it had secured popular support, would shape its policies once it was in power. So, for example, the need to establish local level people's committees as expressions of "popular democracy" dealing with "each level's local affairs", acting "as political forums to discuss relevant issues concerning the whole country" (National Resistance Movement 1986, p. 4). This idea was fleshed out in Museveni's inauguration speech on January 29, 1986, where the importance of the practices the NRM had applied in those areas it had liberated were highlighted, such as the establishment of 'Resistance Committees'. Given that these "have a lot of power", it was clear Museveni saw these as the fulfilment of the NRM's commitment to restore "democracy for the people of Uganda" (Ugandan Diaspora News 2015).

While the NRM's Programme stated it planned to introduce "parliamentary democracy", this was framed in minimalist terms as an "elected parliament, elected at regular intervals", leaving it unclear as to whether political parties would be allowed to operate. Furthermore, the same document argued that "The politics of Uganda at Independence was unabashed sectarianism: DP [Democratic Party] for Catholics, UPC [Obote's United People's Congress] mainly for protestants outside Buganda and KY [a monarchist party] for protestants in Buganda". Coupled with "opportunistic factions" in the army, and "fresh permutations of sectarianism", the consequence had been "Fragmentation of the people so that they can never unite to confront their common enemy – underdevelopment" (National Resistance Movement 1986, p. 5). The document also provided clues as to how the NRM would bring an end to such sectarianism: "As has always been our line, the National Resistance Movement is a home of the former DP, UPC, CP and UPM members" (National Resistance Movement 1986, p. 5). There would therefore be a single national movement where all could—and must if not prepared to run the risk of being labelled sectarian—find a home.

The labelling was itself significant. Not only was the NRM 'National', but it was also a 'Movement' rather than a political party, a self-description which carried within it notions of a dynamic, broad and forward-looking entity, and setting itself apart from a conventional Ugandan political party. In contrast to the sectarian nature of earlier parties, the NRM adopted what came to be known as 'big tent politics', offering a home to all

Ugandans, and through which they could fulfil their economic, political, social and cultural aspirations.

For the NRM, its successful armed struggle confirmed the necessity of employing force to bring about the required radical political change needed if past mistakes were not to be repeated. In addition, it provided the movement and its leadership with the necessary authority to claim they were the saviours of the nation from the ravages perpetrated by their predecessors. Great emphasis was placed after 1986 on the armed struggle as a central component of the NRM's self-legitimising ideology; not only had it been victorious, but the values of discipline and cohesion forged during the insurgency needed to be carried over to a post-victory political dispensation. And for Museveni, the fact that in the run-up to the capture of Kampala he had combined the role of Vice-Chairman of the National Resistance Council (the NRM's political decision-making body), with that of Chairman of the High Command of the NRA, meant that the movement's victory came to be seen as inseparable from the person of Museveni himself.

The emphasis placed by Museveni in his inauguration speech on national unity and national security, as defined by the NRM, also put his opponents on notice regarding the means he was willing to employ to secure these objectives. He made it clear that any efforts to undermine them would be dealt with harshly: "Any individual or group of persons who threatens the security of our people must be smashed without mercy". And he took the opportunity to announce during his inauguration speech: "No one should think that what is happening today is a mere change of guard: it is a fundamental change in the politics of our country" (Museveni 1986).

The RPF and the Deadly Bequests of Pre-genocide Rwanda

If Uganda was burdened with a legacy of extensive internal fault lines, in the case of Rwanda these were even deeper, and expressed themselves in pervasive feelings of entitlement, privilege, subordination, historic wrongs and high levels of mistrust between different ethnic groups. They would also eventually prove to be significantly more deadly.

Rwanda's pre-colonial and colonial history had also been marked by the widespread use of force. In terms of pre-colonial indigenous state-building efforts, this included the establishment of an expansionist Tutsi kingdom during the eighteenth and nineteenth centuries which subjected the majority Hutu to its rule. Force was also integral to colonialisation efforts; firstly, when Germany laid claim to the territory in 1897, and then in 1911 when it assisted the Tutsi kingdom put down a Hutu rebellion. It was present when Belgium took over the territory under a League of Nations mandate between 1919 and 1945 and launched a series of operations against smaller independent kingdoms. After WWII, and until Rwanda's independence in 1962, Brussels was responsible for administering the country as a UN Trust Territory, and Belgian troops violently suppressed widespread unrest in the run-up to the country's independence.

The actions of European powers also deepened existing ethnic divisions. Drawing on nineteenth-century European theories concerning racial hierarchies, the Germans privileged the Tutsi ruling elite and the predominantly pastoralist Tutsis, attributing to them ethnic superiority based on alleged foreign Hamitic origins, and solidifying the subordination of the supposedly indigenous and inferior Bantu Hutu agriculturalists. Under Belgian rule ethnic distinctions were further entrenched with the introduction of identity cards containing information on the ethnicity of the holder, a practice continued by post-independence governments until 1994.[4]

When the colonial authorities granted permission for the establishment of political parties, one analyst argued that the "birth of party politics brought Hutu-Tutsi animosity squarely into the public domain and turned ethnicity into a major arena for political mobilisation" (Golooba-Mutebi 2008b, p. 4). Hutu demands for emancipation led to the formation by Grégoire Kayibanda of the *Parti du Mouvement de l'Émancipation Hutu* (PARMEHUTU - Party of the Hutu Emancipation Movement), which sought to eliminate the Tutsi monarchy and emancipate the Hutu majority. Winning parliamentary elections in 1960, and then a referendum on the abolition of the Tutsi monarchy, Kayibanda and his party led the country to independence in July 1962, forming a government overwhelmingly dominated by Hutus.

Between 1958 and 1961, during what became known as the 'Hutu Revolution', PARMEHUTU militants armed themselves, and in 1959, as independence loomed, fighting erupted between them and members of the Tutsi monarchist party *Union Nationale Rwandaise* (Rwandese National Union – UNAR). The violence spread rapidly, and in a foretaste of things to come decades later it took on the contours of an ethnic civil war. Though eventually quelled by Belgian forces, it led to the flight of large numbers of Tutsis to neighbouring Burundi, Uganda, Tanzania and Zaire.

The period between independence in 1962 and the genocide of 1994 was plagued by military coups, invasions, the rule of strongmen, a short-lived period of multi-party democracy and regular outbreaks of ethnic conflict. In December 1963 Rwandan exiles, linked to an external faction of UNAR, invaded Rwanda from bases in Burundi and Uganda, with such infiltrations continuing throughout the 1960s. The Kayibanda government then embarked on a purge of both moderate Hutu and prominent Tutsi politicians.[5] In another harbinger of 1994, during and after these incursions, retribution was meted out to Tutsis by Hutu militias in what were effectively small-scale pogroms, with new waves of Tutsis then seeking refuge in neighbouring countries. By 1965 Kayibanda had instituted a one-party state, with PARMEHUTU winning all the seats in the legislative elections that year. Kayibanda successfully put himself forward as the sole candidate for President, a feat he repeated in 1969.

While attempting to introduce constitutional amendments allowing him to run again in the elections of 1973, Kayibanda was overthrown in a military coup led by Juvénal Habyarimana, the Minister of Defence and Army Chief of Staff, who would go on to perpetuate single-party and Hutu dominant rule. His *Mouvement républicain national pour la démocratie et le développement* (National Republican Movement for Democracy and Development –MRNDD) as it would be renamed in 1991 became the country's only legal party. As party leader, Habyarimana was the sole candidate in presidential elections in 1978, 1983 and 1988.

Despite Habyarimana declaring he intended to move away from the discriminatory ethnic politics of his predecessor, it soon became clear ethnicity as an organising principle of state policy would be further entrenched, quashing Tutsi hopes the new president might deliver on his initial promises. During his rule a system was established whereby access to both educational opportunities and public sector employment was based on regional considerations, ones which mirrored the country's ethnic composition. The system further eroded the position of the Tutsi, increasing their sense of insecurity and contributing to further outward migration. Strongman politics was the order of the day, with Habyarimana concentrating in his person not only the presidency as leader of the MRNDD, but also the posts of prime minister, Chief of Staff of the Army and Minister of Defence.

Tutsi exile politics were informed by the reality of being squeezed between hostile forces and demographic factors. There was only begrudging tolerance of the presence of Tutsis in countries such as Uganda, and barriers, both formal and informal, were placed in the way of their integration into their host societies, while there was continuous strong resistance from successive Hutu-dominated governments to their return. As a result, the military option increasingly came to be seen by many Tutsi as the only realistic one to pursue. In addition, the experience of the Tutsi with multiparty democracy, and the slim chances their parties had of influencing national policy given their numerical inferiority compared to the Hutu majority,[6] meant many exiled Tutsi came to believe that if they were to reclaim their citizenship, they would have to force their way back into Rwanda.

This objective would have to be achieved in the face of opposition from extra-regional powers such as France, and powerful neighbours such as Zaire, neither of them favourable to the possibility of a Tutsi-dominated government in Kigali. For Paris the primary concern was to prevent an erosion of its influence in Africa by a movement incubated in Anglophone Africa, and for whose leaders—most of whom born and raised in Uganda as English-speakers—the importance of historic and linguistic ties, and the benefits supposedly on offer from membership of the economic, diplomatic and military arrangements within the Paris-led *African Francophonie*, carried little weight. Under the rule of Mobutu, Zaire had developed close ties with the Habyarimana regime, both leaders being staunch supporters of *La Francophonie*. Mobutu also viewed the RPF as an alien 'Anglo-Saxon' intrusion in the region and was likely concerned about the possible negative effect on Zaire's own political stability of a neighbouring country led by a radical liberation movement such as the RPF. When the antagonism of external powers towards the RPF translated into the provision of military assistance to the Habyarimana regime, the experience turned out to be a profoundly formative one for the RPF. It not only raised the premium it placed on developing its own military capabilities, but also led to a recognition that it operated in an extremely hostile neighbourhood, and which it would subsequently use to justify military operations outside Rwanda's borders.

In terms of the RPF's rise, exile politics had their epicentre in Uganda, where the Tutsi monarch had sought refuge. Efforts by a younger generation of exiles to produce a strategy for the diaspora led to the founding in 1980 of the Rwandan Alliance for National Unity (RANU), the RPF's precursor. Rwandans in Uganda had become caught up in the maelstrom of that country's politics, and after the fall of Amin, and Obote's return to power in 1979, the latter would accuse the Rwandan exiles of having provided support to his predecessor. Building on anti-refugee sentiments, Obote tried to strengthen his support base by dispossessing Rwandans of their property, redistributing their assets to his followers and denying Rwandans access to public employment. In 1982 he sought to compel them to relocate back to Rwanda, a move resisted by Habyarimana as well as the exiles themselves, who viewed with dread their prospects in a Rwanda under the rule of the MRNDD.

Against this backdrop, RANU sought to distance itself from the conservative sentiments which pervaded the Tutsi exile circles, dominated as these were by earlier waves of refugees from the late 1950s and mid-1960s, and it adopted a radical platform which included the abolition of the monarchy and creation of a socialist state. This was an ideological position that shifted the focus away from ethnicity as the primary organising principle of politics, and one in tune with the dominant radical political discourse in Africa at the time and the objectives of other liberation movements.

Later, and drawing heavily from the example set by the NRM's Ten-Point Programme, RANU developed its own Eight-Point Plan. Adopted at RANU's Congress in 1987 during which it changed its name to the RPF, the Plan was informed by the NRM's strong anti-tribal stance, and it called for an end to sectarianism and the need for national unity which transcended ethnic distinctions.

Throwing in their lot with the anti-Amin and then anti-Obote insurgencies led by Museveni, large numbers of Tutsi exiles joined the latter's forces, amongst them Kagame, who like many others gained first-hand experience of the strategy and tactics of a guerrilla insurgency. Rwandans took on increasingly prominent roles in the NRM and NRA, and after Museveni's victory in 1986 in Uganda's security institutions. One of them, General Fred Rwigyema, would be appointed Uganda's Deputy Minister of Defence, while Kagame rose through the ranks of the NRA to become its head of military intelligence.

Following the NRM's capture of Kampala, it became increasingly clear a parallel Rwandan Patriotic Army (RPA) had been gestating within the NRA, likely with the blessing of Museveni. As the NRA began its own transformation into Uganda's national army, the RPA also benefitted from further training and materiel, and so when conditions were judged favourable the RPA had the capability to go into action as an independent force.

Pressures of various kinds on the RPF eventually led to the decision to invade Rwanda in 1990. On the one hand, with the return of relative stability to Uganda under NRM rule, the number of Ugandans questioning the continued high-profile of RPF notables within NRM and NRA structures increased, as a result of which Museveni eventually felt the need to dismiss Rwigyema from his post. In addition, and again linked to the restoration of a degree of security within Uganda, there were strong fiscal reasons for the new Kampala government to embark on a process of demobilisation and disarmament, one which would necessarily have included Rwandan fighters.

Conditions inside Rwanda also seemed to have become propitious for an invasion. The Habyarimana government was under growing pressure on the economic front because of a major downturn in the international price of coffee, the country's main export. There was increasing internal contestation by both Hutu and Tutsi political groups calling for the liberalisation of the country's political system, with some of the country's Western donors joining the call for multi-party elections.

In October 1990 RPA units crossed the border into Rwandan territory, led by Rwigyema as Commander in Chief. While it initially made progress, this invasion was eventually turned back by government forces, with the assistance of French troops who were already on the ground as part of an ongoing French military cooperation training programme (*New Times* (Kigali) 2021). Zaire also came to Kigali's rescue, with Mobutu sending members of his own elite Presidential Guard to assist government forces (Prunier 1999, p. 101).

One consequence of the failed 1990 invasion was a closing of ranks amongst many Hutu, and increasing radicalisation of anti-Tutsi sentiment, with state propaganda depicting the enemy as bent on returning the Hutu to their subordinate position pre-independence. It also led to the further militarisation of anti-Tutsi groups as they organised themselves into armed militias linked to the ruling party, most infamously the *Interahamwe* which was to become the main perpetrator of genocidal acts in 1994.

As in so many parts of the world, the end of the Cold War fuelled growing external and internal demands for the country to democratise. Pressure began to be applied on Kigali by France which now, at least in terms of its declared policy, sought to link its aid programmes in Africa to progress on democratisation. In response Habyarimana took some tentative steps to liberalise on the political front. He allowed political parties to operate, with the exception of those which had not taken up arms against the government, which meant continued non-recognition of the RPF as an acceptable negotiating partner. Faced with both an economic crisis and a war, Habyarimana then established a coalition government with several smaller parties.

Despite Habyarimana's unwillingness to engage with the RPF, other Rwanda-based opposition parties opened negotiations with the rebels, with peace talks being held in Brussels in June 1991. These talks continued in Arusha, Tanzania, this time with the participation of representatives of the coalition government, and eventually led to a ceasefire which came into effect on August 1, 1992, and then to the Arusha Accords of August 1993. Amongst the most important items in the latter were agreements to establish a 'Broad-Based Transitional Government' to oversee future general elections, the integration of government and RPF forces into a single national army, and the repatriation of the country's refugees (United Nations Peacemaker 1993). To help ensure the implementation of the Accords, in October 1993 the UN approved a monitoring force, the United Nations Assistance Mission for Rwanda (UNAMIR).

Significantly given how the RPF subsequently went on to govern Rwanda, the Arusha Accords contained several provisions concerning democracy. The signatories agreed that "Democracy is founded on the idea that sovereignty belongs to the people. It is expressed, notably, through regular, free, transparent and fair elections. Popular representation must be the authentic representation of the will of the people". The two sides also recognised "that multipartyism entails the legitimate existence of a democratic opposition and consider as legitimate the aspiration of any Rwandese citizen to accede to power through the democratic process" (United Nations Peacemaker 1993).

Tensions remained high throughout the Arusha negotiations, particularly in January 1993 when the details of the power-sharing arrangements were leaked. The Rwandan military were uneasy about the integration of forces, and the inevitable demobilisation which would follow. There was also disquiet amongst the general Hutu population regarding the negotiations on power-sharing, and as details on the agreements emerged many Hutu saw the results as unduly favouring the RPF.[7] The ranks of Hutu militia swelled amidst such uncertainty, and they armed themselves with the support of Habyarimana and the Rwandan army.

Developments in neighbouring Burundi also fuelled the increasingly volatile situation in Rwanda. Following a military coup in October 1993, the democratically elected Hutu President of Burundi, Melchior Ndadaye, was kidnapped by Tutsi officers of the Burundian army and subsequently executed. The ensuing unrest in Burundi led to widespread ethnic violence and the flight of large numbers of Hutu across the border into Rwanda, compounding anti-Tutsi sentiments there with Hutu hardliners in Rwanda seeing the hand of the RPF in the coup.

On April 6, 1994, Habyarimana was killed, together with the Chief of Staff of the Rwandan army and the new Burundian president, when the Rwandan president's plane was shot down over Kigali. Accusations of responsibility were traded, hard-line Hutu supremacists claiming the RPF had carried out the action, and the RPF in turn attributing responsibility to those Hutu militants seeking a reason to take over the government launch a genocide against the Tutsi and eliminate those moderate Hutus in favour of national reconciliation and implementation of the Arusha Accords. With UNAMIR constrained by a mandate which did not authorise its Blue Helmets to use force, except in self-defence, by May 1994 the genocide was well under way. It would eventually result in the deaths of around 500,000 Tutsi, as well as large numbers of Hutus seen by the Hutu militias as moderates, and therefore traitors.[8] The RPA, now under the command of Kagame following the death of General Rwigyema in the early stages of the 1990 invasion, quickly made gains against both the Rwandan army and the Hutu militias, and in early July 1994 it captured Kigali.

For the RPF, its experiences in 1994 with both UNAMIR and the French military *Opération Turquoise* would profoundly shape its worldview and policies it subsequently pursued. The international community in the form of the UN had shown itself to be impotent, and maybe also disinterested, in the face of mass slaughter. The UN's mission had not only failed to prevent the genocide, but the unwillingness of members of the Security Council to provide it with the means to do so was seen to have encouraged the genocidal forces to believe they had free rein to carry out their plans without fear of an external response. To the extent any Western power had been willing to intervene, this had taken the form of French troops who, after their arrival in Rwanda (in the context of the *Opération Turquoise* and supposedly to set up safe humanitarian areas) were seen by the RPF to have propped up France's Hutu allies. When this no longer proved an option, the RPF believed that Paris enabled the genocidal forces to set up in neighbouring Zaire where Habyarimana's old ally, Mobutu, continued to rule.

Taken together, the country's history of ethnic discrimination, organised violence and the prevalence of both domestic and external hostile actors reinforced the RPF's belief in the utility, if not indispensability, of the use of armed force. Surrounded by enemies, the leadership of the RPF believed that national security could only be secured through the force of arms, that it would have to largely rely on its own human and material resources and internal discipline to achieve its objectives, and that the ends justified the use of any means. Dissidence within its own ranks would be dealt with harshly, and unity and the importance of strict compliance with superior orders became sacrosanct. Furthermore, given the numerical inferiority of its ethnic support base, any form of multi-party democracy would have to be managed by the RPF government in such a way that continued RPF rule was never threatened.

The EPRDF: Absolutist Rule, Warfare and Totalising Ideologies

Like the NRM and RPF, the EPRDF's rise to power under Meles Zenawi and the means it used to rule the country from 1991 to 2019 need to be understood against the backdrop of the country's history, and the political culture within which the movement developed. Ethiopia's long history of indigenous authoritarian rule, under emperors who enjoyed semi-divine status, set important precedents in terms of the role of strongmen and centralisation of authority in a single person at the apex of political structures. This template was one which would be reproduced over time, and in different circumstances. After the fall of the imperial regime in 1974, it was replicated by a totalitarian Marxist-inspired military dictatorship, the Dergue, which seized power and held it until the EPRDF captured Addis Ababa in 1991 and went on to institute its own set of restrictive political governance practices.

Again like Rwanda and Uganda, one factor shaping Ethiopia's political culture throughout its modern history was the pervasiveness of warfare, and employment of violence against political opponents. Reacting to official repression, and in their quest for power, groups targeted by state repression themselves often embarked on the path of violent contestation of the rule of central government, and on occasion against each other as well.

The ubiquity of conflict, and the prominent role played by the country's armed forces, reflected the powerful centripetal ethno-nationalist dynamics at work in the country. Their origins can be traced to the internal colonialism undertaken by successive Ethiopian emperors, in the form of the territorial expansion of a dominant ethnic core with strong unitarist and integrationist aspirations, and the conquest and subjugation of peoples in the periphery. This triggered armed resistance, accompanied by increasing demands from ethnic groups for some form of regional autonomy, up to and including the right to secede. Tensions between autonomist centrifugal and authoritarian centripetal forces were a recurrent feature of Ethiopia's history. They have made themselves felt up to the present day and help explain the strong emphasis placed by successive governments on national unity, and their antagonism towards fissiparous tendencies.

Proof of such intolerance was shared by all regimes in Addis Ababa, irrespective of their ideological colouration, can be seen in the Dergue's responses to the problem of ethnic dissidence. The antithesis of the imperial regime in terms of its avowed ideology nevertheless pursued policies of centralisation in regard to the country's peripheral areas and placed considerable emphasis on the maintenance of the country's territorial integrity. In line with its Marxist-Leninist views, it argued that the revolution of 1974, and most importantly the overthrow of the exploitative feudal system, made any demands for autonomy redundant. The Dergue therefore pursued the same policies as the *ancien régime* on this issue, employing force to repress the secessionist aspirations of the Eritreans, the autonomist demands of Tigrayans, and the separatist ambitions of the Somalis in the Ogaden.

If the precolonial and colonial histories of Uganda and Rwanda had been characterised by periods of intense warfare, the scale of such warfare in Ethiopia throughout the nineteenth century and much of the twentieth century was significantly greater. This was partly a consequence of successive large-scale invasions of Ethiopian territory by European powers and neighbouring countries, and which elicited significant popular resistance from Ethiopians.[9]

The net result of these wars against external powers, the use of force by the political centre to extend its reach throughout the country, and the violent resistance of dissident nationalist movements placed armed conflict at the centre of the development of the modern Ethiopian state. One consequence was the embedding of a highly militarised worldview amongst both the country's elites and general population, one in which the use of purposive organised violence was not treated as an instrument of last resort.

Another consequence was that the country's armed forces, police and associated security agencies expanded significantly over time. By the time of Mengistu's overthrow in 1991, Ethiopia had come to possess the largest armed forces in Sub-Saharan Africa, numbering some 450,000 (Human Rights Watch 1991, p. 287). Regular conscription drives during both the imperial and post-imperial periods meant generations of Ethiopians (and not only those in the regular armed forces, but also large numbers of citizens engaged in local militias) received military training. The same processes were at work amongst the country's numerous armed dissident nationalist movements, adding to the numbers of those Ethiopians exposed to military life, who gained combat experience, and who came to see war as simply a continuation of politics by other means.

In terms of the role of ideological influences in the country's post-imperial political history, what catches the eye of the observer is the tremendous hold of Marxist-Leninist thinking on the country's political protagonists, both before and after 1974. It informed the positions taken by the Dergue as well as groups which contested its right to rule, and in particular that of its eventual nemesis the TPLF/EPRDF. There was widespread adherence to Marxist-Leninist analytical categories and revolutionary objectives, with great emphasis placed by all radical actors on the need for internal discipline, ideological purity, the necessity of a single correct political line, a strong aversion to political pluralism and the imperative of highly centralised control. Both the history of imperial absolutist rule and the pervasive influence of Marxist-Leninist thought as a guide to the capture and then retention of control of the state helped reproduce what has been appropriately characterised as a "specific zero-sum conception and 'indivisibility' of power" (Hagmann and Abbnik 2011, p. 585).

The two main organised civilian political parties of the 1970s opposed to the imperial system were the Ethiopian People's Revolutionary Party (EPRP), and the All-Ethiopia Socialist Movement (known by its Amharic acronym MEISON). Both put themselves forward as 'vanguards' of the revolutionary masses, and each seeing themselves as best positioned to determine where the objective interests of the oppressed masses lay. They would eventually criticise the Dergue for usurping the role of vanguard of the revolution, for its poor grasp of Marxism-Leninism, and specifically its failure to transition from the 'Provisional Military Administration Council' (PMAC) it established and hand over power to the 'People's Government' they demanded, and in which they clearly intended to play the leading role.

Ideological distinctions between the two movements were difficult to discern, their common ground being most apparent in their views on democracy and civil liberties. The EPRP committed to safeguarding "the free activity of all political parties, organizations and individuals", while MEISON promised that "freedoms of expression, of assembly, to demonstrate and to strike shall be guaranteed to all the people absolutely" (Lefort 1983, p. 163). Yet at the same they were more circumspect in terms of commitments to safeguard what, given their Marxist-Leninist inspired views, they saw as 'bourgeois' liberal democracy. On this point there was little to distinguish between the two. While the EPRP undertook, once it had gained power, to ensure all political parties would be able to operate freely, this was not an unqualified right. Rather, this freedom might only be enjoyed by other political groupings "provided they oppose feudalism, the bureaucratic bourgeoisie and imperialism", and it argued for "a ban for a fixed period on political activities by all those...who have acted against the people" (Lefort 1983 p. 163). Both claimed to be the sole authentic vanguard working class party capable of leading the struggle of the 'exploited masses', and "both of them were avowed devotees of a single-party system" (Tiruneh 1993, p. 145). While neither movement would realise its political ambitions, their exclusionary and monopolistic political views set important precedents and were to have a strong influence on those who eventually seized power in 1974. The more radical elements within the Dergue appropriated the Marxist-Leninist ideology of these urban-based revolutionary civilian political groupings, and struck what turned out to be purely tactical alliances with them.

Mengistu's rise to a position of dominance within the Dergue was a bloody one, with a massive culling of ancien régime notables, and internal purges of fellow Dergue members. But such ruthlessness would be dwarfed by Mengistu's subsequent actions against the civilian opposition revolutionary movements which came to oppose him. After the Dergue's announcement that it had transformed itself into the PMAC, democratic rights were suspended in September 1974.

Securing the position of Dergue Chairman in February 1977, Mengistu became the country's new post-imperial strongman, a development which one analyst characterised as essentially "a continuation of Ethiopia's political culture" (Tiruneh 1993, p. 200). The Dergue's intolerance of dissent, and willingness to eliminate those it characterised as 'counter revolutionaries', led to the 'Red Terror' against the EPRP after the latter launched an armed urban guerrilla struggle, resulting in the execution of thousands of EPRP supporters. In a second wave of Red Terror, equally repressive methods were employed against MEISON. Not only did the Red Terror demonstrate the Dergue's extreme intolerance towards opposing political views, but it also set yet another important precedent in the use of violence to deal with political opposition to be emulated by future governments.

After crushing the civilian opposition, the Dergue adopted Marxism-Leninism as the official ideology of the single-party state it went on to establish in 1987, the communist People's Democratic Republic of Ethiopia (PDRE). The Dergue's creation, the Workers' Party of Ethiopia (WPE), became the sole legal party, and the PDRE featured the full panoply of structures and systems common to such states. These included the practice of democratic centralism within the confines of a single revolutionary vanguard party. A vast number of party-controlled mass organisations were set up for groups such as students, women, and workers. A national legislature was created, which despite the powers it was formally granted to initiate and approve legislation was in reality a rubber-stamping entity subordinate to the decisions of the ruling party's Central Committee and Politburo. Power was concentrated in the hands of Mengistu as both the Secretary-General of the WPE and President.

It was the TPLF—allied to a number of other smaller movements that would form the EPRDF in the late 1980s—together with the Eritrean People's Liberation Front (EPLF) would eventually defeat the Dergue militarily and lead to its overthrow in May 1991.[10] In a repeat of the issues which had exercised Ethiopian political activists before, during and after the 1974 revolution, debates within the TPLF/EPRDF had revolved around the economic, social and political objectives of the struggle, the appropriate strategies and tactics to be adopted, the support bases to be nurtured and alliances to be struck, all informed by Marxist-Leninist analytical categories. Much time and effort was expended in defining what constituted a 'genuine' socialist revolution, with particular attention paid to the need to clarify the positions of firstly the TPLF, and then the EPRDF, on the burning 'nationalities question' and its links to the class struggle. This resulted in a platform which merged ethno-nationalist grievances with socio-economic deprivation, and the redefining of the armed struggle it launched in 1975 in increasingly revolutionary terms to include the ending of economic exploitation and the building of an entirely new society.

This change was driven by the Marxist-Leninist League of Tigray (MLLT), a faction within the TPLF which by the mid-1980s had come to exercise decisive control over the movement, and in which Meles Zenawi played a central role. The TPLF would adopt the standard organisational structure and practices of most Marxist-Leninist vanguard parties, with Congresses held at regular intervals, a Central Committee, and a Politburo. As highlighted by a TPLF dissident, Aregawi Berhe, it also possessed a large Propaganda Department which produced a range of training manuals and propaganda material, and a Department of Mass Organisation to encourage popular participation in the armed struggle (Berhe 2008, p. 120). It established a training school for cadres, headed up by Meles Zenawi, which allowed the future leader of Ethiopia to become the principal ideologue within the TPLF and then within the broader EPRDF, and to build a support base imbued with the 'correct' political line he believed should be pursued. The MLLT leaders consolidated their hold over the TPLF, silenced dissonant voices within the Front, and moved it decisively in what they saw as the correct orthodox Marxist-Leninist direction. As Aregawi Berhe observed:

> Free and open debates in CC [Central Committee] circles now became much more limited, as independent-minded members faced purges and later execution. From here on it was only the MLLT that defined the course of the struggle ideologically, politically and militarily. (Berhe 2008, p. 227)

Like Museveni and Kagame, in his rise to power Meles Zenawi also benefited from the legitimacy derived from his combination of extensive political and military experience. As leader of the TPLF, and then in 1988 of the EPRDF, he took part in the long military struggle of both organisations. Imbued with a strong sense of the utility of Marxism-Leninism as a strategy for capturing the state, as a guidebook for the retention of power and for organising society, and the acceptability of using targeted violence to achieve such objectives, another African strongman intolerant of notions of 'bourgeois democracy' would therefore be in power in Ethiopia when the Cold War ended.

Africa's New Leaders and Their Hybrid Regimes

The African 'new leaders' which gained the attention of Western capitals in the early to mid-1990s, and with whom Western capitals felt able to develop privileged relations, made an effort to set themselves apart from the predecessors they blamed for the extremely poor situations they found their countries in when they gained power. Speaking the language of urgent reform to both domestic and international audiences, they took every opportunity to proclaim that their sole interest in governing was to consolidate peace after prolonged periods of conflict and instability and to deliver the urgently required improvements in the living standards of their peoples. The need to arrest the seemingly irreversible institutional decline, which had been a prominent feature of their countries, modernise their economies, tackle corruption, overhaul their justice systems and public sectors, and introduce liberalising political reforms, were all items to be addressed under their leadership.

After what had seemed to be decades of atrophy and drift in SSA, the dynamism and sense of purpose projected by these governments was warmly welcomed by Western powers. There also appeared to be a great deal of common ground between Western donors and these 'new leaders' on the importance of faster economic growth, and of poverty reduction and improvements in other human development targets, most particularly in health and education. In terms of the economic growth component, there seemed to be a meeting of minds on the need to implement a specific set of interventions based on the aforementioned 'Washington Consensus'.

The leaders also made reference, though less frequently, to their intentions to embark on a process of political liberalisation, and for the West this meant they intended to transform their countries into recognisably liberal states. Multi-party elections, held under new constitutions and robust electoral legislation, would help usher in fundamental change in these African polities, changes that would eventually converge upon a liberal democratic model of political and economic organisation. Their declared attachment to such principles was unsurprising, since to secure Western support for the reconstruction of their devastated countries, it was essential that they not be seen as outliers, rowing against the tide of the Third Wave of Democratization.

In the event, the regimes in Addis Ababa, Kampala and Kigali proved extremely skilful in building governance systems and programmes which, while appearing to pay more than simply lip-service to liberal political and economic principles, also enabled them to manipulate or simply ride roughshod over the laws and institutions they had created. These African partners of the West, which had been chosen to showcase the benefits of the novel post-Cold war modalities of Western development assistance, adopted a highly selective 'pick and mix' attitude to the West's recommended menu of reforms.

As detailed in later chapters, they each embarked on what has appropriately been characterised as 'illiberal state building'. Implemented by victorious armed liberation movements, such as those which seized power in Ethiopia, Rwanda and Uganda, this was a process based on strengthening of a core of institutions, foremost amongst which their security apparatus which came to enjoy primacy in terms of decision-making. After their capture of the state, liberation movements constructed and entrenched political economies in which their hegemonic role, based on close ties between their political, military and economic support bases, was secured, and accompanied by a high degree of centralised power.[11]

Despite their formal adoption of many features of liberal democracies, these African regimes have displayed strongly authoritarian and illiberal traits carried over from an earlier period in their evolution. In addition to the concentration of power in the hands of national leaders and their inner circles, reminiscent of the top-down and closed-shop decision-making processes of their years of armed struggle, another carry-over is intolerance of dissent within their ranks, and the importance attached to internal discipline.

When aspects of their rebel movement past were transplanted to the way they subsequently governed, it led to poor levels of accountability in the executive branch and the nurturing of weak legislatures heavily dominated by ruling party representatives, which in terms of their oversight functions were often reduced to a rubber-stamping role. Judiciaries, supposed to be the last line of defence in terms of ensuring compliance with the rule of law and constraining governmental power, likewise came to be composed of members completely beholden to the executive for their appointments. Any countervailing role these institutions might play as constraints on the exercise of Executive power was thus intentionally, and severely, weakened. Government processes therefore embodied many of the features of the closed, strongly hierarchical, top-down features of military-style decision-making these movements had practiced as armed insurgents, with minimal oversight from any external bodies.

Amongst additional practices that violate the Western liberal democratic canon has been their willingness to manipulate laws guaranteeing civil and political liberties, most particularly by restricting the space available to those questioning the status quo (be these organised political opposition parties, civil society groupings, or the media). And, as already noted, these regimes have also shown themselves willing to regularly tinker with their constitutions; through amendments to extend the time limit of mandates or increases in the number of mandates permitted, they have thus able to prolong their shelf-life and that of their leaders.

Given their countries' histories of unchecked, unaccountable and arbitrary exercise of power by former strongman rulers, they claimed to attach great importance to the constitutionally mandated separation of powers between various branches of government, with specific attention paid to the independence of the judiciary, as well as guarantees for civil liberties and political rights, and the rule of law. Free and fair multi-party elections, based on competition between multiple political parties (though in the case of Uganda this was explicitly deferred in 1986, until such time as conditions were judged appropriate for its reintroduction) were supposed to provide for political transitions. However, such features have co-existed with a consistent recourse to exclusionary and authoritarian practices and seemingly arbitrary decision-making, with these regimes regularly making it clear that any organised opposition which threatens to undermine the status quo will not be tolerated. Therefore, behind a façade of liberal policies, legislation and institutions, these regimes have engaged in authoritarian, anti-democratic and occasionally violent practices, ones often all too reminiscent of the dictators they had previously overthrown. Given the post-Cold War Western position on the unacceptability of openly authoritarian practices, they adopted what one scholar appropriately termed 'stealth authoritarianism' deploying,

> The same laws and legal institutions that exist in democratic regimes for anti-democratic purposes. [They] cloak repressive measures under the mask of law, imbue them with a veneer of legitimacy, and render authoritarian practices much more difficult to detect and eliminate. (Varol 2015, p. 1677)

The 'new leaders' of Uganda, Rwanda and Ethiopia therefore came to preside over 'hybrid regimes', prominent examples of an increasingly common political governance system in both developed and developing countries, ones which incorporate both liberal and illiberal elements.[12]

In order to capture the essential elements of such hybridity, scholars developed new typologies and analytical categories to capture 'deviations' from what, at least in line with the West's early post-Cold War triumphalist mindset, was supposed to be linear progress from authoritarian single-party regimes towards liberal multi-party democratic systems and free-market economies. Given that hybrid regime behaviour is often difficult to categorise, a certain amount of definitional confusion was inevitable, with the most easily discernible feature of their hybridity being their attitude towards elections, and on that basis regimes were variously designated as not only 'hybrid' (the broadest category), but also 'electoral authoritarian' and as the slightly less closed 'competitive authoritarian'.

In regard to electoral authoritarianism, this combines a veneer of adherence to liberal democratic principles at the level of political discourse, the existence of formal institutions and regulatory frameworks based on such principles, and most importantly the regular holding of constitutionally mandated elections under conditions of universal suffrage, though the actual behaviour of these regimes indicates they treat the former as purely formal and 'decorative' elements. Electoral outcomes favouring incumbents are a given, with electoral authoritarian regimes using often deadly repression to ensure opposition forces are so weakened they become to all intents and purposes non-existent. The media compliantly toes the ruling party line and provides blatantly pro-government coverage, and national institutions operate solely in accordance with regime directives, while legislation is enacted and laws interpreted by the judiciary in such a way as to benefit the incumbents.[13]

Under competitive authoritarianism, there is a higher degree of electoral competition than under electoral authoritarian regimes. There are elements of a genuine contest, and while opposition parties operate under seriously disadvantageous circumstances, they are not banned outright. They can openly challenge incumbents, and elections are sometimes bitterly fought. Despite the playing field still being heavily skewed in favour of the incumbents, there remains sufficient uncertainty regarding outcomes for opposition parties to be willing to contest elections, for incumbents to devote time and resources to courting voters, and for the electorate to turn up on polling day. In addition, in dealing with the political opposition, the preferred methods of competitive authoritarian regimes fall short of the repressive measures favoured by electoral authoritarians. For example, during elections, while competitive authoritarian regimes may still engage in the use of violence against opposition candidates, their supporters and journalists and also manipulate results, they tend to prefer less violent forms of repression such as co-optation and control over electoral bodies and the judiciary, to secure their political authority (See Levitsky and Way 2002).

Some aspects of the behaviour of the regimes in Uganda, Ethiopia and Rwanda show that rather than openly meting out violence to silence political dissent, they have also occasionally opted for more subtle methods. At the same time, their positioning as either electoral or competitive authoritarian regimes was contingent on the specific challenges they faced at any given moment in time, whether these posed serious threats to regime continuity, the responses judged necessary, the resources at their disposal and the pressures they faced domestically and internationally against their employment of undisguised violent repression. Even if at times they may have been tempted to do so, the attractions and the feasibility of sustaining undisguised dictatorial rule had to be weighed against other considerations. Snapshots of their behaviour at various periods in their recent history therefore show them shifting between the two categories, and often displaying features of both simultaneously.

However, what is clear given the decades they have been in power is that if their leaders ever genuinely intended to move towards the establishment of liberal democracies in their countries, the reality is that any progress is barely discernible. In addition, their significant democratic backsliding during the pandemic indicated that any previous liberalisation which had been permitted had not led to robust institutions capable of safeguarding such gains and was easily reversed.

Donor Rationalisations

Focusing on reconstruction, and the stabilisation of their security situations, such urgent and mammoth tasks helped these governments justify to both external and domestic audiences their often opaque government processes. And the rapid progress they made in rebuilding their countries had important regime legitimising effects; simply reducing armed conflict and lawlessness, ensuring the restoration of a minimum level of service delivery in health and education after years of neglect, and restoring food production were usually sufficient to secure the support of large segments of their population and Western donor approval. This made it easier for political transitions to be deferred to an indeterminant future.

Given the widespread destruction of those countries, it was unsurprising that in their early days these governments should have found listeners receptive to the argument that individual political and civil freedoms, and the most appropriate political system required to safeguard these, should have taken a back seat relative to restoration of the physical safety of citizens and the provision of the basic means of survival. Nor was it surprising that the new regimes would justify their curtailment of freedoms—portrayed as necessary given continued threats to national security and the dangers of a return to conflict, but always as purely temporary and for the greater good—precisely on the grounds that this reflected the relative importance placed by their own peoples on economic and social reconstruction relative to other concerns.

In addition, the early post-Cold War world was one which was expected to be characterised by the sunny uplands of international cooperation based on mutual respect and the pursuit of common interests, and this was accompanied by a strong and palpable Western sense of unease in prescribing to former subject peoples. In terms of international development, the new commitment to cooperation required building relations between donors and aid recipients as equals, the latter now to be treated as 'partners' in a common global endeavour. Notwithstanding the reality of their dependence on Western assistance, such lofty principles provided leaders with compelling arguments for exercising their prerogatives in terms of the national issues they themselves wished to prioritise. Highly sensitive to accusations of neo-colonialism and interference in the internal affairs of sovereign states, the effect was to cause some Western capitals to often take a step back so as not to be seen to be dictating to Africans.

Part of the explanation for this behaviour by Western donor countries, and their apparent downgrading of the importance of democracy relative to other objectives, lies in changes to the goals of Western development assistance and targets set. By the late 1990s, new global frameworks were developed which contained detailed multi-sectoral development priorities and concrete, measurable and sustainable development targets such as those contained in the MDGs. As detailed in the next chapter, such frameworks largely focused on improvements in economic and human development indicators, while remaining deafeningly silent on issues of political governance and civil and human rights. The focus was on the more easily measurable and verifiable improvements in both income and non-income dimensions thrown up by standardised national and international surveys, as well as a restrictive set of non-political governance indicators, in particular those related to restrictive definitions of what constituted 'good governance'.

These in turn helped Western foreign offices and donor agencies justify their continued assistance to these African governments. Foremost amongst the arguments advanced by Western apologists of their 'hybrid' behaviour was that such occurrences were deviations from a more significant and broader picture of progress in terms of economic growth and social development, and which helped justify the continued disbursements of aid. Early post-Cold War Western commitments to strictly link aid disbursements to political reforms gradually weakened, and conditionalities were now devised that largely linked Western development assistance to partner country commitments to improve social welfare indicators and to undertake specific institutional and economic reforms.

This shift eminently suited the regimes in Uganda, Ethiopia and Rwanda. So long as they continued to deliver the necessary results in terms of a set of internationally agreed development priorities and targets—or were at least perceived to be genuinely trying to do so—they could count on repeated injections of Western development assistance. The gradual delinking of Western aid flows from the status of democracy and human rights in recipient countries, and the provision of aid to support progress on frameworks such as the MDGs, therefore reduced Western pressure on these governments to introduce political reforms.

Notes

1. For some conclusions on this aspect of 'rebel-to-ruler' transitions, and the style of post-conflict governance adopted in Rwanda, see Purdeková et al. (2018). "Militarisation of governance after conflict: beyond the rebel-to-ruler frame – the case of Rwanda". *Third World Quarterly* 39 No.1, 2018. pp. 158–174.
2. International Commission of Jurists (1977). "Uganda and Human Rights: Reports to the UN Commission on Human Rights". Geneva: Amnesty International, 1977, p. 167. Amnesty International, in its annual report of 1979, put the figure for deaths during Amin's rule at 300,000 (Amnesty International 1979. *Amnesty International Report 1979*, London, p. 38).
3. University of Dar es Salaam website showing Museveni's biography and degrees awarded: https://www.udsm.ac.tz/web/index.php/alumni/name/3. During a state visit to Mozambique in 2018, Museveni took the opportunity to thank the Mozambicans for the military training they had provided to cadres that would eventually form the NRA. *Independent*(2018).
4. On the consequences of this policy, see Longman (2002).
5. On this period, see Lemarchand (1970).
6. The population census of 1991 estimated the Hutu represented around 91.1 per cent of the population, the Tutsi 8.4 per cent, the remainder composed of the Twa people. (République du Rwanda, *Recensement*

Général de la population et de l'habitat au 15 aout 1991- Analyse des résultats, Kigali, 1991).

7. In terms of the distribution of ministerial portfolios within the Transitional Government, the MRNDD and RPF were each granted five portfolios, the other four other parties sharing the remaining eleven portfolios (Article 55, *Protocol of Agreement between the Government of the Republic of Rwanda and the Rwandese Patriotic Front on Power-Sharing within the Framework of a Broad-Based Transitional Government*, 30th October 1992). However, it was the provisions governing the integration of the armed forces that proved most unsettling for the Hutu in general, and government soldiers in particular. Government troops would be granted only 60 per cent of the vacancies below that of command posts in the new integrated army, the RPF the remaining 40 per cent, while there was to be a 50/50 split between the two parties at command level. These same proportions were to be applied to the country's National Gendarmerie. (Articles 74 and 144, *Protocol of Agreement between the Government of the Republic of Rwanda and the Rwandese Patriotic Front on the Integration of the Armed Forces of the Two Parties,* August 3, 1993.)
8. While the future RPF government claimed a figure of over 1 million killed in the genocide, a more widely accepted figure is that between 491,000 and 522,000 Tutsi were killed. On this see, McDoom (2020).
9. The country faced almost continuous warfare during the second half of the nineteenth century and first half of the twentieth century. This included a British incursion in 1868 during the reign of Emperor Tewodros, while his successor engaged in military operations between 1874 and 1876 against the Egyptian state under Khedive Ismael, and then in 1889 against the Mahdist state in Sudan. There followed the First Italo-Ethiopian War of 1895–1896 as Rome sought to expand into Ethiopia from its bases in Eritrea. The Second Italo-Ethiopian War of 1935–1937 began when Italian forces again invaded and occupied the country, with Ethiopians later contributing to the defeat of Italian forces in the British-led campaign of 1940–1941.
10. In addition to the TPLF, the other members of the EPRDF coalition were the Ethiopian People's Democratic Movement (APDM) (an offshoot of the EPRP), the Oromo Democratic Party (ODP) and the Southern Ethiopian People's Democratic Movement (SEPDM).
11. On this, see Jones et al. (2013).
12. The concept of hybrid regimes is closely associated with the work of Larry Diamond (2002).
13. For an excellent overview of this form of political regime based on case studies, see Schedler (2006).

References

Amnesty International. 1979. *Amnesty International Report 1979*, London 1979.

Berhe, Aregawi. 2008. *A political history of the Tigray People's Liberation Front (1975–1991): Revolt, Ideology and Mobilisation in Ethiopia.* Amsterdam: Vrije Universiteit, 2008.

Diamond, Larry. 2002. "Elections Without Democracy: Thinking About Hybrid Regimes". *Journal of Democracy*, 13 No. 2, April 2002, Johns Hopkins University Press.

Fisher, Jonathan. 2020. *East Africa after Liberation - Conflict, Security and the State since the 1980s.* Cambridge University Press.

Golooba-Mutebi, Frederick. 2008a. "Collapse, war and reconstruction in Uganda – An analytical narrative on state-making". Crisis States Working Paper Series No.27. January 2008, Crisis States Research Centre, The London School of Economics.

Golooba-Mutebi, Frederick. 2008b, 'Collapse, war and reconstruction in Rwanda – An analytical narrative on state-making', Crisis States Working Paper Series No.28, February 2008, Crisis States Research Centre, The London School of Economics

Government of Rwanda. 1991. *Recensement Général de la population et de l'habitat au 15 aout 1991- Analyse des résultats.* République du Rwanda Kigali: 1991.

Hagmann, Tobias and Jon Abbnik, 'Twenty years of revolutionary democratic Ethiopia, 1991 to 2011', *Journal of Eastern African Studies*, Routledge, Vol. 5, No. 4, November 2011.

Human Rights Watch. 1991. *Evil Days: 30 years of War and Famine in Ethiopia.* Africa Watch Report, New York, September 1991.

Independent (Kampala). 2018. "Museveni salutes FRELIMO for role in birth of UPDF". Kampala, May 19, 2018. https://www.independent.co.ug/84994-2/ (Accessed May 2, 2024)

International Commission of Jurists. 1977. "Uganda and Human Rights: Reports to the UN Commission on Human Rights". Geneva: Amnesty International, 1977.

Jones, Will et al. 2013. "Africa's illiberal state-builders", Working Paper Series No.89, Refugees Studies Centre, University of Oxford, January 2013.

Lefort, René. 1983. *Ethiopia: An Heretical Revolution?*, London: Zed Press, 1983.

Lemarchand, René. 1970. *Rwanda and Burundi*, New York: Praeger, 1970.

Levitsky, Steven and Lucan Way. 2002. "Elections Without Democracy: The Rise of Competitive Authoritarianism", *Journal of Democracy* 13, No.2, April 2002.

Lofchie, Michael. 1972. "The Uganda Coup – Class Action by the Military", *Journal of Modern African Studies* 10 No.1 Cambridge University Press, May 1972.

Longman, Timothy. 2002. “Identity Cards, Ethnic Self-Perception and Genocide in Rwanda” in Jane Caplan and John Torpey (eds.) *Documenting Individual Identity – The Development of State Practices in the Modern World*. Princeton University Press, 2002, pp.345–358.

Lyons, Terrence. 2016. “From victorious rebels to strong authoritarian parties: prospects for post-war democratization”. *Democratization* 23 Issue 6 Taylor and Francis, 2016.

McDoom, Omar Shahabudin. 2020. “Contested Counting: Toward a Rigorous Estimate of the Death Toll in the Rwandan Genocide”. *Journal of Genocide Research* 22 Issue 1; 2020. Taylor and Francis, 2020.

Museveni, Yoweri Kaguta. 1986. *Inaugural Speech*. Transcript accessed on May 2, 2024: https://www.scribd.com/doc/297046963/MUSEVENI-Fundamental-Change-Speech-1986.

National Resistance Movement (NRM). 1986. *The Ten-Point Programme*, Kampala, Uganda, 1986.

New Times (Kigali). 2021. “Rwanda: New Report Details France’s Role in Genocide Against the Tutsi”. 20 April 2021. https://allafrica.com/stories/202104210376.html.

Omara-Ottunnu, Amii. 1992. *Politics and the Military in Uganda, 1980–1985*. London: Macmillan, 1987.

Prunier, Gérard. 1999. *The Rwanda Crisis: History of a Genocide*. Kampala: Fountain Publishers, 1999.

Purdeková, Andrea et al. 2018. “Militarisation of governance after conflict: beyond the rebel-to-ruler frame – the case of Rwanda”. *Third World Quarterly* 39 No.1, 2018.

Schedler, Andreas, ed. 2006. *Electoral Authoritarianism: The Dynamics of Unfree Competition*, Boulder, CO: Lynne Reiner Publishers, 2006.

Tiruneh, Andargachew. 1993. *The Ethiopian Revolution 1974–1977: A transformation from an aristocratic to a totalitarian autocracy*. London School of Economics Monographs in International Studies, Cambridge University Press, 1993.

Ugandan Diaspora News. 2015. “Liberation Day 1986 – Revisiting President Inaugural Fundamental Change Speech 31 years later!” January 26, 2015.

United Nations Peacemaker. 1993. Protocol of Agreement between the Government of the Republic of Rwanda and the Rwandese Patriotic Front on the Integration of the Armed Forces of the Two Parties. Kigali, August 3, 1993. https://peacemaker.un.org/rwanda-integration-armed-forces93#:~:text=This%20protocol%20calls%20for%20the,forces%20into%20various%20security%20organs (Accessed 2 May 2024).

Varol, O. Ozan. 2015. “Stealth Authoritarianism”. *Iowa Law Review*, 100, Issue 4, May 2015. University of Iowa College of Law.

CHAPTER 6

The Silences of International Development Frameworks and 'Good Governance'

International Compacts

In the new millennium, the gradual de-prioritisation by Western donors of issues related to the political regime type of aid recipients, specifically the status of democratic freedoms in those countries benefitting from their development assistance, can be linked to various international compacts agreed at a series of global summits. These collectively set out the Western mainstream international consensus on the development priorities to be pursued and detailed the various rights and responsibilities of both sides of the donor-aid recipient relationship. They also solidified a focus on largely apolitical technical and financial solutions to the development challenges facing developing countries, ones which suited authoritarian rulers such as those in Ethiopia, Uganda and Rwanda.

From New York to Accra via Monterey and Paris

The International Conference on Financing for Development, held in Monterey, Mexico, in 2002, brought together over fifty Heads of State and representatives of the UN, World Bank, IMF and WTO. With the aim of securing the resources required to achieve the recently approved Millennium Development Goals (MDGs), its outcome document was circumspect on questions of political governance. There were hortatory references to the "overall commitment" of signatories "to just and democratic

M. Simpson, *Donors, Democracy and Development in Africa*,
https://doi.org/10.1007/978-3-031-74917-9_6

societies", the need for "solid democratic institutions responsive to the needs of the people" and the observation that "good governance is essential for sustainable development" (United Nations 2003, p. 7), formulations which became *de rigeur* in such international frameworks. However, the 'Monterey Consensus' document focused largely, and in significantly greater detail, on the need for more aid and greater effectiveness in development cooperation, such effectiveness defined as the capacity of development finance to deliver positive economic and broader human development outcomes.[1]

The Monterey meeting was essentially a resource mobilisation event, and called for significant increases in ODA which were seen as critical for the achievement of internationally agreed development goals, with the final text reminding developed countries of the longstanding target of 0.7 per cent of GNI they should allocate to ODA.[2] It also emphasised the need for increased Foreign Direct Investment (FDI) in developing countries as a means of eradicating poverty through economic growth, and faster foreign debt relief to free up additional resources for beneficiary governments. External assistance would also be provided to help developing countries better integrate into the world trading system so that international trade played a stronger role as a driver of growth and development by enhancing market access for developing country exports, and by providing financial and technical resources to remove supply-side constraints such as infrastructure and technology deficits. All these initiatives were to be supported by better alignment of donor aid programmes to the development priorities of recipient countries, ones which reflected the shared objectives contained in the MDGs.

As a blueprint for international development in the twenty-first century, the Monterey Consensus was clear in terms of its assumptions. Increased aid, FDI and debt relief from donors, greater integration of developing economies into the international trading system, strengthening the capacity of developing country governments to generate domestic resources, improved targeting of resources by both donors and aid recipients with a specific focus on those interventions contributing to economic growth and poverty reduction, and better policies and systems in aid recipient countries to manage the expected increased ODA would, collectively, deliver the desired results.

Many of these themes were taken up in the Paris Declaration of 2005 (OECD 2005). This became the main template used by both Western donors and developing countries to operationalise what were framed as the 'new partnership' principles to improve aid effectiveness. This Declaration was even more circumspect than the Monterey document in terms of Western donor expectations on the status of democracy and political freedoms in countries receiving their development assistance. The entire document contained a detailed menu of proposed reforms to the ways aid resources were delivered and managed and how development progress should be monitored. Great emphasis was placed on the need to strengthen developing country 'ownership' and 'leadership' of development initiatives. However, it contained only a single reference to the commitment of aid recipients (now designated 'partner countries') to strengthen "as appropriate the parliamentary role in national development strategies and/or budgets" (OECD 2005, p. 8).

The accompanying framework to track progress on the Paris Declaration's objectives of improving 'ownership', 'harmonisation', 'alignment', 'mutual accountability' and 'managing for results' contained a series of detailed targets to be achieved by 2010. These again covered technical progress indicators, such as increases in the number of donors and the percentage of their aid disbursements channelled through the Public Financial Management (PFM) systems of partner countries, changes in the number of theses having "operational development strategies" (for which read PRSPs) and improvements in the predictability of aid flows by halving "the proportion of aid not disbursed within the fiscal year for which it was scheduled" (OECD 2005, pp. 9–10). As at Monterey, increases in ODA, and their improved management, were expected to contribute to better development outcomes. Significantly, even the cursory reference to the role of the partner country legislatures in the development process was conspicuous by its absence in the Declaration's own monitoring framework. No specific target to enable tracking progress in terms of this commitment was set, and necessarily therefore there could not be accountability for progress on this item.

The Accra High-Level Forum on Aid Effectiveness of September 2008 was a follow-up to the Paris Declaration meeting. In contrast to the Paris Declaration, the final statement of the meeting (the Accra Agenda for Action) did make a single, though pointed, reference to democracy as one of the "prime engines of development in all countries" (OECD 2008 p. 3). It noted participants had recognised the "critical role and responsibility of parliaments in ensuring country ownership of development processes and that developing country governments had again undertaken (as they had already committed to do in Paris), to "work more closely with parliaments and local authorities in preparing, implementing and monitoring national development policies and plans" (OECD 2008, p. 4). Yet as with the Paris Declaration, this specific developing country commitment ran the risk of being an open-ended one, likely to remain untested given the lack of any accompanying objectively verifiable benchmarks, indicators and time-bound targets against which progress might be measured.

The Millennium Development Goals (MDGs)

The lodestar of post-Cold War international development agreements were the MDGs, which enjoyed primacy in the international development landscape between 2000 and 2015 until replaced by the Sustainable Development Goals (SDGs) in 2016. The MDGs were the dominant overarching set of international development objectives, containing a time-bound destination for developing countries, detailed benchmarks for evaluating progress and upon which a wide range of development actors were to base their efforts. Their prominence can be seen in the regular references to their importance in the policy documents of UN agencies, the BWIs, both Western and non-Western bilateral donors, partner country governments, non-state actors including local and international NGOs, and international philanthropic foundations.

The MDGs were presented by the UN in the form of a list of eight Goals, each buttressed by detailed targets and indicators. Their genesis can be traced to the adoption of the Millennium Declaration of September 2000 in a UNGA session which followed a Millennium Summit attended by representatives from 189 countries. The precise relationship between the Millennium Declaration and the MDGs is worth examining, as it throws additional light on the gradual process of circumscribing development challenges to a set of resource and capacity constraints, all supposedly susceptible to purely technical fixes, foremost amongst which was the adoption of apolitical, technocratic 'good governance' practices in developing countries.

The Millennium Declaration (United Nations General Assembly 2000) reaffirmed the values of the United Nations Charter and set out a common agenda for the international community in the twenty-first century, bringing together in a single package a wide range of issues to be addressed by all member states. Foremost in terms of the commitments on development entered into by the Heads of State and Government present was that of freeing "our fellow men, women and children from the abject and dehumanizing conditions of extreme poverty" (United Nations General Assembly 2000, p. 4).

Like the Monterey and Paris summits, the Declaration emphasised the need for more resources for development, with calls for industrialised countries to "grant more generous development assistance" and to "deal comprehensively and effectively with the debt problems of low and middle-income developing countries" (United Nations General Assembly 2000, p. 4), as well as to reform existing tariffs and quotas to facilitate access for the exports of least developed countries. Significantly, the increased ODA resources called for were to be directed especially to those countries that were "genuinely making an effort to apply resources to poverty reduction" (United Nations General Assembly 2000, p. 4). However, there were no references to any form of conditionality attached to the release of such funds, notwithstanding the fact the same section of the Declaration had explicitly stated that success in meeting the poverty eradication objective depended "*inter alia*, on good governance within each country" (United Nations General Assembly 2000, p. 4).

The MDGs drew from this Millennium Declaration, and the prior commitments entered into by member states in a series of landmark UN conferences held during the preceding decade, incorporating many of the unmet targets set at these earlier events.[3] When it came to issues of democracy and civil rights, much was again lost in translating the hortatory into the verifiable and monitorable. On the one hand, the Declaration had stated that those heads of state and government present were committed to the fundamental values seen as essential to the conduct of international relations in the twenty-first century, amongst these being the protection of rights such as freedom from "the fear of violence, oppression or injustice" while also recognising that "democratic and participatory governance best assures these rights" (United Nations General Assembly 2000, p. 2). Yet in operationalising the eight MDGs, which were complemented by what would eventually become a total of twenty-one targets and sixty progress indicators, the importance of 'democratic and participatory governance', which world leaders had apparently undertaken to promote, was noticeably absent as a separate MDG. There were therefore no targets or indicators to measure progress on 'democratic and participatory governance'. From Goal 1 on eradicating extreme poverty and hunger to Goal 8 on the development of a global partnership for development, the MDGs and accompanying targets and indicators reflected a purely technical approach to the unblocking of constraints to development. All that was required to achieve the Goals was a supposedly self-evident formula of extra resources, new technology, sound planning and monitoring, better delivery mechanisms and targeting, improved financial management, greater developing country ownership and commitment to the Goals, all based on the idea of 'new partnerships' between donors and recipients characterised by trust and transparency. By the late 1990s, such relations were expressed in terms of 'mutual accountability', with both providers and recipients of development assistance (the latter now re-designated as 'partner countries'), working together to achieve the global public good of development.

The keystone of the expected behaviour changes on both sides of the donor-recipient relationship was therefore to be a 'shared agenda', one based on reciprocal commitments on how aid was to be provided by donors and how it would be applied by partner countries. Such a recasting of the relationship meant aid recipients were able to use the new rules of engagement to push back against unwelcome attention to certain policies they pursued domestically, to resist the intrusion of political governance considerations into their negotiations with donors and to employ their recently granted autonomy in the management of donor resources as a tool for regime strengthening.

Therefore, taken as a whole, the body of soft international law governing international aid and development which emerged in the new millennium was one that proved permissive of the maintenance of authoritarianism in aid-recipient regimes. Subject to the latter declaring they shared with their Western partners the agreed development priorities (with a focus on improvements in social welfare indicators), that they were willing to strengthen the performance of their public institutions, committed to tackle corruption, adopted more market-friendly economic policies, exercised sound fiscal and monetary policies and engaged with local non-state actors to meet 'participatory governance' commitments, they could rest assured that significant ODA resources would flow in their direction. So long as they demonstrated progress on the above items, any shortcomings in terms of the political freedoms they granted their citizens would not be subject to intrusive scrutiny by Western development agencies. As the West went about refining its 'good governance' agenda as a part of its prescriptions for development progress, authoritarian regimes would be able to also use this concept as an additional means to distract their donor patrons from their repressive domestic politics.

The Rise of the 'Good Governance' Agenda

Despite criticisms of American policy on democratization from various quarters, there nevertheless remained a deeply held belief in the US that it remained the bastion of multi-party liberal democracy. The latter was seen as the only political system able to guarantee political freedom and civil liberties, legal equality, the protection of human rights and economic prosperity, and Washington saw itself as having unique responsibilities for its promotion around the world.

The 2000s therefore did see the inclusion of political conditionality linked to progress on democratisation in some of Washington's aid initiatives which were primarily focused on promoting economic growth, such as AGOA's eligibility criteria which linked access to American markets to progress on 'political pluralism' in African countries. Another example was the criteria adopted for the Millennium Challenge Account (MCA), a foreign aid initiative of George W. Bush, launched in 2004, to provide grants to poor countries but subject to them meeting certain standards. Amongst the eligibility criteria for MCA assistance was verifiable progress in terms of democratic governance, with political rights indicators that included free and fair elections, political pluralism and freedom from the rule of totalitarian parties, as well as civil liberties indicators such as freedom of expression and association.

The continued importance attached by Washington to such values stood in contrast to the changing position of other Western bilateral donors. The latter was partly a function of the growing emphasis paid to the new and highly malleable concept of 'good governance', one which first took hold amongst Western European donors and the BWIs in the 1990s. It became an integral component of post-Cold War Western development discourse, an objective which partner countries were expected to pursue and which Western donors committed to support. The elasticity of the term allowed users to set their own parameters based on shifting donor priorities and to include or exclude progress on democracy as an evaluative criterion to be applied to aid recipient countries.

During the 1990s, much effort was expended by Western development actors in defining 'governance'. If the consensus was it concerned relations between state and society, and the rules governing processes and institutions which determined how things were decided and plans implemented by public authority, further work was done to clarify its normative variant, namely 'good governance'. In the case of Africa, deficits in terms of good governance were seen to have been the root cause of post-independence Africa's generally poor development track record. In summary form, this prescriptive version translated into a need to strengthen state capability to get things done through greater policy predictability, better macro-economic management, improved accountability for the use of public funds, greater responsiveness to the need of citizens (in particular the poor) and respect for the rule of law.

Two additional items came to feature prominently in both Western donor and partner country discourse and practice in terms of the good governance agenda and which contributed further to the relegation in Western donor policy of national level democratic reforms to a lower position relative to the pursuit of other forms of citizen engagement in public affairs. These were, firstly, the emphasis placed by Western development agencies on improving participatory and consultative engagements between the state and non-state actors in developing countries and, secondly, on decentralisation as a means of giving communities a greater say on local-level issues. Both themes increasingly featured in Western donor programmes from the mid-1990s onwards and reflected another item in the consensus between donors and their partner countries on how best to achieve development priorities (see, for example, DFID's White Paper of 2000).

Western donor emphasis on the need for partner countries to improve participation and consultation mechanisms, and to embark on decentralisation, was framed as a means of improving poverty reduction and the achievement of other MDGs, with the successor SDGs of 2016 setting out a specific target under Goal 16 to "Ensure responsive, inclusive, participatory and representative decision-making at all levels". In addition, they were expected to help meet other important Western aid objectives; popular participation in PRSP planning and execution was seen as a means of strengthening 'country ownership', a key element of the 'new partnerships' agenda, and was also supposed to allow for greater public scrutiny of state agencies and therefore improved accountability.

According to the World Bank's PRSP manual of 2002, the involvement of organised non-state groups in the design of a poverty reduction strategy would "make it more equitable to and representative of various stakeholder interests, increase the transparency of the policy formulation process, and ultimately make the strategy more sustainable" (World Bank 2002, p. 240). Significantly, this document also argued that multi-party democracy had limited potential to improve development outcomes compared to the more regular participatory processes which it proposed, since "traditional democratic processes usually only allow citizens to make one input in four or five years. Participatory processes allow citizens to actively participate in the governance of their country and their resources between election cycles, on a more regular basis" (World Bank 2002, p. 253).

For the authoritarian regimes of partner countries, consultation and decentralisation were likely seen as unthreatening. They could take many forms, proceed at different speeds and if effectively managed need not weaken central government control over the direction of national economic and political development.

By the new millennium, good governance had established itself firmly in the international development lexicon and generated an entire specialised 'practice area' for development workers. As a critical development goal, it came to be seen as largely a technical challenge, achievable through the implementation of an ambitious menu of institutional reforms and capacity-building interventions.[4] In addition to being seen in instrumental terms as both pre-condition and guarantor of sustainable and robust economic growth and development, good governance policies and programmes would also be developed to help ensure the transparent and effective use of donor funds by aid recipient countries. The latter issue became particularly important following the introduction of the General Budget Support (GBS) modality for aid transfers championed by DFID, which involved a move away from project funding with disbursements tied to a specific project to the channelling of ODA directly to a partner country's treasury to support an overall national development and/or poverty reduction strategy.[5]

Key position papers and statements from the 1990s provide insights into how the good governance concept was interpreted by different Western bilateral donors and Western-dominated multilateral development actors. In 1989 the World Bank released a landmark document, essentially a thirty-year retrospective of the performance of African countries since the 1960s. This profoundly shaped Western development policy towards SSA, by placing institutional reform at the centre of donor attention and linking Africa's poor economic performance with the crisis in its governance systems. In the report's foreword, World Bank President Barber Conable argued that to achieve the required standards of good governance what the SSA region required was "a public service that is efficient, a judicial system that is reliable, and an administration that is accountable to its people" (World Bank 1989, p. viii).

The OECD's Development Assistance Committee (DAC), made up of the donor members of the organisation, took a somewhat different line. Given the political profile of OECD members, who were overwhelmingly liberal multi-party democracies and market economies (these being pre-conditions for membership of the club), it felt less constrained than the World Bank in discussing the political aspects of development, specifically the role played by the political systems of countries in the development equation. A 1993 OECD-DAC document set out the organisation's views on the subject, arguing that "sustainable development requires *a positive interaction between economic and political progress*" (author's emphasis; OECD-DAC 1993, p. 8). Democracy and good governance defined in technical terms were seen as inextricably linked, and while the latter centred on management processes through which political authority was exercised, a key aspect of governance was seen to be the "form of political regime" that existed (OECD-DAC 1993, p. 18).

The document also left little room for doubt as to what it understood by democratic practice. Legitimate governments required "the consent of those who are governed" (OECD-DAC 1993, p. 9). This meant citizens should enjoy "the possibility of withdrawing their consent and participating in a peaceful replacement of one government with another", with periodic "free and fair elections…one of the essential features of functioning democracies". Another key feature of democratic systems was the existence of autonomous non-state organisations representing a diverse range of interests, which could act as "a counterweight to government" and help ensure the latter was "responsive" (OECD-DAC 1993, p. 15).

The UK's Evolving Position on Democracy and Good Governance

DFID's views on the role democracy should play in the development process provide useful insights into the tensions Western bilateral donors faced in reconciling multiple development objectives and in deciding which should be prioritised if congruence between them proved to be elusive and choices had to be made in terms of where to invest time and human and financial resources. The various positions taken by DFID in the face of this conundrum are also worth exploring in detail because of the prominent position it enjoyed within Western donor circles, its role in shaping the international development agenda and influencing the priorities of other Western donors, defining how development progress should be evaluated and the most appropriate forms of donor-partner country interactions.

Produced soon after its establishment, DFID's first White Paper of 1997 captured the new department's worldview and expounded in great detail its plans to engage in a wide range of development activities. In that White Paper, good governance was cast in apolitical instrumental terms as an essential pre-condition for the achievement of economic growth and poverty reduction, and "raising standards of governance is central to the elimination of poverty" (DFID 1997, p. 30). Or, as Clare Short defined it in the course of a Parliamentary debate in 2001, good governance simply meant "effective systems that enable an economy to grow and to provide proper services for people" (House of Commons 2001, Column 166).

Given DFID's influence in the wider international development community, one consequence of its restrictive definition of what constituted good governance was the sidelining of the politics of development in discussions between Western donor agencies and host country representatives. Institutions in aid recipient countries were taken as given, the task being simply to improve their performance in order to achieve other development objectives. How political control over the state apparatus was exercised, the roles of armed forces and non-state actors in decision-making processes, the degree of independence of civil services from political interference and the transparency of appointment procedures within them, what systems (including electoral systems) were in place to ensure governments were representative of their populations, how these systems might be improved, how differing views within society were managed, what checks and balances existed to avoid the excessive concentration of power in any one branch of government and how well any constitutionally prescribed separation of powers operated were not issues that were to play a decisive role in allocating aid. In essence, how power holders determined who got what, when, and why and how they maintained their power were questions which were, grosso modo, off the table in donor and partner country engagements.

DFID's 1997 White Paper also made only cursory references to the status of democracy in its developing country partners. While it committed DFID to work on "encouraging democratic structures which can hold government accountable and give the poor a voice" (DFID 1997, p. 30), and in cooperation with other arms of the British government to seek to "spread the values of civil liberties and democracy" (DFID 1997, p. 69), no detail was provided as what constituted acceptable democratic practice in DFID's eyes, the sorts of democratic structures to be encouraged, how progress would be measured and what sort of assistance would be provided to support reform. Eligibility for aid was defined in terms of recipients' commitment to "the elimination of poverty and [the pursuit] of sensible policies to bring that about" (DFID 1997, p. 38). Depending on the subjective judgement of DFID officials regarding the poverty reduction policies of partner countries, these might or might not include the status of political freedoms in those countries.

The White Paper was also silent on the issue of possible punitive measures against those countries seen to be violating democratic freedoms and civil liberties. While it set out the limited circumstances under which London would not seek to establish a trusting partnership with a new country, these were restricted, significantly, to situations where the partner country was "not committed to the elimination of poverty…not pursuing sound economic policies or is embroiled in conflict" (DFID 1997, p. 39).

DFID's 1997 White Paper made clear that the most important criterion for DFID engagement with low-income countries was that of merit, defined largely in terms of their commitment to technocratic 'good governance' practices. It was on the basis of progress on the latter that DIFD would move away from project-specific interventions, broaden its assistance to benefit entire sectors and provide debt relief and GBS when it had confidence in such aspects of good governance as the "policies and budgetary allocation practices and in the capacity for effective implementation in the partner government" (DFID 1997, p. 38).

Democracy and civil and political rights as criteria for aid disbursements were therefore displaced from the position of primacy they had seemed to briefly enjoy in the immediate aftermath of the Cold War, such as in 1990 when Foreign Secretary Douglas Hurd had established a clear linkage between the status of democracy in recipient countries and British aid disbursements. Furthermore, while the 1997 White Paper did reference certain other aspects of development considered "essential to the attainment of the quantitative [international development] targets", such as "democratic accountability, the protection of human rights and the rule of law", it went on to argue, unconvincingly, that there were difficulties in measuring these targets as they were "not amenable to quantification" (DFID 1997, p. 21). The latter observation provided DFID with an escape route whenever it found it inconvenient to probe too deeply into what was happening in terms of progress on democratisation, human rights and the rule of law in partner countries. It also erroneously juxtaposed the ease of tracking progress in areas such as income poverty, infant and maternal mortality and primary education enrolment rates based on objectively verifiable benchmarks, data and indicators (and which would be used to assess partner country commitments and therefore levels of DFID support), with evaluations of changes in the political governance sphere which were supposedly more dependent on unreliable and subjective criteria. The argument that such aspects of government performance were more difficult to measure was particularly puzzling given the existence of comprehensive surveys on the status of political rights, civil liberties and the rule of law in countries around the world. These included those produced annually since 1973 by Freedom House and which were used by Washington's MCC to determine eligibility for MCA grants.[6]

Under its new Secretary of State, Hilary Benn, DFID issued another White Paper in 2006. This laid out how the UK would work to fulfil the commitments made at the Gleneagles G8 summit the previous year, most importantly the fight against poverty. Significantly, and in marked contrast to the 1997 White Paper, this one highlighted the previously ignored political aspects of 'good governance', the latter now recognised to be "not just about government", but also the role of "political parties, the judiciary, the media and civil society" (DFID 2006, p. 22). While state capability, that is, "the extent to which leaders and governments are able to get things done", continued to be seen as an essential feature of good governance as it had during the Clare Short years, there was nevertheless greater emphasis on the need for this aspect of state capability to be accompanied by 'Responsiveness', defined as "whether public policies and institutions respond to the needs of citizens and uphold their rights", and 'Accountability', determined by "the ability of citizens, civil society and the private sector to scrutinise public institutions and governments and hold them to account". Crucially, it argued that for good governance to be achieved one key requirement was "the opportunity to change leaders by democratic means" and more specifically "opportunities to change leaders in peaceful ways" (DFID 2006, p. 22).

There was also a move away from reliance on previous broad catch-all phrases such as 'respect for the rule of law', with this White Paper specifying, for example, that one key characteristic of this cardinal principle was "an independent judiciary" (DFID 2006, p. 22). In another major shift from the largely technocratic and apolitical definition of good governance which had previously held sway within the organisation, the 2006 White

Paper recognised that development was not a purely technocratic exercise: "This is about politics. Politics determines how resources are used and policies are made. And politics determines who benefits. In short, good governance is about good politics" (DFID, p. 23).

The inclusion of such observations in the 2006 White Paper reflected recognition of a need by the agency to shift to a broader, more nuanced approach in its governance work to examining the political dynamics of partner countries and in particular the status of "democratic accountability". It had clearly come to recognise the hybridity of some of the regimes it was dealing with and the challenges these posed to its decisions on aid allocations and its development efforts. Significantly, the White Paper called for a more incisive analysis of the state of play of democracy in countries receiving British ODA, since "the existence of the formal structures of democracy—political parties, elections and parliaments—does not guarantee the empowerment of poor people, even when they make up the majority of the population" (DFID 2006, p. 23).

Amongst events likely to have contributed to DFID's new thinking at the time was the increasing political turmoil in Zimbabwe, extensively covered by both the Western and African media. By the early 2000s, the country had become a byword for political repression, gross economic mismanagement and a growing humanitarian emergency.[7] This helps explain the 2006 White Paper's reference to the limitations of an excessive focus on the formal structures of democracy (Zimbabwe representing a good example of hybridity). While the existence of political parties (and in particular opposition parties), regular multi-party elections, parliaments and formally independent judiciaries were necessary (all of which had been carefully retained by the regime in Harare), they were not sufficient conditions for democracy to operate as the West believed it should.

Yet while the 2006 White Paper advocated for greater attention to the political aspects of good governance, and provided more detail as to how DFID intended to support this objective, the specific criterion of democratic transitions through elections (presumably also with a preference for ones that were free and fair), and which DFID had stated in that White Paper it would adopt in deciding how to assist partner countries, was then lost in the mix, subsumed again under the broad 'good governance' rubric. More specifically, the performance of partner countries would be scrutinised to provide answers such as whether "people's rights [are] being respected" (without specifying which rights), if "spending on public services [was] going up", if there were "efforts…made to tackle social exclusion" and whether "economic policy [was] promoting growth, and...public finances [are] well managed" (DFID 2006, 23). Therefore, yet again, the focus was on the largely technical rather than political aspects of development.

Notwithstanding earlier arguments in the 1997 White Paper concerning the limitations of such assessment tools, the 2006 White Paper did commit DFID to develop a new 'quality of governance' assessment tool "to guide the way in which we give UK aid" (DFID 2006, p. 10). A 2008 Practice Paper provided operational guidance to DFID country offices on the tool (DFID 2008). Several aspects of this guidance note stand out in terms of the importance to be granted to the state of democracy in partner countries in determining the disbursement of UK ODA. The first was the extensive latitude granted to individual DFID country offices, enjoying as they would "maximum flexibility in their choice of governance indicators...[and allowing them to] focus on specific aspects of governance relevant to their country context" (DFID 2008, p. 3). However, such leeway raised the possibility, if not strong likelihood, of DFID officials operating in-country succumbing to the temptation of painting countries to which they were assigned in a more favourable light than that which might be produced by more disinterested assessments. An additional temptation would be to set the bar so low in terms of the "governance indicators" and the "specific aspects of governance" chosen such that their host easily passed muster, and were reported as making acceptable progress (or at least not backsliding), on any given set of governance indicators (which might or might not include democratization), or as at least making sufficient progress to avoid any withholding of aid. In fact, the note pointedly stated that such governance assessments "will **not** [emphasis in the original] be used" inter alia to "establish indicators that will be used to trigger aid disbursements" or to "outline final judgement...on partnership commitments" (DFID 2008, pp. 5–6). This could only leave external observers wondering what the precise function of such assessments was, other than to project the image of an organisation paying adequate attention to political governance considerations.

Secondly, and further complicating the reality of competing priorities between the promotion of development and the broader interests of donor country governments, the Practice Paper also emphasised the importance of close cooperation with the UK's Foreign and Commonwealth Office (FCO) and its Ministry of Defence (MOD) during such governance assessments and noted that the final assessment would be used to inform not only the UK's aid strategies towards individual partner countries but more broadly the implications for Her Majesty's Government's overall "assistance strategy" (DFID 2008, p. 8). Such a broad remit necessarily enabled the intrusion of 'extraneous' considerations into decisions on development assistance, with the possibility of commercial, diplomatic, geo-political and security interests trumping any concerns about the status of democratic freedoms in beneficiary countries.

A Permissive International Development Ecosystem for Authoritarianism

The Western-dominated international development system set up after the end of the Cold War was therefore one which facilitated the entrenchment of authoritarian rule in certain aid-recipient African countries. The development compacts agreed between Western donors and the recipients of their aid prioritised progress in terms of economic and social rights, to the detriment of political and civil rights. Furthermore, the key assumptions in these frameworks were that such progress could be achieved simply through the increased and more predictable North-South transfers of aid, better use of these resources by recipients through adherence to good governance defined in apolitical terms such as through better planning, budgeting and implementation, a strengthened commitment to poverty reduction and other welfare indicators contained in the MDGs and reforms to the international trading system to enable developing countries to benefit more from exchanges. The solutions to development constraints were presented as not only largely technical, but also easily surmountable once the necessary policies were in place, and any resource constraints overcome through appropriate levels of Western donor funding.

An additional enabler of the trade-off between progress on the MDGs and Western commitments to the promotion of democracy was the ability of regimes, such as those in Ethiopia, Rwanda and Uganda, to adopt the appropriate language du jour in their interactions with Western development agencies and which was another prominent facet of their hybridity. It indicated a major investment on their part in keeping abreast of changes in donor-speak and the latest funding mechanisms and implementation modalities, their discourse always faithfully reflecting the most up-to-date Western development priorities. In their discussions with donors on the development challenges their countries faced, any commitments to introduce political reforms, and in particular multi-party democracy, were likely to remain untested so long as other kinds of results, judged by Western donors to be of greater importance, were being delivered.

In sum, a number of processes converged in the post-Cold War era, and in particular in the new millennium, which created propitious conditions for the entrenchment of authoritarian rule in those African countries which Western donor countries had decided were deserving of special consideration. The priority granted by the West to the achievement of the MDGs which emphasised social welfare indicators, and of economic reforms to trigger faster growth, acted to the detriment of the promotion of political and civil rights which were relegated to the sidelines in negotiations between donor agencies and their hosts on development assistance. The 'new partnership' principles contained in the global development compacts, which emphasised respect for the decisions taken by the governments of beneficiary countries, further limited the scope for linking the flows of Western aid to the performance of those governments in terms of political governance. Restrictive Western definitions of the components of what constituted 'good governance', and used by many donor agencies, would also prove helpful to the leaders of Ethiopia, Rwanda and Uganda as they set about establishing, and then strengthening, their authoritarian hybrid regimes and were employed to push back against Western pressure to reform and liberalise their political economies.

Notes

1. The concept of human development, championed by the UN, goes beyond economic growth metrics to focus on other dimensions of development progress, such as people being able to live a long and healthy life and their ability to access education.
2. This target was first set during the twenty-fifth session of the UN General Assembly in a resolution adopted on November 19, 1970 (see: United Nations General Assembly 1970, p. 49).
3. These included the policies and actions on child protection, survival and development agreed at the UN's World Summit for Children in 1990, which informed MDG2 on universal primary education and MDG4 on child mortality, those concerning global environmental issues agreed at the United Nations Conference on Environment and Development in 1992 which were translated into MDG7 on environmental sustainability, and commitments to promote gender equality negotiated at the Fourth World Conference on Women held in Beijing in 1995 which shaped MDG3 on this

item. The first comprehensive compilation of the goals, which became with minor modification, the MDGs, is contained in a document jointly produced by the UN, World Bank, OECD and the IMF. Entitled *2000 A Better World for All—Progress Towards the International Development Goals*, this was released prior to the Millennium Summit of September 2000 (see United Nations, IMF and World Bank 2000. *2000 A Better World for All—Progress Towards the International Development Goals*. Washington D.C., New York and Paris, 2000).

4. The multilateral institutions were prominent on this front. The World Bank's early views on this subject were contained in its *Governance and Development* report (World Bank 1992), which set out the linkages between good governance and positive economic outcomes. Later, its *Reforming Institutions and Strengthening Governance* (World Bank 2000) detailed its strategy for assisting countries to overhaul poorly functioning public institutions and tackle weak governance.
5. The arguments in favour of GBS included better donor alignment to partner country systems and priorities and therefore greater partner country ownership of development policy, reduced transaction costs for the beneficiary government due to decreased individual project level reporting requirements, greater predictability of resource flows given longer timeframes associated with donor commitments in terms of GBS, more transparent budgetary processes and accountability to the public and national legislatures in partner countries, and reductions in the scope for corruption often associated with project funding. For donor countries, the risks were those associated with the channelling of resources through deficient national public financial management systems, and weakened accountability due to the problem of the fungibility of aid flows which was even greater under GBS given the increased scope for governments to allocate aid funds, and the domestically generated resources freed up by such aid inflows, to activities not in accordance with donor priorities.
6. The MCC relies on independent third-party analysis and ratings. In addition to evidence generated by Freedom House, it uses data and indices compiled by, for example, the World Bank Institute, to evaluate the status of accountability, civil rights and the rule of law.
7. Between 2000 and 2008, Zimbabwe's GDP per capita contracted by an average of 4 per cent per annum (IMF 2010. *World Economic Outlook Database* 2010). According to the government's own figures, by 2003, 72 per cent of the population was living below the 'total consumption' poverty line (which included both essential food and non-food items), while those below the 'food poverty line', based on minimum calorific intake requirements, had increased even more dramatically from 29 per cent in 1995 to 58 per cent in 2003 (Government of Zimbabwe 2006. *Zimbabwe 2003 Poverty Assessment Study Survey*, Harare, 2006).

References

DFID. 1997. *Eliminating World Poverty: A challenge for the 21st Century*, White Paper on International Development, November 1997 Cm 3789.

DFID. 2000. *Eliminating World Poverty: Making Globalisation Work for the Poor*, White Paper on International Development, December 2000. Cm 5006.

DFID. 2006. *Eliminating World Poverty: Making Governance Work for the Poor*, White Paper on International Development, December 2006. Cm 6876.

DFID. 2008. *How to note: Country Governance Analysis*. July 2008.

Government of Zimbabwe. 2006. *Zimbabwe 2003 Poverty Assessment Study Survey*, Harare: 2006.

House of Commons Hansard. 2001. International Development Bill, Second Reading, 6 March 2001, Column166. https://publications.parliament.uk/pa/cm200001/cmhansrd/vo010306/debtext/10306-09.htm.

OECD-DAC. 1993. *DAC Orientations on Participatory Development and Good Governance*, OECD/GD (93) 191, Paris, 1993.

OECD. 2005. *Paris Declaration on Aid Effectiveness*, Paris: OECD Publishing, 2005. https://doi.org/10.1787/9789264098084-en.

OECD. 2008. *Accra Agenda for Action*, Paris: OECD Publishing, 2008.

United Nations General Assembly. 1970. "Twenty-fifth session: Resolutions adopted on the Reports of the Second Committee" Resolution 2641 (XXV) Review and Appraisal of the Objectives and Policies of the International Development Strategy (A/8124/Add.2), November 19, 1970.

United Nations General Assembly. 2000. *United Nations Millennium Declaration*. Fifty-fifthsession,A/RES/55/2NewYork.2000.www.undocs.org/A/RES/55/2.

United Nations, IMF and World Bank. 2000. *2000 A Better World for All – Progress towards the international development goals*. New York, Paris, and Washington D.C., 2000.

United Nations. 2003. *Monterey Consensus on Financing for Development*, New York: United Nations Department of Public Information, 2003.

World Bank. 1989. *Sub-Saharan Africa: From Crisis to Sustainable Growth: A Long-Term Perspective Study*, Washington D.C. 1989.

World Bank. 1992. *Governance and Development Report*. Washington D.C. 1992.

World Bank. 2000. *Reforming Institutions and Strengthening Governance*. Washington D.C. 2000.

World Bank. 2002. *A Sourcebook for Poverty Reduction Strategies, Vol.1*: Core Techniques and Cross-Cutting Issues, Washington DC, 2002.

CHAPTER 7

Democracy and Civil Rights: Securing Political Closure and Western Responses

Uganda: From Hostility to Multi-party Democracy to Manipulation of the Electoral System

In its Ten-Point Programme, issued before it had captured Kampala, Museveni's NRM had declared its deep mistrust of multi-party democracy and political parties; the political system was viewed as a dysfunctional and divisive political arrangement, and the behaviour of parties was seen as the source of many of Uganda's misfortunes since independence. The new government's first legal measure in 1986 was to ban the activities of political parties, and this was used to induce other political actors to join its own 'Movement' political system, an all-inclusive 'big tent' approach to politics putatively aimed at avoiding a return to the deadly violent sectarianism of the past.

While the NRM never entirely dismissed the possibility of an eventual return to multi-party democracy (a hostile posture towards democratisation being difficult to reconcile with its own proclaimed pro-democracy stance, and the need to reassure Western donors of its intentions to democratise Uganda), it regularly argued that such a system would only be appropriate once Uganda had reached a certain level of development. Reflecting some of the Marxist thinking imbibed by Museveni, the rationale put forward for going slow on democratisation was that Uganda was still a predominantly peasant society, and its underdevelopment meant there was insufficient economic class differentiation to justify multiple

M. Simpson, *Donors, Democracy and Development in Africa*,
https://doi.org/10.1007/978-3-031-74917-9_7

political parties representing class interests such as those in industrialised countries. Under existing conditions, Ugandans would easily fall prey to the false promises of ethno-regional or religious entrepreneurs, increasing the prospect of a return to the country's divisive past. Until such time as the required economic transformation had taken place, the NRM's own innovative non-party unifying 'Movement' political system was seen as best suited to help Ugandans exercise their political rights. As Museveni argued:

> What is crucial for Uganda now is for us to have a system that ensures democratic participation until such time as we get, through economic development, especially industrialisation, the crystallization of socio-economic groups upon which we can then base healthy political parties. (Kasfir 1998, p. 61)

Clarifications on when the specific conditions in terms of levels of development and class formation might be met, and the situation judged appropriate for a return to multi-party democracy, were not forthcoming. Needless to say, it would be up to the NRM, and specifically its leader, to decide when and how it would be reintroduced, as well as the 'health' of any political parties which might be allowed to compete for power. In the meantime, legislation would eventually compel all Ugandans to belong to the 'Movement'.

The NRM's views subsequently found their way into the country's new 1995 constitution. While parties themselves were allowed to formally exist (Constitution of Uganda 1995, Article 72), they were in effect neutered by having their rights in terms of freedom of assembly and association proscribed. Article 269 prohibited them from operating branch offices, from holding party conferences and public rallies, from campaigning for or against any candidate in elections and most significantly from "carrying on any activities that may interfere with the Movement political system for the time being in force". And while the constitution granted people the right to eventually chose and adopt any political system through "free and fair elections or referenda" (Constitution of Uganda 1995, Article 69), it also characterised the existing Movement political system as being "broad based, inclusive and non-partisan", one which operated according to the principles of "democracy, transparency and accountability", ensuring "accessibility to all positions of leadership by all citizens", with "individual merit as a basis for election to political office" (Constitution of Uganda 1995, Article 70).

The NRM used the protracted constitution-making process from 1989 to 1995 to consolidate its monopoly on power. Elections for a Constituent Assembly were held in 1994 under the restrictions banning party political activities, meaning parties could not run candidates as their representatives. Candidates had to compete as individuals on the basis of 'merit' in all elections, starting from the base of the political system, the village-level 'movement committees' (inspired by the NRM's Resistance Councils of the Bush War years), all the way up through various higher administrative levels, with such elections framed as an expression of 'popular democracy'. This requirement for individual competition had the effect of severely restricting the scope for other political parties to organise, mobilise and develop as alternatives to the NRM. While the NRM itself operated as a full-fledged political party in all but name, it dodged the constraints on the grounds it was a 'Movement'.

The rules governing the composition of the Constituent Assembly also ensured NRM control of that body. In addition to 214 Assembly members elected at district level, there were to be a further 74 special members, of which a total of 20 were appointed by the President and the NRA, with other special members being selected by bodies beholden to the NRM government.

Furthermore, the members of the Constitutional Commission (CC) charged with soliciting the views of the public, and producing a draft constitution, were also seen to have been appointed based on their support of the NRM government. The process lacked an open nominations system, the result being a body made up of strong supporters of the Movement system. As noted by Aili Mari Tripp, "Not one member of the commission openly opposed the Movement system" (Tripp 2010, p. 162). Under such conditions, it was hardly surprising that during the consultations overseen by the CC, any opinions and suggestions made which were contrary to the NRM's positions were simply set aside. As a result of the rules governing the establishment of the Constituent Assembly and CC, it was a given that the outcome would favour the NRM and its no-party democracy position as against those supporting multipartyism.

The Movement Act, approved in August 1997, detailed the composition, roles and responsibilities of the various organs of the Movement system (Uganda Legal Information Institute 1997). At the level of the country's villages, it stipulated that all adult Ugandans, irrespective of their political leanings, were considered members of their village Movement councils, and therefore of the Movement (Uganda Legal Information Institute 1997. 'Movement Act 1997', Article 24). In addition, all members of Parliament were automatically members of the highest organ of the Movement political system, the National Conference, including all those affiliated with other political parties whether they wanted to be associated with what was effectively an NRM body (Uganda Legal Information Institute 1997. 'Movement Act 1997', Article 4 (1) (j)).

This Act also blurred the distinctions between the NRM as a de facto political organisation and the organs of the Ugandan state. The close ties between the NRM and the country's defence and security forces were clearly on show. The Movement's National Conference was to include ten representatives from the Uganda Peoples' Defence Forces (UPDF), five from the Uganda Police Force and another three from the Uganda Prison Services (Uganda Legal Information Institute 1997. 'Movement Act 1997' Article 4(1)), all three institutions also being granted places on the NRM's Executive Committee (Uganda Legal Information Institute 1997. 'Movement Act 1997' Article 9). Funding of the Movement system would be based on "monies as may from time to time be appropriated by Parliament" (Uganda Legal Information Institute 1997. 'Movement Act 1997' Article 31)—which given the NRM's control of the legislature would undoubtedly be generous—while the system's budget was to be approved by the Minister of Finance "in like manner as for a department of Government" (Uganda Legal Information Institute 1997. 'Movement Act 1997' Article 36). Relations between the NRM, its Movement system, the legislature, government ministries and the country's defence and security forces would therefore be mutually reinforcing and beneficial.

Despite the official proscription on political party activities, this did not mean support for multipartyism did not make itself felt, and at times prove awkward for Museveni. While the parliamentary elections of 1996 were a resounding victory for the NRM, they also returned a number of members linked to four other political parties, who went on to form a National Caucus for Democracy, and openly criticised both the Movement system and the government policies. The disguised presence of other political formations in Parliament indicated the NRM was willing to tolerate some organised opposition in the legislature, and which could be managed in such a way as to show the country was not moving towards a single-party dictatorship.

Notwithstanding the entrenchment of the Movement system, both foreign and domestic voices occasionally came together to pressure Kampala to lift the restrictions on political parties and return to multi-party democracy. Though difficult to determine with precision, the 2001 legislative elections were seen to have returned an even greater number of parliamentarians favouring a return to multipartyism (Carbone 2005). At the time Kampala would also have felt the need to show some progress in this regard given Uganda's position as an early beneficiary of the US's AGOA in 2000, and that advances in democratisation was a key eligibility criterion to be allowed continued access to the trade scheme's benefits.

Feeling secure in its own popularity and that of its leader, and confident of its ability to win under a multi-party system, discussions began within the NRM as to how and when to introduce change. After firing cabinet ministers opposed to his pitch for the third term in office, Museveni launched a campaign to change the constitution. In 2005 the government announced a referendum on the issue of a return to a multi-party system. After a Bill was approved by Parliament in July 2005, a constitutional amendment lifted the previous presidential term limits. With the 'yes' vote winning in the 2005 referendum on multipartyism, and the lifting of term limits, Museveni felt confident in running again for office under the new political system.

To retain power under this competitive system, there was increasing recourse to the electoral toolkit employed by hybrid authoritarian regimes. These centred on the abuse of state resources and machinery to secure advantage during elections, such as vote-buying through the distribution of largesse, the use of intimidatory force by security forces, the politicised prosecution of opposition figures, the harassment of CSOs and the independent media and the manipulation of electoral processes by supervisory bodies which were structured to ensure favourable outcomes for the ruling party.

In the February 2006 General Elections (both Presidential and Parliamentary), and the country's first multi-party elections since the NRM took power, an EU Election Observation Mission (EU EOM) referenced the bias in the state media in favour of Museveni and the NRM, concluding that as a result "the playing field was not level" (European Parliament 2006, p. 7). The more detailed EU observers' mission report on the subsequent 2011 elections stated that "the power of incumbency was exercised to such an extent as to compromise severely the level playing field between the competing candidates and political parties" (European Parliament 2011, p. 5). It also noted its observers had witnessed:

> The distribution of money and gifts by candidates, especially from the ruling party, a practice inconsistent with democratic principles ... [and it] was evident that the National Resistance Movement's dominance and resources were much greater than those of the opposition. (European Parliament 2011, p. 6)

Returning to Uganda to observe the 2016 General Elections—one characterised by significantly heightened political tensions compared to previous ones—the next EU observer mission highlighted evidence of the merger of ruling party and state institutions, referencing "the blurred line between the state and NRM structures which was manifested predominantly in the use of state budget and security at campaign events and by the extensive use of public media (European Parliament 2016, p. 17).

Vote-buying, a practice already flagged in previous EU election reports, was pervasive in 2016, with the EU team reporting that "[d]uring the campaign's final stage ... the ruling party's representatives started distributing cash throughout the country" (European Parliament 2016, p. 19). In terms of media bias in favour of the NRM and Museveni, it referenced the atmosphere of intimidation and self-censorship resulting from the actions of state agents, with journalists subjected to "intimidating phone calls" (European Parliament 2016, p. 22).

It also expressed concerns regarding the impartiality and performance of Uganda's Electoral Commission (EC). Given the pro-government utterances of that institution, the mission concluded that "the EC does not reflect the complete political spectrum and does not enjoy widespread confidence" (European Parliament 2016, pp. 10–11). Amongst its reported shortcomings was its role in the demarcation of electoral constituencies. In 2015, the NRM-dominated Parliament had enacted legislation, significantly increasing the number of counties from 168 to 245; given each county was required to have at least one constituency, the number of constituencies also increased from 238 to 290. Yet there was scant evidence of any attention being paid by the EC to the principle of the equality of the vote in the demarcation process, and the exercise only compounded an existing problem, namely the "profound population discrepancies between electoral constituencies". As a result, the mission found that "231 out of the 290 constituencies are outside a 15 percent range of the average size of a constituency" (European Parliament 2016, p. 2). Given the NRM's electoral strongholds were predominantly rural, the creation of numerous new rural constituencies, while at the same time restricting any increase in urban constituencies, worked to the advantage of the NRM.[1]

Other aspects of the EC's performance were also criticised. These included a lack of transparency in various stages of the electoral process; the uploading of the voters' register onto a new voter verification system took place without the presence of party representatives, while the minutes of its meeting were not made public (European Parliament 2016, p. 11). Poor voter education, delays in the distribution of electoral material, unsealed ballot boxes and the fact the "entire vote tallying process lacked transparency ... [since] party agents and observers [were precluded] from ascertaining the veracity of the results" (European Parliament 2016, p. 3) were other shortcomings noted.

When more subtle forms of manipulation proved insufficient—and in a preview of the outbreaks of violence in the elections held during the COVID-19 pandemic—the 2016 electoral period was marked by the intimidating presence of security personnel, and the selective use of force against opposition groups and their leaders. Referring to the harassment faced by the two main presidential candidates running against Museveni, the 2016 EU mission noted:

> [E]xtensive use of force by police, including tear gas and assault rifles, to disperse crowds during Kizza Besigye's and Amama Mbabazi's rallies. ... On 15 February, police detained Besigye twice, preventing him from addressing scheduled rallies ... and used teargas and live ammunition against his supporters, resulting in one death and several injuries. (European Parliament 2016, pp. 15–16)

All EU observer mission's reports had contained detailed recommendations as to how the Ugandan authorities and other 'stakeholders' might improve the country's electoral framework. In 2018, an EU Follow-up Mission (EUFM) assessed the degree to which the thirty recommendations made by the 2016 mission had been implemented, and which it emphasised in its report were based on Uganda's own laws and its obligations under regional and international agreements. The EUFM was damning in its conclusions:

> As of the date of writing, none of the 30 recommendations ... has been implemented by the Ugandan authorities. There is no draft law or any piece of legislation currently before parliament which addresses a single one of the recommendations of the EU EOM 2016. In general, there is a lack of political will on the part of the governing party, the NRM, to address the electoral process other than through measures designed to entrench their own electoral power. (European Union 2018, p. 8)

Kampala was clearly not overly concerned with possible negative repercussions, such as cuts to ODA from the EU. As the report noted in terms of the government's response:

> Official representatives of the Republic of Uganda, and representatives of public institutions such as the Electoral Commission, expressed views ... that the recommendations of the EU EOM 2016 were misguided, irrelevant and unnecessary. The only concession made on the part of such interlocutors was that there was a need for enhanced voter education in the future, and that the single recommendation in this area was valid. (European Union 2018, p. 8)

And the NRM's insouciance proved justified; between the 2016 and 2017, and after the release of the EU's critical 2016 election report, the EU Commission's aid spent for Uganda actually increased from US$35.2 million to US$57.8 million, and then proved remarkably stable. After the release of the 2018 EUFM report, it fell only marginally to US$53.9 million in 2019 (International Aid Transparency Initiative 2024).

Ethiopia: Yet Another Attempt at Revolutionary Transformation

While the early post-Cold War international environment was one in which Marxist-Leninism was widely discredited, its hold on the leadership of the TPLF would prove enduring. As late as 1984, that is, only a few years before the collapse of communism in the Soviet Union, Eastern Europe and its outposts in the developing world, in a comprehensive policy statement replete with revolutionary communist terminology, the TPLF's Marxists in the MLLT were excoriating rival political movements such as the EPRP and MEISON for their lack of ideological sophistication and poor understanding of the issues at stake.

Significantly, the document clarified what the MLLT meant by democracy and democratic forces, a democratic stance being defined as being "anti-imperialist, anti-feudal and anti-bureaucratic capitalist" (*Tigray People's Liberation Front* 1984, p. 8). The EPRP was attacked on the grounds of its false "proletarian pretensions", its "erroneous line and petty bourgeois character" (*Tigray People's Liberation Front* 1984, p. 15). As far as MEISON was concerned, this group was accused, *inter alia*, of having committed cardinal sins such as its "right opportunism" (*Tigray People's Liberation Front* 1984, p. 6). Given the TPLF's role as a revolutionary Tigrayan nationalist movement, it was unsurprising that the MLLT should have strongly criticised MEISON's for denying "that democratic national movements had any positive role to play in the revolution" (*Tigray People's Liberation Front* 1984, p. 8).

The MLLT also dismissed the Tigray Liberation Front (TLF), the TPLF's older rival nationalist movement, casting it as an embodiment of "Tigrean narrow nationalism", and responsible for spreading "bourgeois nationalist poison" (*Tigray People's Liberation Front* 1984, p. 13). The distinction drawn between its own revolutionary nationalism and that of the TLF helps throw light on how it viewed the 'national question', the arguments it rehearsed in 1984 subsequently informing its decision to form the EPRDF and its policy of Ethnic Federalism once in power. Given the country's long history of Amhara domination and exploitation of other ethnic groups, the national question was seen as the central one facing Ethiopia's revolutionaries. And the best way to organise and lead the mobilisation of the masses in the class struggle was to "form democratic national organizations and multinational democratic organisations ... and coordinate them all by forming an all-Ethiopia united democratic front" (*Tigray People's Liberation Front* 1984, p. 9).

To the extent it was willing to make any concessions to the positions of other political formations, these were initially only granted to the Amhara-dominated Ethiopian People's Democratic Movement (EPDM), which would later unite, as a junior partner, with the TPLF in January 1989 to form the EPRDF, subsequently changing its name to the Amhara National Democratic Movement (ANDM). The TPLF's willingness in 1984 to accept the EPDM's revolutionary credentials was due to the fact that its members had "accepted the overall validity of TPLF's general line for the Ethiopian revolution" (*Tigray People's Liberation Front* 1984, p. 25). In the run-up to the fall of the Dergue, and given its need to expand its support base beyond its Tigrayan heartland, the TPLF brought two other movements into the EPRDF fold (or created them according to some analysts); these were the Oromo People's Democratic Organisation (OPDO), which claimed to represent the country's largest ethnic group, and the Southern Ethiopian People's Democratic Front (SEPDF). Both were judged to also possess the correct ideological leanings, and therefore able to assist the TPLF carry forward its ideas on Ethnic Federalism.[2]

The tide which swept away communist regimes in Eastern Europe and the Soviet Union during 1989–1991, and the abandonment of Marxism-Leninism by self-declared Marxist-Leninist movements such as the MPLA and FRELIMO, meant the TPLF/EPRDF was then confronted by fundamental questions. These included how to hold true to its foundational ideology (the continuing validity of which it portrayed as the key success factor in its victory over the Dergue), given Western hostility to its ideas on the solutions to Ethiopia's problems. Another was how, given the lack of alternative foreign sources of assistance at the time, it might secure the necessary Western support for recovery. Finally, and most importantly given both domestic and Western expectations regarding the introduction of multi-party democracy, it had to decide on the methods it would employ to secure its hold on power, and retain the political vanguard role it had assigned to itself.

After taking the capital in May 1991, concealing its long-term Marxist-inspired revolutionary vision for Ethiopia was essential. The international and domestic environment was one in which the replacement of one Marxist-Leninist dictatorship (the Dergue), for another led by the TPLF/EPRDF, would have been opposed both internally and externally. Furthermore, the TPLF represented a small national minority amongst the country's numerous ethnic groups (particularly so in the Amhara-dominated capital city), and it was unsure of its legitimacy in the eyes of other segments of Ethiopian society.

The solution was the postponement of any immediate moves towards the establishment of a single-party state that would spearhead the transition to socialism, and for the TPLF/EPRDF to declare its adherence to liberal principles, at least during a transitional period. In July 1991, the EPRDF announced the launch of a 'National Conference'. Chaired by Meles Zenawi, this body drafted a transitional constitutional framework to enable the establishment of a transitional government. The resulting 'Transitional Period Charter' contained numerous references to liberal political and civil rights principles. While the latter was welcomed in Western capitals as indicating this might lead to a new and more open

Ethiopia, a closer reading of the document should have raised concerns given its sacralisation of ethnicity, and the relative importance attached to collective group rather than individual rights.

The overthrow of the Dergue was described as the start of a "new chapter in Ethiopian history" in which "freedom, equal rights and self-determination of all the peoples shall be the governing principles of political, economic and social life", and that "the proclamation of a democratic order is a categorical imperative" (Federal Negarit Gazeta 1991, p. 1). Liberal principles to be respected under the new political dispensation included freedom of expression, association and assembly, and to engage in political activity and organise political parties.

The Charter also laid out the principles to be followed to resolve the national question. The right to self-determination of "nations, nationalities and peoples" was guaranteed, which included not only the right to preserve their own languages, cultures and history but also for each group to benefit from a process of decentralisation and administer their "own affairs within its own defined territory" while participating "in the central government on the basis of freedom, and fair and proper representation". Significantly, where such rights were judged by the group in question to have been "denied, abridged or abrogated", the Charter also granted the "right to the self-determination of independence" (Federal Negarit Gazeta 1991, Article 2,2).

The paramount importance attached to ethnicity as the fundamental organising principle in a post-Dergue dispensation was already evident in the convening of the National Conference. Only those movements representing ethnic groups were invited, while the TPLF's old rivals, the EPRP and MEISON, which had always criticised the TPLF for its ethnic-based revolutionary programme and prided themselves on their own supposedly pan-ethnic membership, were excluded from the deliberations.

The Transitional Charter provided for a Transitional Government, composed of a Council of Representatives (CR) and a Council of Ministers. The CR was made up of a total of eighty-seven "representatives of national liberation movements, other political organizations and prominent individuals" (Federal Negarit Gazeta 1991, Article 7,3), and informed by the need to ensure that nominees "shall be from different nations/nationalities" (Federal Negarit Gazeta 1991, Article 9,3). In terms of transitional processes, the CR was to set up a Constitutional Commission (CC), tasked with drawing up a draft constitution to be presented "to the people for discussion" (Federal Negarit Gazeta 1991, Article 11, 4). A final draft would then be submitted for adoption to a Constituent Assembly (CA) elected in June 1994, the Transitional Government then handing over power to the party or parties that gained a majority in a National Assembly established through elections scheduled for December 1994.

One overarching and complex issue needed to be tackled by the TPLF/ EPRDF; this was the need to reconcile a process of decentralisation through the granting of rights of self-government to subnational administrative units, with the political vision of the Marxist-Leninist Core of the TPLF which aimed at the construction of a dominant vanguard party capable of enforcing its decisions throughout the country. The paradox was clear, as the centralisation of power could not but undermine regional autonomy.

Given the strong TPLF/EPRDF presence in the CR, with thirty-two out of the total eighty-seven representatives (Aalen 2002, p. 7), and the support it received from the affiliated parties it had nurtured, it was able to ensure that Meles Zenawi, who was already Chair of the National Conference, was also elected Chairman of the CR, and therefore became Head of State of the Transitional Government. The Prime Minister he appointed, Tamrat Layne, was leader of the Amhara-based EPDM/ ANDM which had merged with the EPRDF.

Like the NRM in Uganda, the EPRDF also initially adopted a big tent approach in the transitional period; for example, the Oromo Liberation Front (OLF)—which fought for an independent Oromia for the Oromo people—was granted a few places in the CR and ministerial posts. This despite the fact it had opted not to join the EPRDF coalition, though the TPLF/EPRDF had also already responded by creating the OPDO to counter the OLF's claim to be the sole representative of the Oromo.

The entire constitution-making process—from the establishment of the CC through to the elections for the CA and final ratification of the Constitution—was carefully managed by the TPLF/EPRDF, through its power to determine who participated in the various stages of this process (with parties compelled to represent ethnic groups), and thereby secure the desired outcomes. A number of political parties chose not to participate in the process of drafting in the CC, and the discussions in the CR, and regularly denounced these processes from the side lines. The 1994 elections for the CA which ratified the new constitution were also boycotted by a large number of parties, again leaving the field open to the TPLF/ EPRDF. The latter's candidates took 484 seats out of a total 547 seats up for grabs, with the CA ratifying in December 1994 what was seen in many quarters as in effect the TPLF/EPRDF's constitution.

There had been some initial optimism that the fall of the Dergue, the period of political decompression which followed the adoption of the Transitional Charter, together with the establishment of local NGOs working on human rights issues such as the Ethiopian Human Rights Council (EHRCO), and the growth of independent media outlets might improve the country's poor record on human rights. Such expectations soon proved to be misplaced. In its 1993 report HRW stated that while the "Transitional Government remains more accountable on human rights than any other government in Ethiopian history", nevertheless in its opinion, 1993 had already witnessed the "dawn of a sober reality" (Human Rights Watch 1993). Replicating the NRM's efforts to extend its influence throughout Uganda through its 'movement committees', the EPRDF had established its own 'Peace and Stability Committees', responsible for the maintenance of law and order. As these were under the control of the local commanders of the EPRDF forces, and were only accountable to the EPRDF, it was clear they acted as the eyes and ears of central government and were used to monitor political opposition. The report also noted an early sign of the merger of state and the TPLF/EPRDF-dominated transitional government; in January 1992 the latter had issued a proclamation designating the EPRDF's military forces as the country's 'State Defence Army' for the duration of the transition.

Repression of opposition forces had already come to the fore as early as the regional elections of June 1992, one marked by manipulation of the exercise by the EPRDF to ensure a favourable playing field. Two American election observer missions—the National Democratic Institute (NDI) and the African-American Institute (AAI)—jointly reported on an extensive range of problems, from the voter and candidate registration stages through to the bias of the state media and balloting procedures (National Democratic Institute for International Affairs and African-American Institute 1992).

Shortly before polling day, the OLF and some other smaller parties withdrew from the elections. The AAI mission subsequently issued a statement, arguing that because of the withdrawal of these parties: "In very few places were there competitive, multi-party elections. The EPRDF and its affiliated parties (*e.g.*, EPDM, OPDO, etc.) were usually the only parties on the ballot" (African-American Institute 1992, p. 103). The election results showed the EPRDF and its affiliated parties winning 1108 out of a total 1147 seats contested, and 96.6 per cent of the votes cast, a margin of victory which would generally be repeated in subsequent elections. The joint NDI-AAI mission report concluded:

> [T]he June 21 elections represented a sterile, surreal and wholly formalistic affair ... no genuine competition between parties or candidates existed. ... The elections, moreover, exacerbated existing tensions, reinforced the hegemonic power of the EPRDF while marginalizing other fledgling parties. (African-American Institute 1992, pp. 6–7)

The country's elections provide unique insights into the ruling party's illiberal state-building exercise, and specifically its ideological underpinnings. Once in power, the authoritarian positions taken by the TPLF/EPRDF were informed by two key concepts in the Marxist-Leninist lexicon and practices of communist parties and governments around the world, namely 'Revolutionary Democracy' and 'Ethnic Federalism'. Their institutionalisation became the TPLF/EPRDF's long-term political objectives, shaping its hybrid political governance system and helping it to defend its dominant position. As stated by a senior TPLF/EPRDF official, using the language of perpetual entitlement which might have been faithfully repeated by any of his counterparts in the NRM or the RPF: "We fought for 20 years, and it is not fair that any party born yesterday should compete with us. We will fight to keep the power" (Aalen 2002, p. 9).

Central to the TPLF's ideas on Revolutionary Democracy (subscribed to by other partners within the EPRDF coalition), was the continued relevance assigned to a vanguard party. As during its armed struggle, this vanguard should continue practising 'democratic centralism', the rigidly hierarchical decision-making processes which allowed for some internal democratic discussion, but which then ceased once an official party-line was decided upon by the leadership. It was therefore only within the confines of the ruling party's higher bodies that debate could take place. It remained committed to reshaping society in a top-down fashion via its control and transformation of the state apparatus, assisted by the mobilisation of the 'masses', and to steadfastly combat both internal 'factionalism' arising from dissenting views within the Front and opposition movements.

The TPLF/EPRDF's enduring attachment to Marxist-Leninist objectives was to become clear after its victory in the 1992 regional elections. The following year it released a detailed document for its members, which provided insights into the long-term goals it intended to pursue after the transitional period, and specifically how it would establish, and then defend, its hegemonic position.

Firstly, it recognised that the end of the Cold War meant "major changes around the world" had occurred, which had led to the "hegemony of the imperialist power led by the United States" (Ethiopian National United Front 1993, p. 2). However, rather than abandoning Marxism-Leninism as the basis for a political programme, these changes called for only "a few adjustments so that we are able to come out victorious under the circumstances prevailing in our country and around the world" (Ethiopian National United Front 1993, p. 2).

Secondly, the document contained ideas on the concessions it was prepared to make, most importantly the adoption of a multi-party democratic system and a new constitution guaranteeing the political and civil rights of citizens. These, however, could still be manipulated to secure the Front's goals. So, for example, the future constitution needed to be drafted such that it contained "laws which protect the rights of the people and outlaw the obstructionist activities of the enemies" (Ethiopian National United Front 1993, p. 3). Concerning multipartyism, while both the 'masses' and the 'ruling classes' would enjoy the right to organise and compete for political power, if the latter sought to "obstruct the masses from exercising their rights", the TPLF/EPRDF would "use the constitution and other laws to punish them and bring under control their illegal activities" (Ethiopian National United Front 1993, p. 3). In the post-Dergue era, it was clear that tolerance of a plurality of views was not going to be a prominent feature of a TPLF/EPRDF dispensation.

Thirdly, the document clarified the TPLF/EPRDF's views on the separation of ruling party and state institutions, and how it intended to circumvent any constitutional provisions governing the non-partisan nature of the latter. In the case of the country's armed forces, the fact that its own military forces, and those of its allies the EPDM and OPDO, would eventually have to be integrated to form a new Ethiopian defence force meant the "severing of its direct links with the EPRDF". However, drawing a sharp distinction between formal and informal ties with the future defence forces, which must "become the army of the State", the document argued it would nevertheless be possible to "organize our Defence Force to carry out the required revolutionary democratic tasks through indirect ties" (Ethiopian National United Front 1993, p. 3).

The imperative of creating institutions to mobilise and control 'the masses' to further the objectives of Revolutionary Democracy also extended to the media, which would have a key role in spreading the TPLF/EPRDF's message. The state media needed to be reorganised so it could influence "the masses to fully support the government", and the educational system transformed into propaganda tools with a revised curriculum so as to "inculcate the basic goals of our revolutionary democratic system" (Ethiopian National United Front 1993, p. 9).

Finally, the document detailed the TPLF/EPRDF's views on multiparty democracy, in particular the dangers posed by elections and the need to ensure the chances of losing them were minimised. If the objective was to establish Revolutionary Democracy as "the governing ideology of society", this would be done by winning elections "successively and holding power without let up". On that basis, it would be possible for the TPLF/EPRDF to construct what was clearly going to be an illiberal hybrid political system, or as the Front put it, "[A] conducive environment that will ensure the establishment of this hegemony" (Ethiopian National United Front 1993, p. 7).

It was around the TPLF/EPRDF's goal of entrenching its political hegemony that Revolutionary Democracy and Ethnic Federalism dovetailed. If the former represented the overall strategic approach, the latter can be seen an essential operational component for its realisation. It enabled the TPLF to reconcile safeguarding of the country's territorial integrity by reducing the scope for a resurgence of ethnic-based armed dissident movements, with its ambition to monopolise political power. With skilful packaging, it also helped the ruling party to display its reformist credentials to Western audiences.

Ethnic Federalism was an approach diametrically opposed to that pursued by the NRM to prevent the politicisation of ethnicity. To the TPLF, the country's historical problems of war, famine and underdevelopment were traced to not only the excessive centralisation of power in Addis Ababa, but more specifically the ethnic characteristics associated with it, with power concentrated in the hands of the elite of one dominant ethnic group (traditionally the Amhara), and the exploitation and marginalisation of others.

What the TPLF believed was needed was a root and branch reform of the political system, and Ethnic Federalism aimed to transform the country into one made up of ethnically defined regional states run by ethnically defined political parties. By granting ethnic groups certain rights of self-expression and self-government, the expectation was that this would neutralise, rather than foster, dissident subnational ethnic sentiments. The policy might be sold to the West, and domestic audiences, as the reversal of centuries of authoritarian centralisation seen to have been the main driver of the centripetal forces, attendant political instability and conflict which had plagued Ethiopia, with the political, fiscal and administrative autonomy it promised as the fulfilment of the right to 'national self-determination' provided for in the 1991 Transitional Charter. It would thus serve to demonstrate the TPLF/EPRDF's *bona fides* in terms of respects for democratic and human and civil rights (even if the focus was on group-based rather than individual rights), and its commitment to setting the country on a new development-oriented trajectory.

The creation in 1992 of ethnically defined regional states (initially nine sub-units, in addition to Addis Ababa which enjoyed its own status as capital city), and elevation of the principle of ethnicity to that of primary and only acceptable source of political legitimacy, enabled the TPLF/EPRDF to expand its influence throughout the country while maintaining its control over the levers of power at central level. Ethnic federalisation, and the introduction of a particular form of multi-party democracy, helped the TPLF/EPRDF achieve these objectives in a number of ways; by supposedly granting 'nations and nationalities' the right to manage their own affairs, it stole some of the thunder of ethnically based opposition groups such as the OLF which continued to operate on the basis of a secessionist agenda. At the same time, as individual parties were required to be based on ethnicity, this weakened the scope for any political opposition to develop an openly pan-ethnic platform to challenge the ethnic federalist position of the TPLF/EPRDF, or the EPRDF-affiliated parties led by the compliant ethnic elites it had cultivated in the regions.

Following the overwhelming victory of the TPLF/EPRDF and its affiliates in the June 1992 regional elections, another opportunity to further entrench its ethnic federalist project arose in the context of the constitution-making process. Since opposition parties such as the OLF boycotted elections to the CR, this ensured the TPLF/EPRDF's ethnic federalist project featured prominently in the approved draft, and that those political forces in favour of a unitary state were side lined during the deliberations.

Article 39 of the 1995 Constitution enshrined the right to self-determination, up to and including secession. It is significant that the deliberations within the CC and CR had taken place against the backdrop of a referendum on Eritrea's independence, held under the provisions of the Transitional Charter. Set in motion by the victorious EPLF which had played a decisive role, in alliance with the TPLF, in the military defeat of the Dergue's forces in 1991, a UN-supervised referendum was held in April 1993. The results were overwhelmingly in favour of Eritrea's independence, which was declared on April 27, 1993. Therefore, faced with the real possibility of further dismemberment of the country, while the TPLF/EPRDF reaffirmed its commitment to the principle of national self-determination, including the right to secede, it also sought to ensure that a repetition of the Eritrean case was made more difficult. Therefore, Article 39 of the 1995 Constitution also stipulated that the exercise of the right to secession required approval by "a two-thirds majority of the legislative Council of the Nation, Nationality or People concerned", following which the Federal government would then organise a referendum in which a simple majority in favour of secession would suffice (Federal Negarit Gazeta 1995, Article 39).

Given TPLF/EPRDF concerns about the precedent set by Eritrea, it was significant the Constitution also made provision for further subdivisions of the nine 'Member States' of the new Federal Democratic Republic of Ethiopia (FDRE), granting peoples "within" those existing States the right "at any time" to form their own states, subject again to meeting referenda requirements and approval of their respective regional councils (Federal Negarit Gazeta 1995, Article 47). When the earlier boundary delimitation exercise had been carried out, none of the eventual nine States ended up being ethnically homogenous. Granting the right to further self-determination at sub-regional state level could serve to further mitigate the risk of an outbreak of violent ethnic-based dissidence. But more importantly, it also meant that the TPLF/EPRDF, when faced with secessionist pressures from any existing Member State, could engage in 'divide and rule' tactics, encouraging sub-groups to demand autonomy from the State in which they might feel themselves entrapped, and thereby weaken any regional government it found problematic.

In addition to capitalising on the withdrawal of many opposition forces from the transitional processes, and carefully selecting those it allowed to take part, the TPLF/EPRDF used other means to deal with dissent and prevent other regions going down the route of Eritrea. These included extending TPLF/EPRDF control over regional and sub-regional administrative structures by ensuring they were staffed by TPLF/EPRDF cadres or those from trusted affiliated parties. As a result, these structures came to operate "in ways which often make them indistinguishable in practice from the ruling party itself", acting as transmission belts for the TPLF's Revolutionary Democracy and Ethnic Federalist ideologies, while local-level administrators became the ruling party's eyes and ears, "reporting any 'anti-revolutionary' and 'anti-government' activities back to the party and intelligence services" (Vaughan and Tronvoll 2003, pp. 40–41).

The methods it would adopt to contain secessionism following Eritrea's departure were soon employed throughout the country. As the TPLF/EPRDF placed its OPDO acolytes in positions of power in the administrative structures of what became the Member State of Oromia, the OLF continued to call for an independent Oromia, and made clear it was willing to put to the test the provisions of firstly the Transitional Charter, and then the new Constitution, concerning the right to secede. In December 1993, the OLF and other opposition groups attempted to convene their own Conference to review the transitional process and propose reforms. The TPLF/EPRDF government announced it considered the initiative illegitimate and an incitement to violence, and simply arrested their leaders (Parmelee 1993).

In the case of the State of Somalia, another member state of the federation, its dominant political party, the Ogaden National Liberation Front (ONLF), also continued to entertain secessionist ambitions. Initially a willing participant in the transitional process, the ONLF took part in the regional elections of 1992, easily winning control of the Regional Assembly. However, when it became clear that the ONLF was also prepared to test the Transitional Charter's guarantees of a right to self-determination, the government sought to neutralise this additional threat to Ethiopia's territorial integrity. Not only did the TPLF/EPRDF nurture the formation of a Ethiopian Somali Democratic League (ESDL) to counter the influence of the ONLF, but when in January 1994 the ONLF called for a referendum on self-determination for the Ogaden (in accordance with the requirements of the Transitional Charter), central government security forces simply arrested a number of prominent ONLF regional office-holders on charges of corruption, and replaced the regional government administrative staff with ESDL personnel (Human Rights Watch 2008, p. 22).

The transitional process culminated in the May 1995 regional and federal elections. Given the continued boycott of most opposition parties, and with TPLF/EPRDF, its affiliated parties and a few independents left to contest the elections, the result was a foregone conclusion. The EPRDF and its affiliates took 417 of the total 547 seats in the CR, which elected

Meles Zenawi as Prime Minister, the largely ceremonial post of President being granted to a leading figure from the TPLF-nurtured OPDO.

One expert argued that many independent candidates had been artificially created by the TPLF/EPRDF, the aim being to convey an impression of genuine competition, and that at least as far as the Tigray region was concerned "some if not most had clearly been recruited by the TPLF" (Lyons 1996, p. 133). Where such methods were judged inadequate, the same tactics employed in the 1992 regional elections were used. These included the arrest of opposition leaders, amongst which the leader of the All Amhara People's Organization (AAPO), a party believed to have a significant following in the Amhara region, and which represented a threat to the EPRDF's own coalition ANDM party which claimed to represent the Amhara.

Following its victory in the 1995 elections, which placed the TPLF/EPRDF in an unassailable commanding position at the end of the transition, it continued to tighten its political control. It launched a civil service reform programme which included a 'purging' of those senior public functionaries at the central level (largely Amharic speakers based in Addis Ababa who had remained in post after 1991 and were seen as hostile to Revolutionary Democracy and Ethnic Federalism). Due to the decentralisation programme and urgent need for large numbers of civil servants at regional level, a massive training programme was launched at the country's Civil Service College. Though it had no formal relations with the EPRDF, and according to its statutes was an autonomous body, not only was the College's Board chaired by a senior figure from the EPRDF, but it was also accountable to Meles Zenawi as Prime Minister, and it was hardly surprising it came to be known as the TPLF/EPRDF's 'cadre school' (Vaughan and Tronvoll 2003, p. 25).

In terms of constitutionally guaranteed media freedoms, the immediate aftermath of the new post-1991 dispensation had seen a flourishing of new newspapers. However, as the latter became increasingly critical of the government, the authorities used certain provisions contained in the transitional government's Press Proclamation of October 1992 to silence critical voices, such as Article 10 which was used to detain and prosecute journalists on the grounds of alleged "defamation or false accusations against any individual, nation, nationality or organization" (Federal Negarit Gazeta 1992). By 1996, the Committee to Protect Journalists was reporting Ethiopia had become "one of the world's most frequent jailers of journalists" (Committee to Protect Journalists 1996).

The ruling party's intolerance of dissent would be most clearly displayed in the aftermath of the May 2005 federal and regional elections, ones in which the major opposition party, the Coalition for Unity and Democracy (CUD), made significant gains, and the ruling party's hegemony was seriously threatened for the first time. After protracted delays in the vote-counting, which led to accusations of election fraud committed by the TPLF/EPRDF, the ruling party was declared to have won an overall majority in the Lower House of the country's Parliament (the Council of People's Representatives). However, the new opposition parties—principally the CUD and the United Ethiopian Democratic Forces (UEDF)—significantly increased their presence in the Parliament's lower chamber, with the number of opposition MPs growing from 12 in the previous Parliament to 174. Opposition parties also made significant inroads in the elections for regional government councils: the most significant of such setbacks for the TPLF/EPRDF being its loss of control of the Addis Ababa region to the CUD.

The TPLF/EPRDF's intolerant and authoritarian style of governance then came to the fore in the form of a general crackdown on opposition political parties, critical civil society organisations, domestic media outlets and an increasingly unwelcoming environment for foreign journalists. In the face of growing popular anger with the slow progress in vote-counting (the final results were only released in mid-September 2005), the government issued a ban on demonstrations and arrested opposition figures. Further raising the political temperature were critical reports of the electoral process issued by international observers, most notably that of an EU mission. Its report was detailed and scathing, noting that while the pre-election period and the voting itself were peaceful and orderly:

> The human rights situation rapidly deteriorated in the post-election period when dozens of citizens were killed by the police and thousands were arrested. Overall, therefore, the elections fell short of international principles for genuine democratic elections. (EU Election Observation Mission Ethiopia 2005, p. 1)

Continued TPLF/EPRDF rule was secured through widespread use of targeted violence by the security forces which were, constitutional niceties aside, now seen to have been successfully moulded into the regime's Praetorians. An official commission of inquiry concluded that a total of 199 people (including 6 members of the police) were killed.

The elections of 2005, and its bloody aftermath, severely undermined the TPLF/EPRDF's claims that its policies represented a clean break with the country's authoritarian past. However, the response of Western donors to the incidents of 2005 was muted, and the head of the EU's election observer mission, the Portuguese Member of European Parliament (MEP) Ana Gomes, accused EU leaders of complicity, and of "turning a blind eye because they want to turn a blind eye. … They just pretend this is not true because they want to continue dealing as usual with the Ethiopian regime" (BBC News 2006). While Addis Ababa might expect some temporary turbulence in the aid relationship, and maybe even harsh words from some donors concerning backsliding on the political front, it could also be confident that over time such transgressions would be overlooked if both substantial development progress could be showcased and more importantly the country's role as a strategic partner on security matters continued to be treated as critical to Western interests.

Meles Zenawi's calculus proved to be correct. At a time when external observers were failing to detect any significant improvements in the country's democratic political space and human rights situation, but rather the opposite following the events of 2005, the EU's ODA to Ethiopia saw significant increases, rising each year from US$163 million in 2005 to US$460 million in 2008 (Human Rights Watch 2010b, p. 28). ODA disbursements to Ethiopia from the wider group of OECD-DAC members did fall marginally in 2005 from US$1.18 billion (in constant prices) to US$1.02 billion in 2006, but by 2007 they had already recovered US$1.24 billion, and by 2008 had reached US$1.84 billion (OECD Statistics 2022). If there were some bilateral donors such as the UK, which did cut ODA to Ethiopia from US$143 million in 2004 to US$75.5 million in 2005, by 2006 the UK aid flows had also rebounded to US$164.6 million, and by 2007 had reached US$291 million. Canada's disbursements fell marginally from US$65 million in 2005 to US$62.5 million in 2006, and then increased substantially to US$152 million by 2008. Italy, another major donor, increased its disbursements from US$11.2 million in 2004 to US$103 million by 2006 (Human Rights Watch 2010b, p. 28).

It is noteworthy that at a time when the US had become the largest bilateral donor to Ethiopia, and Washington therefore enjoyed the greatest potential leverage over decision-making in Addis Ababa, significant amounts of American ODA funding also continued to flow despite the state violence unleashed in 2005. While Washington did reduce its ODA disbursements from US$608 million in 2005 to US$315 million in 2006, by 2008 its disbursements had recovered to US$811 million (Human Rights Watch 2010b, p. 28). Such increases continued despite the EPRDF government, long after the violent repression of 2005, proceeding to further tightening its control on society, by neutering the political opposition and silencing critical civil society and media voices. Employing Orwellian doublespeak common to legislation produced by such hybrid regimes, a new Mass Media Law was passed in 2008; its Preamble stating the Law had been drafted:

> Cognizant of the necessity of preserving and consolidating past achievements and positive practices pertaining to freedom of expression while removing structural and institutional impediments that hinder the independent operation of the mass media and the free exchange of information and ideas. (Federal Negarit Gazeta 2008, Preamble)

In reality the legislation placed severe restrictions on the development of the free media it claimed to protect. It granted public prosecutors the right, on grounds of a "clear and present grave danger to national security", to "issue and order to impound" printed matter (Federal Negarit Gazeta 2008, Article 42), with the government left to define where and when such dangers arose. Defamation and libel remained criminal offences subject to terms of sentences of imprisonment, and the registration and licencing requirements for media houses meant unlimited discretionary powers for the state to refuse applications.

This was followed by the enactment of legislation on NGOs, which given the important role they had played as observers and reporters of electoral malpractices and human rights violations had become increasingly inconvenient to the government. As with the Mass Media Law, the Preamble of the Charities and Societies Proclamation of 2009 was couched in the language of liberal principles, more specifically the need to "enact a law in order to ensure the realization of citizens' right to association enshrined in the Constitution of the Federal Democratic Republic of Ethiopia", and to "aid and facilitate the role of Charities and Societies in the overall development of Ethiopian peoples" (Federal Negarit Gazeta 2009a, Preamble).

However, rather than opening up space for civil society, it clearly aimed to reduce the scope for organisations to operate freely, in particular those working on human rights and democratisation issues, by placing the operations of NGOs under the direct supervision of central government. The

Proclamation established a Societies and Charities Agency, whose Chairperson and Director-General were appointed by the Government. Given the requirement for all NGOs to register to obtain an operating licence, the Agency was granted wide discretionary powers to deny one to any NGO. Grounds for refusal to register a charity included that in the Agency's opinion an NGO was "likely to be used for unlawful purposes or for purposes prejudicial to public peace, welfare or good order in Ethiopia" (Federal Negarit Gazeta 2009a, Article 62). This in effect meant the government could disband any organisation it disliked.

In the run-up to 2010 parliamentary elections, another government initiative to stifle dissent took the form of an Anti-Terrorism Law (Federal Negarit Gazeta 2009b). Like similar laws around the world, it provided the government with additional means to suppress critical voices within civil society and weaken organised political opposition forces. It delegitimised non-violent protest and dissent by conflating political opposition with terrorism, criminalising behaviour that should rather have been considered the lawful exercise of the rights to freedom of expression and association guaranteed by the Constitution.

The government was quick to use the anti-terrorist legislation to silence potential challengers, banning a number of opposition parties such as the OLF and ONLF (Keita & Rhodes 2011). The year 2011 saw a major crackdown on critical voices, with Amnesty International reporting that at least 108 opposition figures, and 6 journalists, were arrested for alleged links with proscribed entities designated as terrorist groups. Reviewing the evidence, the charges brought against these individuals, as well as their trials, Amnesty concluded that "the overly broad definitions of the Anti-Terrorism Proclamation are being used to prosecute individuals for any display of dissent" (Amnesty International 2011, p. 5).

Most Western donors were silent, at least in public, as they witnessed these additional disturbing developments taking place in one of their African donor darlings. Commenting on the situation in 2009, HRW observed that even though the country was one of the most aid-dependent countries in the world (which should have provided donors with strong leverage over the government's policies), "major donors have been unwilling to confront the government over its worsening human rights record" (Human Rights Watch 2010a), and attributed this partly to their concern that if they were too vocal in their criticisms the government might close down their aid programmes.

Even a temporary suspension of budget support to the government in 2005 had proved insufficient to compel the government to abandon its repressive measures. The stand-off with Western donors had been quickly resolved when the Ethiopian Finance Minister played a card much favoured by aid-dependant authoritarian governments when faced with pressure from donors to introduce reforms through threats to cut their development assistance; this was to argue that those who would suffer most from such decisions would be the most vulnerable. As he stated in December 2005, with a touch of bravado, "[T]he impact should be insignificant although it is the poor who will suffer" (*The New Humanitarian* 2005).

In the event, rather than reductions in the total volume of Western ODA, funds previously earmarked for budget support were simply redirected through alternative schemes which donors believed gave them greater control over targeting. There was no net loss to the country in terms of ODA, which in fact continued its steep upwards trajectory despite ongoing governmental repression of civil and political rights. Though the temporary suspension of aid resources transferred directly to its treasury would have been inconvenient for the government, there was nevertheless no weakening of governmental control over those external flows channelled outside central government systems given its ability to manipulate new programmes and funding modalities for its own ends (on this see Chap. 9).

The ruling party's key objective in the 2010 elections was to prevent a recurrence of the strongly contested elections of 2005, and in this it was very successful. It won 499 out of the total 545 parliamentary seats, its allied parties picking up the remainder, with a single seat going to an opposition party representative and another to an independent candidate. The results showed how accomplished the ruling party had been in weakening the ability of opposition parties to build on their 2005 gains. This was achieved through the harassment of leaders and their supporters, intimidation of the independent media and critical voices within wider civil society who were regularly depicted as pursuing a treasonous regime change agenda, targeting those sections of the electorate which supported opposition parties through a variety of positive and negative inducements and engaging in other breaches of electoral protocol such as ballot box stuffing and barring opposition party agents from observing the voting process.[3]

After the events of 2005, the government's sales pitch also changed, and it sought to shift the attention of both Western donors and the

Ethiopian electorate away from issues of political governance to the improvements in development indicators and economic growth it attributed to its rule. Most prominent amongst these new campaigning elements was the ruling party's declaration of an intention to establish a 'developmental state' (explored in greater detail in the next chapter), an economic model associated with the fast-growing economies of East and South East Asia and successful state-led capitalist development.

Developmental state discourse came to occupy pride of place in official government pronouncements. It was argued that the success of the model required regime continuity; if the EPRDF's policy of Ethnic Federalism had earlier been sold as a means to put an end to the country's propensity for ethnic-based conflict, now the developmental state model held out the promise of rapid economic transformation of the country. But this would only be possible if the necessary visionary and determined leadership remained at the helm. If the ruling party had previously characterised political opponents who objected to Revolutionary Democracy and Ethnic Federalism as counter-revolutionaries, restorationist Amhara ethnic chauvinists hiding behind the disguise of non-ethnic or pan-ethnic political platforms or 'narrow nationalists', now developmental state discourse was used to denigrate them as anti-developmental and anti-modernisation, self-interested economic elites focused on growing their personal wealth and preventing the masses from escaping poverty.

Even after its landslide victory in the 2010 elections, the government continued to harass and imprison opposition political leaders, and assiduously applied the media, NGO and anti-terrorism laws to silence critical voices. The results of the general elections of May 2015 again showed the extent to which these measures had proven effective. The TPLF/EPRDF and its allies (now under the leadership of Hailemariam Desalegn, following the death of Meles Zenawi in August 2012) won all 546 seats in the House of Representatives, and also swept the board in the regional state elections. Opposition political voices were effectively shut out of the country's legislative processes, and the ruling party had to all intents and purposes achieved its longstanding ambition of complete political hegemony.

And Western largesse continued to flow to Ethiopia, even after one of the bloodiest episodes in the history of TPLF/EPRDF rule. Between November 2015 and May 2016, protestors in Oromia (the largest of the country's regions, populated by its largest ethnic group the Oromo) demonstrated against a government proposal to expand the municipal boundaries of Addis Ababa into Oromia. Deep and longstanding feelings of discrimination and political and economic marginalisation amongst the

Oromo were compounded by the government's outlawing of the OLF as a terrorist group, and the fact that the national budget appeared to grant priority to Tigray's call on national resources.

Federal security forces moved into Oromia, brutally repressing the unrest. HRW reported the use of live ammunition to disperse protestors, with estimates of loss of life ranging from the 27 persons documented by HRW up to over 400 deaths reported by local NGOs. Thousands were arrested, including anyone associated with the promotion of Oromo identity and interests (Human Rights Watch 2016).

Western governments were well aware of the continual and severe deterioration in political freedoms and civil and human rights taking place under the EPRDF's rule. The US State Department's 2011 report on human rights in Ethiopia, which covered developments both before and after the May 2010 general elections, referenced incidents of "unlawful killings, torture, beating and abuse and mistreatment of detainees and opposition supporters by security forces", and "restrictions on freedom of speech and of the press" (U.S. Department of State 2011, pp. 1–2). Its 2016 report, which covered the crackdown in Oromia, contained the now-familiar references to the harassment of opposition party leaders and supporters, journalists and civil society activists, arbitrary arrests, forced disappearances and use of torture by the security forces, and noted what it characterised as the "only limited ability of citizens to choose their government" (U.S. Department of State 2016, p. 2).

Yet once again, despite ever-growing evidence that all was not well in terms of political governance in one of the West's African donor darlings, the disconnect grew between, on the one hand, the deterioration in the country's democracy and human rights indicators, the declared interest of Western donors in the promotion of democracy and willingness to hold aid-recipient countries to account for their repression, and, on the other hand, the totals of Western development assistance disbursed to Ethiopia. If in the aftermath of the 2005 crackdown this had fallen marginally from US$1.35 billion in 2005 (in current US$), to US$1.22 billion in 2006, the downward trend was quickly reversed such that by 2007 total disbursements had reached US$1.61 billion, and increased significantly to US$2.29 billion by 2008. The total value of bilateral disbursements by Western countries then remained above the US$2 billion mark per annum between 2008 and 2015, reaching US$2.42 billion in 2017 (World Bank 2024). Together with ODA received from multilateral bodies such as the EU and the World Bank, Ethiopia was able to retain its position as the largest recipient of Western ODA in SSA.

Rwanda: Unwavering Repression of Political Dissent

A major factor shaping the RPF's political governance style concerned its views on multi-party politics, and their links to ethnicity and conflict. Like the NRM's analysis of Uganda's post-independence travails, the RPF traced Rwanda's problems to the ethnic divisions nurtured by the colonial powers, which were then instrumentalised by post-independence politicians pursuing narrow rather than national interests. However, in sharp contrast to the TPLF/EPRDF which sought to take the sting out of the tail of ethnicity and ethnic-based conflict by granting collective rights to ethnic groups on the basis of a shared commitment to Revolutionary Democracy and Ethnic Federalism, the RPF claimed it wanted to totally replace ethnicity as a defining characteristic of state-society relations in Rwanda with another set of ties, one based on the restoration of a supposed historic pre-contact unity between the country's ethnic groups, and the nurturing of a post-1994 sense of common citizenship.

Given the RPF's views on the close links between ethnic-based competitive politics and violence, it was clear the post-genocide regime would always be reluctant to nurture political pluralism. Like the EPRDF and NRM, the RPF therefore set out to 'game' any constitutionally enshrined political pluralism, while in fact concentrating power in its own hands.

In July 1994, a coalition Government of National Unity (GNU) and a Transitional National Assembly (TNA) were established in accordance with the power-sharing provisions of the 1993 Arusha Accords. However, some of the Accord's clauses were unilaterally modified by the RPF through a 'Declaration' it issued on July 17, 1994. These changes were later accepted by the representatives of eight political parties in a Protocol of Agreement signed in November 1994, and in turn incorporated into the Fundamental Law of May 1995 which served as a de facto interim constitution, with the RPF justifying the amendments in terms of the profound changes to national realities brought about by the genocide.

Given the RPF's initial position of weakness (the significant numerical inferiority of the Tutsi relative to the majority Hutu, and the devastated country it inherited in 1994), as well as its stated desire to promote national reconciliation, early bans it imposed on some political parties (contrary to the provisions of the Arusha Accord) were also accompanied by overtures to its political and military opponents. These initially included the Hutu-dominated *Mouvement Démocratique Républicain* (MDR) with which the RPF had negotiated in Arusha, as well as members of the

Hutu-dominated former Rwandan armed forces. Most GNU ministerial portfolios and TNA seats—members of both the GNU and the TNA being appointed by the parties to the Arusha Accords on the basis of a predetermined distribution formula—were held by Hutus. The new President, Pasteur Bizimungu, was a Hutu who had held several senior posts in the previous regime until joining the RPF in 1990.

At the same time, the RPF announced that the former government's official party, the MRNDD (which in the Accords had been granted posts in the Government of National Unity, and a number of TNA seats), and the smaller Hutu *Coalition pour la Défense de la République* (CDR), which had rejected the Arusha peace process, were banned on the grounds that they had planned and executed the genocide. The RPF thus effectively granted itself the right to act as sole judge and jury in attributing responsibility for the events of 1994. Changes were made to the Arusha provisions governing the executive branch, most particularly the creation of the post of vice-president which was to be held by Kagame.

Kagame also became the country's Minister of Defence, and this enabled him to oversee the elevation of national security considerations to a position of primacy in the government's decision-making, with a wide range of seemingly unrelated issues all refracted through the prism of national security. A close association was established between the defence of Rwanda's territorial integrity, its citizens, economy and national institutions, on the one hand, and regime continuity and maintenance of the political status quo, on the other. Within the ranks of the country's defence and security forces, and those personnel attached to other state institutions, definitions of national security and the security of the RPF regime became synonymous, and any threats to public institutions, the economy and the Rwandan people were all interpreted as threats to the RPF and vice versa.

The official promotion of the idea of ever-present security threats facing post-genocide Rwanda has helped justify a continuous state of alert and preparedness. Adversaries are depicted as lurking everywhere, waiting only for an appropriate opportunity to put their pernicious plans to overthrow the RPF, and return Rwanda to the dark days of 1994, into practice. This in turn has enabled the RPF to justify the use of any means to neutralise its enemies, and that any curtailment of political freedoms and civil rights is both necessary and acceptable. This has been accompanied by the significant strengthening of the country's defence, security and intelligence institutions, and the construction of a Rwandan 'national security state' which is key to the preservation of RPF rule.

If the NRM depicted its political opponents as vehicles of 'sectarianism', and the TPLF/EPRDF labelled its rivals as purveyors of 'narrow nationalism', 'counter-revolution' and later 'anti-developmentalism', the RPF delegitimised its foes by labelling them as the purveyors of 'genocidal' plans, because they either entertained eliminationist anti-Tutsi ideas or engaged in genocide denial. The latter is treated as only a marginally less serious threat than the former, as they might raise uncomfortable questions around the RPF's official account of events leading up to the 1994 genocide and subsequent developments, and might thereby undermine the RPF's efforts to project itself as the sole bulwark against the clear and present danger of another genocide.[4]

As with the NRM and the TPLF/EPRDF (though arguably more deftly employed by the RPF), additional legitimising tools were brought into play to justify both the policies adopted and the need for its continued rule. To the dangers of a repeat genocide would later be added the objective of 'development' as critical overarching national and party objective. The priority it attached to development, and the need to defend the development progress made and ensure further gains, helped the RPF demand a degree of forbearance from its foreign supporters for its shortcomings in the political realm, as it insisted the enormous tasks the country faced in terms of national reconstruction and reconciliation required 'strong government'.

The RPF also developed its own particular interpretation of democracy. While the NRM had sought to disguise its authoritarian political programme behind the promotion of 'no-party democracy', and the TPLF/EPRDF did the same through its espousal of Revolutionary Democracy, the RPF invested in what it argued was an appropriate political governance system for post-genocide Rwanda, namely 'consensual democracy'. Again echoing the rationalisations put forward by the NRM and the TPLF/EPRDF for their political system, the RPF claimed the form of democracy it had chosen best reflected Rwanda's specific history and culture, its current needs and the imperative of removing the perennial scourge of violence from Rwandan politics.

The emphasis of consensual democracy was on 'popular empowerment' and 'popular participation', rather than the confrontation within the political arena of parties with different visions for the country, and with citizens freely exercising their right to choose between them. Translating consensual democracy into a programme, it was clear that national unity and reconciliation, as defined by the RPF, would be used to fend off early demands for a return to multi-party politics, and then when political parties were eventually permitted to run in the 2003 elections it would be used to control them. The 'consensus' sought would be determined by the RPF, and the boundaries of political discourse delimited and rigorously patrolled by the ruling party.

The first concrete translation into practice of consensual democracy was the launching of a decentralisation programme in 2000, followed by local elections in 2001. Popular mobilisation at local level was meant to enhance decision-making and the identification of citizen priorities at that level, always based on 'consensus'. It involved the direct election of local councillors, though candidates were subjected to clearance by the RPF-dominated National Electoral Commission (NEC), with the degree of their adherence to the RPF's policies undoubtedly looming large in the evaluative criteria applied.

The role of Rwanda's NEC in the 2001 elections set the pattern for its performance in all subsequent elections and referenda, and helped clarify what consensual democracy meant in practice. The President of the NEC and its executive secretary were senior RPF figures, and its permanent secretariat was also dominated by the RPF. The latter selected the provincial electoral commissioners responsible for conducting elections in the country's twelve provinces, and these in turn approved candidates for the district-level commissioners proposed by local authorities. As one foreign organisation observed, "Since the government nominated all prefects and *bourgmestres* [mayors of communes] as well as the permanent secretariat of the commission, commissioners were invariably in line with the interests of the RPF dominated government" (International Crisis Group 2001, p. 13). The NEC closely monitored the campaigns of candidates for mayorships or positions on the district executive committees to ensure these were restricted to the bread-and-butter issues of development, and that there were no political overtones in their platforms. The results of the local elections meant the majority of incumbent *bourgmestres* (which had been appointed by central government) were returned to office.

Prior to the reintroduction of multi-party politics in 2003, and based on the ideas of consensual democracy, a National Consultative Forum of Political Organisations (NFPO) was established. According to the 2003 constitution the NFPO was meant, inter alia, to facilitate the "exchange of ideas on major issues facing the country", help "consolidate national unity" and act as "mediators in conflict arising between political organizations", while its decisions "would always be taken by the consensus of its constituent organizations" (Constitution of the Republic of Rwanda 2003, Article 56). Yet Article 57 also made it clear that participation would be less than voluntary, as only those parties registered with the Forum would be entitled to state grants and that a forthcoming organic law would "determine the modalities for the establishment of political organizations, their functioning, the conduct of their leaders" (Constitution of the Republic of Rwanda 2003, Article 57). This was a clear indication of the intrusive role the NFPO intended to play in the operations of political parties.

In addition, Organic Law 16/2003 (Official Gazette of the Republic of Rwanda 2003) then faithfully rehearsed the RPF's views on the links between political parties and ethnic conflict. It stipulated that the parties were prohibited from basing their platforms on a range of criteria such as race, ethnicity, region or religion "or any other division which may give rise to discrimination". They were also required to "constantly reflect the unity of the people of Rwanda ... whether in recruitment of members, putting in place organs of leadership and in their operations and activities" (Official Gazette of the Republic of Rwanda 2003, Article 4), which given the vagueness of these regulations granted the NFPO significant scope for subjective interpretations of breaches of these provisions. Such discretion was reinforced by other Articles, such as that party media was "prohibited from disseminating information with a denigrating or divisive nature likely to undermine national security, territorial integrity and national unity" (Official Gazette of the Republic of Rwanda 2003, Article 20), and prohibited from "negationism and trivialization of Genocide" (Official Gazette of the Republic of Rwanda 2003, Article 40-14). Sanctions for breaches of this law ranged from formal warnings to suspension of any political activities for fixed periods of time and outright dissolution (Official Gazette of the Republic of Rwanda 2003, Article 42).

The NFPO's operations clearly showed it to be yet another instrument of RPF political control. The 'consultative' and 'consensus building' elements of its mandate took a back seat to its primary functions, which were to discipline any wayward political party, sanction any politician who posed a serious challenge to the RPF and more generally to apply the RPF's definitions of acceptable political behaviour. After observing the NFPO's initial operations, the African Union (AU) concluded in its African Peer Review Mechanism Report on Rwanda of 2006 that "it became patently clear that competitive political pluralism was consciously contained within clearly defined guidelines by the Consultative Forum of Political Organizations" (African Union 2006, p. 37).

As events were to prove, the RPF's introduction of a new constitution in 2003—many provisions of which were prima facie guarantees of liberal political and civil freedoms and human rights—seemed to have less to do with any deeply rooted adherence to liberalism within the upper echelons of the RPF, and were more a reflection of the need to strengthen its presentability to the West and its African peers. The marketing of the liberal credentials it claimed to hold dear, and its regular public commitments to strengthen political and civil freedoms and human rights, helped it access international development assistance and dial down any Western pressure for faster progress on democratisation. Legislation reflecting liberal principles was either interpreted or applied in ways contrary to their original intention, replaced by new illiberal legislation or simply ignored. It became increasingly evident that the RPF's modus operandi resembled that of other hybrid authoritarian regimes; the goal of perpetuating its hold on power was the key determinant of its actions, any moves towards greater pluralism and greater democratic freedoms and strengthened civil rights would be tightly controlled and managed, and it showed its willingness to use violence for regime maintenance purposes.

Political opposition was systematically stifled. Following the banning of the MRNDD and CDR, the RPF's next move to neutralise opposition from political parties occurred during 2000–2001. Growing tensions between President Bizimungu and Vice-President Kagame—which some sources attributed to Bizimungu's criticisms of the RPF's increasingly repressive policies during the transitional period (BBC News 2004)—led to the President's resignation in March 2000, with Kagame eventually taking on the post of President. Bizimungu then established a new political party, the Party for Democracy and Renewal (PDR), but he was immediately arrested and charged with conducting illegal political activities on the grounds that the Cabinet had decided that no new political parties could be established during the transitional period. The PDR was labelled a security threat, and Bizimungu was eventually sentenced to a fifteen-year jail term for, inter alia, fomenting ethnic divisions, embezzling of public funds and threatening national security by planning to overthrow the Kagame government.

Bizimungu's arrest and quashing of the PDR were part of a broader RPF strategy of neutering any political opposition, strengthening RPF hegemony and merging party and state. Regarding the latter process, a HRW report of May 2003 observed that during the period between establishment of the GNU and TNA in 1994, and in the run-up to the presidential and parliamentary elections of August and September–October 2003,

> the RPF increased its official share of posts to more accurately reflect the real extent of its power. As of late 2002, the president of the republic, twelve of fifteen ministers (and most of the secretary-generals of ministries), the chief judges on the Constitutional Court and the Court of Cassation, the prosecutor general of the republic, eleven of twelve governors, thirteen of fifteen ambassadors, seven of nine heads of security services, and nineteen of seventy-four assembly members ... were members of or affiliated with the RPF. (Human Rights Watch 2003, pp. 2–3)

Furthermore, notwithstanding the RPF's official discourse of ethnic unity and its denial of the importance of ethnicity in determining the composition of government and state institutions, such claims came to be seen as a cover-up for ethnic favouritism and the gradual 'tutsification' of the Rwandan polity. A 2003 study highlighted the extent of Tutsi dominance, noting that fourteen of the country's twenty-two Supreme Court judges were Tutsis, as were twenty-three of the twenty-eight heads of state enterprises, with Tutsis also dominating the country's diplomatic service at ambassadorial level (on this see Gakusi and Mouzer 2003).

In another effort to silence opposition voices prior to the 2003 elections, the RPF moved against the MDR, its principal partner in the GNU, and by then the only remaining political party other than the RPF. It neutralised the MDR by attributing to it the Hutu-supremacist and anti-Tutsi genocidal ideology of the former pre-1994 ruling party, the already banned MRNDD, and associating the MDR with its previous incarnation, the MDR-Parmehutu, which had played a decisive and murderous role in the events of 1994. To develop the necessary evidence, the RPF established a Parliamentary Commission.

In its March 2003 report to Parliament, this Commission unsurprisingly concluded that the MDR was in fact the bearer of 'divisionist' and genocidal plans. The Commission report even argued that its opposition to specific government policies constituted evidence of divisionism, a tactic subsequently used to neutralise other parties. It also accused the MDR of seeking to create discontent within the armed forces, of minimising the genocide and, in particular for committing the cardinal sin (one which the

RPF was particularly sensitive to), of claiming that there had in fact been a 'double genocide' in 1994, one in which the RPF had sought to eliminate the Hutu in the same way the latter has targeted Tutsi (Republique Rwandaise 2003).

In April 2003 the TNA accepted the Commission's recommendations and formally denounced the MDR. When the latter failed, in accordance with the aforementioned Organic Law 16/2003, to re-register prior to the 2003 parliamentary elections, it was then banned from partaking in political activities and effectively dissolved. Its presidential candidate, Faustin Twagiramungu, was then forced to run as an independent.

To ensure a favourable outcome in the 2003 elections, not only did the RPF shape the electoral playing field in its favour by ensuring any serious rival parties and candidates were eliminated, but it also interfered with the electoral process itself. In its report on the 2003 Presidential election, a delegation of observers from the EU Parliament was scathing in its conclusions, setting a tone in terms of critical foreign views on elections in Rwanda repeated in subsequent reports by external bodies. It highlighted the abuse of the advantages of incumbency by Kagame and the ruling party: "[C]ampaign resources were totally one-sided. The delegation did not see a single poster or leaflet for an opposition candidate during its travels" and concluded that since the candidature of the main opposition figure was invalidated "the opposition had no real chance of winning these elections" (European Parliament 2003, p. 2). It also referenced another feature of the party-state merger underway in Rwanda, namely the lack of any clear distinction between RPF officials and supporters, on the one hand, and state officials, on the other, both appearing together at RPF rallies. Intimidation of voters was ensured through the heavy presence of RPF representatives, the delegation observing that they were "often threatening and they were allowed to stand very close to the ballot boxes" (European Parliament 2003, p. 4).

The actions of the NEC provided further evidence of the extent to which the RPF had used the transitional period to blur the distinction between the interests of the ruling party and those of state bodies. Not only did the NEC act as the custodian and watchdog of the electoral rules, but it exercised a high degree of discretion as to whether candidates had abided by those rules. It repeatedly called opposition candidates such as Twagiramungu to task for sowing 'divisionism', which given the vagueness of the concept meant anyone who disagreed with the RPF. A team of

Norwegian human rights specialists, who also observed the 2003 elections, commented acerbically:

> While arrests, interrogations and summons were reported on the part of many opposition candidates ... hardly any were reported on the RPF side. It is improbable that this imbalance reflected an actual imbalance of the lawfulness of the actors on the ground. (Samset and Dalby 2003, p. 16)

Kagame won the 2003 presidential race with 95.05 per cent of the vote, with Twagiramungu running as an independent securing 3.7 per cent. In the Parliamentary elections held later that year, of the fifty-three seats out of a total eighty seats up for grabs in the lower house Chamber of Deputies (the remaining twenty-seven members being indirectly elected by special interest groups such as the state-sponsored and RPF-supported women's groups and the National Youth Council), the RPF and its coalition allies won a total of forty seats. The other two parties which were not part of the RPF's coalition secured the remaining thirteen seats. Given they were allowed to run at all clearly meant they were not seen to represent a significant threat to the RPF, with one Western think-tank arguing that "the political parties that exist today in Rwanda are only tolerated if they agree not to question the definition of political life drawn up by the RPF (International Crisis Group 2002, p. 2). Their existence enabled the ruling party to stage an appropriate display of electoral theatre for Western eyes, and demonstrate its adherence to the ideal of multi-party democracy.

Yet notwithstanding the seemingly unassailable position the RPF and Kagame enjoyed after the 2003 elections, repression was still judged necessary as powerful enemies continued to be unmasked on a regular basis. Since the Parliamentary Commission investigation into the MDR had referenced links between this party and certain CSOs and media outlets, the regime further tightened restrictions on the latter. Kagame repeatedly calling for tight controls of the media in the interests of national unity in order to prevent a return to inter-ethnic violence. The closure of newspapers became a common occurrence, as did the intimidation, murder, disappearance and exile of journalists.

A 2002 media law had introduced sanctions, including prison terms, for the by now familiar list of ill-defined and already proscribed offences such as "apology for genocide and massacres and crimes against humanity" (Official Gazette of the Republic of Rwanda 2002, Article 85). Additional crimes and draconian punishments were now added, such as for contempt of "the President of the Republic of Rwanda", such crimes being susceptible to being "punished by the maximum of the related penalties provided for in the Penal Code" (Official Gazette of the Republic of Rwanda 2002, Article 84.2). A High Council of the Press, responsible for issuing broadcasting licences and accrediting journalists, was placed "under the supervision of the Office of the President of the Republic" (Official Gazette of the Republic of Rwanda 2002, Article 73). The legislation contributed to a general atmosphere of fear within media circles, and a hardly surprising tendency towards self-censorship. One foreign journalist, who worked in Rwanda between 2009 and 2013, witnessed a succession of newspapers being shut down, and many journalists fleeing the country, being arrested, murdered or simply disappearing, and concluded:

> The press had been decimated in its widest sense, and profoundly. Newspapers were meaningless: merely repeating government propaganda, publishing public announcements, inventing flattery. ... The president's words had become the news, indeed were becoming the sole voice in the country. (Sundaram 2016, p. 58)

In 2012 the Committee to Protect Journalists reported that eighteen Rwandan journalists had been forced into exile between 2001 and 2011, and that between 2007 and 2011 seven media outlets had been suspended, leaving "a subdued and largely state-dominated press landscape" (Committee to Protect Journalists 2012). International accolades of the wrong kind were regularly bestowed on Kagame by Western NGOs monitoring press freedoms around the world, and he became a permanent feature in the list of 'Predators of Press Freedom' published by the international NGO Reporters Without Borders.

In the 2010 presidential elections, efforts were again made to ensure there was no genuine opposition to Kagame as he ran for another seven-year term. All the other three candidates—the leaders of the Social Democratic Party, the Liberal Party and the Party of Progress and Concord—headed up organisations widely seen as supportive of the RPF and Kagame, and ran on platforms indistinguishable from those of the RPF. This was hardly surprising, as the leader of the Social Democratic Party had been nominated by Kagame as Minister of Health in 2006, the Tutsi leader of the Liberal Party had served as Minister of Industry in the Government of National Unity headed by the RPF and the leader of the

PPC had withdrawn before the 2003 race and gone on to announce her support of Kagame's candidature (*France 24* 2010).

Parties with a track record of criticising the government were simply not allowed to field candidates; amongst the most notorious cases of exclusion was that of the UDF-Inkingi (United Democratic Forces-Inkingi). Established by exiles in 2006, its leader, Victoire Ingabire Umuhoza, returned to Rwanda in January 2010 to contest the elections, and central to her platform was a demand that the government officially recognise the Hutu victims of the genocide. In April 2010 she was arrested and charged with promoting genocide ideology, divisionism and collaboration with terrorist groups. Though subsequently released on bail, she was prohibited from running in the elections, and would later be sentenced to a fifteen-year custodial sentence. Following an election campaign in which other opposition figures were the targets of what were clearly politically motivated killings—with the UN Secretary General calling on the Rwandan authorities to conduct an investigation into the murders (Beaumont writing in the *Observer* 2010)—Kagame won 93 per cent of the votes, the remainder being shared between the three other parties allowed to compete.

A constitutional amendment in 2015 then allowed Kagame to run for a third seven-year term, and also reset the clock in terms of presidential terms already served. The run-up to the 2017 presidential elections would again be marred by harassment of opposition party leaders and supporters, most notably Diane Rwigara (referenced in Chap. 2), who had intended to run as an independent candidate, as well as human rights activists and journalists. The NEC eventually disqualified Rwigara and two other candidates on technical grounds, leaving Kagame to face an independent candidate and the leader of the small Democratic Green Party. After a campaigning period heavily criticised by external observers, Kagame won these elections with 98.79 per cent of the vote. The US State Department reported on the by now familiar litany of electoral malpractices, which included difficulties faced by opposition parties in registering their candidates, instances of ballot stuffing, observers being denied access to the process of vote tabulation at polling stations and vote consolidation, with some election observers having "noted that reported results in some polling stations exceeded the number of registered voters, the number of voters observed throughout the day, and the number of physical ballots counted by elections officials in the presence of observers" (U.S. Department of State 2017, pp. 28–29).

As the RPF conducted a relentless campaign to undermine the country's constitutionally enshrined guarantees of liberal political and civil freedoms, and sought to dress this up as implementation of its policy of consensual democracy, it was clear to the Western press, international NGOs, Western governments and multilateral bodies such as the AU and EU that the policy was nothing more than a façade behind which it strengthened its hegemonic position. Yet after the transitional period and the controversial 2003 multi-party parliamentary and presidential elections, Western ODA to Rwanda had continued to flow in ever-increasing amounts. Between 2003 and 2004, net ODA from the OECD-DAC group of donors rose from US$267.4 million to US$282.2 million (in current prices), and continued to increase thereafter. By 2011 (the year after the controversial 2010 presidential elections), OECD-DAC member disbursements to Rwanda reached US$681.4 million. While the 2011–2020 period saw greater volatility in aid flows, the totals disbursed on an annual basis never fell below US$513 million, and by 2020 were back up to US$642 million (World Bank 2024).

It was clear that despite a well-documented track record of electoral malpractices and repeated violations of political and civil rights, Western donor countries were unwilling to use the country's high levels of aid dependency as leverage to secure the reforms they themselves repeatedly stated were essential. The net ODA disbursements of DAC members to Rwanda in 2020 represented 6.3 per cent of that country's GDP per capita. Even more significant in terms of scope for applying pressure on the RPF, as late as 2020 such aid flows represented 38.4 per cent of total government expenditure on goods and services (World Bank 2024). Yet the taps were never turned off. Given such high volumes of aid, it was also clear that Western aid flows were effectively providing the RPF with financial resources to construct the repressive state structures which secured its monopolistic grip on political power. As was the case with the regimes in Uganda and Ethiopia, the discrepancy between what Western donors and Kigali both claimed as their priorities in terms of political liberalisation and democratisation, and the reality of relentless political repression under Kagame, was increasingly stark.

Again, as with the NRM and EPRDF, political governance was not the only issue where there was increasing divergence between the declared objectives of both sides of the Rwandan donor-recipient relationship, and evidence of what was happening on the ground. Western donor demands for progress on democratisation was always accompanied by an insistence that recipients of their aid also undertake market-friendly economic reforms, one which translated into a downsizing of the state's presence in the economy, and greater transparency and accountability in terms of economic management. However, as all three regimes set about rebuilding their economies, and simultaneously set about constructing their respective party-states, their adoption of market-friendly reforms would be an extremely selective one as they found ways to implement economic policies which supported regime continuity.

Notes

1. The report referenced the extreme example of the country's smallest constituency in the far northern district of Kaabong with 2051 voters, while the largest constituency in Kampala had an electorate of close to 208,000.
2. On the view that other members of the EPRDF, such as the OPDO, were in fact TPLF creations, see Young (1997, p. 166).
3. For an in-depth analysis of those factors which influenced the outcome of the 2010 elections, see Tronvoll (2010).
4. Amongst the provisions of the May 2003 Constitution, which replaced the pre-genocide 1991 Constitution, were that "[r]evisionism, negationism and trivialisation of genocide are punishable by the law" (Article 13), the vagueness of the terms facilitating the penalisation of political opponents and exclusion from the political arena. Room for the exercise of judicial discretion was expanded by Article 54, which ruled that "[p]olitical organizations are prohibited from basing themselves on race, ethnic group, tribe, clan, region, sex, religion or any other division which may give rise to discrimination" (Constitution of the Republic of Rwanda 26 May 2003). The "Law Relating to the Punishment of the Crime of Genocide Ideology" of 2008 was widely criticised for its excessively broad definition of the crime of promoting or carrying out actions that reflected a 'genocide ideology', as it could be used to criminalise a range of legitimate forms of association and expression and exclude opposition voices from the country's political processes.

References

Aalen, Lovise. 2002. "Ethnic Federalism in a Dominant Party State: The Ethiopian Experience 1991–2000" Bergen, Norway: Chr. Michelsen Institute, 2002.

African Union. 2006. African Peer Review Mechanism—Country Review Report of the Republic of Rwanda, Africa Peer Review Mechanism Secretariat, Midrand, South Africa, June 2006.

African-American Institute. 1992. "Revised Statement of the African-American Institute on the June 21 Elections in Ethiopia", Appendix V in:, "An Evaluation of the July 21, 1992 Elections in Ethiopia", Washington D.C.: National Democratic Institute for International Affairs and African-American Institute, June 25, 1992.

Amnesty International. 2011. "Dismantling Dissent: Intensified Crackdown on Free Speech in Ethiopia". London, 2011.

BBC News. 2004. "From president to prison". June 7, 2004. (http://news.bbc.co.uk/1/hi/world/africa/3728807.stm).

BBC NEWS. 2006. "Ethiopia row over 'massacre' leak" 19 October 2006. http://news.bbc.co.uk/1/hi/world/africa/6067386.stm.

Beaumont, Peter. 2010. "Deadly attacks on Rwandan opposition spark warning by UN". *Observer*, Sunday 18 July 2010.

Carbone, Giovanni. 2005. "'Populism' Visits Africa: The case of Yoweri Museveni and No-Party Democracy in Uganda". *Crisis State Programme*, Working papers series, No.1. December 2005, Development Studies Institute, London School of Economics.

Committee to Protect Journalists. 1996. "Clampdown in Addis: Ethiopia's Journalists at Risk" July 1996.https://cpj.org/reports/1996/07/ethiopia-journalists-at-risk/

Committee to Protect Journalists. 2012. "Attacks on the Press in 2011-Rwanda", https://cpj.org/2012/02/attacks-on-the-press-in-2011-rwanda/

Constitution of the Republic of Rwanda. 2003 https://www.ilo.org/dyn/natlex/docs/ELECTRONIC/64236/90478/F238686952/RWA64236.pdf

Constitution of Uganda 1995. (https://www.ilo.org/dyn/natlex/docs/ELECTRONIC/44038/90491/F206329993/UGA44038.pdf)

Ethiopian National United Front. 1993. *TPLF/EPRDF's Strategies for Establishing its Hegemony and Perpetuating its Rule*, (abridged version of 1993 document, translated from Amharic), Washington D.C. 1993.

EU Election Observation Mission to Ethiopia. 2005. "Legislative Elections 2005 Final Report" European Union 2005.

European Parliament. 2003. Report—"Ad-hoc delegation to observe the presidential election in Rwanda, on Monday 25 August 2003", September 5, 2003.

European Parliament. 2006. "Account of the mission to observe the presidential and parliamentary elections in Uganda 23 February 2006", March 16, 2006.

European Parliament. 2011. "EU Election Observation Mission, Uganda Final Report- General Elections 18 February 2011", March 10 2011.

European Parliament. 2016. "EU Election Observation Mission, Final Report-Uganda Presidential, Parliamentary and Local Council Elections 18 February 2016", April 2016.

European Union. 2018. "Election Follow-up Mission to Uganda, 26 February–17 March 2018", 2018.

Federal Negarit Gazeta. 1991. "Transitional Period Charter of Ethiopia", Addis Ababa, July 22, 1991.
Federal Negarit Gazeta. 1992. "Freedom of the Press" (Article 10) Proclamation No 34 of 1992, Addis Ababa.
Federal Negarit Gazeta. 1995. "Constitution of the Federal Democratic Republic of Ethiopia", 21st August 1995, (Article 39).
Federal Negarit Gazeta. 2008. "Freedom of the Mass Media and Access to Information" Proclamation No. 590/2008 (Preamble).
Federal Negarit Gazeta. 2009a. "Charities and Societies" Proclamation No.621/2009 (Preamble).
Federal Negarit Gazeta. 2009b. "Anti-Terrorism" Proclamation No.652/2009.
France 24. 2010. "Rwanda's presidential elections: Four candidates, but same old policies". August 4, 2010. https://www.france24.com/en/20100804-three-candidates-challenge-kagame-what-looks-like-presidential-election.
Gakusi, Albert-Enéas and Frédérique Mouzer. 2003. *De la Révolution Rwandaise à la contre-révolution: contraintes structurelles et gouvernance 1960-2003*, Paris: L'Harmattan, 2003.
Human Rights Watch. 2003. "Rwanda—Preparing for Elections: Tightening Control in the Name of Unity", Briefing Paper, May 8, 2003.
Human Rights Watch. 1993. "Ethiopia", World Report 1993. New York. (https://www.hrw.org/reports/1993/WR93/Afw-01.htm#P47_21729).
Human Rights Watch. 2008. "Collective Punishment -War Crimes and Crimes Against Humanity in the Ogaden area of Ethiopia's Somali Regional State", New York, June 2008, p.22.
Human Rights Watch. 2010a. World Report 2010—Ethiopia Events of 2009, New York. (https://www.hrw.org/world-report/2010/country-chapters/ethiopia).
Human Rights Watch. 2010b. "Development without Freedom—How Aid Underwrites Repression in Ethiopia". New York, October 19, 2010.
Human Rights Watch. 2016. "Such a Brutal Crackdown—Killings and Arrests in Response to Ethiopia's Oromo Protests". New York, 2016.
International Aid Transparency Initiative (d-portal). http://d-portal.org/ctrack.html?country_code=UG&year_min=2016&year_max=2020&/transaction/transaction-type@code=3#view=donors&year=2017. Accessed 2 May 2024.
International Crisis Group. 2001. "'Consensual Democracy' in Post-Genocide Rwanda—Evaluating the March 2001 District Elections". ICG Africa Report No.34, October 9, 2001, Nairobi/Brussels.
International Crisis Group. 2002. "Rwanda at the End of the Transition: A Necessary Political Transition", ICG Africa Report No.53, November 13, 2002, Nairobi/Brussels.
Kasfir, Nelson. 1998. "African Ambiguities: 'No-party democracy in Uganda'", *Journal of Democracy*, Vol 9, No 2, April 1998.

Keita, Mohammed and Tom Rhodes. 2011. Committee to Protect Journalists, 'In Ethiopia, anti-terrorism law chills reporting on security', June 24, 2011. https://cpj.org/africa/ethiopia/2011/

Lyons, Terrence. 1996. "Closing the Transition: The May 1995 Elections in Ethiopia", *Journal of Modern African Studies*, Vol 34, No 1, March 1996, Cambridge University Press.

Uganda Legal Information Institute. 1997. 'Movement Act 1997'.

National Democratic Institute for International Affairs and African-American Institute. 1992. "An Evaluation of the July 21, 1992 Elections in Ethiopia", Washington D.C., 1992.

New Humanitarian. 2005. "Halt in budget support will affect the poor, says minister". December 30 2005.

OECD Statistics. "Aid (ODA) disbursements to countries and regions". https://stats.oecd.org/Index.aspx?datasetcode=TABLE2A#ns'. Accessed 2 May 2022.

Official Gazette of the Republic of Rwanda. 2002. "Law 18/2002 of 11/05/2002 Governing the Press". Kigali, 2002.

Official Gazette of the Republic of Rwanda. 2003. "Organic Law governing political organizations and politicians, No.16/2003 of 27/06/2003". Kigali, 2003.

Parmelee, Jennifer. 1993. "Ethiopia arrests dissident political leaders", *Washington Post*, December 18, 1993.

République Rwandaise. 2003. *Rapport de la Commission Parlementaire de control mise en place le 27 décembre 2002 pour enquêter sur les problèmes du MDR*. Kigali: National Transitional Assembly, 2003.

Samset, Ingrid and Orrvar Dalby. 2003. "Rwanda: Presidential and Parliamentary Elections 2003". Oslo: Norwegian Institute of Human Rights/ NORDEM. 2003.

Sundaram, Anjin. 2016. *Bad News—Last Journalists in a Dictatorship*, London and New York: Bloomsbury, 2016.

Tigray People's Liberation Front. 1984. "Some Stands of the Marxist-Leninist Core in the Tigray People's Liberation Front", TPLF, May 1984. https://www.marxists.org/history/erol/ethiopia/tplf-ml.pdf.

Tripp, Aili Mari. 2010. "The Politics of Constitution Making in Uganda", in Framing the State in times of transition: case studies in constitution making, Washington D.C.: United State Institute of Peace, 2010.

Tronvoll, Kjetil. 2010. "The Ethiopian 2010 Federal and Regional Elections: Re-Establishing the One-Party State", *African Affairs*, Vol 110, No 438, Oxford University Press, 2010.

U.S. Department of State. 2011. Country Report on Human Rights Practices 2010—Ethiopia. Washington D.C., April 8, 2011.

U.S. Department of State. 2016. Country Report on Human Rights Practices 2016—Ethiopia. Washington D.C.

U.S. Department of State. 2017. Country Reports on Human Rights Practices 2017—Rwanda.

Vaughan, Sarah and Kjetil Tronvoll. 2003. "Structures and Relations of Power—Ethiopia, Background Documents". Stockholm: SIDA, March 2003.

World Bank. World Development Indicators, The World Bank Group, Accessed March 1 2024. http://data.worldbank.org

Young, John. 1997. *Peasant Revolution in Ethiopia*, Cambridge University Press, 1997.

CHAPTER 8

Controlling Economic Liberalisation

Western Pressures for Reform

The prevailing Western view that SSA's economic regression in the 1970s and 1980s had been driven by highly interventionist economic policies, such as manipulation of exchange rates, protectionist trade policies and the operations of large and inefficient state-owned enterprises (SOEs), was one shared by many reform-minded African governments. What was required was the freeing of markets and increased competition through deregulation and the removal of what were seen as state-induced distortions such as marketing restrictions and price controls, the implementation of currency devaluations, the adoption of stricter monetary and fiscal policies, the privatisation of state enterprises, the granting of independence to central banks to focus primarily on the control of inflation and broader programmes of public sector reform. Such prescriptions, embodied in the aforementioned Washington Consensus, therefore centred on the need for states to withdraw from intervening extensively in the economy and to allow market forces to operate freely. Faced with the urgent need to secure Western financial assistance to deal with their increasingly onerous foreign debts, most African governments had little choice but to embark on the necessary reforms.

M. Simpson, *Donors, Democracy and Development in Africa*, https://doi.org/10.1007/978-3-031-74917-9_8

Holding the Line

Under the NRM, TPLF/EPRDF and RPF, Uganda, Ethiopia and Rwanda faced similar economic challenges to those of most African countries and would implement reforms aimed at reducing economic distortions by permitting a greater role for market forces and the private sector as drivers of economic growth. However, these regimes never allowed their economies to become test sites for an undiluted Washington Consensus. They not only shared a strong aversion to political pluralism but also adhered in varying degrees to the Marxist-Leninist tenet that it was economic factors that determined politics, and therefore the need for the state to play a strong role in shaping economic processes such that they aligned to their political interests. Given the risk of autonomous sources of economic power emerging (i.e., ones not beholden to the state and ruling party), and which might in turn become alternative sources of political power, continued and tight control over economic developments was necessary to preserve their monopoly on political power.

Such views were the flipside of their positions on the political 'underdevelopment' of the countries and societies they had inherited. If for various reasons their citizens were judged not ready for full multi-party democracy, so the underdeveloped state of their economies, in particular their weak financial systems and private sectors, required an activist role for the state in the economy. They therefore strongly resisted the small state model advocated by the supporters of what they viewed as fundamentalist 'neo-liberalism'. If capitalism was the only economic system left standing with the end of the Cold War and the demise of communism, in their opinion it was nevertheless the case that only their states had the means to mobilise, control and direct the necessary resources to implement a comprehensive plan for capitalist development, at least until such time as their respective private sectors had matured sufficiently to take on the role of primary drivers of growth.

The regimes in Uganda, Ethiopia and Rwanda were also reluctant to forgo the opportunities for patronage made possible through control of economic resources, and which would be severely restricted by any wholesale implementation of the Washington Consensus reform menu. The nurturing of patron-client relations through dispensing preferential treatment to favoured economic actors and the distribution of largesse at specific moments in the electoral cycles to secure support for the ruling party were features of the neo-patrimonialism seen to be prevalent in Africa. Kampala, Addis Ababa and Kigali thus had to manage Western pressure to replace the economic cronyism of the past with the impersonal state-private sector relations held to prevail in the West, and to liberalise their economies, downsize their states, increase the transparency and accountability of their public financial management systems and reduce levels of corruption.

One way they resisted such pressure was to critique Western demands for wholesale and rapid economic liberalisation, on the grounds these were inappropriate remedies for the economic constraints their countries faced. This went hand in hand with their adoption of a developmental state discourse, promoting this model to Western donors as the only rational alternative to neo-liberalism. Yet another was to advertise their ambitious development visions, and the progress they had already made in terms of improvements in the welfare of their citizens. Taking every opportunity to trumpet their development achievements was mutually beneficial; if their Western benefactors could display these African countries as success stories for their aid programmes, this also reduced their willingness to pressure their African counterparts to meet strict economic conditionalities attached to their aid.

Other instruments could be employed to counter Western blandishments to pursue greater economic liberalisation. Rwanda regularly took advantage of the West's sense of genocide guilt to deflect criticism of aspects of its rule, including on occasion its economic policies. And in the context of a changing post-Cold War international aid and development architecture, these regimes were also adept at capitalising on tensions between competing Western priorities. If on the one hand they often faced strict economic conditionalities from the BWIs, on the other they were able to take advantage of an evolving Western consensus on the need to reform donor-partner country relations, and specifically for donor countries to grant developing countries greater autonomy to determine their development priorities in the form of 'new partnerships'. Together with the appearance of aid delivery mechanisms such as GBS which had fewer strings attached to disbursements, such shifts made it easier for recipient countries to restrict any economic conditionalities tied to new Western grants, loans and debt relief (the latter effectively another form of budget support given it released funds for governments that previously were dedicated to servicing external debt). The three African regimes were thus able to pursue what were unorthodox economic policies when measured against the benchmark of the Washington Consensus list of reforms and maintain a high level of control over their economies as an integral component of their regime preservation efforts.

The Developmental State and Justifications for Economic Dirigisme

The downgrading of democracy promotion as a central objective of Western aid policy from the position it briefly enjoyed in the early post-Cold War period was hastened by a growing interest within both academic and development practitioner circles in the rapid progress made earlier by a group of East and Southeast Asian countries. These shared certain characteristics seen as conducive for the unleashing of very rapid economic growth and structural transformation of their economies, such as highly competent bureaucracies[1] and leaders committed to the realisation of long-term objectives, both of which had provided strong support to their private sectors. This enabled their countries to shift from being predominantly agriculture-based economies, to ones dominated by their manufacturing and/or service sectors, a process accompanied by the adoption of new technologies, increased engagement in higher value-added economic activities and sustained rises in productivity, employment, output and incomes which fundamentally transformed their economies. They developed a strong export-orientation, making rapid gains in terms of international competitiveness and market share for their exports. In addition, they oversaw significant improvements in social welfare indicators such as rapid reductions in poverty rates, increases in life expectancy and levels of schooling, as well as falls in infant and maternal mortality rates.[2] Most significantly, they had achieved this within a relatively short space of time, such progress being achieved over the course of one or two generations. However, and contrary to the Washington Consensus rejection of strong state intervention, they had all adopted varying degrees of activist state-led approaches to development and engaged in various forms of indicative planning[3] and infant industry protectionism.

The economic performance of East Asian countries such as Japan, Korea and Taiwan between the 1950s and 1980s, of Southeast Asian countries such as Singapore which embarked on its rapid growth trajectory in the 1970s, followed by Malaysia in the 1980s and 1990s and that of more recent 'Asian Tigers' such as Thailand and Vietnam were all seen as representative of the phenomenon of 'developmental states'. For Western donors concerned with assisting Africa's development, and for many African governments amongst which the regimes in Kampala, Kigali and Addis Ababa, the possibility of replicating such experiences proved extremely attractive, if not irresistible. Efforts were therefore made to identify the common development constraints these Asian countries had faced, and the solutions applied, which might be transferred to Africa, and thereby justify the provision of development assistance to those countries which committed to replicating such Asian experiences.

For authoritarian African governments, one of the most attractive Asian economic success stories was that of the post-Mao PRC. As a result of Beijing's growing international economic and military power, and its increased activism on the African continent as it projected itself as a valued partner for all developing countries (a market for their exports, source of FDI, development finance and technical expertise), the alternative Chinese development model was one many African governments were increasingly attracted to. In addition to unprecedented economic growth rates and poverty reduction following the launch of its economic reform programme in 1979, the ruling Chinese Communist Party (CCP) also seemed to provide an example of how to reconcile aspects of market economics, stellar economic growth rates and significant social upliftment, with high levels of economic interventionism and zero tolerance towards political dissent, indicating such objectives might be achieved simultaneously.

Two additional developments help explain the growing interest in these Asian development experiences. Firstly, meeting the MDG targets by 2015 placed significant responsibilities on developing country governments, and meant attention had to be paid to the capacity of their bureaucratic/administrative and decision-making bodies. The MDGs helped move the state, and issues related to its responsibilities and capacity to deliver, back into the centre of attention of development practitioners, and this reflected the nature of the Goals themselves. MDGs objectives such as ensuring the provision of basic universal health and education services, the eradication of extreme poverty and hunger, the combating of diseases such as HIV/AIDs and policies aimed at improving gender equality meant the primary responsibility for designing, implementing and coordinating the required activities would lie, if not solely then at least largely, with public institutions.

This went hand in hand with a second development, namely an ongoing re-evaluation of the role of the state in the development process. Following the dominance of a minimalist state paradigm in Western prescriptions on development during the 1980s—reflected in the policy advice contained in both the Washington Consensus and the SAPs overseen by the BWIs—what were seen as the sub-optimal results achieved (particularly in SSA), led to efforts by the 1990s to reassess the state's role in the development process, one strongly informed by the experiences of the Asian success stories and the activist role played by their states.

The World Bank released a report in 1997 which triggered extensive discussions and contributed to a new Western development consensus (World Bank 1997) centred on bringing the state back into focus. The report examined the key features of effective states, such as their governance systems and public agencies, and the optimal relationship between states and markets and non-state actors such as business and private sector actors. According to the World Bank, a re-evaluation of the state's role was needed because the pendulum had swung too far away from the "state-dominated development model of the 1960s and 1970s to the minimalist state of the 1980s" (World Bank 1997, p. 24), and it attributed poor development results, most obvious in the case of Africa, to an indiscriminate rollback of the state and a neglect of its key functions. While in no way entailing abandonment of the market-based reforms it had previously advocated, a new list of public sector institutional reforms was now added, and which came to characterise a new 'Washington Consensus Plus' which aimed to strike the right balance between the state and markets.

The rapid progress of some East and Southeast Asian countries—for extended periods of time many of them under the rule of authoritarian governments in the form of military governments or dominant or single-party political systems—also informed the World Bank's conclusions on the links between democratic practices and development. So, for example, the World Bank noted in its 1997 report that in terms of the relationship between growth and democracy, its researchers had "found no statistically significant correlation between the two" (World Bank 1997, p. 149). Elsewhere in the report, the World Bank came close to endorsing authoritarian practices as a positive factor contributing to the Asian success stories, contrasting the high levels of state effectiveness of the latter with the anti-development combination of both authoritarianism and low levels of state effectiveness in Africa, and which was seen to explain the continent's economic decline:

> [T]he link between authoritarianism and economic decline, so evident in Africa, has been inoperative in Asian countries, largely because of their powerful commitment to rapid economic development, strong administrative capability, and institutionalized links with stakeholders such as private firms, as well as their ability to deliver on the economic and social fundamentals:

sound economic management, basic education and health care, and infrastructure. (World Bank 1997, p. 163)

The Asian combination of both highly effective, development-focused administrations, on the one hand, and their authoritarian practices, on the other, was seen as a winning one, and many African leaders regularly referenced them as examples to be emulated.

Western bilateral donors and the BWIs also came to view such cases of rapid Asian progress as providing both justification and guidance for pursuing particular forms of engagement with African states they identified as potential developmental states. The positive results of the Asian examples therefore seemed to offer a solution to an uncomfortable problem faced by Western donors, namely the unwillingness of their favoured African governments to engage on issues related to the status of political freedoms and civil rights in their countries. A partial solution to the conundrum donors faced was, therefore, to highlight the critical role they themselves played in supporting the achievement of objectives such as the MDGs and improved rates of economic growth, with such development progress helping them explain away their lack of success in terms of pressing for political reforms in their authoritarian partners. This effectively meant that Western support was granted to these regimes based on an unstated trade-off, namely that the fulfilment of economic and social rights manifest in the MDGs, and faster economic growth, was granted greater importance than the advancement of political and civil rights, and on the understanding this was an acceptable one to the West. As the West's favoured 'new leaders' came to promote their countries as developmental states, they were held to merit special consideration given their potential to catalyse and oversee significant economic and social progress notwithstanding (and often according to the leaders themselves, because of) their authoritarianism.

The term 'developmental state' had yet to become common currency in Africa when its 'new leaders' were identified as favoured partners by the West. But in the new millennium, and as they moved to the centre of attention of Western donors, their anointing as leaders of developmental states was a natural and seamless progression. The performance of Ethiopia, Rwanda and Uganda measured in terms of high economic growth rates, accompanied by significant improvements in human development indicators, was deemed by Western donors to be of ground-breaking import for SSA, demonstrating what might be achieved if the correct focus was adopted, if the proper economic and social sector policies were designed and implemented, if good governance principles were adhered to and if the right amounts of external assistance was provided. And such progress enabled Western countries to overlook their serious shortcomings in other areas.

Committing to the Developmental State

Despite Ethiopia's extremely high levels of aid dependency, the TPLF/EPRDF proved to be highly effective in ensuring its positions on economic matters prevailed in the face of Western demands for greater and faster economic liberalisation. This is partly attributable to the fact that Meles Zenawi was comfortable in discussing economic affairs. Whenever granted an international platform, he took the opportunity to put forward his case for the state playing a significant role in Ethiopia's economic development. He went further than either Museveni or Kagame in arguing for the creation of a developmental state, and successfully defended a number of red lines against external pressures to deregulate and privatise specific enterprises and sectors.

The TPLF/EPRDF's case for transforming the Ethiopian state into a developmental one acted as a domestic source of regime legitimisation, one which comfortably sat alongside its political model of Revolutionary Democracy in which the state was also omnipresent. The party regularly put forward its views that only through the building of such an interventionist state could Ethiopia overcome its formidable development challenges. As Meles Zenawi argued, "[D]eveloping countries face formidable market failures and institutional inadequacies which create vicious circles and poverty traps which can be addressed only by an activist state" (Zenawi 2006, p. 9). If there were trade-offs to be made in terms of restrictions on economic freedoms as a result of centralised and authoritarian economic policy-making and implementation practices, this was seen as an acceptable price to be paid for improvements in economic and welfare indicators. In addition, while the historical record showed that the Asian developmental states, which were a source of inspiration for the EPRDF, were all characterised by de jure or de facto single-party or military rule and varying degrees of political authoritarianism, the TPLF/EPRDF argued the Ethiopian variant would be an exception to the rule, able to reconcile both economic and political freedoms in the form of a 'democratic developmental state'.

The timing of the EPRDF's adoption of the model can be linked to its own political fortunes following the 2005 elections. Faced with weakened democratic legitimacy domestically (and criticisms from some of its Western partners for the country's growing democratic deficits), the adoption of 'developmentalism' and in particular the importance attached to rapid economic growth and poverty reduction were components of a strategy to rebuild its credentials. The developmental state was marketed as an instrument to achieve the country's extremely ambitious economic growth and development targets (including the one set by Meles Zenawi that Ethiopia should achieve Middle-Income Country status by 2025). It also provided the ruling party with the means to shift Western donor attention away from its shortcomings in terms of political governance, providing donors with rational arguments to continue supporting the EPRDF to achieve its important development objectives.

Analysis of Meles Zenawi's musings on the subject clarifies what he meant when he argued there was "no reason why a developmental state should necessarily become undemocratic" (Zenawi 2006, p. 14). What he aimed for was a broad national 'consensus' on development issues (similar to the consensus on which the TPLF/EPRDF had constructed its system of political dominance), one in which "politics is confined to dealing with trivialities and personalities" (Zenawi 2006, p. 14). The most prominent feature of such a construct was that it would be headed by a hegemonic party such as the TPLF/EPRDF, acting as a custodian of the national consensus on development issues. Only such a dominant party would be immune to the messy horse-trading and procedural delays in policy formulation and execution associated with elections and democratic transitions, and able to use its position to engage in the long-term planning and wide-ranging reforms required for rapid economic growth and social upliftment. Since policy continuity was essential for sustained and rapid growth, a key requirement was "stable long-term coalitions which stay in power for a long period but do so by democratic means [and which] can provide the needed continuity and stability of policy" (Zenawi 2006, p. 12). In the eyes of the Prime Minister, the existing situation in Ethiopia, updated through the injection of the necessary developmental ambitions, met the requirements for the rise of a democratic developmental state, since the "most likely scenario for a state that is both democratic and developmental to emerge is in the form of a dominant party [such as the TPLF] or a dominant coalition democracy [such as that of the EPRDF and its affiliated parties]" (Zenawi 2006, p. 14).

One key responsibility of such a state would be to capture and centralise the 'rents' enjoyed by individual economic agents, redirecting them to what were seen as more productive uses. The objective was to eliminate "socially wasteful rent-seeking behaviour" (Zenawi 2006, p. 9), seen as an extremely damaging feature of Africa's neo-patrimonial political economies. This required the elimination of 'excess' profits and incomes.[4] An Ethiopian developmental state would target rent-seekers on the grounds they were not only parasitic and economically inefficient but also growth retarding (even if the ruling party's own distribution of largesse was not cast in such negative terms).

Reflecting concerns on the economic power of an autonomous and vibrant private sector might undermine the ruling party's monopoly on patronage and become a source of alternative political power. Meles Zenawi adopted a strong anti-rentier discourse to justify the attitude he believed a developmental state should adopt towards the private sector. The core of the argument was that the state needed to distinguish between the "developmental or rent seeking" activities of private sector actors, and "punish the rent-seeking part and reward the value-creating part" (Zenawi 2006, p. 12). Needless to say, the ruling party would determine what constituted rent-seeking, monopolistic or oligopolistic behaviour, and excessive and undeserved profits, rewarding or punishing private economic agents accordingly.

'Rent-seekers' became a ubiquitous, elastic and convenient catch-all socio-economic category, employed to delegitimise any group of economic actors the ruling party disapproved of. Like its labelling of those opposed to its revolutionary democratic ideology and ethnic federalist political system as variously 'counter-revolutionaries', 'ethnic chauvinists' or 'narrow nationalists', so in the economic sphere 'rent-seekers' were cast as selfish, anti-people and anti-development actors, justifying any restrictions imposed on them.

However, despite the government's efforts to convince Western bilateral donors and the Bretton Woods Institutions (BWIs) that it remained committed to a critical role for the private sector, by 2013 the IMF had concluded that, notwithstanding its repeated undertakings on privatisation, "an economic structure had evolved where the public sector is deeply involved and state ownership is widespread in many activities" (IMF 2013, p. 4). The IMF explicitly linked the relegation of the private sector to a support role, rather as the main driver of economic growth, to the government's adoption of a developmental state model "whereby a proactive public sector leads the development process and the private sector is *oriented* [author's emphasis] to support the development goals" (IMF 2013, p. 4). It also concluded the "dominance of the public sector has meant that the private sector has not contributed as much as it could in the growth process" (IMF 2013, p. 14).

Amongst the government's most significant economic controls were those linked to its consistent refusal to relinquish state ownership of land. Its policy was to all intents and purposes a continuation of the Dergue's which had nationalised all land in 1975, seizing the large land holdings of the feudal elite and granting usufructuary rights to small holders. In an effort to consolidate its position in a predominantly agrarian peasant economy, when it took power the EPRDF promised to guarantee the access of peasants to land without payment, the rationale being framed in terms of the need to prevent them being exploited and displaced by the operations of a land market. During a visit to the US in 1995, Meles Zenawi justified the land policy in terms of the need to protect the Ethiopian peasantry, since land was "the only social security the peasants have" (Marcus 1995).

While disallowing private ownership of land, new legislation would later be introduced permitting its leasing. Yet the central government's control of this basic factor of production remained intact, and it successfully resisted all pressures, both domestic and external, to privatise land. At local level this gave party-state officials enormous powers of patronage, land being one of the many resources of which they were the gatekeepers. Land policy was therefore a critical tool of social control in a context of high levels of land scarcity, and widespread fears of expropriation amongst the peasantry.

Yet when the EPRDF later decided small-scale agriculture as the primary engine of economic growth was not yielding the desired benefits and following the adoption in the mid-2000s of the developmental state model, its attention then switched to the potential of export-oriented and large-scale commercial agriculture which entailed major infrastructure projects and the need to attract foreign investment through tax breaks and subsidised land leases. The scene was thus set for its top-down authoritarian economic decision-making to come to the fore, and the government went on to demonstrate it was prepared to ride rough-shod over the rights of not only regional governments to determine land allocations but also the tenure security of communities.

The government set about implementing an extensive programme of leasing land to both domestic and foreign investors for agricultural and industrial projects. Provisions in the 1995 Constitution, which reflected the ruling party's initial position on the need to proscribe the development of a land market, were largely ignored, and it oversaw what many saw as a legalised and non-transparent form of state 'land grabbing' disguised as development projects, as the ruling party engaged in patronage to the benefit of its supporters.

The Oakland Institute, an American think-tank with extensive experience on land issues in Ethiopia, found that as of 2011 approximately 3.6 million hectares of land had been awarded to investors under generous lease agreements with significant tax incentives (Oakland Institute 2011, p. 18). Furthermore, it also found "[l]arge discrepancies between publicly stated positions, laws, policies and procedures and what is actually happening on the ground". Despite Addis Ababa's insistence that consultations with affected communities had taken place, that no farmers had been displaced and that the land granted had been 'unused', the Institute "did not find a single incidence of community consultation". Significant displacement had occurred, and it reported that "the vast majority of locals receive no compensation" (Oakland Institute 2011, p. 1).

Furthermore, the government's measures also revealed its willingness to ignore its own stated objective of decentralising decision-making which was supposedly integral to its Ethnic Federalist project. The programme of land leases revealed the tension between, on the one hand, the government's use of Ethnic Federalism to neutralise dissident ethno-nationalist sentiments and, on the other, the centralising aspects of decision-making associated with the developmental state model. Its decision to prioritise the needs of investors over those of peasants, and to use its policy of state ownership of land to do so, meant the federal government had in fact re-centralised authority away from regional administrations in order to lease land to investors.

The EPRDF's developmental state, and specifically its land policy, increasingly came to be seen by opposition groups as a means for the ruling party to use its monopoly on economic decision-making to avoid the establishment of open and competitive markets, and to extract resources and concentrate them in the hands of the ruling coalition, and specifically those within the dominant TPLF. The Oakland Institute reported that the translation of the political power of Tigrayans into preferential economic treatment was a widespread practice, as they benefitted from not only privileged access to land being leased but also credit. Rather than tackling speculative rent-seeking behaviour as the EPRDF claimed it wanted to do, the Institute instead found that significant amounts of land transferred to domestic investors had been left idle, or had not been used for the intended purpose, leading it to conclude that land was being held for speculative purposes in the expectation that land markets would eventually be formalised.

In Rwanda, the RPF government also announced ambitious economic growth and development targets and committed to withdraw the state from intervening extensively in the economy, to free markets from regulation, to embark on a programme of privatisations and to support the private sector to take on the role of primary driver of growth. However, as with Ethiopia, there were clear tensions between the RPF's adoption of economically liberal discourse and its desire to exercise strong control over the country's direction of travel on all fronts, including the economy.

The RPF government's long-term vision for the country was launched in 2000. 'Vision 2020' showed the RPF was an early convert to the idea that the desired economic change (embodied in the ambition to transform the country into a technological and knowledge centre of excellence on the continent) needed to be overseen by an effective developmental state. Though at this stage the latter term was not used officially (and was a label more commonly attributed to Rwanda by external commentators and analysts), it was nevertheless clear the objective was to create one, as the realisation of the government's development aspirations were seen to lie in emulating the "development experience of the East Asian 'Tigers'" (Republic of Rwanda 2000, p. 26).

Rwanda's Vision contained a vaulting ambition to achieve Middle-Income Country status by 2020.[5] It also stated that "in order to achieve sustainable development, the private sector will have to become the major engine of growth" (Republic of Rwanda 2000, p. 3). Rehearsing key items in the Washington Consensus, in addition to trade liberalisation, privatisation and market-determined interest and exchange rates, the government would "desist from providing services that the private sector can deliver more efficiently and effectively" (Republic of Rwanda 2000, p. 12). The role of the state would be restricted to that of facilitating the growth of the private sector, and it would "only act as a catalyst; ensuring that infrastructure, human resources and legal frameworks are geared towards stimulating economic activity and private investment" (Republic of Rwanda 2000, p. 18)

Like the TPLF/EPRDF's ideas on the feasibility of creating a 'democratic developmental state', Kigali's Vision argued the Rwandan state would not only be able to reconcile its rapid growth economic model based on private sector growth with the country's aspirations in terms of democratisation, but that the two processes were in fact intimately linked. The line of argument reflected the assumptions of modernisation theory,[6] according to which rapid economic transformation and expansion of democracy walked hand in hand, as "the emergence of a vibrant middle class of entrepreneurs [will] help develop and embed the principles of democracy" (Republic of Rwanda 2000, p. 18).

Furthermore, at a time when the international development agenda increasingly highlighted the importance of popular consultation and participation in the design of development interventions, Rwanda's Vision sought to reassure Western donors the views and interests of citizens would not be ignored in the rush towards rapid economic growth. It therefore emphasised that the government would ensure 'popular participation' at the grassroots level and "that local communities would be empowered in the decision-making process, enabling them to address the issues which affect them the most" (Republic of Rwanda 2000, p. 15).

The decisive test to be applied, and which revealed the RPF's red lines on economic liberalisation, concerned its commitment to the development of a vibrant (and independent) private sector. In accordance with the Washington Consensus prescriptions, interactions between the state and business should be restricted, and the government should not engage in neo-patrimonial patronage (or even when viewed more favourably, 'developmental patrimonialism'[7]), by granting preferential treatment to a targeted group of entrepreneurs.

However, given concerns regarding the possible emergence of powerful economic interests not beholden to the ruling party, the RPF did in fact engage in highly selective clientelist practices, using privatisation and private sector development to shore up the RPF's support base within the country's entrepreneurial class. Business would clearly understand its dependence on the goodwill of the country's political leadership for its profits, and therefore be amenable to responding positively to any demands for support from the ruling party.

Attitudes towards privatisation, liberalisation and the operations of a free market, and how rents were managed, allocated and certain private sector interests excluded, varied according to the specifics of each economic sector and overall economic considerations, but party interests always loomed large. Through its control of SOEs, and those companies it either owned or with which it developed close relations, the RPF set about creating a business elite dependant on the RPF.

Often intense pressure from institutions such as the IMF to adopt market reform, and specifically to privatise SOEs, gave rise to clear tensions "between facilitating rent creation and pursuing an agenda of liberalisation" (Behuria and Goodfellow 2016, p. 3). Behuria and Goodfellow have shown how the RPF managed to navigate the crosscurrents. Their work on the RPF's protection of specific 'nodes' in certain sectors helps throw light on the political considerations informing economic policy, and the evolution of state-business relations and growth dynamics in Rwanda. They drew on the work of Pritchett and Werker, specifically their concept of 'deals environments' in developing countries—the fundamental distinction made being that between 'open deals' available on an impersonal basis between governments and private sector agents, and 'closed deals' which could only be struck by those in the private sector with the necessary political connections (Pritchett and Werker 2013)—and applied this to the liberalisation of a number of economic sectors in Rwanda.

Amongst their key findings were that the country's coffee sector, a 'closed deal' sector under previous regimes, underwent a significant degree of liberalisation under the RPF, with many new traders and exporters entering the marketplace. The government largely restricted itself to regulatory activities in terms of this sector, and therefore as far as coffee was concerned they concluded that while "many individuals who set up companies were closely linked to the RPF, there is no evidence to claim that benefits they received ... would not have been available to other investors" (Behuria and Goodfellow 2016, p. 14). This stood in contrast, for example, to the mining sector, one in which concessions were regularly awarded to individual investors on a non-competitive basis, and which therefore became an industry characterised by 'closed deals', as well as "a good example of a rentier sector" (Behuria and Goodfellow 2016, p. 11).

Rwanda's privatisation programme, launched in 1997, was meant to reduce the burden on the fiscus of SOEs through their sale to domestic and foreign interests, and contribute to the development of the country's private sector. Between 1997 and 2003 a small number of companies were privatised, the pace of privatisation picking up following the establishment of the Rwanda Development Board (RDB) in 2008. The RDB has the broad mandate of ensuring rapid economic growth through private sector growth, including carrying out and monitoring privatisation processes.

This allowed it to take on a role as one of the key actors in the RPF's economic patronage arrangements.

A 2016 report on the country's privatisation initiative was produced by a state institution (Office of the Auditor General of State Finances 2016). Covering the period between 1997 and 2015, it provided copious evidence of the intrusion of 'closed deal' considerations into the exercise and raised uncomfortable questions for a regime which sought to project itself, both domestically and externally, as a leader in terms of applying 'good governance' principles such as transparency and accountability in its Public Financial Management, its anti-corruption stance and the professionalism of the country's civil service. The audit report identified a series of breaches of established procedures by the RDB. These included its non-participation in the identification of several companies to be privatised and its failure to monitor the performance of privatised companies in line with its responsibility to support private sector development. It detailed cases where companies were privatised without a reference value having been established, and others sold at values below the reference value. But possibly the most significant evidence of a 'closed deal' environment and clientelism were observations it made concerning the non-receipt by the RDB of payments from investors in some privatised enterprises, "for a period ranging from 6 to 10 years" (Office of the Auditor General of State Finances 2016, p. 3), and deviations from established privatisation procedures in instances of companies sold to investors "without competition" (Office of the Auditor General of State Finances 2016, p. 2).[8]

While Kigali made strenuous efforts to portray Rwanda as 'open for business' and emphasised its commitment to apply international 'best practices' for market-led growth, the reality, however, was that the RPF's approach to the development of free markets and the private sector was a highly selective one. It was able to sustain a 'closed deals' environment in the areas of privatisation, while simultaneously winning plaudits for its apparent economic liberalism.

Many upbeat views of Rwanda's economic progress since the genocide have been attributed to the RPF's adoption of a strongly interventionist state. Any 'developmental patrimonial' measures, such as centralisation, accumulation and subsequent allocation of rent opportunities, are seen as linked to its pursuit of supposedly economically rational growth-oriented criteria (and efforts to 'crowd in' other private sector players). Scholars such as Booth and Golooba-Mutebi have drawn a connection between the country's economic progress and the RPF's direct involvement in the private sector. The regime's developmental patrimonialism is thus seen to have been beneficial for economic growth and development, and on that basis Rwanda is put forward as a model developmental state worthy of emulation (Booth and Golooba-Mutebi 2012).

Others have critiqued such a positive narrative. Mann and Berry have argued that as the RPF advanced its economic 'modernisation' project and sold to Rwandans the need for development and the important roles played by entrepreneurship and markets, its predisposition for centralised decision-making and control of economic activity has had significant negative consequences. As it sought to shape capitalist accumulation "it had a specific vision of what types of markets are acceptable" (Mann and Berry 2015, p. 31), and restrictive views on the kinds of private entrepreneurship it considered admissible and compatible with its ambition to transform the country into a technological and knowledge hub in Africa. So, for example, in a country where the informal sector dominates economic transactions, and informal activities are the main sources of employment and livelihoods, the RPF's desire to project an image of modernity has led to regular harassment of informal sector operators. The burden has fallen, in particular, on women who are disproportionately represented in the informal sector workforce and dominate activities such as street vending which have been made illegal.

By ensuring the current political-military elite enjoy close, if not incestuous, relations with an entrepreneurial class created by the RPF (to the point where these groups are often indistinguishable), the country's business elite has been compelled to respond to the political interests of its benefactor. Rather than spearheading a growing national product and economic diversification, the RPF's control over the private sector has constrained the development both of a more competitive free market and of a larger and more efficient private sector. As economic power has become increasingly concentrated in the hands of a few large party-affiliated and party-owned enterprises, so they have come to dominate a small formal private sector. An enterprise census conducted in 2011 showed that only 5.2 per cent of all enterprises in the country were formal (the figure including state-owned enterprises), the remainder being composed of informal micro and small enterprises (National Institute of Statistics of Rwanda 2011, p. 156). A follow-up census in 2020 revealed only a small rise in the percentage of formal enterprises to 7.4 per cent of all enterprises (National Institute of Statistics of Rwanda 2020, p. xi). This was hardly the stellar rate of progress in terms of the growth in the number of formalised enterprises which might have been expected given the government's declared commitment to economic liberalisation and private sector growth.

In the case of Uganda, and like the TPLF/EPRDF and RPF, the NRM inherited a devastated economy. The predatory activities of the Amin regime and other former presidents such as Obote, protracted civil wars, the exodus of the country's entrepreneurial class with the expulsion of the country's Asian community, the flight of other skilled nationals and general institutional and infrastructural decay, all contributed to a rapid decline in sectoral output, imports, exports and GDP per capita,[9] and then by the mid-1980s to the final collapse of the Ugandan economy. The NRM faced the unenviable tasks of both restoring political stability and national security and having to plan and implement comprehensive post-conflict economic recovery. It had to do while also having to consider the demands of Western development agencies (the BWIs foremost amongst these) for economic liberalisation. Given the parlous state of the country's public finances, and its high levels of dependence on Western aid, it was clear its room for manoeuvre on economic policy would be extremely restricted.

In 1987, the new government adopted the first of a series of World Bank and IMF-supported SAPs. The Economic Recovery Programme (ERP) focused on the urgent restoration of macro-economic stability and implementation of structural reforms to reverse negative growth rates. Measures included devaluation of the currency and tighter controls of the monetary base, fiscal discipline through tightening expenditure, rationalisation of the public sector workforce and improvements in Public Financial Management, liberalisation of the export and import sectors and domestic trade, deregulation of the financial sector and the restructuring and divestiture (sale or liquidation) of public enterprises.

Mirroring the later economic reform programmes of Ethiopia and Rwanda, one of NRM's declared aims was to reduce government interventions in the economy and nurture competition and free markets to enable the private sector to become the main engine of economic growth and source of employment. In a letter requesting support from the World Bank in July 1987, Uganda's Minister of Finance stated that the NRM government would "continue to rely on markets and is committed to maintaining a policy environment free from unnecessary price fixing and control" (World Bank 1987, Annex 1 p. 5).

In a retrospective of its efforts in terms of private sector development, the government's 'National Strategy for Private Sector Development' of

2017 felt able to claim that ever since taking power the NRM government had placed the private sector "at the forefront of the growth and development process of the Country" (Republic of Uganda 2017, p. ii). It committed to continue supporting the development and growth of private companies through measures ranging from the provision of infrastructure, further trade liberalisation, facilitating access to credit and encouraging FDI, additional legal and regulatory reforms to improve the business environment and investments in the upgrading of the skills of the workforce.

For the NRM, one of the difficulties presented by its adoption of an SAP in 1987 had been how this might be reconciled with the strong suspicion of markets expressed in its 1984 Ten-Point Programme. The latter had called for an interventionist state and greater economic self-sufficiency. While it had argued for a "mixed economy", which meant "allowing the majority of economic activities being carried out by private entrepreneurs", and rejected copying the "over nationalisation of the socialist economies", at the same time it had warned of the dangers of the "laissez-faire of pure capitalism". In an attempt to square the circle, and given its belief the state should be allowed to "guide the economy as a whole", amongst its specific proposals were that the state should control imports and exports on the basis of "licensing with very clearly defined priorities", "commercial banking so as to control the loaning policy" and "ownership of certain basic industries like iron and steel" (National Resistance Movement 1986, p. 15).

Despite its early views on economic matters, once it took power the NRM government set about implementing the bulk of the orthodox economic remedies prescribed by the BWIs. And the results of the ERP, and its 1993 successor programme the Rehabilitation and Development Plan, were positive; if in 1985 (the year before it took power), GDP growth had been −3.3 per cent, by 1986 it was back in positive territory (World Bank 2024). Annual GDP growth over the 1990s averaged a robust 7 per cent, even though a high population growth rate meant per capita GDP growth was a much lower 3.4 per cent (World Bank 2010, p. 2). Inflation, which had stood at 100 per cent in 1985, and peaked at 215 per cent in 1987, was also slowly brought under control, and by 1995 had fallen to 6.8 per cent (IMF 2024). Uganda quickly came to be regarded as another committed economic reformer and applier of Western economic reform advice. Flows of Western donor and BWI development assistance reflected such positive assessments of progress, over two decades increasing from US$192 million in 1986 to US$1.7 billion by 2007 (World Bank 2010, p. 15).

In parallel with its economic recovery, scholars began to attribute developmental state status to Uganda. The government's commitment to the 'fundamental change' Museveni had announced in his 1986 inauguration speech, and the positive results of the economic recovery programmes, showed Kampala's determination to channel its administrative capacity and resources to achieving clear development objectives. Its strong focus on poverty reduction, evidenced in the fact that Uganda was the first country to have developed a PRSP in the form of its own Poverty Eradication Action Plan (PEAP) of 1997, also contributed to such positive impressions.

One notable aspect of the country's economic recovery was the new government's abandonment of specific forms of predatory behaviour, most notably the gradual dropping of a policy pursued by previous governments to impose punitively high taxes on the country's exports (primarily agricultural products). An easy way of capturing revenue, this unsurprisingly had a negative impact on both output and export levels. While the new government was slower in terms of its abolition of import taxes, its overall policy of tariff reduction meant that by the end of the 1990s Uganda had one of the lowest tariff structures in Africa. This was accompanied by other trade liberalisation measures, most notable in the case of coffee (the country's major cash crop export), with the ending in the early 1990s of the state-owned Coffee Marketing Board's monopoly on processing and exports, and which led to better prices for producers and increased output and exports.

In the early 1990s, the government also embarked on the privatisation of public enterprises, entities notorious for constituting a major drain on public finances, and the site of corrupt practices and patronage. In 1987 the World Bank had emphasised the urgent need to privatise them, noting that most public industrial enterprises were "operating below 20 percent capacity, and two thirds have been making losses for an extended period of time" (World Bank 1987, p. 21). Amongst the objectives of the privatisation exercise was that their sale would constitute a source of urgently needed revenue for the government. Other objectives included improving efficiency in those to be restructured and retained as public enterprises, with an emphasis on greater accountability for performance and adoption of a commercial orientation and financial self-sufficiency. Competitors to SOEs were not to be restricted from entering the market, while those

SOEs operating in natural monopolies would be subjected to increased oversight to ensure greater efficiency.

According to a 2001 World Bank study, by 1999 the government had completed its divestiture of a total of ninety-three enterprises, of which sixty-two had been privatised (a significant number being sold to foreign investors), and the remainder liquidated. The same study opined that in most cases "privatization led to increased output and efficiency, higher tax payments, significant new investment, and some job creation" (Collier and Reinikka 2001, p. 37). Yet at the same time, and bearing strong similarities to the Rwandan experience, the extent to which the ruling party had taken the opportunity presented by its privatisation drive to construct a 'closed deals' environment was also flagged, the study referencing

> stakeholder perceptions ... that the process through which the firms were sold was perceived to have been corrupt ... shortcomings included ... lack of broadly based ownership of the program and transparency in a number of transactions, and the executing agency's failure to collect payment from buyers. (Collier and Reinikka 2001, p. 38)

Research by David Kibikyo into the privatisation of a number of enterprises, and their beneficiaries, led him to conclude that the President had used the divestiture process to "enrich party supporters, his relatives, [and] Asian investors" (the latter group benefitting from Museveni's efforts to attract back to Uganda those expelled by Amin by returning their confiscated properties), and that a number of SOEs had been "undervalued and sold to cabinet ministers, presidential advisers ... and Members of Parliament" (Kibikyo 2009, p. 18). Kibikyo also referenced the views of media and opposition figures who believed such divestitures were not only part of a wider strategy of power retention, but also attributed the government's apparent preference for foreign investors compared to local investors to the fact that "in a crisis, the former were likely to support the government in power in order to protect their investments, unlike the latter that could ally with the opposition to change government" (Kibikyo 2009, p. 19).

The phenomenon of 'closed deals' was also examined by Muriisa Roberts. He catalogued a series of problems which included regular accusations of foul play during tendering such as the payment of bribes to ministers, senior army officers and members of the President's family to influence the outcomes of sales. He noted concerns expressed by members of Parliament that there had been "little transparency in the activities of the Privatisation Unit", most particularly surrounding the undervaluation of SOEs which had been sold "at give-away prices" (Roberts 2005, p. 131).

In 2007 the country's own public agency with regulatory responsibilities in this area reported violations of the legal framework governing public procurement, with only 33 per cent of processes conducted using open tendering and therefore competitive bidding (Public Procurement and Disposal of Public Assets Authority 2007). After its earlier positive reviews of Uganda progress since 1986, by 2010 the World Bank was pointing out a number of issues tarnishing the country's image, foremost amongst which rising levels of corruption. It highlighted problems with public procurement and the development of a 'closed deals' environment which undermined transparency and stifled the growth of free markets and development of a competitive private sector. It referenced a review conducted by the AU which had noted that "petty and high-level corruption are prevalent and affect every institution in the country, and are most rife in *procurement*, *privatization* [author's emphasis] ... [and that] few if any high-level officials involved in major corruption scandals have been tried" (World Bank 2010, p. 11), and situated the problem in the wider context of the weakening of Uganda's economic governance environment.

Regime-strengthening and Party-Business Empires

With economic transactions taking place behind closed doors in all three countries, of all aspects of TPLF/EPRDF, NRM and RPF economic governance it is their relations with business which are some of the most opaque. They constitute one of the clearest examples of how these regimes successfully built up their power bases by securing the loyalty of key economic actors. All three regimes established 'party-statals', commercial enterprises they owned and directly controlled. These became their 'business empires', operating in what were effectively parallel economies. As a result of the significant preferential treatment party-statals received from political elites, they came to occupy dominant positions within their respective economies, acting as a source of employment for party members, the security forces and civil servants. Given the close ties they enjoyed with SOEs and other private concerns, they could also be used as levers to influence the wider economy and shape the development of the private sector to their advantage.

Most importantly, they represented sources of reliable independent finance for their political masters, and their operations fell outside the purview of PFM systems. Given the significant costs of running party machineries, such financial flows from party-controlled enterprises supplemented the advantages of incumbency which ruling parties already enjoyed as a result of their control of the state apparatus and state resources. Thanks to 'closed deal' environments, these firms could themselves benefit disproportionately from state procurement processes, public monies representing another source of funds which could then be channelled to their political masters and their economic power could be deployed in interactions with other private sector enterprises (both domestic and foreign) to leverage additional support for the ruling party, including funding in the form of regular 'donations'.

In the case of Ethiopia, the TPLF/EPRDF set up businesses in sectors ranging from construction, road haulage to mining and finance, and encouraged other parties within the EPRDF coalition to do the same. Regarding the TPLF's own companies, shares and management positions were held by party members, on the understanding they were to act on behalf of the TPLF. In 1995 these enterprises were consolidated into a single umbrella vehicle, the Endowment Fund for the Rehabilitation of Tigray (EFFORT), with senior positions dominated by members of the TPLF's politburo and central committee and the EPRDF government. In terms of commercial law, this transformation into an endowment allowed the TPLF to claim EFFORT was now a legally separate entity from the Front. However, close ties between those occupying senior positions in EFFORT companies and those holding political power in Ethiopia, and the fact EFFORT responded to the political and economic agenda of the Front, were both open secrets and further proof of the gradual extension of the ruling party's reach into all walks of national life (Weis 2015/16). Above all, what the conglomerate provided the TPLF/EPRDF were the means for it to indulge its predilection for the centralisation of rents and top-down planning and fulfil its plans to intervene in the private sector and strengthen its role as the vanguard of development. The EFFORT conglomerate became the largest 'private' investor in the country. Given its regional focus on Tigray, it also became associated with a particular form of privileged ethnic entrepreneurship, fuelling growing resentment of Tigrayan dominance amongst other ethnic groups.

By the late 2000s, it had become clearer what had taken place in terms of private sector development and market liberalisation in Ethiopia; a

World Bank report of 2009 noted that amongst firms it had interviewed there was "an impression that endowment and state-owned enterprises benefit from privileged access to policymakers and resources and are consequently able to compete on unfair terms" (World Bank 2009, p. 50).

In Rwanda, the RPF also proved adept at reconciling Western donor pressure for improvements in the investment climate and growth of the private sector with its interest in building its own business empire. Central to the RPF's efforts was Tri-Star Investments, subsequently renamed Crystal Ventures Ltd (CVL), a holding company wholly owned by the RPF. Tri-Star/CVL would, directly or through its majority share ownership of other companies, go on to secure significant market share in many sectors of the economy. It enabled the ruling party to determine how economic rents were centralised and then employed to help secure the RPF's rule, creating a private sector deeply beholden to the RPF. Together with other 'private' companies owned by the country's armed forces, these enterprises also played leading roles in the pillaging of the neighbouring DRC's natural resources in the wake of Rwanda's successive interventions in that country (see Chap. 11).[10] As with Uganda and Ethiopia, and in line with the logic of illiberal state-building, the overall aim was to create a strong support base bringing together political, military and economic elites based on shared interests, most importantly that of enhancing the regime's security, with Kagame at the apex of the decision-making pyramid and able to determine who gained economically, when and how.

Booth and Golooba-Mutebi, sympathetic to the developmental patrimonial argument that enterprises such as Tri-Star/CVL enabled the centralisation of rents, thereby reducing the opportunities for corruption, and that their activities led to progress in key sectors which would otherwise not have obtained, nevertheless also recognised that the RPF's campaign funding needs were, at least in part, met through Tri-Star's profits. However, they viewed the latter in positive terms, arguing it had "the side-effect of removing pressure on the ruling party to raise political funds by methods that involve fraud, kickbacks, or other corruption", though they nevertheless conceded that those who viewed such practices from "the angle of democratic ideals may well find it unfair that an already dominant political party can finance its activities in this way" (Booth and Golooba-Mutebi 2012, pp. 391–392).

The RPF's development of a 'closed deals' environment and centralised economic control required extensive window dressing. Nilgün Gögkür has argued that any positive views on progress made on privatisation should be tempered by the fact that while the government did sell off a number of SOEs, contrary to its declared intention to diminish the role of the state in the economy, it then simultaneously established a raft of new ones, while in the case of those that were privatised, the regime's party-statals became the new owners, such that they have "replaced the former SOEs, under the guise of having been sold to private owners and operators" (Gögkür 2012, p. 16).

Such non-transparent privatisation practices were common knowledge, both inside and outside the country. *The Economist* reported in 2017 that the RPF "does more than help business: it runs its own conglomerate", that CVL had funded half of the RPF's 2010 election campaign and that together with its sister holding company controlled by the Ministry of Defence they get "cushy government deals which mask the failure of their enterprises, several of which are said to be loss-making" (*Economist* 2017). As recently as its 2020 'Investment Climate Statement' on Rwanda, the US State Department reported that "the financial performance of most SOEs is only detailed in an annex [of the national budget] that is not publicly available", and that "SOEs are governed by boards with most members having other government positions" (U.S. Department of State 2020).

Contrary to the argument that such RPF 'party-statals' played positive developmental and private sector enhancement roles, the protection they have enjoyed has been detrimental to the development of an open market and stymied the entry of new competitors and growth of a broader private sector (notwithstanding repeated government commitments to the promotion of SMEs). As a result, privatisation processes since the 1990s, intended as far as the Western donors were concerned to lead to significant reductions in levels of state intervention in the economy and market-led growth spearheaded by an independent and wider private sector, have been manipulated to secure continued government control over the economy, even if the means used have been indirect ones. And this aspect of the ongoing entrenchment of the RPF regime has been facilitated by what has been called a "shared concealment" (Mann and Berry 2015, p. 33) on the part of Kigali and its Western partners, the former using its hold on the private sector to strengthen its political control, while the latter are able to present a development success story which is attributed to the country's apparent adoption of their liberal economic prescriptions.

In Uganda, the NRM adopted similar measures to those of the RPF and TPLF/EPRDF as it set about creating its own business empire. This involved the establishment of NRM-affiliated companies, ensuring that specific roles were played by SOEs which favoured the ruling party, managing private sector development in ways which facilitated the NRM's access to non-public resources, and that these efforts collectively responded to regime-strengthening imperatives.

As in Rwanda and Uganda, an early opportunity for shaping this pillar of the NRM's regime-supporting architecture presented itself through Uganda's privatisation process. Tangri and Mwenda have shown the latter was quickly plagued by accusations of lack of transparency and favouritism in the sale of assets, and that it had allowed the concentration of economic power in the hands of a new elite with close ties to the NRM, and in particular Museveni's family members (Tangri and Mwenda 2001). By 1998 the World Bank, a provider of technical assistance for the privatisation initiative, was expressing concerns about the programme, observing that it was "widely criticised for non-transparency, insider dealing, conflict of interest and corruption", and that "questions have been raised about the use of funds in the divestiture account" (World Bank 1998, p. xi).

The regime's use of its links to business to support its political financing needs, particularly during elections and referenda, has been well documented. One method of ensuring the NRM's elections war chest was filled was that of providing favours to specific businesses, such as tax exemptions, concessional loans and preferential treatment in state procurement processes. As noted by Tangri and Mwenda, "[B]y extending assistance to specific companies of the politically well-connected, Museveni was able to cultivate individual businessmen who were personally indebted to him, and who were a source of campaign finance at election time" (Tangri and Mwenda 2013, p. 110).

One novel instrument used by Museveni referred to above, and which distinguished his approach from that of his Ethiopian and Rwandan counterparts, was to nurture Ugandan Asian companies, its owners having benefitted from the government's invitation to return and reclaim their properties, in exchange for which they made 'voluntary contributions' to the NRM's election war chest. The NRM's likely calculation was that the growth of these Ugandan Asian enterprises did not represent a political threat; their economic power was unlikely to translate into a political challenge given their sense of vulnerability to persecution and expulsion which would, despite the passage of time, still have run deep within this group of entrepreneurs. If anything, should the NRM be under threat, the logic would have been for those Asian companies to rally in support of the government to protect their investments.

To secure revenue streams it could control more directly, in the run-up to the 1994 Constituent Assembly election campaign, senior NRM figures established trading companies. These would enjoy a range of privileges not available to other companies, and in return profits were channelled to the NRM. Other components of the NRM's business empire included its control of the country's remaining SOEs. These were not only used as cash cows but also as sinecures to be granted by Museveni to important regime supporters such as senior military figures. In addition, the NRM's encouragement of military entrepreneurship meant the UPDF was granted the right in 1989 to establish its own state-owned commercial enterprise, the National Enterprise Corporation (NEC). This engaged in activities ranging from agriculture to construction and pharmaceuticals. Its board is dominated by senior military figures, and its chair, appointed in 2018, was a UPDF Lt. General and former Presidential advisor on Defence. The preferential treatment it had received from the state in the context of a 'closed deals' environment, and the uneven playing field faced by its private sector competitors, was made clear in September 2021 when the State Minister for Investment and Privatisation announced that all future local government and schools construction contracts would be awarded, without competitive tendering, to the UPDF's NEC. And the Chair of the NEC expressed his gratitude to President Museveni for this decision, highlighting the fact that amongst the advantages of such a 'closed deal' arrangement was that there would be "no whistle-blowers to raise investigations to stall the process" (*Real Muloodi News Network* 2021).

All three regimes were able to entrench their authoritarian governance practices by structuring their political and economic systems so as to strengthen their ability to fend off Western pressures for both democratic and market reforms. However, their high levels of aid dependency also meant they had to remain attentive to, and continually responsive to, changes in Western development interests and priorities. This required them to continually update and market their development ambitions and achievements in order to retain their status as leaders committed to leading their peoples onto the path of peace and development after decades of regression and repression under previous regimes, and on the basis of which they had received Western approval in the 1990s. And as with the tactics they adopted to counter Western demands such as liberalisation of their economies, when donors pushed for improvements in terms of popular participation and decentralisation as a means to improve development outcomes and accountability, similar ways were found to manage such Western pressure.

Notes

1. The positive performance of the Asian Tigers, and the prominent role played by their bureaucratic elites, generated an interest in the role of core state economic agencies in the growth equation. On the various causal paths connecting the quality of those bureaucracies' performance and economic growth, see Evans and Rauch (1999).
2. By way of example, amongst the later generation of Asian Tigers, Malaysia saw the percentage of its population in extreme poverty, that is, those living below the PPP-adjusted US$1.90 a day metric, fall dramatically from 2.9 per cent to 0.4 per cent over the two decades 1984–2004, while Thailand witnessed an even more impressive decline in the incidence of extreme poverty: its poverty headcount dropping from 19.3 per cent of the population to 0.7 per cent between 1981 and 2004 (World Bank 2024). Between 1980 and 2000, Malaysia's infant mortality rate (number of infants dying before the age of 12 months per 1000 live births in a given year) fell from 25.2 to 8.7, and Thailand's fell from 46.7 to 18.7. Over the same period, life expectancy in Malaysia rose from 68.1 years to 72.5 years and in Thailand from 64.4 years to 70.6 years (World Bank 2024).
3. Detailed indicative planning, such as that practised by the Asian Tigers, often took the form of sectoral industrial policies. These involved the identification of specific industries and sectors which were encouraged to expand, with output targets being set and plans for the relevant support to be provided. Such plans and targets created a set of expectations which firms could rely on, and reduced the element of uncertainty for corporate decision-making, with firms thereby more willing to undertake investments, increase production and achieve the growth targets set by governments.
4. The essence of 'rents' is that these constitute 'excess' profits and income derived from, for example, ownership of assets such as land, rental properties and shares and bonds, or the enjoyment of monopolistic advantages, access to preferential subsidies or the fruits of corruption. Such rent-seeking behaviour is contrasted with the 'normal' profits accruing to enterprises and individuals operating in open and competitive markets.
5. Despite significant progress between 2000 and 2020, this target was missed due to lower than expected GDP growth and high population growth. However, rather than postponing the deadline for achievement of the required GDP per capita for Rwanda to be considered a Lower Middle-Income Country, the next iteration of the Vision introduced an even more ambitious target, namely reaching Upper Middle-Income Country status by 2035, and High-Income Country status by 2050 (Republic of Rwanda 2020, p. 9).

6. In the late 1950s and early 1960s, American modernization theorists suggested a positive correlation between levels of socio-economic development and democracy. The emergence of democracy was brought about by changes in class structure (in particular the emergence of a bourgeoisie), rising levels of urbanisation, education and literacy, and as a result of these increased demands for rights and representation from both the bourgeoisie and a growing industrial working class.
7. What are seen as 'relationship-based' or 'clientelist' economic governance practices are normally associated with extensive and unproductive rent-seeking, corruption, waste, low levels of investment and growth rates and lack of economic transformation. The central premise of developmental patrimonialism, however, is that in certain circumstances patrimonial practices can generate rapid economic growth, economic transformation and significant poverty reduction. The proper management of rent opportunities by the holders of political power—more specifically their centralisation and subsequent targeted distribution by a development-oriented political leadership in accordance with a long-term planning horizon—can result in positive development outcomes. In other words, certain kinds of neo-patrimonialism, and the management of certain kinds of rent (the important distinction being that between growth-promoting and growth-retarding rents), can yield positive development results. This is particularly so in economies with weak private sectors, low levels of domestic and foreign investment or those recovering from prolonged conflict. So, for example, growth-promoting rents include those created by the erecting of tariffs and other barriers to specific imports to protect an infant industry from competition while it is absorbing new technology and methods of production, and which subsequently enable it to grow and adopt an export-orientation. For a useful discussion of the concept, and its application to a group of Asian and African examples, see Kelsall and Booth (2010).
8. It is noteworthy that in its response to this specific audit observation on cases of lack of competitive bidding, the Rwanda Development Board (RDB) confirmed that this had not taken place in six out of a total eighty-seven privatizations. Without providing explanations for this lapse, the RDB simply responded to the finding by stating that "[g]oing forward, we shall improve to make sure public calls for competitive bidding is respected" (Office of the Auditor General of State Finances 2016, p. 22).
9. One source estimated that between 1971 and 1986 per GDP per capita fell over 40 per cent (Collier and Reinikka 2001, p. 9).
10. In the UN's 2001 report on the illegal exploitation of the DRC's mineral wealth, a Tri-Star subsidiary, Rwanda Metals, was named as one of a number of Rwandan companies engaged in such activities. In line with the RPF's logic of rent centralisation, the report noted that "all key managers

have personal relationships with different army commanders who themselves report to the leadership. This pyramidal and integrated structure, coupled with the strict discipline of the group, has made the exploitation of the resources of the Democratic Republic of the Congo more systematic, efficient and organized" (UN 2001, p. 17).

References

Behuria, Peter and Tom Goodfellow. 2016. "The political settlement and 'deals environment' in Rwanda: unpacking two decades of economic growth", ESID Working Paper No 57, University of Manchester, 2016.

Booth, David and Frederick Golooba-Mutebi. 2012. "Developmental patrimonialism? The case of Rwanda". *African Affairs* Vol 111, Issue 444, July 2012.

Collier, Paul and Ritva Reinikka. 2001. "Reconstruction and Liberalization: An Overview" in Paul Collier and Ritva Reinikka (Editors). 2001. *Uganda's Recovery—The Role of Farms, Firms and Government.* Regional and Sectoral Studies, Washington D.C.: World Bank, 2001.

Economist. 2017. "Party of Business: The Rwandan Patriotic Front's Business Empire" March 4, 2017.

Evans, Peter and James Rauch. 1999. "Weberian Bureaucracy and Economic Growth: A Cross-National Analysis of the Effects of "Weberian" State Structures on Economic Growth", *American Sociological Review*, American Sociological Association, Vol 64, No 5, October 1999.

Gögkür, Nilgün. 2012. "Rwanda's ruling party-owned enterprises: Do they enhance or impede development", Discussion Paper/2012.03, University of Antwerp: Institute of Development Policy and Management, October 2012.

International Monetary Fund (IMF). 2013. "The Federal Democratic Republic of Ethiopia—Selected Issues". Washington D.C.: IMF Country Report No.13/309, October 2013. https://www.imf.org/external/pubs/ft/scr/2013/cr13309.pdf (Accessed 4 May 2024).

International Monetary Fund (IMF). 2024. "Country Data, Uganda: Inflation rate, average consumer prices (Annual percentage change)" https://www.imf.org/en/Countries/UGA (Accessed 2 May 2024).

Kelsall, Tim and David Booth. 2010. "Developmental Patrimonialism? Questioning the orthodoxy on political governance and economic progress in Africa", Working Paper No 9, London: Africa Power and Politics Programme, Overseas Development Institute, July 2010.

Kibikyo, David L., 2009. *Assessing privatization in Uganda*, Denmark: Roskilde University, 2009.

Mann, Laura and Marie Berry. 2015. "Understanding the political motivations that shape Rwanda's emergent developmental state", London School of

Economics Research Online, 2015. https://doi.org/10.1080/13563467.2015.1041484.

Marcus, Harold. 1995. "A Breakfast Meeting with Prime Minister Meles", Michigan State University, 20 October 1995. http://hartford-hwp.com/archives/33/008.html. Accessed 4 May 2024.

National Institute of Statistics of Rwanda. 2011. Establishment Census 2011, Rwanda.

National Institute of Statistics of Rwanda. 2020. Establishment Census 2020, Rwanda

National Resistance Movement (NRM). 1986. *The Ten-Point Programme.* Kampala, Uganda, 1986.

Oakland Institute. 2011. *Understanding Land Investment Deals in Africa: Ethiopia*, Oakland, CA, 2011.

Office of the Auditor General of State Finances. 2016. *Performance Audit Report on Strategic Management of Privatization Activities.* Government of Rwanda, May 2016.

Pritchett, Lant and Erik Werker. 2013. "Developing the guts of GUT (Grand Unified Theory): Elite commitment and inclusive growth". ESID Working Paper No.16, University of Manchester, 2013.

Public Procurement and Disposal of Public Assets Authority. 2007. "A Report on the Compliance and Performance Indicators for the Uganda Procurement System", Final Draft Report, Kampala, August 2007.

Real Muloodi News Network. 2021. "UPDF Will Handle All Local Construction Projects", September 4, 2021. https://realmuloodi.co.ug/updf-will-handle-all-local-construction-projects/ (Accessed 2 May 2024).

Republic of Rwanda. 2000. *Rwanda Vision 2020.* Kigali: Ministry of Finance and Economic Planning, 2000.

Republic of Rwanda. 2020. *Rwanda Vision 2050.* Kigali: Ministry of Finance and Economic Planning, December, 2020.

Republic of Uganda. 2017. "The National Strategy for Private Sector Development 2017/18-2021/22". Ministry of Finance, Planning and Economic Development, Kampala, 2017.

Roberts, Muriisa. 2005. "The Privatization Experience in Uganda: Prospects and Challenges in its Implementation" *in* Pamela Mbabazi and Ian Taylor (eds). 2005. *The Potentiality of 'Developmental States' in Africa: Botswana and Uganda Compared*, Dakar: CODESRIA, 2005.

Tangri, Roger and Andrew Mwenda. 2001. "Corruption and Cronyism in Uganda's Privatization in the 1990s", *African Affairs*, Vol 100, No 398, January 2001.

Tangri, Roger and Andrew Mwenda. 2013. *The Politics of Elite Corruption in Africa: Uganda in Comparative African Perspective*, Routledge, 2013.

The World Bank Group. World Development Indicators, *World Bank*, Databank (2024).
U.S. Department of State. 2020. "2020 Investment Climate Statements: Rwanda", Section 7 State-Owned Enterprises. 2020. U.S. Department of State webpage: https://www.state.gov/reports/2020-investment-climate-statements/rwanda/ (Accessed May 4 2024).
United Nations. 2001. "Report of the Panel of Experts on the Illegal Exploitation of Natural Resources and Other Forms of Wealth of the Democratic Republic of Congo (S/2001/357)", 12 April 2001.
Weis, Toni. 2015. "Vanguard Capitalism: Party, State and Market in the EPRDF's Ethiopia", Thesis submitted for the degree of Doctor of Philosophy in Politics, Exeter College, University of Oxford, Michaelmas 2015/16.
World Bank. 1987. "Report and Recommendation of the International Development Association to the Executive Directors on a proposed credit of SDR 50.9 million and a proposed African Facility credit of SDR 18.8 million to the Republic of Uganda for an Economic Recovery Program", Washington D.C.: World Bank, August 19, 1987.
World Bank. 1997. *The State in a Changing World*, World Development Report 1997, N.Y.: Oxford University Press, 1997.
World Bank. 1998. "Recommendations for Strengthening the Government of Uganda's Anti-Corruption Programme". Poverty and Social Development, Africa Region, Washington D.C.: World Bank. November 1998.
World Bank. 2009. "Ethiopia Toward the Competitive Frontier—Strategies for Improving Ethiopia's Investment Climate", Washington D.C.: World Bank, June 2009.
World Bank. 2010. "Country Assistance Strategy for the Republic of Uganda for the Period FY 2011–2015", Washington D.C.: World Bank, April 27, 2010.
Zenawi, Meles. 2006. *African Development: Dead Ends and New Beginnings*, Preliminary Draft, 2006. http://www.ethiopiantreasures.co.uk/meleszenawi/pdf/zenawi_dead_ends_and_new_beginnings.pdf. Accessed May 4 2024.

CHAPTER 9

Ambition, Authoritarianism, Participation and Decentralisation

Visions and Results

All three African countries had leaders who skilfully marketed their ambitious development visions for international audiences. This was an important precondition for Western donor support; the level of ambition of a partner country's development plans, and in particular its focus on poverty reduction, coupled with a track record of being able to deliver on commitments, constituted key factors in determining the extent and nature of Western development assistance.

Rwanda's development aspirations were contained in the already referenced Vision 2020 document, and the government's goal to transform Rwanda from a low- to medium-income country within two decades easily passed muster in terms of ambition criteria. The intended final destination of Rwanda's post-genocide development roadmap could be summed up as its transformation from a poor, aid-dependant, predominantly agrarian economy reliant on the production and exporting of coffee and tea into one dominated by internationally competitive, knowledge-based economic sectors, and with significantly reduced levels of poverty and major improvements in health and education (Republic of Rwanda 2000).

Kigali's pronouncements on the kind of state needed to oversee Rwanda's transformation would also have been well received by the Western donor community, with the Vision document stating that to achieve its ambitious goals what was required was "an effective state"

M. Simpson, *Donors, Democracy and Development in Africa*,
https://doi.org/10.1007/978-3-031-74917-9_9

which would be "capable of formulating and implementing policies that will lay the foundations for private sector growth" (Republic of Rwanda 2000, p. 3). Western capitals would also have taken note of the government's intentions on the governance front, in particular its commitment to practising 'good governance', which in line with prevailing understandings was defined in restrictive instrumental terms as "accountability, transparency and efficiency in deploying scarce resources". But in a nod to the political values of Western donors, Vision 2020 also argued that a state which practised good governance was "respectful of democratic structures and processes and committed to the rule of law and the protection of human rights in particular" (Republic of Rwanda 2000, p. 15).

During its first decade in office, the RPF government was able to demonstrate both seriousness of intent and an ability to deliver on its promises to turn the country's fortunes around and improve the welfare of its citizens. On both the economic and social fronts, progress was plain for all to see (though as noted in Chap. 12, some of the achievements claimed by Kigali would be queried on the grounds of both the questionable quality of data used and its manipulation by the government). The country's GDP (in current US$) was reported to have more than doubled from a low of US$754 million in 1994 (the year of the genocide) to US$2.07 billion by 2000 (World Bank 2024). In 1993, the year before the genocide, GDP per capita (in current US$) had stood at US$249; in 1994 this had collapsed to US$112. However, over the course of a decade the Kagame government oversaw a process of economic growth, which by 2004 had restored GDP per capita to US$270. And over the next decade between 2004 and 2014, this grew to US$724 per capita, an increase of 168 per cent (World Bank 2024).

There was also rapid progress in critical welfare indicators. Life expectancy at birth showed improvement, increasing between 1993 and 2002 from 42 years to 50 years (World Bank 2024). The country's adult literacy rate also improved between 1991 and 2000, rising from 57.8 per cent to 64.8 per cent.[1] Between 1995 and 2004, the infant mortality rate fell from 129 to 73 per 1000 live births (World Bank 2024), and the child mortality rate was reduced even more dramatically from 221 to 119 per 1000 live births.[2]

Such rapid positive development outcomes (regularly trumpeted by Kigali) not only made it easier for Western donors to explain to home audiences why they were supporting such a highly authoritarian African government, but they also provided Kigali with a means to blunt Western pressures for political reforms. Highlighting the connection between the country's development progress and the latitude granted to Kigali by Western countries regarding its widely known poor record on political and civil rights, one reporter commented, "It is easy to see why other African leaders look enviously at what Kagame has achieved. He can not only boast development statistics that his peers can only dream of, but he also gets away with the routine human rights abuses that everyone else is so regularly censured for" (Allison 2017). Such occultation was succinctly captured by a representative of HRW at a 2015 hearing of the US House of Representatives Foreign Affairs Subcommittee Hearing on Developments in Rwanda:

> Because Rwanda is held up as an all too rare model of successful development in Africa, the focus stays there, to the exclusion of all else. The repressive domestic environment has been treated as an ancillary problem—or not treated at all—for the most part because, it seems, it is just too difficult to reconcile with the positive narrative. (Human Rights Watch 2015)

Ethiopia also came to be seen in Western eyes as a developmental state led by a visionary leader, a country which had embarked on an extremely ambitious development programme and left behind its notorious history of protracted civil wars and devastating famines. The ruling party's aspiration to create an Ethiopian developmental state which would oversee rapid economic growth, with the poor as the main beneficiaries, always featured prominently in government documents, with its 2002 PRSP emphasising the need for such a state to oversee "the envisaged socioeconomic transformation in Ethiopia" (Federal Democratic Republic of Ethiopia 2002, p. 48).

The government's grandiose long-term development vision was reiterated in a follow-on document launched in 2006, namely the Plan for Accelerated and Sustained Development to End Poverty (PASDEP) (Ministry of Finance and Economic Development 2006). If Western donors required the plans of their partner governments to be not only visionary, but also aspirational, neither element was lacking given the government's forecast that over a twenty- to thirty-year timeframe its policies would result in an "increase [in] per capita income of citizens so that it reaches the level of those in middle-income countries" (Ministry of Finance and Economic Development 2006, p. 44).

Ethiopia had suffered from extremely poor per capita growth rates in the 1980s—reaching a nadir in 1985 with a negative per capita growth of close to −14 per cent. However, over the decade 1995–2005 its GDP per capita (in current US$) grew modestly but steadily from US$137 to US$160 and then increased rapidly to reach US$758 per capita by 2017 (World Bank 2024). It also registered marked progress on the non-income dimensions of deprivation which featured prominently in the MDGs and the successor SDGs. Foremost amongst these was the infant mortality rate, which fell from 81.7 per 1000 live births in 2002 to 42.6 in 2015 (World Health Organization (WHO) 2024). In the field of basic education, it also reported the desired progress in line with Western donor priorities. One key indicator used to track progress in this area was that of the gross primary school enrolment rate;[3] in the case of Ethiopia, this increased over the two decades between 1995 and 2015 from 30 per cent to 97 per cent (World Bank 2024).

Uganda initially saw slow but nevertheless positive growth in GDP per capita (in constant US$) between 1992 and 2002, rising from US$152 to US$242. Thereafter, however, it experienced rapid growth, such that by 2015 its GDP per capita had increased to US$864. It made rapid progress in infant mortality reduction, which declined from 79 deaths per 1000 live births in 2002 to 39.2 by 2015 (World Bank 2024). Uganda's primary school enrolment rate also rose, from 69.2 per cent in 1995 to 135.4 per cent in 2003 (World Bank 2024).

Increasing economic growth rates were seen by Western donors as a precondition for achieving their other central objective, namely poverty reduction, and the latter was used by Western bilateral development agencies as a proxy for the effective use of their funds. The leaders of Uganda, Ethiopia and Rwanda would not disappoint their Western partners in terms of both their poverty reduction aspirations and their recognition of the importance of economic growth in achieving poverty targets.

Ethiopia's PRSP of 2002 committed to Goal 1 of the MDGs to halve the proportion of people living below the extreme poverty threshold of US$1.00 a day, unequivocally stating that poverty reduction was "the core objective of the Ethiopian government" (Federal Democratic Republic of Ethiopia 2002, p. 36). Presiding over one of the world's lowest incomes per capita (estimated at US$100 per capita), and with an absolute poverty rate of 44 per cent in 1999/2000 (based on the country's own national poverty line rather than the internationally comparable daily US$ per capita rate), it undertook to reduce the latter to 40 per cent by 2004/2005

(Federal Democratic Republic of Ethiopia 2002, p. 155). Furthermore, recognising that achieving its poverty reduction objectives required "enhancing rapid economic growth", it also set out to achieve a real average annual GDP growth rate of 7 per cent over the period (Federal Democratic Republic of Ethiopia 2002, p. 42).

Rwanda's first PRSP of 2002 pointed out that, notwithstanding significant progress since the genocide, poverty continued to affect an estimated 60 per cent of the population in 2000 (Government of Rwanda 2002, p. 13). The approach to poverty reduction adopted by the government was one based on rapidly increasing the economic growth rate to between 7 and 8 per cent per annum (Government of Rwanda 2002, p. 29). This was expected to result in the proportion of those below the poverty line falling to 25 per cent by 2015 (Government of Rwanda 2002, p. 31).

Uganda's PRSP of 2000 also set an ambitious target of reducing the country's absolute poverty headcount to 10 per cent by 2017, down substantially from an estimated 44 per cent in 1997 (Government of Uganda 2000, p. 10). The Museveni government made clear to Western interlocutors it recognised that economic growth (and the employment creation which accompanied it) was an essential precondition for poverty reduction, and it targeted an annual GDP growth target of 7 per cent over the PRSP's timeframe (Government of Uganda 2000, p. 18).

All three countries reported significant progress on poverty. Ethiopia—in the consciousness of many in the West the very poster child of African destitution during the 1980s—saw its extreme poverty headcount fall dramatically from 69 per cent in 1995 to 27 per cent by 2015. Rwanda, with an extreme income poverty headcount of 75 per cent in 2000, reported this had fallen to 60 per cent by 2010. Rapid progress was also achieved by Uganda, which saw a fall in the incidence of extreme poverty from 68 per cent in 1999 to 38 per cent in 2012 (World Bank 2024).

Taken together with their progress on other human development indicators, such advances in poverty reduction lent credence to claims the 'new partnerships' between Western donors and these African countries were yielding the desired results. Such visible returns on their investments also seemed to validate the Western donor emphasis, shared with its African partners, on the importance of good governance practice defined largely in apolitical technical terms as the fundamental prerequisite for achieving such gains. Any shortcomings in terms of political or economic liberalism could then easily be considered being of secondary importance.

Development Progress, Justifying Authoritarianism and Contrary Evidence

During their early days in power, Kagame, Zenawi and Museveni often asserted that competitive multi-party democracy was not an appropriate political system for their societies and certainly not an urgent matter. Priority had to be given to preserving peace and national unity as essential preconditions for their post-conflict reconstruction and development plans. In addition, all three regimes argued the success of their recovery programmes, and progress on ambitious objectives such as the MDGs, required not only a long-term focus on targets and delivery but also an absence of distractions and sudden changes in policy and political leadership which they associated with multi-party democracies. Not only was the centralisation of power essential to enable rapid decision-making and strong oversight of implementation, but given the scale of the challenges their countries faced, it also required a monopoly on political power by a single actor capable of overcoming resistance from vested interests to critical reforms. In other words, what was required was a replication of the political conditions associated with the authoritarian regimes which had overseen many of the Asian success stories they admired. The argument thus posited a trade-off between broader and deeper democracy, on the one hand, and faster and better development and preservation of national unity, on the other.

The RPF regime explicitly linked development and the safeguarding of national unity as overarching and paramount national objectives, which helped it rationalise its attitudes towards political dissent:

> The regime's position that poverty is the cause of conflict...[this] means that development becomes a justification for the policing and curtailing of dissent, and thus a further means for maintaining a monopoly of power at home. (Mann and Berry 2017, p. 20)

To disagree with RPF policies was therefore to be anti-development, and any repressive measures it implemented were cast in terms of not a desire to perpetuate its hold on power, but rather the need to fulfil the more worthy development goals it sought for the country, which according to the regime's Vision 2020 document reflected "ambition and imagination in overcoming poverty and division" (Republic of Rwanda 2000, p. 2).

Meles Zenawi wrote extensively on such matters while in office. In regard to the tensions between the imperative of development-focused policy continuity and democracy. Though he also argued that the two might be reconciled by the TPLF/EPRDF, he summarised well the argument often put forward to justify authoritarian developmental states:

> Development policy is unlikely to transform a poor country into a developed one within the time frame of an election cycle. There has to be continuity of policy if there is to be sustained and accelerated economic growth. In a democratic polity uncertainty about the continuity of policy is unavoidable...It is argued therefore that the developmental state will have to be undemocratic in order to stay in power long enough to carry out successful development. (Zenawi 2006, p. 12)

These African leaders believed a hard choice had to be made (one they had already made on behalf of their peoples), in terms of the priority to be granted to the developmental or democratic aspects of their governance. The social contract they claimed to have struck with their populations was one in which transformative rates of economic growth, rising incomes and better health and education services, were provided in exchange for acceptance of political stability defined as maintenance of the political status quo. The transaction was based on the foregoing of competitive and free and fair multi-party elections and the opportunity to change political leadership, for the sake of more jobs, less poverty, improved services, and peace and stability.[4]

Yet leaving aside the normative point that democracy facilitates participation and human choice, and that freely elected governments are more likely to enact policies which best reflect the interests of the electorate, it is important to note that more recent empirical research—part of the longstanding debate on causal relations between democracy and growth—has helped counter the argument that democratic regimes are less capable of triggering and managing economic growth than authoritarian ones. The evidence also contradicts the more extreme position presented by authoritarian states, namely that democracy in fact acts as a hindrance to economic growth. So, for example, the seminal work of Daron Acemoglu and his colleagues, using data from a large panel of 175 countries over a fifty-year period (from 1960 to 2010), was able to show that "democracy does cause growth and that its effect is significant and sizeable" (Acemoglu et al. 2019, p. 48). Given the poverty levels in the three African countries, the results of their research also undermined an argument often advanced by their ruling parties, namely that democratisation needed to be postponed until their countries reached a certain level of income. Significantly, their findings enabled them to conclude that "democracy does not have a negative effect for countries with low income levels" (Acemoglu et al. 2019, p. 93).

Controlling Participation and Decentralisation

Reflecting the Western focus on poverty reduction as the overarching international development objective, in the late 1990s PRSPs became the principal development planning document used by donors and aid recipient countries and around which agreements were reached as to the priority areas which would be supported by Western ODA. One prominent feature of their production process was the emphasis placed on the need for extensive consultations to determine the extent and nature of poverty, as well as the priority needs of target groups on the basis of which poverty reduction measures could be designed and implemented. More specifically, consultations were seen as a means of not only improving the targeting of resources, but in line with Paris Principles they would also strengthen country ownership and accountability by giving citizens a 'voice' in public affairs in PRSP countries.

In their assessment of Uganda's PRSP, on the basis of which Kampala would be granted significant amounts of debt relief, World Bank and IMF staff were effusive in their praise of the consultations which had taken place during its preparation, judging them to have been "highly participatory and transparent processes". This resulted in improved prioritisation and targeting of poverty reducing public expenditures and also "a measure of public accountability for the spending choices made by the government" (IMF and IDA 2000, p. 3).

Addis Ababa also quickly grasped the importance attached by Western donors to consultations and participatory processes. It emphasised the extent to which its PRSP was the product of popular consultations which it characterised as "extensive, inclusive and transparent", carried out in the presence of donors, the press and NGOs who "independently monitored the various consultations" and submitted "positive reports". It also took the opportunity to stress that the results of the consultations confirmed the correctness of "the broad development strategy, sectoral and cross-sectoral priority actions followed by the government" (Federal Democratic

Republic of Ethiopia 2002, p. 31), thus strengthening the government's hand in its negotiations with the donor community.

Ethiopia's first PRSP was also favourably assessed by the BWIs in terms of the consultations component, which were seen as "deep and wide-ranging" and "open and free of interference by the government or the ruling party" (IMF and IDA 2002a, p. 2). The staff of both BWIs therefore concluded the PRSP "provides a sound basis for World Bank and Fund concessional assistance...[and recommended] that the respective Executive Directors of the World Bank and IMF reach the same conclusion" (IMF and IDA 2002a, p. 10).

In the case of Rwanda's PRSP, in 2001 the country's stakeholders were invited to attend a national workshop to comment on an initial draft. This event was preceded by a Participatory Poverty Assessment, during which local communities were given an opportunity to identify solutions to the challenges they faced. Together with the circulation of draft versions of the PRSP amongst both national and international actors, the feedback received through such participatory processes was held by Kigali to have "greatly enriched the final document" (Government of Rwanda 2002, p. 12).

Kigali's commitment to pursue poverty reduction policies and ensure that measures implemented were based on such prior consultations meant the final assessment by the BWIs of its PRSP was also extremely positive. The World Bank and IMF noted the document "reaffirms the commitment of the government to sustainable poverty reduction", while "participation in the PRSP process and sense of ownership are impressive" (IMF and IDA 2002b, p. 1).

The importance attached by Western donors and the BWIs to consultations and participation in poverty reduction efforts went hand in hand with the increasing attention paid to decentralisation in Western donor discourse and praxis. 'Going local' was presented as a solution to many of the inefficiencies associated with planning and service delivery in developing countries and a way of countering centralising and dirigiste tendencies. According to the World Bank's PRSP manual, the fundamental change brought about by decentralisation would be a downward shift in accountability, whereby "households can turn to locally elected leaders to demand better public services" (World Bank 2002, p. 280). Local governments would be more responsive to the needs of communities (and in particular the poor), and this would result in improved allocative efficiency through better matching of local public expenditure patterns with local preferences, improved accountability and reduced corruption.

For this to happen, local communities had to benefit from not only administrative decentralisation, that is, the transfer of planning and implementation responsibilities from central government to subaltern administrative units, but also fiscal decentralisation, that is, the granting of revenue raising and expenditure autonomy, as well as political decentralisation. According to the World Bank's PRSP manual, political decentralisation implied "transfers [of] policy and legislative powers from central governments to autonomous, lower-level assemblies and local councils that have been democratically elected by their constituencies" (World Bank 2002, p. 322). All three forms of decentralisation were seen as complementary and needed to take place simultaneously if national poverty reduction efforts were to be responsive to the specific needs of the poor. If successful, and given the priority attached to poverty reduction, this also reduced any pressures felt by Western donors to continue pushing for national-level democratic reforms amongst their African partners as a precondition for their ODA.

The governments in Kampala, Addis Ababa and Kigali drew selectively upon such arguments to support their authoritarianism. They regularly insisted that the voices of their peoples could more appropriately be heard through means other than solely the representatives of independent political parties in national legislatures elected through competitive multi-party elections. The local-level participatory structures they established were portrayed as forms of direct democracy and were more relevant to the state of development and the pressing welfare and security needs of their countries.

The NRM had always committed to ensuring the voices of the Ugandan people could be appropriately heard. While its 1984 Ten-Point Programme had referenced the need for parliamentary democracy, much greater emphasis was placed on the need to introduce 'people's power' through the transfer of its experience with 'people's committees' in its liberated zones to a post-conflict Uganda. By giving people a voice at the local level, these bodies reduced the need for multi-party democracy, since not only could they "deal with each level's local affairs…but, above all, they would be political forums to discuss relevant issues concerning the whole country…They would be a channel of communication between the top and the bottom" (NRM 1986, p. 4).

The Ugandan government committed to pursue decentralisation through the gradual transfer of responsibilities to the district level. As local council office bearers came to be directly elected, this allowed Kampala to claim that the "democratisation of Uganda has been pursued in a context of decentralisation" (Government of Uganda 2000, p. 15), even though at the time the activities of political parties remained restricted.

Decentralisation also featured prominently in Ethiopia's PRSP and was marketed as a means to improve the efficiency, responsiveness and accountability of state programmes at the local level, thereby enhancing their impact on poverty. Over and above its policy of Ethnic Federalism, which at least on paper granted the country's federated regional ethnic states substantial autonomy, the government also framed additional decentralisation in terms of strengthening and deepening the process of democratisation, with the planned transfer of powers (including revenue raising and expenditure powers), from the federal and regional governments to locally elected governments at *woreda* (district) and *bekele* (municipality) levels. The granting of greater autonomy to lower levels of government would be carried out with the "objective of deepening the democratization process and bringing about improved governance", which in turn had already "helped create peace and stability in Ethiopia" (Federal Democratic Republic of Ethiopia 2002, p. 108).

Decentralisation also featured prominently in Rwanda's PRSP and was likewise depicted as strengthening the country's democratic governance structures. The national decentralisation policy of 2001 had spoken of the need to reverse the centralisation of power during both the colonial and post-colonial periods which had resulted in "inappropriate, highly centralised dictatorial governance" and "excluded the Rwandese population from participating in the determination of their political, economic and social well-being" (Republic of Rwanda 2001, p. 3).

To counter this, the Kigali government engaged in the rolling out of what it called 'democratic decentralisation'. This involved mobilising Rwandans to participate in the management of their own affairs, with the decentralisation policy document highlighting the fact that there had already been "elections at the *Akagari* [village] and *Umurenge* ['sectors'] levels in 1999 as part of the democratisation process" (Republic of Rwanda 2001, p. 6). Its PRSP argued Rwanda's decentralisation programme would help achieve a number of other developmental objectives on the Western donor checklist, namely create "a sense of local ownership of public programmes...[allow] local Governments to respond to local needs…[and] increase the accountability of Government to the people" (Government of Rwanda 2002, p. 62).

However, the praise lavished by the BWIs on the consultative and decentralisation initiatives launched by Addis Ababa, Kampala and Kigali failed to take account of the extent to which ruling parties were able to make their presence felt at local level and thereby ensure the outcomes they desired. Since a clear framework for PRSP consultations was lacking, let alone a precise definition of what constituted participation, the glowing reviews of this component by the three governments, and the validations forthcoming from the BWIs, should be treated with scepticism. The careful selection of those invited to attend consultative events, and the fear of speaking out in a repressive political system, meant it was unlikely that any substantive discussions took place which might have altered the existing plans of central government.

Consultations, participation and decentralisation could, and were, manipulated in accordance with ruling party interests. One example can be seen in the efforts of the EPRDF to manage consultative and decentralisation processes following the violent 2005 elections. There was initially tough talk from Western donors in response to the government's violations of political, civil and human rights. Those engaged in providing budget support to the Ethiopian government (the UK, Canada, Ireland, Germany and Sweden), together with a number of multilateral organisations (the World Bank, the EU and the African Development Bank), had come together to form the Development Assistance Group (DAG), and before the end of 2005 the DAG announced it would be reviewing its assistance to Ethiopia. It was reported that members were planning to withhold a total of US$375 million in budget support funds and were willing to apply political conditionality to their assistance to secure, *inter alia*, the release of political detainees and the lifting of restrictions on the press and freedom of assembly imposed after the elections (Reuters 2006).

However, threats of punitive and lasting cuts in overall aid flows went unfulfilled. What happened instead was the redirecting of budget support funds to programmes which were supposed to afford greater donor control over the use of these resources, as well as promote decentralisation and consultative mechanisms to improve development outcomes.

Most prominent amongst the novel programmes set up by the Western donor community was the 'Protection of Basic Services' (PBS) programme. Approved in May 2006, and implemented by the World Bank with significant bilateral donor contributions, the PBS sought to address donor concerns about the EPRDF's use of budget support funds to shore up its political hegemony. The rationale put forward by the World Bank for the PBS was that "in an increasingly divided environment, a new instrument was needed to ensure that resource flows to local authorities could be protected from political capture through an enhanced set of checks and balances" (World Bank 2006, p. 3). It aimed to do so by ensuring that funds to the federal government were then channelled to subaltern administrative units at district and village levels, where they would be used for sector-specific activities in health and education, agricultural extension, and water and sanitation. Beneficiaries were to be identified based on consultations and needs assessments of communities and households.

However, at the same time the PBS was being designed, the EPRDF was strengthening its systems of control to prevent a recurrence of the previous year's closely fought elections. A detailed report subsequently produced by HRW, and based on extensive field work, showed how successful the regime had been in boosting its control mechanisms. It found that Western development assistance resources, channelled through programmes such as the PBS, were in fact being widely used by local officials affiliated with the ruling party as both carrots and sticks to control the population, with criteria such as the political affiliation of beneficiaries applied to discriminate between individuals. It concluded that "donor funded services, resources and training opportunities were being used as threats and rewards for citizens to join the ruling party and cease supporting the opposition" (Human Rights Watch 2010, p. 26). It was clear—assuming that one of the objectives was to weaken central government and ruling party control over aid resources—that Western donors had failed to grasp the extent to which the TPLF/EPRDF party-state had extended its presence down to the local level:

> The strategy of providing funds to district government rather than to the federal government was seen as a way to avoid political risks. But giving money to district governments carried exactly the same risks. While Ethiopia's national government created the repressive policies, district governments actually implemented them; meanwhile, foreign donors found it hard to monitor and detect misuse of funds at the local level. (Human Rights Watch 2010, pp. 20–21)

Or if donors were aware of such developments, other considerations trumped such concerns, and the result was that any withholding of ODA turned out to be a very temporary measure. Like its counterparts in Uganda and Rwanda, who also proved adept at riding out occasional Western opprobrium, the EPRDF government benefited from an apparent compact of silence between Addis Ababa and many Western capitals, based on the understanding that the latter's concerns regarding the state of political and civil liberties in Ethiopia would not be prioritised over development progress. What also became apparent over time was that even the latter would come to be treated as a secondary consideration as a result of a meeting of minds between the three regimes and Western capitals regarding common security threats and the appropriate responses required. The regimes in Uganda, Ethiopia and Rwanda were again able to position themselves so as to benefit from this new Western focus, one which provided them with additional means to tighten their grip on power by enhancing their capacity to deploy deadly force against domestic and external opponents.

Notes

1. The indicator measures the percentage of people aged fifteen years and over who can read, write and understand a simple statement about their everyday lives.
2. The child mortality rate measures the probability of dying before reaching age five years per 1000 live births.
3. This indicator measures the ratio of total enrolment of children, regardless of age, to the population of the age group that officially corresponds to the level of education. Therefore the possibility of the ratio exceeding 100 per cent if there is a large presence of overage children in each primary school grade.
4. The argument was that precisely because of the downgraded importance assigned to human rights and democratisation, gains in development were possible, and that a 'right to development' (often framed in terms of a 'full belly') could only be delivered by an authoritarian state, and this trumped the 'luxury' of civil and political rights.

References

Allison, Simon. 2017. "Like it or not, Rwanda is Africa's future", *Mail and Guardian*, July 7, 2017. https://mg.co.za/article/2017-07-07-00-like-it-or-not-rwanda-is-africas-future/. Accessed 2 May 2024.

Daron Acemoglu et al. 2019. "Democracy Does Cause Growth", *Journal of Political Economy*, Vol 127, No 1, University of Chicago, 2019.

Federal Democratic Republic of Ethiopia. 2002. Ministry of Finance and Economic Development, Ethiopia: Sustainable Development and Poverty Reduction Program, July 2002, Addis Ababa.

Government of Rwanda. 2002. Poverty Reduction Strategy Paper, Ministry of Finance and Economic Planning, June 2002.

Government of Uganda. 2000. Uganda's Poverty Eradication Action Plan: Summary and Main Objectives, Ministry of Finance, Planning and Economic Development, March 24, 2000, Kampala.

Human Rights Watch. 2010. Development without Freedom – How Aid Underwrites Repression in Ethiopia, New York: HRW, October 2010. https://www.hrw.org/report/2010/10/19/development-without-freedom/how-aid-underwrites-repression-ethiopia https://www.hrw.org/report/2010/10/19/development-without-freedom/how-aid-underwrites-repression-ethiopia

Human Rights Watch. 2015. "Human Rights Watch Testimony at House Foreign Affairs Subcommittee Hearing on Developments in Rwanda", 20 May 2015. https://www.hrw.org/news/2015/05/20/human-rights-watch-testimony-house-foreign-affairs-subcommittee-hearing-developments

IMF and IDA. 2000. Uganda – Poverty Reduction Strategy Paper, Joint Staff Assessment, March 31, 2000.

IMF and IDA. 2002a. Ethiopia - Poverty Reduction Strategy Paper, Joint Staff Assessment, August 27, 2002.

IMF and IDA. 2002b. Rwanda - Poverty Reduction Strategy Paper, Joint Staff Assessment, July 18, 2002.

Mann, Laura and Marie Berry. 2017. "Understanding the political motivations that shape Rwanda's emergent developmental state". London School of Economics Research Online, November 2017.

Ministry of Finance and Economic Development. 2006. *Ethiopia: Building on Progress – A Plan for Accelerated and Sustained Development to End Poverty* (PASDEP) (2005/06-2009/10), Volume 1: Main Text, Addis Ababa, September 2006.

National Resistance Movement (NRM), The Ten-Point Programme, Kampala, Uganda, 1986.

Republic of Rwanda. 2000. *Rwanda Vision 2020*. Kigali: Ministry of Finance and Economic Planning, 2000.

Republic of Rwanda. 2001. National Decentralisation Policy, Ministry of Local Government and Social Affairs, May 2001.

Reuters. 2006. "Donors to withhold $375 million from Ethiopia". December 29, 2006.

WHO, Global Health Observatory, World Health Organization, Geneva. Accessed 10 March 2024.

World Bank. World Development Indicators, The World Bank Group, Accessed August 2 2024. http://data.worldbank.org

World Bank. 2002. *A Sourcebook for Poverty Reduction Strategies*, Vol.1: Core Techniques and Cross-Cutting Issues, Washington D.C.: World Bank. 2002.

World Bank. 2006. *Interim Country Assistance Strategy for the Federal Republic of Ethiopia*, Washington D.C: World Bank. May 1, 2006.

Meles Zenawi. 2006, *African Development: Dead Ends and New Beginnings*, http://www.ethiopiantreasures.co.uk/meleszenawi/pdf/zenawi_dead_ends_and_new_beginnings.pdf

CHAPTER 10

Development Assistance and the West's Changing Security Agenda

From the Red Peril to African Transnational Threats

In the wake of the September 9, 2001 (9/11), attacks on the US, followed by other terrorist incidents in Europe, the West's ensuing global 'War on Terror' meant national security objectives aimed at countering a new set of threats featured prominently in the West's policy towards Africa. During the Cold War, they also came to play a decisive role in decision-making on development assistance. If fears of the spread of communism had shaped the Africa policy of Western powers during the Cold War, its place was now taken by the problem of fragile states linked to the emergence of an Islamist threat in SSA.

Signs of reassessment of Western security interests in Africa were already apparent before 9/11. A few months after Bill Clinton had completed his tour of African countries and given his blessing to the continent's new leaders, the Islamist threat was brought home to the Americans in the clearest possible manner. On August 7, 1998, the US embassies in Nairobi and Dar es Salaam were the targets of simultaneous truck bomb attacks, subsequently claimed by Al-Qaeda and its affiliates.

The rise of a new ideological adversary operating in Africa was linked to the substantial number of fragile, failed and conflict-affected states on the continent. Now, in a post-9/11 world, these states were seen to suffer from extensive 'ungoverned spaces'; characterised by the severely

M. Simpson, *Donors, Democracy and Development in Africa*,
https://doi.org/10.1007/978-3-031-74917-9_10

deficient, or total absence, of formal state institutions, extreme deficits in health and education provisioning as well as public security and the rule of law, these were seen to constitute threats to global security, ideal breeding grounds for Islamic terrorist groups in Africa which used such states as springboards for their operations inside and beyond the continent.

Consequently, increasing Western attention was paid to fragile African states and those African countries willing to join the West in countering this terrorist threat and stabilising their respective neighbourhoods. It led to the growth of policy-relevant academic research in the West on the phenomenon of terrorism, and its links to fragile and failed states in Africa.[1] This went hand in hand with analysis of those obstacles impeding the better integration of Western defence, development and diplomatic policies in counterterrorism activities.

One result of these new Western concerns was the rapid securitisation of development assistance to Africa, as well as a significant increase in Western resources available for security-related programmes. Uganda, Ethiopia and Rwanda all came to benefit from this new focus. And as relations deepened between Western donor countries and the three African regimes based on security cooperation, their Western benefactors came to view them as important allies and were even more disposed to overlook their violations of the political and civil rights of their citizens and of international law in regard to their behaviour towards their neighbours.

Donors and the Securitisation of Development

In addition to the need to combat security threats to the West posed by terrorist groups based in aid beneficiary countries, the securitisation of development, that is, the linking of security concerns to the objectives and targeting of development assistance (and more specifically the prominence of the national security objectives of donor and recipient countries in aid programmes), was rationalised in terms of the creation of the necessary conditions for development. This was the main argument deployed by both Western donors and countries benefitting from securitised aid, to justify the merging of security and development objectives. Aid, if properly designed and appropriately targeted, could therefore meet the security and development interests of both donors and aid recipients, and this new thinking spread rapidly throughout the Western donor community.

While the expansion of the definition of development assistance led to increased resource transfers to the military and broader security sectors of developing countries, this was hardly a radical departure from the practice of major Western powers during the Cold War, when aid disbursements had also been linked to geopolitical and security considerations. In one sense, Western aid budgets had always been used to support strategically important partnerships. Now, however, they were more directly and explicitly linked to the problem of fragile and failed states, entities seen as the source of new transnational threats to Western security which therefore needed 'fixing'.

The arguments put forward for this post-Cold War 'securitisation of aid' are easily identified in the debates within Western donor circles during the 2000s. One common thread running through them was a strong element of Western self-interest married to development altruism. Poverty, underdevelopment and inequality bred resentment and strife. This was compounded by the poor political governance record of many states which further fuelled unrest, increasing the likelihood of conflict and the emergence of 'ungoverned spaces' which terrorist groups could exploit. In simple terms, Western security at home required improvements in security abroad, and spillovers could only be contained through a deeper understanding of the roots of the problem and the adoption of a new set of customised tools.

A year after 9/11, the new US National Security Strategy of September 2002 provided an early statement on how the problem of 'weak states' and the dangers they posed were viewed in Washington:

> The events of September 11, 2001, taught us that weak states, like Afghanistan, can pose as great a danger to our national interests as strong states. Poverty does not make poor people into terrorists and murderers. Yet poverty, weak institutions, and corruption can make weak states vulnerable to terrorist networks and drug cartels within their borders. (White House 2002, p. iv)

The transnational operations of such organisations, facilitated by growing global interdependence, meant a fundamental review of the sources of threats to Western security was required. The EU's Security Strategy of 2003 stated, "In an era of globalisation, distant threats may be as much a concern as those that are near at hand…Our traditional concept of self-defence—up to and including the Cold War—was based on the threat of invasion. With the new threats, the first line of defence will be abroad" (Council of the European Union 2003, p. 4).

Given Africa's underdevelopment and high levels of conflict, the continent's problems therefore represented a global security threat. Development needed to be understood as a security issue and vice versa. Since Western development assistance had the potential to help reduce levels of conflict in Africa, Western donor agencies needed to be cognisant of the security dimension of their development programmes.

DFID's White Paper on International Development of 2000 highlighted the negative consequences for development of Africa's numerous wars:

> Violent conflict is one of the biggest barriers to development in many of the world's poorest countries...This problem is particularly acute in Africa where twenty percent of the population live in countries affected by armed conflict. (DFID 2000, p. 28)

Development could only occur in secure environments, without which there could be no investment, no trade, no growth, no service delivery and no development. And since conflict is one of the major causes of poverty, conflict reduction and prevention should be treated as an instrument in the poverty-reduction toolkit.

The need for substantial changes to how development was understood, and development work conducted, was also recognised by Scandinavian bilateral donors. For example, in 2005 the Danish International Development Agency (DANIDA) observed in its annual report:

> Security is a necessary prerequisite for development. Therefore, contributions to re-establishing security and promoting peace in countries and regions where there has previously been systematic violence, crime and terror are also an investment in reducing poverty and promoting economic growth. (DANIDA 2005, p. 27)

The Canadian government also incorporated such thinking into its 2005 International Policy Statement. Fragile states constituted a security threat to Canada, since "the weakness of failed states makes them obvious breeding grounds for terrorist networks and organized crime, which can directly threaten the security of Canadians" (Government of Canada 2005, 13). It followed that Canadians needed to recognise that "any solution to their dilemma must operate within this security-development nexus" (Government of Canada p. 22).

The operational implications of such linkages were teased out in a 2001 UK government consultation document. In a foretaste of what became the standard practice of 'whole of government approaches' to the problem of conflict in the developing world—and which would see a blurring of the distinction between development, diplomatic and security work in tackling the security-development/insecurity-poverty nexus—DFID, the FCO and Ministry of Defence (MOD) teams were brought together to improve "the effectiveness of Britain's contribution to peace keeping, conflict prevention and conflict management in Sub-Saharan Africa and elsewhere in the world" (DFID 2001, p. 3).

In addition to drivers of violent conflict in Africa, such as the proliferation of small arms or the lack of adequate conflict-resolution and mediation capacity in regional and continental bodies (such issues normally treated as within the purview of the UK's MOD or FCO), the consultation document referenced DFID's areas of endeavour, such as inequality reduction and improving access to goods and services for the poor. By helping contain inter-group inequality which was seen as a major driver of conflict, the objectives of the UK's development agency were seen to align with the UK's security interests. Further eliding development and security considerations, DFID's responsibilities in the areas of economic growth, employment and education had the potential to solve security problems, since countries "with high levels of unemployment among young men and where educational levels are low face a far higher risk of conflict" (DFID 2001, p. 14).

In 2010, a UK Minister of State for International Development provided an American audience with an overview of changes which had taken place since 9/11 in his government's approach to the security threats posed by fragile states. Significantly, he argued that these had allowed the British government to now "look at security in the round, not in the compartmentalised boxes that treat development, diplomacy and defence as stand-alone efforts" (Duncan 2010).

Following a Strategic Defence and Security Review in 2010, the UK government committed DFID to a new objective. In addition to its traditional focus on poverty reduction, DFID was now also tasked with "making an optimal contribution to national security within its overall objective of poverty reduction". This entailed "coordinated cross-government efforts overseas to build the capacity of priority national security and fragile states to take increasing responsibility for their own stability" (HM Government 2010, p. 11).

Western Programmes for the Securitisation of Aid to Africa

As part of the global 'war on terror', Western countries launched several initiatives to strengthen the capabilities of African states to deal with their security threats. Such assistance programmes were extensive in terms of the number of countries covered and the range of multi-faceted interventions rolled out.

Washington led these efforts, undertaking a fundamental re-assessment of the role of its development assistance programmes in its global war on terror. A review conducted by the Center for Strategic and International Studies (CSIS) showed that following 9/11, the Department of Defence (DOD) share of American ODA had rapidly increased from 5.6 per cent to 21.7 per cent between 2002 and 2005 (CSIS 2008, p. vi). In terms of Africa's place in such programmes, a US Army War College document of 2008 observed that "the African continent, SSA in particular, has become a prominent front in the global front in the fight against Islamic extremists" (Chau 2008, p. 1) with increasingly securitised development assistance to Africa reflected in a growing share of Department of Defence (DOD) expenditures in the ODA budget allocated to the continent.

In 2005, a Trans-Sahara Counterterrorism Partnership (TSCTP) was launched, with the State Department as the lead agency working in cooperation with USAID and the Pentagon (U.S. Department of State 2019). This targeted West and North African states facing threats from organisations such as Al-Qaeda in the Islamic Maghreb[2] and later Boko Haram.[3] The multi-faceted approach adopted required extensive multi-agency cooperation, with programmes ranging from capacity-building of the military and law enforcement agencies for counterterrorism operations, which included the monitoring of terrorist group activities and disruption of their financing mechanisms, to those tackling the underlying developmental constraints seen to facilitate the recruitment efforts of terrorist organisations, such as unemployment, poor access to health and education, and weak local governments unable to provide law and order.

In 2009 another regionally focused initiative was launched by the first Obama administration: the US State Department's Partnership for Regional East Africa Counterterrorism (PREACT). Targeting twelve countries (including Ethiopia, Uganda and Rwanda), it had as its overarching objective to "build the capacity and cooperation of military, law enforcement, and civilian actors across East Africa to counter terrorism in a comprehensive fashion". As with the TSCTP, PREACT would bring to bear "law enforcement, military and development resources to achieve its strategic objectives" (U.S. Department of State 2011).

American assistance to those African states facing security challenges was also increasingly framed in terms of the principle of 'African solutions to African problems', with the building of African capacity as the long-term solution to the continent's security problems. The objective of African self-sufficiency can be partly attributed to Washington's reluctance to commit American troops to future peacekeeping missions in Africa after the failed 1993 US operation in Somalia to capture the Somali warlord Farah Aideed, which had resulted in many American casualties and eventual American withdrawal from Somalia.[4] Under the second Clinton administration from 1996 to 2001, the focus on improving the capabilities of African forces to participate in peacekeeping activities was given a boost in 2002 by the AU's decision to take on primary responsibility for ensuring peace and security in the continent and to establish an African rapid response Standby Force.

Post-Somalia, an increasingly important form of American engagement with Africa's trouble spots was Washington's financing of peacekeeping operations through regular assessed American contributions to the UN's peacekeeping budget and voluntary and direct financial contributions to support AU peace operations. The US was also involved in training, equipping and deploying African troops to UN missions and other operations authorised by continental or regional bodies. The largest Africa-specific programme of this 'train and equip' variety was the Africa Contingency Operations Training and Assistance (ACOTA), launched in 2001. The focus of ACOTA was on the training of African trainers, including in peace enforcement capabilities, that is, for situations where there is no peace to keep, where parties remained hostile both to each other and to intervention forces and where the latter might be given a mandate under the UN Charter's Chapter VII to employ lethal force. ACOTA activities included boosting 'Force Protection' capabilities in hostile situations, training in areas such as planning and communications, and transfers of military equipment to the contingents of participating countries. Rwanda, Ethiopia and Uganda were all partner countries in the ACOTA initiative.

In 2014 President Obama announced yet another American initiative aimed at improving the capabilities of African armed forces engaged in peace operations. As its name suggested, the aim of the African Peacekeeping Rapid Response Partnership (APRRP) was to increase the capabilities of such forces in areas such as air transport, communications and information gathering in order to quickly respond to crises (U.S. Department of State 2021). Amongst the initial six African countries identified to benefit from this Partnership were, once again, Uganda, Rwanda and Ethiopia.

London also made programmatic adjustments in line with its identification of new security threats, the evolving analytical work on fragile states and its thinking on the security-development nexus. The UK government had cut its teeth early on in terms of applying its resources to fragile and post-conflict state situations. In 2000 British forces intervened in Sierra Leone to end a protracted civil war. This was followed by extensive engagement in post-conflict reconstruction activities in that country, central to which reform of the country's security sector. In the context of a collapsed state in which security institutions were widely discredited, this required military, diplomatic/political and development expertise to be brought to bear simultaneously, and Sierra Leone saw field testing of 'whole of government approaches' to the securitisation of the UK's aid, with intensive collaboration between DFID, the FCO and the MOD.

In 2001 the UK government established a set of Conflict Prevention Pools (CPPs) with three principal areas of focus, namely conflict prevention, security sector reform[5] and post-conflict stabilisation. In line with the UK's presentation of the securitisation of its aid being a merging of altruistic concern for the world's poorest with the national interest, Foreign Secretary Jack Straw characterised these Pools as "a form of forward defence…[a way] in which we can safeguard our security at home by contributing to stability and prosperity overseas" (Straw 2002).

One of the UK's main vehicles to implement its securitized aid policy was its Defence Advisory Teams. Composed of both military and civilian personnel (including DFID Governance Advisors), Defence Advisory Teams were tasked to provide technical advisory support for security sector reforms through reviews of defence policy and training in financial management and on civil-military relations (including the democratic management of the defence sector). Within their first two years of operations from 2001 to 2003, amongst the five African countries benefiting from such assistance were Ethiopia, Rwanda and Uganda.

Defining Terms of Engagement, Objectives and Conditionalities

Western donors were well aware of the risk of 'dual use' of their securitised aid, namely, that Western support to enhance the capacity of the security sectors of their African allies to deal with terrorist threats might have the perverse effect of Western assets and training also being employed for purposes of internal repression. Securitised aid might not only enhance the capacity of armed forces to carry out operations within and beyond national borders against enemies which were also in the cross hairs of Western governments, but Western assets and training given to what were already highly militarised regimes could be used to suppress peaceful political dissent. This was simply a variation of the more general problem of 'aid fungibility', whereby once resources were handed over, the giver had little control over the subsequent use to which they were put. The capacity-strengthening aspect of securitised aid meant the enhanced capabilities might easily be turned inwards for regime preservation purposes.

In 2005, the OECD-DAC felt compelled to fine-tune the criteria it had used to classify the foreign assistance activities of its members as ODA, a clear indication of the very rapid expansion of Western donor activities into the field of conflict prevention and security activities that involved the diplomatic, development and defence wings of Western governments. The aim was to clarify what activities in the area of security and development it would consider to be ODA (OECD-DAC 2005a). It later felt the need to produce a casebook, setting out the criteria it would use to assess what kinds of activities (and within these, which specific components) might be reportable as ODA, that is, as government aid that specifically targeted the economic development and welfare of developing countries. Amongst the general principles highlighted in the casebook was that development cooperation "should not be used as a vehicle to promote the provider's security interests" (OECD-DAC 2017, p. 63)[6] and that if this was the primary objective then such transfers would not be considered by the DAC as ODA.

As Western aid agencies' programmes gradually factored security objectives into their development programmes, and increasing resources were programmed for security-related activities, this did not prove unproblematic for Western bilateral donors. Firstly, security objectives were not part of the global development frameworks such as the MDGs, as the agreed goals, sectors and targets contained in the latter set the boundaries for what international development actors should focus on. Secondly, the OECD-DAC's proscription on aid being used to pursue the security interests of donors sat uncomfortably beside the arguments put forward by Western capitals that security was a precondition for development, that strengthening the security of aid recipient states was a win-win situation for both sides and, therefore, that the inclusion of work on security issues in their aid programmes married their international development undertakings with their national security interests.

For example, in the case of the UK's aid programmes, which increasingly contained security and development components, DFID proceeded with caution. Given its existing commitments to the achievement of the MDGs, and in particular poverty reduction, a 2002 DFID guidance note on Security Sector Reform (SSR) made clear that "since the point of any DFID intervention is to reduce poverty, DFID should not intervene without being satisfied that what is proposed will contribute to the reduction of poverty" (DFID 2002, p. 9). In terms of a division of labour between the FCO, MOD and DFID, it would focus only on what it saw as its primary role, which was to "help with the governance agenda—the government, political and judicial framework for accountable management of national security" (DFID 2002, p. 8), all aspects seen as directly related to the objectives of both conflict prevention and improving the security of the poor in particular. The document highlighted the fact that, in contrast to the MOD, DFID did "not provide direct assistance to the military" (DFID 2002, p. 8) along the lines of the standard 'train and equip' approach to capacity-building of security forces. In other words, DFID's intention was to abstain from providing support aimed solely at improving the operational effectiveness of the military, police or intelligence services.

Later, in 2005, another DFID policy document made a strong case for its development work incorporating security considerations on the basis the two were closely linked. But it also warned that a single-minded focus on improving the security of the state might translate into growing insecurity of the poor and increased repression of the most vulnerable in society. From DFID's point of view, while it might prove possible, even if difficult, to rationalise the security-enhancing components of its development assistance programmes so long as its focus remained firmly on the security of the poor, to justify such assistance in terms of improving the security of the UK was more problematic. Therefore, the same document emphasised that DFID was constrained by its own enabling International Development Act of 2002 from using "UK development assistance to finance programmes whose primary objective is tackling threats to UK or global security considerations alone" (DFID 2005, p. 23). However, by the time of the UK's 2010 Defence and Security Review, the Conservative government had overruled DFID's position on the integration of the UK's national security considerations into its development programmes.

Other Western donors also sought to clarify the conditions under which they would be prepared to provide support to partner countries committed to improving their security and when they would not. The declared aim was to ensure that, either through acts of commission or omission, their assistance did not strengthen the security props of authoritarian regimes and thereby contribute to increased political repression and violation of human rights.

In the George. W. Bush administration's 2002 American National Security Strategy, the US undertook to ensure its newly strengthened foreign policy focus on global anti-terrorism activism, the cooperation arrangements it entered into and the allocation of foreign assistance resources it provided would be based on certain principles linked to "the non-negotiable demands of human dignity", amongst which "the rule of law; limits on the absolute power of the state; free speech" (White House 2002, p. 3). Aid disbursed in the context of the new Strategy would also be used to ensure "that nations moving towards democracy are rewarded for the steps they take", and the US would make the "development of democratic institutions key themes in our bilateral relations" (White House 2002, p. 4).

Such concerns were evident in Washington's anti-terrorism assistance programmes, with training courses emphasising "the importance of the rule of law and respect for human rights" (U.S. Department of State 2011). Its ACOTA programme to enhance the capacity of African states to take part in peace operations stressed that "respect for international standards of human rights is a fundamental concept throughout the training" (U.S. Department of State 2013), with the State Department responsible for vetting candidate countries on the basis of their human rights record.

Similar principles were echoed in the EU's strategy for Africa of 2005. Its commitment to enter a strengthened partnership with the continent, which included support for dealing with Africa's security challenges, would be shaped by the EU's values, in particular the belief that successful development required "adherence to human rights, democratic principles and the rule of law". In terms of specific objectives, this meant its programmes, including those touching on security issues, would include the promotion and protection of human rights, the improvement of public accountability and the "growth of participatory democracy" (Council of the European Union 2005).

Amongst other multilateral organisations, the OECD-DAC was possibly the clearest in terms of setting out what it saw as the essential principles and conditionalities which should govern the engagement of member countries in security matters. A set of guidelines from 2005 framed the issue as one in which the objective of both donors and partner countries should be that of helping the latter "meet the range of security needs of their societies in a manner consistent with democratic norms and sound governance principles, including transparency and the rule of law" (OECD-DAC 2005b, p. 11). OECD-DAC members were enjoined to apply to SSR processes the same overall approach and principles they used to embed good governance practices in the public sectors of partner countries. These included ensuring security sector decision-making was transparent and accountable, that the necessary information was made available to policymakers, that expenditure management was sound and SSR activities were linked to overall governmental planning and budgeting processes. In other words, OECD donors should encourage partner country governments to treat security as a public policy issue, subject to the same set of good governance principles applicable to the activities of all state agencies.

An OECD-DAC Handbook from 2007 acknowledged the high levels of sensitivity surrounding SSR. It noted that in addition to defence of the territorial integrity of the state, and its role in suppressing internal rebellions, the military might also be used "for the purposes of repression and the protection of sectional interests", that "control over the military is central to the exercise of power" and that they "have frequently been involved in politics and usurped governments or had significant influence over them" (OECD-DAC 2007, p. 124). It alerted donors to the need to exercise caution to avoid their assistance programmes having perverse consequences, with the resources they provided being used to strengthen repressive regimes, and that "external supporters need to be aware that the defence reform process can be manipulated and be clear about boundaries in advance. Support may have to be suspended or terminated" (OECD-DAC 2007, p. 133).

Such words of caution were repeated by many Western bilateral donor agencies. Individual donor countries, as well as Western multilateral organisations, were clearly aware of the dangers of African governments misusing external resources provided to deal with their security challenges. Those of an authoritarian persuasion such as Uganda, Rwanda and Ethiopia might use any assets and training they received to not only improve their contribution to peacekeeping operations but also to neutralise domestic movements they designated as terrorists, intimidate domestic political opposition groups, the media and CSOs or even conduct military operations in neighbouring countries where valuable natural resources could be extracted.

Capitalising on Western Security Concerns

After their prolonged and victorious insurgencies, all three regimes in Kampala, Addis Ababa and Kigali would continue to face threats from armed opposition groups, both within and outside their borders, and sought external assistance to deal with their security threats. Having emerged from armed liberation movements, in their engagements with those taking decisions in Western capitals on Africa's security challenges they were comfortable with the language of national security. Post-9/11, their leaders showed themselves to be extremely capable, through their intelligent use of the lexicon of global security, of connecting the security threats their regimes faced to those confronted by Western countries. Building on the rationales already rehearsed in Western development circles, they also argued that eliminating such security threats was an essential precondition for the achievement of the Western-backed global development objectives. Directing their public statements at both domestic and external audiences, they sought to discredit internal and foreign opposition forces by depicting them both as threats to the national unity and stability of their countries and as dangers to Western security. Opposition figures, defectors from the ruling party and critical voices from within civil society were all classed as security risks. Their perfidious activities were often explained in terms of their treacherous links to external enemies, real or imagined, and regularly used to justify invoking 'emergency measures' to neutralise them on the grounds they constituted significant threats to national security and therefore deserved the harshest responses.

By skilfully reading the runes and correctly interpreting the West's security concerns, by announcing they subscribed to the West's anti-terrorism security objectives and indicating they were willing to act as its forward listening posts, and by marketing themselves and their security forces as reliable allies in the West's struggle against terrorism, all three African regimes ensured that Western aid they received became increasingly securitised in terms of both the reasons it was provided and the forms it took. To ensure that these pipelines remained open, their leaders took every opportunity to remind the West of the important roles they played as protectors of the citizens of the West from the long arm of international terrorism. Like their adoption of 'development speak' which had greatly facilitated common understandings on development to be reached with Western donors and the BWIs, these African regimes rapidly internalised the new 'security speak' generated by the West's focus on international terrorism, which they then successfully fed back to their Western interlocutors.

They also depicted their countries as islands of relative peace and stability on a continent not noted for either. At the same time, and whenever necessary, they juggled this picture of internal peace and security with the need to draw the attention of Western capitals to the continued presence of 'existential threats' to their states, and in particular the risks posed to the development progress made under their rule which the West should have a vested interest in helping them protect.

To manage Western concerns about any political repression or human rights violations which might be connected to the enhanced capabilities that resulted from securitised Western aid, the leaders of the three African regimes constantly reminded their benefactors of the critical role they were playing in preventing the expansion of terrorist activities on the continent. They suggested that as long as progress was being made in tackling security threats, and they continued to show improvements in their human development indicators, too many questions should not be asked as to how they employed the assets received through Western security assistance programmes. This was a golden rule that outsiders were expected to respect.

This joint venture with Western powers was not restricted to participation in the US-led 'coalition of the willing' against terrorism. These leaders also tried to be seen as responsible African states seeking to give substance to the idea of 'African solutions to African problems'. The most significant form this commitment took was their contribution to the resolution of Africa's numerous conflicts, and the peacekeeping and peace-enforcement tasks this required. Engagement in such multilateral initiatives provided all three regimes with substantial diplomatic leverage, raising their profile within the international community. In addition, as the increasing securitisation of their relations with Western capitals had a negative impact on the governance style which evolved in those countries, further limiting the prospects for democratisation, respect for civil liberties, human rights and the rule of law, their role as Western security allies provided them with additional means to fend off criticism for their political governance shortcomings, ones which became increasingly difficult to ignore.

Notes

1. In the new post-9/11 environment dominated by American concerns about terrorism, Washington-based think tanks moved quickly to produce work on international Islamic terrorist networks operating in Africa continent and their implications for American national security. See, for example, the United States Institute for Peace (USIP) report of January 2004 on the theme of terrorism in the Horn of Africa (USIP 2004).
2. This group's origins lie in the Algerian Civil War, which began in 1992 when the results of national elections, won by an Islamist movement (the *Front Islamique du Salut* (FIS)), were overturned by the Algerian military. The subsequent banning of the FIS triggered a protracted and bloody conflict. One of the Islamist armed groups to emerge eventually allied itself with Osama bin Laden's Al-Qaeda and became known as Al-Qaeda in the Islamic Maghreb which expanded its operations into the Sahel region.
3. Boko Haram is an Islamist armed group originating in Northern Nigeria in 2002, whose aim is to overthrow the Nigerian government and establish an Islamic state. Initially it maintained close ties with Al-Qaeda in the Islamic Maghreb, but then switched its primary allegiance to the Islamic State of Iraq and Syria (ISIS). Its insurgency would eventually spread to neighbouring Cameroon, Chad and Niger, and the group was declared a terrorist organisation by the US, the UN and the EU.
4. In 1992, Aideed's militia carried out attacks on UN peacekeepers deployed to safeguard humanitarian relief operations. Following a mandate granted by the UN Security Council (Resolution 794), which authorised a US-led coalition to "use all necessary means" to enable humanitarian operations to be carried out in Somalia, this led to the deployment of 21,000 American troops and 17,000 from other coalition countries. The US became involved in a manhunt for Aideed following the killing of twenty-four peacekeepers from Pakistan in June 1993. This eventually resulted in a showdown in Mogadishu in October 1993 between US forces and Aideed's militia in which eighteen American soldiers were killed, following which President Clinton announced the withdrawal of American forces from Somalia.

5. Security sector reform gained prominence in the aftermath of the Cold War, arguably initially driven by unresolved security issues in the aftermath of the large number of UN peacekeeping operations in the 1990s linked to civil wars in Africa, Central America and the Balkans. Its importance increased when it came to be seen in Western countries as a means of contributing to the 'war on terror', through its potential to strengthen state capacity in developing countries to extend their control over their territories and deal more effectively with domestic and regional security threats.
6. That the DAC's work in terms of defining members' activities in this area as ODA was problematic is evidenced by the fact that several cases, present in an earlier draft, were removed, "as one member disagreed with the eligibility assessment" (OECD-DAC 2017, p. 1).

References

Center for Strategic and International Studies (CSIS), "Integrating 21st Century Development and Security Assistance – Final Report of the Task Force on Non-traditional Security Assistance" Washington D.C., January 2008.

Chau, Donavan C. 2008. "U.S. Counterterrorism in Sub-Saharan Africa: Understanding Costs, Cultures and Conflicts", U.S. Army War College: Strategic Studies Institute, September 2008.

Council of the European Union. 2003. *European Security Strategy: A Secure Europe in a Better World*, Brussels, December 12, 2003.

Council of the European Union. 2005. "The EU and Africa: towards a strategic partnership", 15961/05 (Presse 367), Brussels, December 19, 2005.

DANIDA, *Annual Report 2005*, Copenhagen: Ministry of Foreign Affairs of Denmark, 2005.

DFID, "Fighting Poverty to Build a Safe World - A Strategy for security and development", March 2005, London.

DFID. 2000. *Eliminating World Poverty: Making Globalisation Work for the Poor*, White Paper on International Development, December 2000. Cm 5006.

DFID. 2001. "The causes of conflict in Africa -Consultation document", London: DFID. March 2001.

DFID. 2002. "Understanding and Supporting Security Sector Reform", London: DFID, 2002.

Duncan, Alan. 2010. *Development, Diplomacy and Defence: An Integrated Response to Conflict and Fragility Overseas.* Carnegie Endowment, Washington D.C., December 14, 2010.

Government of Canada.2005. *Canada's International Policy Statement – A Role of Pride and Influence in the World, Overview*, Ottawa, 2005.

HM Government, Securing Britain in an Age of Uncertainty: The Strategic Defence and Security Review, London, October 2010.

OECD-DAC 2005a, *Conflict Prevention and Peacebuilding: What counts as ODA?* Paris, March 3, 2005.
OECD-DAC 2005b, *Security System Reform and Governance*, DAC Guidelines and Reference Series, Paris, 2005.
OECD-DAC 2007, *OECD DAC Handbook on Security System Reform*, Paris, 2007.
OECD-DAC 2017, *Casebook on Conflict, Peace and Security Activities* [DCD/DAC (2017) [22/Final]. Paris, October 20 2017.
Straw, Jack. 2002. "Re-Ordering the World", Speech by the Foreign Secretary to the Foreign Policy Centre, March 25, 2002.
U.S. Department of State. 2011. "Bureau of Counterterrorism, Programs and Initiatives". Washington D.C., 2011.
U.S. Department of State. 2013. African Contingency Operations Training and Assistance (ACOTA) Program. Washington D.C., February 6, 2013.
U.S. Department of State. 2019. "Trans-Sahara Counterterrorism Partnership". Washington D.C. 2019.
U.S. Department of State. 2021. "U.S. Peacekeeping Capacity Building Assistance, Fact Sheet". Washington D.C., January 20, 2021.
United States Institute for Peace (USIP). 2004. "Report of January 2004 on the theme of terrorism in the Horn of Africa". Terrorism in the Horn of Africa, Special Report No.113, Washington D.C., USIP. January 2004.
White House. 2002. *The National Security Strategy of the United States of America*, Washington D.C., September 2002.

CHAPTER 11

Western Security, Regime Security and the Fruits of Plunder

President George W. Bush's Manichean post-9/11 worldview was perfectly encapsulated in his speech to Congress on September 20, 2001. Launching America's global war against terror, he warned all that "you are either with us, or you are with the terrorists" (Bush 2001). The leaders of Uganda, Ethiopia and Rwanda eagerly stepped up and embraced the arguments put forward by Washington on the need for a crusade against terrorists. They would also have taken note of Washington's National Security Strategy of 2002, in which a veritable cornucopia of goodies was promised to those who joined the global war on terror and which would provide them with additional means to secure regime continuity:

> We will continue to encourage our regional partners to take up a coordinated effort that isolates the terrorists. Once the regional campaign localizes the threat to a particular state, we will help ensure the state has the military, law enforcement, political and financial tools necessary to finish the task. (White House 2002, p. 6)

Uganda

One of the NRM's first actions as government had been to formalise the status of its military wing, the NRA, which became the country's new national defence force, the Uganda People's Defence Force (UPDF). This

M. Simpson, *Donors, Democracy and Development in Africa*,
https://doi.org/10.1007/978-3-031-74917-9_11

ensured from the outset that the new military was staffed and controlled by reliable Museveni loyalists and that it became a critical regime prop.[1]

A National Security Council was established in 2000, charged with informing and advising the President on all matters relating to national security. Chaired by the President, it included amongst others the Ministers of Defence, Security, Internal Affairs and Foreign Affairs, the Attorney General and selected Members of Parliament appointed by the President, together with ex officio members such as the Army Commander, the Inspector General of the Police and the Director of the Internal Security Organisation. At lower administrative levels, District Security and Intelligence Committees, composed of local representatives of central-level agencies, were also set up and tasked with informing the National Security Council on matters relating to security in the districts, acting as Kampala's eyes and ears at local level. The pattern was replicated at the sub-county level (Parliament of the Republic of Uganda 2000). As a result, the intelligence-gathering and surveillance capacity of the state were significantly enhanced and used to monitor the activities of all who opposed the Museveni government.

Even before the 1998 bombings of the American embassies in neighbouring Kenya and Tanzania, and the 9/11 attacks on the US in 2001, Museveni had been well positioned to influence the decisions of Western donor countries in terms of their support to Uganda and so ensure Kampala's efforts to address its own security priorities received Western inputs. He was able to do so even though, initially at least, the most serious domestic security threats Uganda faced from armed groups were not primarily Islamist in origin, which meant at first it proved challenging for Kampala to use militant Islam, the dominant Western bugbear, as a basis for building common ground with the West on security issues. The most significant of these early non-Islamic security threats was that posed by the Christian millenarian Lord's Resistance Army (LRA), which came to the fore after 1986. Initially basing itself in Northern Uganda, and to the extent that its poorly articulated programme enables one to grasp its grievances and objectives, the LRA sought to establish a Christian theocracy in Uganda and declared that this required the removal of Museveni and the NRM from power.[2]

However, when Uganda found itself engaged in a proxy war with the Sudanese government because of Khartoum's evolving links with the LRA, this helped Kampala argue it also faced challenges from radical Islam. Beginning in the early 1990s, and due to suspicions Khartoum intended to expand the domain of Islam throughout the Great Lakes region, Uganda began supporting the secessionist Sudan People's Liberation Army (SPLA), forcing Khartoum to divert resources to contain the Southern Sudanese separatists. Even before the 1998 Entebbe summit with President Clinton, Uganda had taken on the role of conduit for American support to the SPLA in its struggle for Southern Sudan's independence. In turn Khartoum, under the National Islamic Front government of Omar El-Bashir, decided to support the LRA, granting it bases in southern Sudan to launch attacks inside Uganda.

An additional rebel group Kampala had to contend with was the Allied Democratic Forces (ADF). This movement was based on an uneasy alliance between a dizzying array of anti-Museveni forces. They included disgruntled members of the old armies of former Presidents Idi Amin and Milton Obote who had resisted integration into the armed forces of the new NRM dispensation, Ugandan Islamists in the Uganda Muslim Liberation Army (UMLA) who came to dominate the ADF's forces, and longstanding ethno-regional separatist forces in the west of Uganda which had coalesced into the National Army for the Liberation of Uganda (NALU). Khartoum oversaw the merger of these forces, and in addition to supporting the LRA, it became the ADF's chief sponsor. In addition, both Khartoum and Mobutu had reached an agreement that the anti-Museveni LRA and ADF rebels could be based on Zairean territory bordering Uganda and supplied by Sudan.[3] Kampala was therefore able to market its struggle against the ADF as having a strong anti-Khartoum and anti-Islamist component.

For Kampala, the regional security situation was further complicated by Kagame's decision in 1996 to invade then Zaire, officially to eliminate remnants of the former Armed Forces of Rwanda and *Interahamwe* militia who had sought refuge amongst their fellow Hutu in camps in Zaire, and which according to Kigali were intent on returning to Rwanda to complete their genocidal project. The existence of Khartoum and Kinshasa-backed anti-Museveni forces along the Zaire-Uganda border, and the opportunities presented by Rwanda's invasion, led to Kampala's increasing involvement in the expanding conflict in the Great Lakes region centred on eastern Zaire, with both Museveni and Kagame supporting the anti-Mobutu forces of the *Alliance des forces démocratique pour la libération du Congo-Zaïre* (AFDL) led by Laurent-Désiré Kabila.

The interlinked conflicts on Zairean territory sucked in a wide range of actors, and what came to be designated Africa's First and the Second

Congo Wars involved rapidly shifting alliances between government armies and rebel groups. As interests changed, ties formed and dissolved with ease as dancing partners were quickly swopped, and what was renamed the DRC in 1997 was used by both internal and external actors as the stage upon which numerous scores could be settled.[4] The DRC conflict also offered significant opportunities for plunder, with the latter increasingly looming large in the decisions of those with the most interests in the outcomes of the various conflicts.

Uganda's security situation changed again when the country became involved in the AU's peacekeeping operation in Somalia, the African Union Mission in Somalia (AMISOM), launched in 2007. Backed by Western countries, this mission was mandated to create an appropriate environment for the delivery of humanitarian assistance and to train the Somali government's fledgling security forces. Uganda not only was the first African country to deploy troops to the mission area, but also became its largest troop contributor. The mission quickly became a de facto peace-enforcement as opposed to peacekeeping operation, as it became clear there was no peace to be kept. One of the roles AMISOM forces therefore eventually played was that of assisting the federal government in Mogadishu to defeat armed opposition groups, most notably Al-Shabaab, the Somali jihadist group affiliated to Al-Qaeda which had been designated a terrorist group by Washington. AMISOM's Ugandan troops were increasingly targeted by Al-Shabaab, and in July 2010 Al-Shabaab also carried out bomb attacks in Kampala which resulted in heavy local and Western civilian casualties (*Al-Jazeera* 2010).

Uganda's involvement in Somalia allowed the government to claim it was demonstrating in practical terms what it meant for African countries to meet their responsibilities in terms of the principle of 'African solutions to African problems'. In addition, Kampala portrayed Somalia as a key theatre of operations in the global war on terror, providing a safe haven for radical Islamists which Western intelligence linked to, amongst others, the deadly attacks on US soldiers in Mogadishu in 1993 and the bombings of the American embassies in East Africa in 1998. Somalia was therefore a problem which Uganda, in line with its responsibilities in both its own neighbourhood and further afield, made clear it was willing to tackle if the necessary Western assistance was forthcoming.

In May 2002, the Ugandan Parliament approved an Anti-Terrorism Act. This provided for the prosecution and punishment of those involved in activities ranging from planning, financing and executing terrorist activities to attending meetings of terrorist organisations. The Minister of Internal Affairs was granted the right to authorise surveillance and interception of communications between citizens which could be justified simply on the grounds of 'safeguarding the public interest'. The same Act also listed the LRA and the ADF as terrorist organisations, both joining the only other organisation specified in the relevant Schedule, namely Al-Qaeda (Parliament of the Republic of Uganda 2002). The 2002 Act thus further extended the surveillance powers of the State granted in the National Security Council Act of 2000.

During a working visit to the US in 2002, Museveni delivered a speech at the Woodrow Wilson Center in Washington. He linked Africa's and particularly Uganda's anti-terrorist efforts to those of the Western-led global war on terror, highlighting the importance of the African continent as a theatre of operations in that wider conflict:

> Africa has a key role to play in the Global Campaign Against Terrorism... Uganda has also been a direct target of terrorism from brutal attacks against local and American civilians by the Lord's Resistance Army and the Allied Democratic Forces...In accordance with the African Pact Against Terrorism, signed last October,[5] African leaders have demonstrated their solidarity to fight terrorism and its breeding grounds that span the continent from Cairo to Cape Town. (Woodrow Wilson International Centre for Scholars 2002)

Kampala also made clear it subscribed to the linkages between security and development. Using language that might have been lifted verbatim from any post-9/11 Western aid policy document, Uganda's White Paper on Defence of 2004 stated that "Uganda recognises that security and development are mutually reinforcing and interlinked. Development without security is not sustainable, and security without development is not durable" (Republic of Uganda 2004, p. 15).

Museveni's efforts to find African solutions to the continent's numerous security challenges included his longstanding efforts to set up continental security frameworks. In May 1991, and while Chairman of the OAU, he hosted a meeting which brought together current and former Heads of State and representatives of the private sector and civil society to deliberate on the theme of 'Security, Stability, Development and Cooperation in Africa'. The meeting resulted in the 'Kampala Document' which contained an early post-Cold War African statement on the linkages between security, stability, development and cooperation and recognised the need to treat all these variables in a comprehensive and integrated manner (Organization of African Unity 1991). Such high-profile external initiatives burnished Uganda's image as a model African state, one willing to take on its responsibilities to make the aspirational 'African Renaissance' a reality.

At the same time, they also helped Kampala deflect criticism of its less commendable actions, both domestically and in its immediate neighbourhood. It was not difficult to link Museveni's decision in 2007 to send troops to Somalia, and Kampala's characterisation of the latter as the African frontline of the West's 'war on terror', with Western pressures for political reform following the controversial February 2006 presidential and legislative elections. As noted in Chap. 7, in addition to widespread reports of intimidation against other candidates and their supporters by security forces, these elections had seen the arrest and detention in November 2005 of the main challenger to Museveni on grounds which included treason given his alleged links to the LRA.

Western donors expressed their concerns, and some of Uganda's major budget support donors such as DFID, the Swedish International Development Cooperation Agency (SIDA), the Norwegian Agency for Development Cooperation (NORAD) and the Netherlands temporarily withheld some budget support funds (Molenaers et al. 2013, pp. 12–13). The punitive measures were, however, short-lived; by 2007 DFID had signed a ten-year partnership deal with Uganda worth £700 million, cementing the country's position as one of the UK's 'donor darlings' (Guardian 2009). In the case of the US, the same reluctance to censure Kampala for violations on the political governance front was clearly linked to the importance Washington had come to attach to Uganda's role as a security partner. While in 2005 total US foreign aid disbursed to Uganda was US$254 million, and in the year of the elections fell marginally to US$234 million, by 2007 it had increased to above 2005 pre-election levels to US$291 million (USAID 2019). In addition, it was significant that American security sector assistance to Uganda also proved resilient during this turbulent period and did not suffer from any interruptions. Uganda's military capacity continued to be enhanced by a range of programmes which included military training, credits for military expenditures with repayments waived, donations of excess military hardware and support for its participation in peacekeeping operations. Museveni's success in convincing Washington of their shared interests in helping Kampala deal with its enemies can be gauged from a specific programme of the US

State Department entitled 'Peacekeeping Operations: Counter Lord's Resistance Army Efforts', which in 2010 cost over US$16 million (U.S. Government Foreign Assistance Tracker 2024).

Museveni also used the country's role as a Western military ally to resist demands for reductions in defence expenditure. One notable case involved a Defence Efficiency Study, conducted in 1998 at the request of the Uganda government and funded by DFID. This initiative had been driven by Western donor concerns that despite a significant donor and World Bank-funded Disarmament, Demobilisation and Reintegration (DDR) exercise in the early 1990s, defence expenditures remained high, absorbing a large share of the country's resources. Kampala on the other hand argued that given the security situation in the north where the rebel Lord's Resistance Army (LRA) continued to operate, such high military expenditures were justified. In 2000, under renewed pressure from donors to reduce military expenditure, Museveni forcefully told donors that Uganda's expenditures on this item would be based on his country's own assessment of the security threats it faced rather than external views (*Daily Monitor* 2000).

Uganda's significant and longstanding participation in AMISOM also helped tone down international criticism of its involvement in other regional conflicts which did not have the sanction of regional or international organisations. Foremost amongst these was the highly militarised and interventionist stance Kampala had adopted towards the conflict in the DRC.

In the course of 1996 Ugandan and Rwandan forces moved deep into DRC territory to confront their respective rebel movements based there and also supported the insurgents led by Laurent Kabila who would eventually overthrow Mobutu in May 1997.[6] However, after Mobutu's ouster, growing tensions between Kabila and his foreign backers in Kampala and Kigali following eventually led Ugandan troops, together with RPF forces, to intervene again in the DRC in 1998. This time they sought to oust Kabila, both directly and through the support they provided to a Zairean Tutsi movement, namely, the *Rassemblement Congolais pour la Démocratie* (RCD). In a further twist to the conflict, between 1999 and 2002 UPDF and RPF forces would each end up supporting rival factions of the RCD and eventually came to blows in the Congolese city of Kisangani, an important centre of the DRC's diamond trade which both sides sought to control, with the violence resulting in heavy civilian casualties documented by Western organisations (Human Rights Watch 1999).

The economic motive for intervening in the DRC loomed large in Kampala's calculations and was referenced in numerous reports, amongst which that produced by a UN Panel of Experts established in July 2000 by Secretary-General Kofi Annan and which presented its findings in 2001. The report contained an in-depth examination of the role of external forces in the DRC and damning evidence of the involvement of Ugandan actors and those from other countries in what it termed "mass-scale looting and the systematic and systemic exploitation" of the DRC's natural resources (United Nations 2001, p. 3). Furthermore, it characterised this as an "organized and embedded venture" (United Nations 2001, p. 5).

The pillaging of the DRC's wealth by Ugandan forces, all meticulously detailed in the report, included the harvesting of forestry products such as timber, the exploitation of wildlife such as elephants for their ivory, and the seizure of agricultural produce such as livestock and coffee. But the most financially lucrative for Ugandans was the exploitation of the DRC's vast mineral resources. These included diamonds, gold and other precious metals such as coltan, the latter an increasingly expensive metal essential for the manufacture of mobile phones and other electronic devices.

The UN Panel estimated the value to Uganda of this illegal exploitation of the natural resources of its neighbour. In the case of diamonds, Uganda's rough diamonds exports increased from US$198,000 in 1997 to US$1.81 million by 1999. While its gold exports metal stood at 0.22 tons in 1994, between 1996 and 1999 these rose from 5.07 tons to 11.45 tons. As for coltan (for which it did not register any exports prior to 1997), Uganda exported 2.57 tons in 1997, 18.57 tons in 1998 and then 69.5 tons in 1999 (United Nations 2001, pp. 21–22).

One consequence of the income generated through its DRC operations was Uganda's ability to significantly increase military expenditure. The country had implemented successive Structural Adjustment Programmes, monitored by the BWIs, under which defence expenditures were to be held at 2 per cent of GDP. However, the operation of what the Panel termed the 're-exportation' economy, that is, the system whereby resources brought in from the DRC were "repackaged or sealed as Ugandan natural resources or products and re-exported" (United Nations 2001, p. 30), provided Kampala with significant fiscal space to finance its own security priorities. Foreign exchange inflows from such exports improved Uganda's balance of payments situation, while activities associated with this re-exportation economy were taxed by the Ugandan Treasury which helps throw light on the Panel's finding that "the tax collection level has increased dramatically over the past five years" (United Nations 2001, p. 31). Due to the trickle-down effects of growth in the relevant export sectors, and their positive impact on overall GDP growth rates (for which the government was praised by Western donors), the Panel concluded that this enabled an increase in absolute terms of the military budget while enabling the government to keep the military budget within the 2 per cent of GDP limit agreed with the BWIs. According to the Stockholm International Peace Research Institute (SIPRI), Uganda's military expenditure increased from US$135 million (in current prices) in 1996 (the year it invaded the DRC) to US$141 million in 2000 (the year prior to the release of the UN Panel Report), and by 2010 had increased significantly to US$608 million (SIPRI Military Expenditure Database 2024).

The Panel also pointedly linked these developments to the phenomenon of 'aid fungibility' and the unintended side-effects of aid transfers, most specifically that such external resource inflows (both external development assistance and revenue from activities such as those carried out by Uganda in the DRC) enabled recipient governments to then reallocate their own resources to priorities which might not be aligned to those of donors, most particularly those linked to the global poverty reduction agenda. In a textbook summation of the fungibility problem faced by donors, the report noted:

> The apparent strength of the Ugandan economy has given more confidence to investors and bilateral and multilateral donors who, by maintaining their level of cooperation and assistance to Uganda, gave the government room to spend more on security matters while other sectors, such as education, health and governance, are being taken care of by the bilateral and multilateral donors. (United Nations 2001, p. 31)

Amongst those identified in the 2001 UN report for their roles in the plunder of the DRC were senior UPDF figures, including a Major General and a younger brother of President Museveni (United Nations 2001, p. 17). In addition, the pivotal role of Museveni in the exploitation of the DRC's resources was spelled out in the strongest possible terms. Given his "very good knowledge of the situation on the ground", the Panel argued it was safe to assume that:

> when the information is passed to the President and he chooses not to act, when he appoints the very people who carry out criminal activities, and

> when his family members get away with criminal activities, it becomes overwhelming that the President has put himself in the position of accomplice. (United Nations 2001, pp. 40–41)

Given post-9/11 Western donor interest in eliminating 'ungoverned spaces', and severing their links to organised crime and terrorism, it was ironic that Uganda as one of their donor darlings, and a major beneficiary of Western security assistance in the expectation it would act as a stabilising force on the continent, became a major driver of insecurity in the DRC. As noted in the Panel's report:

> Plundering, looting and racketeering and the constitution of criminal cartels are becoming commonplace in occupied territories. These criminal cartels have ramifications and connections worldwide, and they represent the next serious security problem in the region. (United Nations 2001, pp. 41–42)

Kampala's military interventions, driven at least partly by pecuniary interests, belied the image Kampala sought to project as a stabilising factor in the region. But if in the wake of the 2001 report, there was some Western censure, and the US temporarily suspended military assistance, Kampala was able to head off any severe and lasting punitive measures by leveraging its participation in operations mandated by the AU and UN Security Council, as well as issuing veiled and sometimes direct threats to withdraw from these peace missions. The priority given by the West to securing African allies in the war on terror, and the increasingly important role Ugandan contingents played in peace operations, would all come to Kampala's rescue. The figures on Western aid disbursements noted above showed a willingness to overlook Uganda's activities in the DRC, and the country continued to benefit from aid resources, amongst which military assistance.

Kampala's skills in pre-empting punitive measures were again required in 2010. That year the UN's Office of the High Commissioner for Human Rights (OHCHR) released a report on human rights abuses and violations of international humanitarian law committed in the DRC over the period 1993–2003. Ugandan troops were accused of rape, acts of pillage, the murder of civilians, the use of torture and attacks on humanitarian convoys. Reiterating the findings of the earlier UN report of 2001, the UPDF was again linked to the illegal exploitation of the DRC's natural resources, either directly or through Congolese proxies (OHCHR 2010).

The response of Uganda's Minister for Foreign Affairs to a leaked draft of the OHCHR report was swift. Not only did he reject it on the grounds that it was simply a "compendium of rumours", and demand it not be published, but in a less than veiled threat he stated that one of the consequences of its production had been to "undermine Uganda's resolve to continue contributing to, and participating in, various regional and international peace-keeping operations" (Republic of Uganda 2010, pp. 1–2).

When yet another UN report on the DRC was released in 2012, which described it as a country "plagued by dozens of foreign and national armed groups" (United Nations Security Council 2012, p. 3), Kampala again strenuously denied involvement in its neighbour's affairs (Biryabarema 2012). This UN report noted not only Uganda's continued military presence in eastern DRC but also its support of yet another Congolese rebel movement, the M23, which was largely made up of Congolese Tutsis fighting against both the central government in Kinshasa and residual Rwandan Interahamwe Hutu elements. Ugandan aid to the M23 took the form of arms, training, rear military bases in Uganda, planning and logistics support, and the deployment of UPDF forces to assist in M23 operations. This report highlighted the fact that the provision of such military equipment was a violation of an arms embargo on combatants operating within the DRC which had been imposed by a UN Security Council Resolution in 2003 (United Nations Security Council 2003). In areas controlled by M23, it reported on the continued looting of DRC minerals, in particular gold smuggled into Uganda and re-exported by Ugandan-based dealers in a trade "worth hundreds of millions of United States dollars" (United Nations Security Council 2012, p. 5). The report's findings on the links between the Ugandan (and Rwandan military), and their DRC protégé, were detailed and comprehensive. What was not spelled out, though implicit, was a recognition by the authors of the report that the capability of Uganda and Rwanda to intervene in the DRC had been built up partly thanks to external military assistance. It is in this light that one should view one of its recommendations, namely when it called for "Member States to review and reconsider future military assistance to Rwanda and Uganda" (United Nations Security Council 2012, p. 55).

Rwanda

Kigali also capitalised on the West's new post-Cold War security concerns to strengthen its capacity to contain its enemies and entrench the RPF regime. Rwanda had an additional advantage in terms of negotiations with the West, namely the 1994 genocide. As a result of the West's failure to stop the slaughter, Kigali felt entitled to demand significant latitude in terms of how it dealt with its post-genocide national security concerns. It successfully argued that strengthening its security forces was the only way to prevent a repetition of the events of 1994 and feeding Western sentiments of guilt resulted in more restrained criticism of not only the RPF's repressive internal policies but also its destabilising role in conflicts in its immediate vicinity such as the DRC.

Kigali invested significant time and resources to demonstrate that not only was it a provider of security for post-genocidal Rwandans, but the role it played in various UN-mandated peacekeeping operations meant it operated as a force for good for others. Its first forays in this area began in 2004 in Darfur, Sudan. Kigali framed its involvement there—firstly under the African Union's Mission in Sudan (AMIS) and then under the joint UN/AU mission in Darfur[7]—as meeting an international obligation, namely that of a Responsibility to Protect (aka R2P), a doctrine which had evolved as a result of genocide, war crimes, ethnic cleansing and crimes against humanity which had occurred in the 1990s in Rwanda and during the wars in former Yugoslavia.[8]

Rwandan troops went on to participate in, amongst others, the UN missions in South Sudan,[9] in the Central African Republic,[10] in Mali[11] and through elements from the Rwanda National Police (RNP) in the UN Mission in Haiti.[12] Such commitments to help secure peace in conflict zones around the world help Kigali project an image of Rwanda not only as a country that had risen from the ashes of its genocide, but as one now able to provide security assistance to other countries and their vulnerable populations, helping to bolster Kagame's reputation as one of Africa's 'new leaders' and as a faithful implementer of the principle of 'African solutions to African problems'.

Arguably even more so than either Uganda or Ethiopia, post-genocide Rwanda was subjected to a process of deep militarisation. The Rwanda Defence Force (RDF) established in 2002, and the successor to the RPF's RPA, was the lynchpin for the realisation of Kagame's vision for Rwanda. Pointing out the key role it has played in national life, a team of Rwanda specialists characterised it as "the core institution for the implementation of state policy, the key space for the socialisation of the elite and a link to the citizenry" (Purdeková et al. 2018, p. 159). The integration of members of the pre-1994 national army, and elements of the RPA, into the new renamed RDF, allowed the government to portray the country's national defence forces as the crucible of a new non-ethnic national identity which bridged the Hutu-Tutsi divide.

Given the critical role as essential regime props played by the RDF, and associated security sector bodies such as the police, the intelligence agency and the large number of militias brought together in Local Defence Forces,[13] it was logical that Kigali should have sought additional resources to strengthen Rwanda's security sector. The Kagame regime successfully secured support in all the areas targeted by Western donor countries as part of the growing securitization of their aid, namely SSR, and the training and equipping of African military and police for international peace operations.

In terms of peace operations, Kigali derived significant benefits, both domestically and internationally, from Rwanda's role as a major contributor to peace operations. The deployment of large numbers of its troops and police to peacekeeping operations, and their performance in various missions around the world, was sold to domestic audiences as one in which all Rwandans could justifiably take pride. Rwanda's participation in such operations helps explain a high-water mark in terms of international respectability, namely its election in 2012 to a non-permanent seat in the UN Security Council. As of December 2021, it had over 5208 troops deployed to various UN peace operations and stood in second place (behind Bangladesh) in the ranking of troop contributing countries (United Nations Peacekeeping n.d.).

In addition to international appreciation of Rwanda's prominent role in peacekeeping, the financial benefits accruing to Rwanda were significant. The UN made reimbursement payments in hard currency to the Kigali government for each Rwandan peacekeeping soldier and police officer; in 2020 this stood at US$1428 per month (many times a multiple of the average pay of Rwandan military or police personnel), with the government also receiving reimbursements for use of its equipment and any support services it provided. According to SIPRI data, Kigali's military expenditure for 2020 was US$147 million (SIPRI Military Expenditure Database 2024). The number of Rwandan troops and police on deployment in UN operations that year was 6383 (United Nations n.d.). These peacekeepers would therefore have earned the equivalent of around 62 per cent of the country's military expenditure. Such reimbursements were important in enabling Rwanda to maintain a relatively large number of armed forces personnel (currently around 33,000) to safeguard the country's national security.

The importance Washington attached to Rwanda as a security partner can be seen in the increases in total costs of American support to the Rwandan military following 9/11. If in 2001 the share of military assistance[14] in total US foreign aid disbursements to Rwanda was nil, by 2005 disbursements for this category had reached 11 per cent of the total (US Government Foreign Assistance Tracker 2024). In terms of capacity-building programmes, post-9/11 Rwanda benefitted from the US' ACOTA programme. American support to enhancing the country's anti-terrorism capabilities also figured prominently, with Rwanda participating in the Pentagon's Combating Terrorism Fellowship Program (CTFP). It also benefitted from significant amounts of US military assistance through the DOD's 'Foreign Military Finance' Programme, a credit line for the procurement of defence assets, with waivers of repayment a standard practice. US military assistance also took the form of the provision of training to military students, both in the US and overseas. Rwanda first became a beneficiary of the DOD's International Military Education and Training (IMET) programme in 2003, and over the period 2003–2019 the total value of such IMET assistance to Rwanda amounted to US$7.4 million (US Government Foreign Assistance Tracker 2024). Further cementing the military relationship between the US and Rwanda was the signing in July 2014 of an Acquisition and Cross-Servicing Agreement, a reciprocal defence logistics arrangement granting the Pentagon the legal authority to provide logistic support and supplies to Rwanda in the context of joint operations with Rwandan forces. Another indication of American appreciation for Rwanda's efforts in peacekeeping was the country's inclusion in the Obama administration's APRRP initiative to build up Africa's rapid response capacity to deploy to trouble spots on the continent. With a total budget of US$267.5 million for the period 2015–2017, APRRP obligations for Rwanda amounted to US$36.25 million (US Government Forei gn Assistance Tracker 2024).

As one of London's African 'donor darlings', Rwanda also became a significant beneficiary of British security assistance. One researcher traced the origins of the military relationship between London and Kigali to 2002 when the Rwandan government first requested British assistance to train RDF personnel in peace operations (Beswick 2010, p. 746). One form of support was through the British Peace Support Team Africa (BPSTA) based in Nairobi. Part and parcel of the UK's Ministry of Defence efforts to strengthen the capacity of African forces in peace support operations, this initiative had a specific focus on 'pre-deployment mission-specific training' for soldiers and police and senior officers. Later, when Rwanda went on to establish its own peacekeeping training centre, the Rwanda Peace Academy, the UK's Ministry of Defence continued to provide support to the RDF (*New Times* 2019).

In terms of assistance to SSR in Rwanda, the UK was a major contributor to a regionally focused World Bank trust fund to support the Multi-Country Demobilization and Reintegration Program (MDRP). This covered activities not only in Rwanda but also in other conflict-affected countries in the region such as Angola, the DRC, the Central African Republic, Uganda and Burundi, with the MDRP aiming to demobilise and reintegrate hundreds of thousands of ex-combatants from these various conflicts. Through the trust fund, London provided support to the Rwanda Demobilisation and Reintegration Programme (RDRP) launched in 1997, which aimed to disarm, demobilise and reintegrate into civilian life members of the former regime's *Forces Armées Rwandaises* (FAR), *Interahamwe* (both those inside Rwanda and those who continued to operate across the border in the DRC) and former members of the RPA and RDF, and also provided additional resources on a bilateral basis directly to the RDRP.

The role played by the RDRP in improving the security of the Kagame regime occurred through several channels. Firstly, the disarmament and demobilisation of large numbers of members of opposition armed groups, and their reintegration into civilian life or inclusion in the country's new security forces, lowered the likelihood of successful armed insurrections against the RPF government. The reduced availability of small arms, after those who signed up for the programmes had surrendered their weapons, also helped the RPF to be seen to be delivering on its promise to restore law and order and improve the personal security of its citizens.

Secondly, the integration of former members of dissident groups into institutions designed and operated by the RPF meant large numbers of Rwandans underwent a comprehensive process of socialisation. They were expected to internalise the norms and values of the RPF's official narrative of Rwanda's history, one in which the RDF as the successor to the RPA occupied centre stage as the country's saviour. They would be pressured to abandon their affiliations with other opposition political groups and develop a sense of indebtedness and loyalty to the country's liberators and new political masters.

At the same time, these various Western security assistance programmes contributed to the creation of well-equipped and highly motivated security forces which became critical to the preservation of the RPF regime. As institutions vested in the maintenance of security and stability in terms defined by Kagame, a major article of faith within its ranks was that of the need to ensure the perpetuation of the RPF's grip on power, and they became powerful coercive instruments to be deployed against any who dissented from the RPF.

The enhanced capabilities of the RDF also helped the regime engage in less commendable activities. These included its deployment to neighbouring DRC, which like Uganda proved to be a highly lucrative intervention for Rwanda. Its invasion of the DRC, in conjunction with Ugandan forces, to destroy rebels based there, firstly in 1996 and then again in 1998, enabled Rwanda's illegal exploitation of that country's mineral wealth and other natural resources, with significant revenues flowing into Rwandan coffers. What initially began as attempts to address justifiable security concerns soon gave way to what Filip Reyntjens characterised as "a logic of plunder" (Reyntjens 2004, p. 177).

What was then still the RPA rapidly gained control of large swathes of Congolese territory, either directly or in cooperation with its military proxies, and exploited their resources. Such predatory behaviour was detailed in numerous reports, amongst which the aforementioned report of the UN Panel of Experts of 2001. The Panel identified a complex web of participants which included members of the RPF, the then RPA, and Rwandan private sector companies, all working together with Western firms in the illegal extraction, transport and commercialisation of DRC resources. Based on its in-depth investigation, the Panel concluded that "most companies with important activities related to the natural resources of the Democratic Republic of Congo are owned either by the Government or by individuals very close to the inner circle of President Kagame" (United Nations 2001, p. 16).

The Panel characterised Kagame's role in such illegal activities as "pivotal". His ties to Rwandan businesses operating in the DRC, and his control over the army as Minister of Defence (between 1994 and 2000), meant he would have been aware of the "structures involved in the illegal activities". It concluded this translated into "his implicit approval of the continuation of the illegal exploitation of the resources of the Democratic Republic of the Congo and somehow his complicity as well as his political and moral responsibility" (United Nations 2001, p. 40).

The Panel's report contained a forensic analysis of the volumes and export values of a range of plundered goods. In the case of coltan, which was actively mined by Rwanda Metals, an RPF-owned company, the Panel calculated that between late 1999 and late 2000, the country "must have made at least $250 million over the period" from sales of the mineral, and stated that:

> Here lies the vicious circle of the war. Coltan has permitted the Rwandan army to sustain its presence in the Democratic Republic of Congo. The army has provided protection and security to the individuals and companies extracting the mineral. These have made money which is shared with the army, which in turn provides the enabling environment to continue the exploitation. (United Nations 2001, p. 30)

Amongst punitive measures recommended in the report were UN Security Council sanctions on those responsible for such activities. They included a ban on the import or export of Congolese natural resources to and from Rwanda. Governments were called upon to ensure that those companies registered in their jurisdictions, and their nationals, who broke this embargo were punished, and their financial assets frozen. It also recommended an arms embargo on "the rebel groups operating in the Democratic Republic of the Congo", and that the Security Council should consider "extending this embargo to the States that support or assist these groups" (United Nations 2001, p. 42). Another recommendation, one which would, if applied, have led to a cessation of Western assistance to Rwanda's security sector, was that the Security Council should "decide that all military cooperation with States whose military forces are present in the Democratic Republic of the Congo in violation of its sovereignty be suspended immediately until those armies withdraw from the Democratic Republic of the Congo" (United Nations 2001, p. 43).

Rwanda's plundering of the DRC's resources was accompanied by massive human rights violations. Reports from NGOs[15] and multilateral bodies such as the OAU[16] meant that by 2001 such activities were common knowledge. Allegations of war crimes, crimes against humanity, genocide and violations of human rights perpetrated by Rwandan forces were thoroughly investigated by the UN Team responsible for the OHCHR Report of 2010. This showed that over the course of 1996–1997, and in numerous locations, the then RPA, in conjunction with its AFDL and Burundian allies,[17] had carried out massacres of Hutu refugees, committed torture and rape, and denied access to humanitarian assistance for survivors. The pattern was repeated in 1998–1999 when Rwandan forces again invaded the DRC and was also extensively documented by the OHCHR team.

The OHCHR report also concluded that the AFDL, depicted by Kigali as a domestic Zairean anti-Mobutu rebel movement, was in fact a recent creation of Kigali's dating back to 1996, "whose own troops, weapons and logistics were supplied by Rwanda" (OHCHR 2010, p. 70). It characterised the uprising headed by the AFDL in eastern DRC as a cover, used by Rwandan and Ugandan forces to capture North and South Kivu provinces which they were then able to exploit.

Kigali's reaction to the damning findings of the 2010 OHCHR report was swift and forceful; in line with previous efforts to deflect possible punitive measures, it relied on its prominent role in UN peacekeeping operations. According to Filip Reyntjens, the country's Foreign Minister wrote to UN Secretary-General Ban Ki Moon, warning him that "attempts to take action on this report—either through its release or leaks to the media—will force us to withdraw Rwanda's various commitments to the United Nations, especially in the area of peacekeeping" (Reyntjens 2011, p. 7). That Kigali's threat was viewed as credible can be seen in the UN's reaction, with Ban Ki Moon diverting to Kigali during a trip to various European countries in September 2010 in order to mollify the RPF.

The report produced by the UN's Group of Experts in 2012 again contained comprehensive and compelling evidence of Rwanda's extensive and multi-faceted support to the DRC's rebel movements, in this case to the M23 (which as of this writing Kigali continues strenuously to deny), as well as the presence of its armed forces on DRC territory, and the participation of Rwandans (both private and state officials), in the continued looting of the DRC's resources. Notwithstanding such evidence, both substantial Western development aid and security assistance continued to flow to Rwanda.

Ethiopia

During the Cold War Ethiopia's leaders, of widely differing political persuasions, had expertly played the security card to obtain the necessary external assistance to deal with their security issues. This history provided the new EPRDF leaders in Addis Ababa with important pointers as to how best to take advantage of great power interests and rivalries.

During the long reign of Emperor Haile Selassie, relations with Washington had been particularly close, and in 1953 Addis Ababa granted the Americans access to a communications base in Kagnew (now in Eritrea). Following the signing of a Mutual Defence Assistance Agreement between Washington and Addis Ababa, linked to a twenty-five-year lease agreement on the Kagnew base, Ethiopia became the largest beneficiary of American military assistance in SSA, with the US training and equipping over 40,000 Ethiopian troops (Human Rights Watch 1991, pp. 355–356). This helped the imperial regime combat the armed secessionist movement in Eritrea which Ethiopia had annexed in 1962[18] and the irredentism sponsored by Somalia in Ethiopia's Ogaden region dominated by ethnic Somalis.

In pursuit of its irredentist objectives, Somalia had in turn established close ties with the USSR, signing military assistance agreements with Moscow. With the onset of the Ethiopian revolution in 1974, and chaos which accompanied it, Mogadishu felt an opportunity had been presented to press its 'Greater Somalia' claims on Ethiopian territory, and it launched an invasion of the Ogaden in July 1977 in support of its secessionist brethren across the border.

Relations between the new Marxist Dergue government in Addis Ababa and Washington were unsurprisingly tense from the outset, with the Americans having lost an old and firmly pro-Western ally in Emperor Haile Selassie. The Carter White House also expressed growing concerns with the Dergue's violations of human rights, most evident during the 'Red Terror' of 1977. The Dergue, faced with growing tensions with Washington and rapidly diminishing prospects the Americans would provide the necessary military assistance to enable it to counter the Eritrean and Somali insurgencies, turned to Moscow for support. Already in December 1976, a military assistance agreement estimated to be worth US$100 million had been signed with Moscow (Porter 1984, p. 194), followed by another in May 1977 valued at between US$350 and $400 million (Porter 1984, p. 196). Following Somalia's invasion of the Ogaden in July 1977, and given the richer prize of Ethiopia as an ally on offer, in November 1977 the Soviets switched sides. Moscow launched a massive military operation in support of Addis Ababa, transporting thousands of Cuban troops, Soviet advisors and military hardware to Ethiopia, forcing Somali troops to then withdraw from the Ogaden.

For whoever held the reins of power in Addis Ababa, amongst the lessons to be drawn from the country's experiences during the Cold War was that Ethiopia was seen by external powers to be of significant geo-strategic importance. Evidence for this could be found in the extended American support to the imperial system and then Moscow's decision to bring its substantial assets to bear to rescue the Dergue regime. The interest of external powers in the country's fortunes would continue in the aftermath of the Cold War, with the West then seeing the Horn of Africa as a region hosting Islamic terrorists and believing a post-Dergue Ethiopia might act as a stabilising force.

As the country's history showed, the essential skill required by Ethiopian rulers of any ideological persuasion was an ability to convince foreign powers of the gravity of the threats the country faced, to argue these also undermined the security and national interests of those powers, and that there was a common interest in dealing with them. In the post-Cold War, and then post-9/11 eras, through targeted messaging and carefully calibrated actions, Addis Ababa repeatedly projected an image of being a reliable ally in whatever crusade was on the current Western *ordre du jour* and presented the strengthening of the Ethiopian state's coercive capacity in terms digestible to any Western donor which might have reservations in terms of its negative impact on the status of civil and political liberties in Ethiopia.

The EPRDF offered itself to Washington and other Western capitals as an essential ally in the West's global struggle against Islamic terrorism, highlighting its long history of combating the forces of radical Islam in the region. Beginning in the period of monarchical rule, Addis Ababa under firstly Haile Selassie, then the Dergue and eventually the EPRDF had provided support to the Southern Sudanese SPLA movement and its predecessors in their struggle against successive Islamist governments in Khartoum, most particularly that of Omar El-Bashir and his NIF government.

Smarting from Khartoum's diplomatic support of Saddam Hussein's Iraq during the first Gulf War of 1990–1991, in 1993 Sudan would be placed on the US list of state sponsors of terrorism. In 1997 it was subjected to comprehensive US economic sanctions, and following the attacks of the US embassies in Nairobi and Dar-es-Salaam, the Americans bombed what they claimed was a factory in Khartoum producing nerve agent precursors, with its owner allegedly having links to Al-Qaeda which was seen to be behind the US embassy bombings in East Africa.

Washington's hardening attitudes towards Sudan provided an opportunity for the EPRDF to demonstrate its worth as a trustworthy ally. Ethiopia joined the American-sponsored 'Front Line States' initiative, an anti-Sudan alliance launched in 1995 which brought together Eritrea, Ethiopia and Uganda[19] and which acted as a conduit for American support to the SPLA (Fisher and Anderson 2015, p. 142).

By the early 2000s the EPRDF was also emphasising the country's need for enhanced security and stability as a prerequisite for realising its ambitious national development agenda. This theme was brought up in Ethiopia's PRSP of 2002, success on poverty reduction seen to be dependent on a range of "structural factors", amongst which the achievement of "peace and stability in Ethiopia and in the region" (Federal Republic of Ethiopia 2002, p. 27). Given the increasing importance placed by the West on security as an enabler of development, and growing Western concerns with terrorism, armed conflict in fragile states and the growth of 'ungoverned spaces', Ethiopia was well positioned when it offered to take on specific responsibilities in efforts to deal with these problems.

The Obama White House's counter-terrorism strategy of 2011 designated the broad East Africa region as one of nine priority areas, with specific attention given to the situation in Somalia, a country which suffered from "persistent instability and disorder" and which meant "the United States faces terrorist enemies in East Africa that threaten our people, our interests and our allies" (White House 2011, p. 14). By highlighting the dangers to its own security emanating from outside Ethiopia's borders, and those it faced from internal centrifugal forces, Addis Ababa was able to convince the West to provide it with the necessary assistance to deal with such threats and prevent further instability in the wider region. The question faced by Western donors was whether, in exchange for such a security partnership, they were willing to accept restricted leverage in their discussions with the Ethiopian government on liberalisation of the country's political governance and to overlook the fact that as a former armed liberation movement the EPRDF's use of violence to deal with rivals had always been integral to its political ambitions.

The principal partner in the ruling party, the TPLF, was like the RPF in Rwanda and the NRM in Uganda a highly militarised movement, whose armed wing had successfully taken on and defeated the Soviet-backed Dergue. Again, like its Rwandan and Ugandan counterparts, it had done so through an emphasis on the need for strict internal discipline, secrecy, top-down decision-making, centralised leadership and the internalisation of the principle of the utility of force to achieve political ends. The myriad enemies it had confronted during its rise to power, and its successful application of force to ensure its final victory, meant the TPLF-dominated EPRDF subscribed to a worldview in which opposition forces were not only ubiquitous but needed to be dealt with harshly.

After capturing Addis Ababa in May 1991, the TPLF's military leadership moved quickly to dominate the newly formed Ethiopian National Defence Force (ENDF), the Ethiopian Federal and State Police, the National Intelligence and Security Services, as well as local militia, inculcating in the personnel of these state institutions the principles of both the use of force as a rational tool of statecraft and the need for a strong sense of loyalty to the ruling party coalition and its ethnic support base made up of Tigrayans.[20] The end result was similar to that in Rwanda and Uganda; Ethiopian bodies responsible for security came to be dominated by TPLF/EPRDF loyalists, and membership of the ruling party was seen as essential for career advancement. Notwithstanding constitutional provisions concerning the non-partisan nature of the country's security forces, they were widely seen as enforcement agencies of the ruling party, to be used against opposition forces (both armed and unarmed), in a context in which national security became coterminous with the security of the ruling party and its continued hold on power.[21]

The international atmospherics created by the West's growing concerns with security issues in Africa were permissive of the TPLF/EPRDF's securitisation project. As Museveni and Kagame had done, in order to strengthen Ethiopia's security forces Meles Zenawi took advantage of Western anxieties about ungoverned and conflict-ridden areas of Africa and their links to international terrorism, and repeated the mantra of 'African solutions to African problems'. The external resources that were forthcoming enabled Addis Ababa to not only deploy Ethiopian troops in multilateral peace operations in situations that were of concern to both Addis Ababa and Western capitals, but as would later be demonstrated, such capabilities could easily be turned inwards whenever necessary to deal with domestic political challenges to the EPRDF's rule.

Addis Ababa's willingness to use force as an instrument of statecraft against both domestic and external enemies came to the fore on numerous occasions under Meles Zenawi (and would surface again under his successors Hailemariam, who applied a punishing violence to deal with the 2015–2016 protests in Oromia, and the Abiy Ahmed government in its conduct of the war in Tigray). It was evident, for example, in the decision by Meles Zenawi to deploy the ENDF against its erstwhile ally Eritrea. Despite the EPLF and EPRDF having enjoyed a history of close cooperation during their joint struggle against the Dergue, a border dispute between Eritrea and Ethiopia led to a bloody war from 1998 to 2000. The conflict ebbed and flowed over land which did not appear to have any major economic or strategic significance. By the time a ceasefire and an interim peace agreement were brokered in 2000, sources estimated that up to 100,000 soldiers from both armies may have been killed in the conflict (International Crisis Group 2003).

At around the same time, the security situation in neighbouring Somalia, which had been deteriorating since the collapse of Siad Barré's regime in January 1991, worsened significantly, and to all intents and purposes there would be no central government in the country until the formation of the Transitional Federal Government (TFG) in 2006. Somalia came to represent the paradigmatic example of that bugbear of Western securocrats, namely an 'ungoverned space', as it not only suffered from centrifugal forces exemplified by the secession of the self-declared Republic of Somaliland in 1991, followed by a declaration of the autonomy of the Puntland region in 1998, but also from seemingly endless internal strife as various factions (including Islamic fundamentalist groupings), fought for control of what remained of the rump country.

Between 1999 and 2003, ENDF troops regularly crossed into Somalia in hot pursuit operations, targeting the Al-Ittihad Al-Islamiya, a Somali Islamist group which claimed as its key objective the creation of an Islamic State in the Horn of Africa. Later, the internationally recognised TFG, backed by Ethiopia, came under pressure from the forces of the Islamic Courts Union (ICU),[22] an organisation which many Al-Ittihad fighters joined to eventually form the Al-Shabaab[23] and which operated as the armed wing of the ICU. When in June 2006 the ICU gained control of Mogadishu, there were concerns in Addis Ababa, given its own large Muslim population, of a spillover of jihadist violence into Ethiopia, as well as of a possible resurgence of secessionist sentiments in the Ogaden and irredentist ambitions in Mogadishu.

The US government had come to believe not only that Al-Shabaab had close ties with Al-Qaeda, but that the ICU was protecting terrorists on Washington's most wanted list, including figures linked to the bombings of the American embassies in East Africa. Capitalising on such concerns, Ethiopia secured American backing for a major military intervention in Somalia. This was launched in early December 2006 and involved both

ENDF and TFG troops. Enjoying the advantage of Ethiopian armoured units and air support, by December 28, 2006, the joint ENDF and TFG troops were able to enter Mogadishu, and by March 2007 the last pockets of ICU resistance in the capital had been eliminated.

Data on flows of American security assistance to Ethiopia show the extent of Addis Ababa's success in presenting threats to Ethiopia's national security as threats to Western donor countries, most particularly the US, and in depicting Ethiopia as an essential partner in Washington's global war on terror. They also indicated the primacy of security considerations in American decision-making on policy towards Ethiopia, and Washington's reluctance to apply any meaningful pressure on the Ethiopian government for its lack of progress on democratisation and its poor human rights record.

Ethiopia under the EPRDF was significantly less reliant than either Uganda or Rwanda on Western military hardware. The Dergue's heavy dependence on Eastern bloc armaments, and in particular Soviet weaponry, meant significant imports of the latter from Russia, and other former Eastern bloc countries such as Bulgaria and Hungary, would continue under the new rulers in Addis Ababa (SIPRI, Arms Transfer Database 2024). However, after 9/11 the Pentagon did become a significant provider of military assistance to Ethiopia. In 2002 Ethiopia benefited from the DOD's 'Foreign Military Financing Program' to the value of US$2.8 million and continued to do on an annual basis until 2020. In 2006, the year of the controversial elections in Ethiopia, and despite clear evidence of state violence against opposition forces following the controversial elections of the previous year, the Pentagon nevertheless provided assistance to the tune of US$1.9 million to Ethiopia. Beginning in 2002, Ethiopia also regularly benefitted from the DOD's 'International Military Education and Training Program' for the training of Ethiopian military students in the US. Ethiopian security sector personnel participated in the Pentagon's 'Combating Terrorism Fellowship Program' and in its 'Global Train and Equip Program—Logistics Enhancement' which aimed to boost the ENDF's "expeditionary logistics capabilities", as well as the US Department of State's APRRP (US Government Foreign Assistance Tracker 2024).

Notes

1. For example, the UPDF Act of 2005 stated all officers were required to swear an oath of allegiance. It was significant that "true allegiance" was owed firstly to "the President", followed by the "Republic of Uganda",

and they were "duty-bound" to defend "him/her against all enemies". (Parliament of the Republic of Uganda, The Uganda Peoples' Defence Forces Act, 2005. Fifth Schedule.)

2. Framing itself as a millenarian religious movement with the stated objective of ruling according to Christian principles, the LRA was accused of widespread human rights abuses by Western governments and NGOs, including the routine recruitment of child soldiers, rape of civilian women and use of torture. In 2001 Washington classified the LRA as a terrorist group. Kampala's success in influencing Western perceptions of security threats in East Africa can also be seen in the US State Department's classification in 2008 of the LRA's leader, Joseph Kony, as a 'Specially Designated Global Terrorist', the relevant Department of State's Notice declaring that Kony "has committed, or poses a significant risk of committing, acts of terrorism that threaten the security of the US nationals or the national security, foreign policy, or economy of the United States" (https://www.govinfo.gov/content/pkg/FR-2008-08-29/pdf/E8-20164.pdf).
3. For a comprehensive analysis, which disentangles the myriad actors and their interests in the interlinked Ugandan, Zairean, Sudanese and Rwandan conflicts, see Prunier (2004, pp. 359–383).
4. In the First Congo War of 1996–1997, Angola joined forces with Uganda, Rwanda and Burundi in their invasion of what was still Zaire, one of their shared strategic objectives being to overthrow Mobutu, install Laurent Kabila in power and end Kinshasa's support for their respective rebel movements which had set up operations on Zairean territory. For Luanda, the conflict was an opportunity to remove Mobutu, a longstanding backer of Angola's various rebel movements, most notably UNITA. Following a rapid military advance on Kinshasa planned by Kigali, with significant involvement of elements of the RPA (but passed off by Kigali as an AFDL victory to evade international opprobrium over the violation of Zaire's territorial integrity), Kabila was installed as the renamed DRC's new head of state in May 1997. However, relations between Kabila and his Ugandan and Rwandan backers quickly soured, largely due to growing tensions with Rwanda whose dominant military presence (Kabila's Chief of Staff was a Rwandan), which was increasingly resented by others in the new DRC government. When Kabila ordered Rwandan and Ugandan military forces to leave the country in July 1998, the stage was set for the Second Congo War, which raged until 2003. The Tutsis of the eastern DRC, who constituted the rump of Kabila's AFDL forces, faced attacks from both Congolese and Rwandan Hutu forces and rose up against Kinshasa. Rwandan forces again intervened in support of their ethnic brethren who came together to form the *Rassemblement Congolais pour la Démocratie* (RCD). As Mobutu

had done, Kabila responded by backing both Congolese Hutu and Rwandan Hutu elements. This time around the Angolans, concerned another government in Kinshasa might renew its support to Savimbi, backed the Kabila government against its former allies, and Angolan troops fought both Rwandan troops and Kigali's proxies.

5. At a meeting in Dakar in October 2001, several African states signed up to the *Dakar Declaration Against Terrorism*.
6. Given Mobutu had provided succour to both the anti-Museveni ADF forces based in the area bordering Uganda, as well as anti-RPF Hutu elements from the former regime in Kigali, growing anti-Mobutu sentiment within Zaire represented an opportunity for both Kampala and Kigali to secure their border areas.
7. Known as the United Nations-African Union Mission in Darfur (UNAMID), this joint AU and UN operation was mandated to bring stability to the war-torn Darfur region of Sudan. Rwanda was a major troop-contributing country to UNAMID, deploying both Rwandan police and soldiers to Darfur. Kigali claimed its involvement was based on the R2P norm, one that was particularly apposite given Rwanda's own recent history, and Rwanda's contribution was presented as an effort to prevent the genocide of Darfur's non-Arab population by Sudanese government forces allied with the Janjaweed (local Arab militia).
8. The R2P principle was unanimously endorsed by the UN's General Assembly in 2005. While the primary responsibility to protect their own populations from mass atrocities rested with individual states, it also placed an obligation on the international community, in cases where national governments had failed in their duties, to take collective action to protect populations from such crimes, including the use of force under Chapter VII of the Charter.
9. The UN Mission in South Sudan (UNMISS) was established on July 8, 2011, prior to that country's independence on July 9, 2011. Its primary mandate was to assist the government in Juba with post-conflict peace consolidation.
10. Known by its French acronym MINUSCA, the United Nations Multidimensional Integrated Stabilization Mission in the Central African Republic was established in April 2014 in response to the complex humanitarian, political, human rights and security crisis in that country. As of January 2021, Rwanda was the largest contributor to the mission in terms of both troops and police (https://peacekeeping.un.org/en/mission/minusca).
11. The United Nations Multidimensional Integrated Stabilization Mission in Mali, known by its French acronym MINUSMA, was established in 2013 with a mandate to stabilise the country following the outbreak of a rebel-

lion led by Tuareg and other groups living in the north seeking the independence of the region.

12. Known by its acronym in French as MINUSTAH, the United Nations Stabilization Mission in Haiti operated until 2017. Its original 2004 mandate aimed to restore stability following the overthrow of President Aristide in February 2004 by armed opposition groups. The Rwandan police contingent was sent in the context of a major increase in the mission's force levels following the devastating earthquake of January 2010, the objective being to provide greater security for the country's recovery efforts.
13. These militia groups were established in the immediate aftermath of the RPF's victory and, after a short period of military training, were then tasked with providing security, in conjunction with the police, to their communes. In 2014 the Local Defence Forces (LDFs) were replaced by District Administration Security Support Organs (DASSOs). Unsurprisingly given the RPF's extended exposure to Ugandan practices, these mirrored the local level Security and Defence Committees set up by Kampala and were, like their predecessors the LDFs, mandated to support law enforcement at local level, as well as inform local administrations of "any suspicious security threat" ("Govt creates new force to replace local defence", *The New Times*, June 23, 2014, Kigali).
14. Defined, according to USAID, as "programs primarily for the benefit of recipient government armed forces, or aid which substantially enhances military capabilities".
15. HRW reports provoked the most forceful responses from Kigali, an indication of the importance it attached to being able to continue drawing down on its 'genocide credit', and its general hostility towards those NGOs it did not control. (See, for example, Human Rights Watch 2000a, 2000b.) Amongst the government's accusations levelled at HRW were that it was an organisation sympathetic to genocidal forces, intent on provoking ethnic division and undermining Rwanda's national unity and on souring the relations between the government and the donor community, all under the guise of a declared concern for human rights.
16. For example, an International Panel of Eminent Persons (IPEP) was established by the OAU in 1998. Led by the former President of Botswana, Ketumile Masire, it was mandated to investigate the 1994 genocide in Rwanda and its aftermath, including the fall of Mobutu and the installing of Laurent Désiré Kabila as President of the DRC in May 1997. Amongst its findings on the actions of the RPF, before and after the genocide, were that after the RPF's invasion of Rwanda in 1990, its forces had shown "little restraint in dealing with Hutu civilians in the areas they 'liberated', a pattern they have followed throughout the past decade...Although the precise numbers are in question, RPF troops committed crimes against

humanity as they advanced through the country" (OAU 2000, p. 38). Following the RPA's invasion of the DRC in 1996 as part of an anti-Mobutu alliance, the IPEP affirmed that Kigali's pursuit of what it termed 'genocidal forces' was seen to have become a "virtual doctrine of RPF policy", one which translated into a "unilateral right to eliminate the threat of Hutu Power, wherever it exists, wherever it must be pursued". One of the consequences was that "in that hunt, the distinction between a Hutu mass murderer and a Hutu civilian is often far from self-evident, and there seems little doubt to us that the RPA rarely stops to ask" (OAU 2000, p. 223).

17. Like neighbouring Rwanda, Burundi suffered from tensions between its minority Tutsi and majority Hutu populations which occasionally led to inter-ethnic violence. Tutsi domination of the Burundian state, in particular its armed forces, and outbreaks of violence in the mid-1990s, led to a growing number of Burundian Hutu refugees fleeing to South Kivu in the DRC. Paralleling Rwandan Hutu Power bases in the refugee camps in North Kivu, Burundian Hutu organisations set up similar structures in South Kivu, recruiting and training Burundian Hutu refugees with the avowed aim of returning to Burundi and overthrowing the Tutsi-dominated government in Bujumbura. Faced with this threat, Burundi took the opportunity provided by the Ugandan/Rwanda decision to also invade the DRC in 1996 to deal with its own Hutu rebels on its neighbour's territory.
18. Following the British defeat of Italian occupying forces during the Second World War, Eritrea became a British protectorate until 1952 when the United Nations General Assembly voted in favour of the territory's federation with Ethiopia, an arrangement under which Eritrea enjoyed considerable freedoms granted in a UN-drafted constitution, such as its own parliament, administration, judicial system and control over taxation. Following gradual encroachments by Addis Ababa on Eritrea's autonomy, in 1962 Haile Selassie sent Ethiopian troops into the territory and then formally incorporated Eritrea into Ethiopia as one of its fourteen regions.
19. The Front Line States coalition proved, however, to be of limited effectiveness, as Uganda's attention turned to its fight against the LRA, while Ethiopia and Eritrea would soon fall out with each other and engage in their bloody border conflict which began in May 1998.
20. One survey, conducted by a local democracy and human rights NGO in 2014, and therefore twenty-four years after the defeat of the Dergue, showed the extent of continued TPFL Tigrayan dominance of the armed forces, with forty-nine out of a total sixty-four Generals in command positions being Tigrayans (Ginbot 7 Movement for Justice, Democracy and Freedom 2014).

21. On these points, based on interviews with key players, see van Veen (2016).
22. The ICU was a coalition of social, political and religious forces which through a network of Sharia courts and their sheikhs based its administration on the implementation of Sharia law.
23. For an overview of the rise of Al-Shabaab, its links to the ICU and its impact on Ethiopian decision-making regarding military options in Somalia, see Wise (2011).

References

Al-Jazeera. 2010. "Al-Shaba claims Uganda Bombings", June 13, 2010. https://www.aljazeera.com/news/2010/7/13/al-shabab-claims-uganda-bombings.

Beswick, Danielle. 2010. "Peacekeeping, Regime Security and 'African Solutions to African Problems': exploring motivations for Rwanda's involvement in Darfur". *Third World Quarterly*, Vol 31, No 5, 2010.

Biryabarema, Elias. 2012. "Uganda's army denies supporting Congo Rebels". *Reuters*, July 30, 2012.

Bush, George W. 2001. "Address to the Joint Session of the 107th Congress", Washington D.C. September 20, 2001.

Daily Monitor. 2000. "Stop questioning Uganda's military expenditure, Museveni tells donors", Kampala, January 22, 2000.

Federal Republic of Ethiopia. 2002. *Sustainable Development and Poverty Reduction Program*, Ministry of Finance and Economic Development, Addis Ababa, July 2002.

Fisher, Jonathan and David M. Anderson. 2015. "Authoritarianism and the securitization of development in Africa", *International Affairs*, Chatham House, Vol 91, Issue 1, January 2015.

Ginbot 7 Movement for Justice, Democracy and Freedom, "TPLF's Minority Ethnic Monopoly of the Armed Forces in Ethiopia (A revisit after four years)". October 6, 2014, http://www.ginbot7.org/2014/10/07/tplfs-minority-ethnic-monopoly-of-the-armed-forces-in-ethiopia-a-revisit-after-four-years/.

Guardian. 2009. "Aid to Uganda: How the UK government is supporting the country", January 30, 2009.

Human Rights Watch. 1991 *Evil Days: Thirty Years of War and Famine in Ethiopia*, New York, September 1991.

Human Rights Watch. 1999. *Civilian Killings by Warring Parties in Kisangani*, News Release, August 18, 1999.

Human Rights Watch. 2000a. *Rwanda: the search for security and human rights abuses*, New York, April 2000

Human Rights Watch. 2000b. *Eastern Congo ravaged: killing civilians and silencing protest*, New York, May 2000.

International Crisis Group, *Ethiopia and Eritrea: War or Peace?* ICG Africa Report, No.68, Brussels, September 24, 2003.

Molenaers, Nadia et al. 2013. "What determines the suspension of budget support in Sub-Saharan Africa?". *Working Paper/2013.08,* Institute of Development Policy and Management, September 2013.

New Times. 2014. "Govt creates new force to replace local defence", Kigali, June 23, 2014.

New Times. 2019. "UK keen to renew peacekeeping training partnership". Kigali, December 15, 2019.

Office of the United Nations High Commissioner for Human Rights (OHCHR), *DRC Mapping Exercise – Mapping of the Most Serious Human Rights and International Humanitarian Law Violations Committed in the Democratic Republic of the Congo between 1993 and 2003*, Geneva, August 2010.

Organization of African Unity (OAU). 1991. *The Kampala Document: Towards a Conference on Security, Stability, Development and Cooperation in Africa.* Kampala, Uganda, 19–21 May 1991.

Organization of African Unity (OAU). 2000. *The Preventable Genocide.* The Report of the International Panel of Eminent Personalities to Investigate the 1994 Genocide in Rwanda and the Surrounding Events, July 7, 2000.

Parliament of the Republic of Uganda. 2000. *The National Security Council Act, 2000.*

Parliament of the Republic of Uganda. 2002. *The Anti-Terrorism Act*, 2002.

Parliament of the Republic of Uganda. 2005. *The Uganda Peoples' Defence Forces Act*, 2005. Fifth Schedule, Kampala.

Porter, Bruce D. 1984. *The USSR in Third World Conflicts – Soviet Arms and Diplomacy in Local Wars 1945–1980.* Cambridge University Press, 1984.

Prunier, Gérard. 2004. "Rebel Movements and Proxy Warfare: Uganda, Sudan, and the Congo (1986–99)". *African Affairs*, Vol 103, No. 412, (July 2004), Oxford University Press: Royal Africa Society.

Purdeková, Andrea et al. 2018. "Militarisation of governance after conflict: beyond the rebel-ruler framework – the case of Rwanda". *Third World Quarterly*, Vol 39, No 1, Routledge, 2018.

Republic of Uganda. 2004. *White Paper on Defence Transformation*, June 2004, Kampala.

Republic of Uganda. 2010. *Uganda's Position on the Draft DRC Mapping Exercise Report* (MFA/X/33), Kampala: Ministry of Foreign Affairs, September 27, 2010.

Reyntjens, Filip. 2004. "Rwanda Ten Years On: From Genocide to Dictatorship". *African Affairs*, Vol 103, Issue 411, April 2004.

Reyntjens, Filip. 2011. "Constructing the truth, dealing with dissent, domesticating the World: Governance in post-genocide Rwanda", *African Affairs*, Vol.110, Issue 438, 2011.

Stockholm International Peace Research Institute (SIPRI). 2024. *Arms Transfer Database* (https://armstransfers.sipri.org/ArmsTransfer/TransferData/transferResults?logic=on).

Stockholm International Peace Research Institute (SIPRI). 2024. *SIPRI Military Expenditure Database*. https://doi.org/10.55163/CQGC9685 (https://www.sipri.org/databases/milex).

US Government Foreign Assistance Tracker. Accessed August 2 2024. https://www.foreignassistance.gov/

United Nations Peacekeeping. n.d. "Troop and Police Contributors". https://peacekeeping.un.org/en/troop-and-police-contributors.

United Nations Security Council. 2003. Resolution 1493 (2003), July 28 2003, (S/RES/1493 (2003).

van Veen, Erwin. 2016. "Perpetuating Power: Ethiopia's political settlement and the organization of security", CRU Report, September 2016, Clingendael Netherlands Institute of International Relations, The Hague, The Netherlands.

United Nations Security Council. 2012. *Final Report of the Group of Experts on the DRC submitted in accordance with paragraph 4 of Security Council resolution 2021 (2011) (S/2021/843)* November 15, 2012.

United Nations. 2001. *Report of the Panel of Experts on the Illegal Exploitation of Natural Resources and Other Forms of Wealth of the Democratic Republic of Congo*, (S/2001/357) 12 April 2001.

United Nations. n.d. *Contributors to UN Peacekeeping Operations by Country and Post Police, UN Military Experts on Mission, Staff Officers and Troops* (https://peacekeeping.un.org/sites/default/files/01_summary_of_contributions_33.pdf).

USAID. 2019. *Foreign Aid Explorer* (https://explorer.usaid.gov/).

White House. 2011. *National Strategy for Counterterrorism*, June 2011.

White House. 2002. The National Security Strategy of the United States of America

Wise, Rob. 2011. 'Al Shabaab', AQAM Futures Project Case Study Series, Case Study No.2, July 2011, Center for Strategic and International Studies, Washington D.C.

Woodrow Wilson International Centre for Scholars. 2002. *Speech by His Excellency Yoweri Museveni, President of the Republic of Uganda*, Washington D.C., May 14, 2002.

CHAPTER 12

Working the Compacts: Western Aid and the Consolidation of Authoritarianism

See No Evil, Hear No Evil, Speak No Evil

The democratic regressions in Uganda, Ethiopia and Rwanda—which preceded the COVID pandemic but which came to the fore during the global health emergency—were made possible by both the political and economic governance systems set up by their ruling parties and the role played by external actors, in particular Western donors, who through their actions over the course of many years facilitated (and continue to enable) the consolidation of authoritarian practices in these countries. However, the favourable report cards produced by donors on the development progress in these countries meant less effort was expended in scrutinising the state of the rule of law, human rights and democratic space in their African partners, and as argued below this was accompanied by a lackadaisical approach on the part of donors concerning the reliability of some of the glowing statistics on their development progress disseminated by these regimes. So long as Ethiopia, Rwanda and Uganda continued to play the role of strategic partners, and delivered on the more easily quantifiable and verifiable outcomes in terms of international development goals—and which Western donors often appeared to judge more important than any slow to non-existent progress, and even deterioration, in standards of political governance, the rule of law and respect for human rights—slippages in the latter were set aside. As during the Cold War, and notwithstanding indications in the early post-Cold War years that aid would be

M. Simpson, *Donors, Democracy and Development in Africa*,
https://doi.org/10.1007/978-3-031-74917-9_12

contingent on the liberalisation of the political systems of beneficiaries, Western donor behaviour towards these countries prioritised political stability, effective government, policy predictability and strategic partnerships over political freedoms and civil and human rights. Over time there developed what appeared to be a conspiracy of silence, if not collusion, between many Western donors and these African regimes.

Pushing for More, Faster and Better Aid

In the new post-Cold War global development environment based on 'new partnerships', a core interest of Addis Ababa, Kampala and Kigali lay in securing as much aid as possible from their Western benefactors, and for this to be delivered in ways which gave them maximum autonomy in how it was used. One benefit they expected to derive from the application of Paris Declaration principles—in addition to securing as large a share as possible of an enlarged ODA envelope as donors strived to meet the target of 0.7 per cent of GNI for ODA—was improved predictability (i.e. their levels of confidence regarding the actual amounts of aid to be disbursed, as opposed to simply committed) and reductions in the volatility of aid flows (which could take the form of both irregular and unexpected aid 'shortfalls' as well as 'windfalls').[1] This was particularly important given that analysts regularly flagged the large gap between donor commitments and disbursements, such that commitments were often poor predictors of expenditures.[2] In the Paris Declaration, donors had therefore committed to provide "reliable indicative commitments of aid over a multi-year framework and disburse aid in a timely and predictable fashion according to agreed schedules" (OECD 2005, p. 7) and to halve by 2010 the proportion of aid not disbursed in the year for which it was scheduled.

Other items in the Paris Declaration also had a significant impact on donor relations with these countries. These included donor commitments to move away from their earlier, more tightly controlled, project-based approach to development assistance[3] and enable partner country governments to receive and channel aid resources in accordance with their own priorities and thereby strengthen 'national ownership', helping them to adopt longer timeframes in their planning and also reducing the administrative burden of having to report to donors on large numbers of individual projects. Many major Western donors would partially replace project-based aid with significant GBS transfers to partner country treasuries (in effect making such resources indistinguishable from other government revenues), though the modality, after its heyday in the first decade of the new millennium, would then fall out of fashion for a range of reasons, not least the 2008 global financial crisis and the election of more fiscally conservative governments in some Western donor countries. Benefits from GBS modality were also supposed to accrue to donors, as it not only precluded the need to design and implement a wide range of programmes and projects, but was a quick and easy way to offload large amounts of aid. So long as partner countries could demonstrate the external resources provided were impacting positively on a set of agreed indicators such as those in the MDGs, increasing Western donor funds in the form of budget support would flow in their direction.

All three regimes proved extremely successful in pushing their demands for both more and better aid through debt relief, new concessional loans and grants, budget support transfers and other forms of assistance such as securitised aid. In particular, they took advantage of the appearance of PRSPs in the late 1990s, with financial transfers increasingly taking the form of Poverty Reduction Budget Support to those countries which demonstrated that poverty reduction was receiving top priority in their development plans and budgets, which declared they subscribed to technical 'good governance' principles, and which could show they had reached the required standards in terms of their administrative and financial systems such that donors were reassured the funds transferred were properly managed.

Kampala, Kigali and Addis Ababa felt sufficiently confident in their status as donor darlings to hold the feet of Western donors to the fire in terms of their undertakings. They regularly expressed a clear preference for donor assistance to be provided through budget support. For example, in its PRSP of 2000, the Ugandan government stated approvingly that it had witnessed "an increasing commitment by our development partners to the provision of budgetary support...this is extremely welcome" (Government of Uganda 2000, p. 21). In the case of Rwanda, some donors were clearly more hesitant in moving towards budget support, with its PRSP noting that "many donors prefer to provide project support rather than budget support", though the Kagame government nevertheless made it clear that it preferred "to receive resources on the most flexible terms", that is, through budget support (Government of Rwanda 2002, p. 81). Addis Ababa likewise announced in its PRSP its "clear and strong preference for budget support" (Federal Democratic Republic of Ethiopia 2002, p. ix).

However, one of the consequences of the shift in funding modalities to budget support was it became increasingly difficult to 'follow the money'. Donors promoting budget support seemed to have disregarded the enduring, uncomfortable and fundamental problem of 'aid fungibility', whereby resources freed up in national budgets through such direct transfers might then be used for less laudable priorities, such as strengthening the means of repression. As succinctly put by one eminent economist, "Aid is fungible: a recipient can promise to spend aid on health care and do so with projects that would have been undertaken in any case, freeing up funds for nonapproved purposes" (Deaton 2015, p. 302). This problem is particularly acute in situations where national budgets in fact represented only a portion of the resources available to certain governments that are able to draw on not only parallel sources of revenue generated by business empires such as those controlled by the ruling parties in Uganda, Ethiopia and Rwanda, but also those obtained through the exploitation of other countries' resources such as the DRC.

Turning on the Taps

During the Clinton administrations, the US approved significant increases in foreign aid to Sub-Saharan Africa. Benefitting from strong bipartisan support, the upward trend was maintained by George W. Bush and Barack Obama; US foreign economic assistance to the region rose from US$2.3 billion in 2001 to US$12.1 billion by 2016 (US Government Foreign Assistance Tracker 2024).[4] And countries led by Washington's favoured 'new leaders' benefitted disproportionately from such increases. In the case of Uganda, US economic assistance obligations to that country stood at US$73 million in 1993 (the year Clinton took office), and by 2016 they had reached US$730 million (in 2016 constant dollars), a tenfold increase. Over the same period the pattern was repeated for Ethiopia, with a rise in American economic assistance from US$153 million to US$1.1 billion, while Rwanda benefitted from an increase from US$54 million to US$231 million (US Government Foreign Assistance Tracker 2024).

The prominent positions Washington and London occupied on the Executive Boards of both the IMF and World Bank also helped these African countries benefit from significant debt relief. In 1998 Uganda became the first country to access the West's Highly Indebted Poor Countries (HIPC) debt relief initiative channelled through the World Bank and IMF. Faced with high levels of external debt distress, and the accumulation of significant arrears, Kampala eventually benefitted from debt relief provided by HIPC, its successor programme the Enhanced HIPC (IMF 2000), and the Multilateral Debt Relief Initiative (MDRI), a programme championed by the UK Chancellor of the Exchequer Gordon Brown and unveiled at the G-8 summit at Gleneagles in 2005. As a result of these various debt-relief initiatives, as of August 2018 Uganda had benefitted to the tune of US$5.3 billion (IMF 2019, p. 31).

Ringing Western endorsements of Uganda's development policies, and in particular its repeated commitments to poverty reduction, resulted in not only substantial inflows of Western aid but more specifically large amounts of budget support aid. Uganda became one of the first countries to take advantage of the West's new modality of direct transfers to the treasuries of partner countries that were based on assessments that a given country's budget formulation and execution processes, and its overall public financial management systems, were sound. As a result, not only did total ODA flows to Uganda—dominated by resource flows from members of the OECD-DAC—increase in absolute terms from US$909 million in 1998 to US$1.335 billion in 2004, but budget support disbursements rose at an even faster rate, growing from US$66 million to U$409 million over the period. This represented an increase from 7 per cent to 31 per cent in the weight of GBS in total ODA received by Uganda over the period. In addition, ODA as a percentage of GNI increased from close to 10 per cent to 17 per cent between 1998 and 2004 (IDD and Associates 2006, Box B2) and as a percentage of total government expenditure GBS funds rose from just under 5 per cent to 22.5 per cent (IDD and Associates 2006, Table B6). In a further sign of the Western donor community's embrace of Uganda, while the World Bank, the Netherlands and the UK were the only countries and multilateral agencies to provide Kampala with budget support in 1998, by 2004 they had been joined by a further ten OECD bilateral donor countries, as well as the European Commission (EC) (IDD and Associates 2006, Table 3.5).

In the course of a Parliamentary debate on March 25, 1998, on the UK government's White Paper on International Development, Secretary of State Clare Short singled out post-genocide Rwanda for a special mention, stating she was committed "to doing everything we can to work with the Government of Rwanda to achieve reconciliation, to rebuild the economy and to help with debt" (House of Commons Hansard 1998: Column 484). Clare Short's staunch support of the government in Kigali resulted in DFID becoming Rwanda's largest bilateral donor partner, with transfers amounting to £168 million over the period 2000–2005, which represented 5 per cent of total UK aid to Africa.

In addition, DFID's influence within the Western development community meant Rwanda also enjoyed significant debt relief. Between HIPC and MDRI, as of August 2018 Kigali had received close to US$1.78 billion in debt relief from the BWIs, the African Development Bank (AfDB) and the Paris Club of bilateral creditors (IMF 2019, p. 31). Total ODA to Rwanda more than doubled between 1997 and 2004, rising from US$247 million in 1997, which represented 17.5 per cent of GNI, to US$500 million and nearly 26 per cent of GNI in 2004. In 2000 DFID also became the first donor to provide GBS assistance to Rwanda to the tune of US$13.7 million. After DFID's vote of confidence in the Kagame government, by 2004 it had been joined by SIDA, the World Bank and the EC as providers of GBS to Rwanda. That year the two bilateral donors and two multilateral institutions were responsible for transferring close to US$130 million directly to Rwanda's Treasury, with GBS representing around 26 per cent of total ODA to Rwanda, a rapid rise from the 4 per cent registered in 2000 when GBS transfers had first begun (IDD and Associates 2006, Table B5).

In 2002 Ethiopia became one of the first African countries to finalise a PRSP. By 2018 it had received significant debt relief through HIPC and MDRI amounting to US$6.4 billion (IMF 2019, p. 31). World Bank and IMF approval of Ethiopia's PRSP made further concessional assistance from the two organisations available. It also signalled to the wider donor community that in their view the strategy constituted a sound basis for their continued engagement in support of the government's development policies. Given the apparent congruence between the policies pursued by the Ethiopian government and Western donor priorities, it quickly became a 'country of focus' for Western bilateral donors. Total bilateral ODA from OECD-DAC countries increased from US$494 million in 1998 (in constant 2016 prices) to just over US$2 billion by 2016, while assistance from multilateral agencies such as the IMF, World Bank, AfDB and UN agencies also rose from US$367 million to US$2 billion over the same period. By 2016 Ethiopia had become the world's largest recipient of ODA from OECD-DAC bilateral donors and the multilateral institutions (OECD 2023).

PRSPs and Marketing the 'New Partnerships'

The priority attached to apolitical progress indicators in documents such as PRSPs provided significant scope for African leaders to substitute these for any democratic reforms their benefactors might demand, and they could do so, confident there would be no interruptions in Western aid flows. In any case, if judged necessary to meet donor expectations, statements of intent to liberalise their political systems and move their countries down the democratisation path (but without any precise definition of concepts or firm timelines being attached) could easily be included in such documents.

Taking the example of Ethiopia, in a statement which would have been warmly welcomed by Ethiopia's Western donors given the links between the economic and political liberalisation processes they believed should ideally be implemented by partner countries, Ethiopia's PRSP specifically referenced the government's recognition of the "significance of conducting economic and political transformations simultaneously" (Federal Democratic Republic of Ethiopia 2002, p. 39). The PRSP committed the government to improve the country's democratic institutions, since:

> a democratic system, which is based on the people's participation in the development process, and which ensures good governance, is a vital instrument for combatting poverty and backwardness. It is therefore mandatory that democratisation be one of our major objectives. (Federal Democratic Republic of Ethiopia 2002, p. 50)

This pledge would have been taken at face value by Western capitals, without bothering to delve deeper into the EPRDF's understanding of what constituted 'democratisation' given its adherence to the ideology of Revolutionary Democracy and the limitations this placed on political pluralism.

Another feature common to the PRSPs of the three countries was how they framed relations with Western donors, which showed their mastery of 'development speak'. All three documents highlighted the important role of donors in their development processes, how these African governments saw the 'new partnerships' developing, and the warm and open relations which they believed characterised such interactions.

In the case of Uganda, its PRSP drew attention to the fact donors had been present at a range of meetings during the preparation of the document, during which their views had been sought on the government's resource allocation plans. A working group had brought together government, civil society and donors, specifically "to make policy and program recommendations on how the government could strengthen its poverty eradication efforts" (Government of Uganda 2000, p. 3).

Rwanda's PRSP referenced the involvement of donors in its drafting and stressed that the "assistance of development partners is very much appreciated" (Government of Rwanda 2002, p. 31). In addition, it stated that future relations between Kigali and donors were to be governed by a mutually agreed set of rules of engagement, namely the 'Guidelines for Productive Aid Coordination in Rwanda', which would help ensure optimal coordination during the PRSP's implementation. In their assessment of Rwanda's PRSP, World Bank and IMF staff noted approvingly that "government officials at all levels have embraced poverty reduction as the key objective of government policy" (IMF and IDA 2002, p. 2) and mentioned that the government had consulted BWI missions and other development partners.

Ethiopia's government also used its first PRSP to put forward its views on the role of donors. The PRSP made numerous references to donor support to various sector-specific programmes and their participation in the national consultations on poverty reduction priorities. As a result, the document noted, in line with the Paris Principles on 'new partnerships', such interactions had led to a "strong partnership between the government and donors that focused on poverty reduction" (Federal Democratic Republic of Ethiopia 2002, p. 150). Furthermore, the government's hope was that progress made in terms of improving the management of public resources and accountability of the public sector would help reassure donors their funds were being spent properly, so they could continue to provide resources in support of "a common goal, i.e., poverty reduction" (Federal Democratic Republic of Ethiopia 2002, p. 150).

Stellar Progress, Really?

Marketing their countries' gains in areas such as economic growth, and progress on the MDGs and the SDGs, has been central to the aid diplomacy of Uganda, Ethiopia and Rwanda, enabling them to reassure Western donors their funds were being well spent on the agreed and shared priorities. Even more importantly, their progress was used to argue that more aid would yield even better and faster results. While it was undeniable that significant progress has been achieved in all three countries, there is, however, evidence which casts doubt on some of the claims made.

Where a political centre seeks a monopoly on all information reported to both the outside world and domestic audiences, data manipulation to present a more favourable picture on progress is made even easier in situations where ruling party and state institutions have been merged, and countervailing structures (such as a free media or strong political opposition) are weak and unable to freely access, scrutinise and question official statistics. In addition, where national statistical agencies suffer from significant capacity deficits, and given their dependence on the favours of incumbents in authoritarian systems and their vulnerability to political interference, questions inevitably arise around the reliability of national statistics. The widespread statistical capacity problem in many developing countries, and particularly in SSA,[5] came to the fore as a result of the tremendous challenges they faced in collecting, analysing and disseminating a wide range of statistical information on the MDGs and the current SDGs (the latter requiring data on a total of 247 indicators). Large amounts of ODA were then earmarked to improve statistical capacity in developing countries, with the SDGs setting a specific target (17.19) to track the resources made available to support statistical capacity-building in developing countries.

The specific issue of authoritarian regimes in developing countries manipulating data to boost their reputation domestically, and transmitting the results to international organisations and donors in order to show themselves as continued worthy recipients of assistance, is one that has received increasing attention from researchers.[6] However, the implications for donors of possible political interference in the production of development statistics, the skewing of the latter to produce more politically acceptable results and the dangers of relying on such data for decision-making on aid allocations are still rarely openly recognised by donor agencies.

An example of data manipulation by one of the West's African donor darlings was flagged in 2011 by the IMF and World Bank in the course of their joint review of Ethiopia's third PRSP (and it is worth noting this occurred at a time when the EPRDF's developmental state discourse, centred on the achievement of extremely ambitious growth targets, was in full flow). Concerning the official estimates of the annual GDP growth rates of 11 per cent achieved between 2005/2006 and 2009/2010 under the preceding PRSP, in a footnote the BWI staff opined that these "appear to significantly overstate actual growth" and that as opposed to 11 per cent their own estimates were that this was in the 7–8 per cent range (IMF 2011, p. 1). The grounds on which they cast doubts on the government's GDP growth figures included that they implied "productivity increases that appear implausible", noting that in regard to agriculture "the survey by the World Food Programme and FAO indicated a production decline of 4.5 percent in 2009/10 whereas the government's Agricultural Survey showed a growth of 7 percent" (IMF 2011, p. 10). The issue would be raised in subsequent IMF reports; following its 2015 Article IV consultations with the Ethiopian authorities, the Fund's Staff Report stated its own "projections for GDP are based on an underlying growth rate that is lower than that of the authorities, and that reflect identified weaknesses in national accounts data" (IMF 2015, p. 4) and that "data on economic growth, savings and investment are subject to considerable uncertainty" (IMF 2015, p. 20). Two years later, the IMF Staff Report of 2017 highlighted the persistence of the problem, observing that "improvements in economic statistics and their upgrading to current international standards are urgent tasks" (IMF 2018, p. 18).

A particularly stark case of data manipulation concerned Rwanda and the findings of its household survey conducted in 2013/2014 by its National Institute of Statistics. In its report, the Institute stated the results showed that since the previous survey of 2010/2011, there had been "substantial progress in poverty reduction and improvements in other socio-economic indicators", with poverty incidence falling from the 44.9 per cent reported in 2010/2011 to 39.1 per cent in 2013/2013 (National Institute of Statistics of Rwanda 2015, Foreword).

However, analysis by Rwanda expert Filip Reyntjens showed that rather than the reported 6 per cent fall, what had in fact happened (which enabled the Kagame government to report the positive news on poverty reduction) was that significant changes were made to the methodology used in 2014/2014 compared to that of previous surveys. These included altering the composition of the basic household consumption basket through substitution of more expensive for cheaper items. This had the effect of lowering the poverty line and meant that any comparison with the previous survey to show progress was invalid. As Reyntjens concluded, the alteration of the basket allowed the government to find (and report) "progress where it cannot be found" (Reyntjens 2015, p. 20).

Embarrassingly for Kigali, the Western press also picked up on the controversy. The *Financial Times* carried out its own analysis of the data, concluding that its results also contradicted the reported fall in poverty, and suggested that "there has been a consistent attempt since 2015 to misrepresent the results". Even more uncomfortable for Kigali was the fact the article linked the government's efforts to spin a good news story on poverty reduction to the upcoming December 2015 referendum on the extension of presidential terms, one which Kagame won by a large margin (Wilson and Blood 2019).

Keep Your Money and Mind Your Own Business

Whenever pressured by Western donors to improve their political governance and human rights performance or curtail their violations of the sovereignty of neighbouring countries and other aspects of international law, these governments used various means to resist such blandishments. Foremost amongst these were shrill nationalist responses, clearly aimed at giving Western donor countries pause for thought if they did not want to be accused of neo-colonial arrogance.

In the case of Uganda, the government regularly warned Western donors they could keep their monies if they were going to use these as leverage to change government behaviour. In February 2014, after Museveni had signed into law legislation which criminalised homosexuality, several Western donors, including the US, Norway, Sweden and Denmark, introduced punitive measures through changes to their aid disbursements, with the Obama administration also introducing visa bans on certain Ugandan officials and postponing a planned US military training exercise for Uganda's armed forces. In the face of such pressures, Uganda's official government spokesperson responded that "Uganda is a sovereign country and can never bow to anybody or be blackmailed by anybody on a decision it takes in its interest, even if it involves threats to cut off all financial assistance" (Reuters 2014). In this specific case, normal service was quickly resumed when the legislation was struck down by Uganda's Constitutional Court in August 2014.

At his swearing-in ceremony on May 12, 2021, Museveni took the opportunity to push back against Western criticisms of the recently held general elections won by the ruling NRM. Arguing that Uganda's political system devised by the NRM was "a most elaborate democratic structure", he expressed doubts there "are many comparable pro-people democratic structures in the World" and declared it was "quite comic to hear of some actors in the World giving us lectures about democracy" (Uganda Media

Centre 2021). Reacting to the EU Parliament's resolution of February 2021, which had called for punitive measures to be introduced against certain Ugandan officials for their roles in the repression which had accompanied the 2021 elections, in a letter to the President of the EU Parliament Uganda's Foreign Minister refuted the allegations levelled at the conduct of the government during the elections. Referring to the concerns expressed about the performance of the Electoral Commission, he labelled these EU statements "an assault on the independence of our institutions", while the threat of sanctions was "regrettable, unwarranted and an unwelcome and barely disguised attempt to intimidate officials" (Ministry of Foreign Affairs 2021).

Kagame likewise proved adept at countering Western criticism of his domestic and foreign policies and threats of punitive measures against Kigali. As a result of the critical role he carved out for Rwanda's military forces in Western-backed UN and African Union (AU) peace operations on the continent, he skilfully deployed the bargaining capital he had accumulated to blunt external pressure on Kigali to undertake liberalising political reforms and end its operations in the DRC.

Critiques of Western aid policy also featured prominently in Kagame's public diplomacy. These were intended to clarify the parameters under which Rwanda was prepared to accept assistance and to establish a relationship with donors in which Kigali was 'aid-recipient dominant'. Given its high levels of aid dependency, the messaging was also carefully calibrated so as not to lead Western donors to redirect their flows of aid elsewhere. Kagame would regularly remind his Western interlocutors of the importance of the Paris Declaration principles, in particular the importance of ensuring 'national ownership'. Rwanda became a pioneer in terms of setting up the necessary systems and processes to monitor the implementation of those components of the Paris Declaration which granted Rwanda greater control over how development priorities were identified, how aid flowed through government systems, how the resources were managed and how their use was reported.[7]

At the same time, in his inauguration speech following his election victory in September 2010, Kagame took issue with Africa's dependence on foreign aid. According to him, this dependence allowed "some governments, even NGOs—who are not accountable to anyone—to think they have a right to dictate the conduct of legitimate state actors". Furthermore, he characterised such unnamed external actors as "promoting the ideas of adventurers who have no legitimacy…and deserve nothing more than to be ignored". In a clear statement of where he saw Rwanda's priorities lying (and therefore of the importance outsiders should attach to economic and social rights relative to political and civil freedoms), he stated that "political rights without a matching reduction of poverty and improved quality of life would be meaningless" (Kagame 2010).

Kagame also used his 2010 inauguration speech to remind the West of its own declared international development priorities. For the benefit of those attending the ceremony, he drew attention to the fact these priorities were integral to the agreed post-Cold War international development policy package, one which the West had motivated strongly to adopt at a global level. His government had agreed with these priorities and had assiduously been implementing them, and in his view other aspects of development had, necessarily, to be treated as less important: "we do what every government is expected to do—deliver services; instil accountability, transparency and efficiency; build social and economic infrastructure; and raise living standards". While the fulfilment of such social and economic rights was the priority, he saw other extraneous considerations as having crept into Western donor decision-making, as a result of which "the goalposts change, and we are then accused of forcing progress on the people and of being repressive...it is evidence of hypocrisy and a patronising attitude towards our entire continent" (Kagame 2010).

Pushing back against what he characterised as Western arrogance was one of Kagame's favoured strategies to ensure Western capitals continued to abide by the implicit bargain he believed had been struck, namely development progress in exchange for donor silence on political freedoms. As he was later to argue in response to the aforementioned controversy over the reliability of Rwanda's poverty statistics: "I think it originates from stereotypes and prejudices that are always there that Africa cannot do fine, Africans have to do things which must be validated by others somewhere. But we don't need any validation" (Uwimana 2019).

Western threats to withhold aid to change the behaviour of the Ethiopian government were also always met with robust responses and demands the country's sovereignty be respected. In November 2020, with the war in Tigray raging, and faced with EU pressure to allow humanitarian aid to flow to the region, backed up by threats from Brussels to review its aid programme, Abiy Ahmed responded that "we may be poor but we are not a country that will negotiate our sovereignty. Threatening Ethiopia for coins will not work" (*Politico* 2021). Strong words were also reserved for the new administration of US President Biden following the imposition of American sanctions, with Addis Ababa warning that should "such a resolve to meddle in our internal affairs and undermining the century-old bilateral ties continue unabated, the government of the Federal Democratic Republic of Ethiopia will be forced to reassess its relations with the United States" (Embassy of Ethiopia Washington D.C. 2021).

As the West's relations with its former African donor darlings deteriorated during the pandemic, this might have been taken as indicating a newly found (or rediscovered) Western enthusiasm for promoting democracy on the continent similar to that which had prevailed in the early post-Cold War years. Yet the likelihood that such a renewed pro-democracy posture on the part of Western donors would endure had to be evaluated against the track record of extremely changeable Western commitments to the promotion of political freedoms in its favoured protégés. The Cold War era had shown any such undertakings were usually hostage to the pursuit of other foreign policy objectives by the West, and this would not have gone unnoticed by its donor darlings in Africa.

Playing the China Card

As Uganda, Ethiopia and Rwanda sought to increase their room for manoeuvre and bargaining power vis-à-vis Western donors, the rapid rise of the PRC as a challenger on the international stage to the West, and specifically its growing influence in Africa, assisted them in pursuing this objective. As already noted, the possibility of replicating the PRC's authoritarian political model, in combination with its historically unprecedented economic growth rates, had proven an enticing prospect to the regimes in Addis Ababa, Kigali and Kampala as they embarked on their illiberal state-building projects.

As its economy grew, so China's presence in Africa increased. Initially driven primarily by the need to secure the necessary raw materials to feed its booming economy, the PRC's interests on the continent rapidly expanded to other areas. Both state and private Chinese enterprises became a prominent feature in many African economies, with Chinese FDI in Africa growing from US$75 million in 2003 to US$5 billion by 2021 (China Africa Research Initiative 2024), and the PRC became Africa's largest trade partner. Beijing also became an important donor. Through grants and concessional loans, the construction of large infrastructure projects and the provision of goods ranging from medical supplies and agricultural equipment to military hardware and security and intelligence equipment, it challenged Western donor and BWI influence on every front.

Adding to its allure, in its dealings with African partners Beijing made a point of emphasising its strict policy of non-interference in the internal affairs of other countries, and on numerous occasions showed itself willing to overlook even their most egregious violations of political, civil and human rights. It also demonstrated it was prepared to flex its diplomatic, economic and financial muscle to shield African countries from Western punitive measures, be this through vetoing of Security Council Resolutions tabled by Western members or by helping African countries circumvent Western sanctions.[8] As Beijing extended its influence in Africa, its interest in closer relations with the continent was reciprocated by African governments, and Uganda, Ethiopia and Rwanda all found this to be a useful counterweight to their dependence on the West. Whenever the possibility of Western sanctions against them was raised, in addition to threats to withdraw from participation in the West's global anti-terrorist campaign, they intimated an intention to pivot further towards Beijing as the primary source of development funding, technical assistance and trade.

For example, against the backdrop of possible Western sanctions following criticisms of Uganda's January 2021 General Elections, in February 2021 Museveni received Yang Jiechi, the PRC's highest-ranking diplomat and personal envoy of President Xi Jinping. In the official communiqué put out by the PRC's Ministry of Foreign Affairs, Museveni was reported to have highlighted China's "selfless help in infrastructure construction, agriculture and anti-pandemic efforts" and also "China's expansion of investment in the country". In turn Yang Jiechi emphasised the fact that "China and Uganda have always supported each other on issues involving each other's core interests and major concerns, and opposed interference in other countries' internal affairs in the name of human rights and democracy". In addition, at a time when Western attitudes to China were hardening, and Western efforts at containment of China's global ambitions were taking shape, note would have been taken of Museveni's commitment "to work with China to facilitate high-quality Belt and Road cooperation" (Ministry of Foreign Affairs of the People's Republic of China 2021),[9] Beijing's showcase global infrastructure initiative.

Playing the China card also served Kagame well, enabling him to remind Western donors that Rwanda possessed alternatives in terms of its dependence on external powers. Following Kagame's visit to China in

March 2017, President Xi Jinping was received in Rwanda in July 2018. During this state visit, a total of fifteen bilateral agreements were reportedly signed, with the Chinese President noting that China had already become Rwanda's most important trading partner and contractor (Deutsche Welle 2018). In an article by Xi Jinping prior to his departure for Africa, he noted that relations between the two countries were based on "mutual respect" and that Beijing "supports Rwanda in following the development path it has independently chosen" (Mission of the People's Republic of China to the European Union 2018). His warm words were reciprocated by Kagame. In what were clearly comments directed at the West, he highlighted the fact that "China relates to Africa as an equal", adding that "this is a revolutionary posture in international affairs, and more precious than money" (Kagame 2018).

Meles Zenawi never hid his admiration for the PRC's authoritarian development model, and despite his close ties with individual Western leaders, he took every opportunity to make clear his respect for what Beijing had achieved under the rule of the Chinese Communist Party following the introduction of economic reforms in 1978. During his time in office, Ethiopia played an important role in helping institutionalise Africa's relations with China, a process which eventually led to the establishment of a Forum on China-Africa Cooperation, with Ethiopia hosting the first of its meetings in 2003. At an AU summit meeting in Addis Ababa in January 2012, Meles Zenawi took the opportunity to not only lambast Afropessimists by highlighting the progress the continent had made since the end of the Cold War, but also heap praise on the Chinese who had built, as a gift, the new AU headquarters building in which the summit was being held. He noted that the PRC's "amazing re-emergence and its commitments for a win-win partnership with Africa is one of the reasons for the beginning of the African Renaissance" (African Union 2012, p. 5).

Selective Myopia and Sunk Costs

Since the MDGs and SDGs prioritised socio-economic rights (and in the case of the SDGs, global environmental targets and the reduction of inequalities), as already noted one consequence of their rise to prominence was a focus amongst many Western donors on apolitical development goals and provision of the necessary funding to achieve them. In many ways this signalled the triumph of the pursuit of economic and social rights over political and civil rights as development priorities. With rare exceptions—only in cases of the most egregious violations of human, civil and political rights in partner countries which became sources of embarrassment to Western governments, often due to media coverage which could not be ignored—progress in terms of democratic freedoms and respect for civil and human rights was regularly left out of the picture when it came to Western donor engagement with these regimes, and such a trade-off became a matter of convenience for both parties.

Given the significant increase in the volumes of Western aid which flowed to countries such as Rwanda, Ethiopia and Uganda once they were seen as worthy recipients, donors faced a conundrum. They had invested so heavily in the success of those countries—their progress being regularly trumpeted by donor agencies themselves for domestic consumption and attributed directly to the resources they had provided to their 'donor darlings'—that any backpedalling on their support was a highly unattractive option. When faced with evidence that they might have, through acts of commission or omission, and directly or indirectly, contributed to the establishment of highly repressive regimes, their enormous sunk costs constituted a serious disincentive to the withholding of additional funds and downsizing their country operations, as this would have required recognising errors in past decision-making.

The easier option was therefore to allow institutional inertia to come to the fore and simply continue spending resources to fulfil prior commitments to support progress on socio-economic issues. Institutional pressures to meet international obligations, such as the 0.7 per cent of GNI on the ODA target, meant the field offices and in-country staff of Western bilaterals were pressured to help meet this target (in the case of the EU and its member states, by 2015 based on a commitment made in 2005) by spending increasing amounts of ODA. Some countries, such as those governed by the three African regimes, therefore not only became 'donor darlings' in terms of the volumes of Western ODA they received. They also came to be seen as 'easy spends' given the solid understandings reached through many prior rounds of negotiations regarding their development priorities and what their Western-supplied ODA should be spent on.

The strong temptation for Western donors was therefore to believe any reported regressions in terms of political and personal freedoms were merely temporary lapses, which paled into insignificance when set against progress made in other important areas of development, or alternatively that any backsliding needed to be understood in the wider context of efforts to democratise from an extremely low base and therefore that these governments were liberalising their political governance systems at the fastest pace possible under adverse circumstances. Any shortcomings should therefore not be treated as deal-breakers, with donor officials often excusing ruling party malfeasance regarding, for example, elections, as nevertheless constituting improvements on what occurred before (such as no elections at all). Such attitudes were assisted by an apparent belief that additional donor transfers, and thereby securing an opportunity to discuss with their government counterparts how to improve agricultural exports or modernise cold chains for vaccination programmes, might also provide an opportunity to engage substantively with their hosts on issues of democracy and human rights (assuming the need to do so was strongly felt by donors). In any case, given that the focus of most Western donor agencies and the BWIs was on progress in a restricted set of largely social sector and economic growth objectives, and on 'stability' as defined by their hosts, once they had identified governments able to deliver on the latter objectives they were inclined to put on blinkers and concentrate on supporting measurable and reportable progress in those sectors which both sides had agreed were the really important ones. They became, in effect, apologists for those regimes.[10]

Notes

1. Though less obviously than aid shortfalls, which usually quickly led to cuts in government expenditure, aid windfalls also had a negative impact on GDP growth, particularly over the longer term. This occurred because windfall funds could be used for unplanned and discretionary consumption expenditure by governments rather than capital investment projects, to the detriment of longer-term growth.
2. One IMF study, based on a sample of thirteen countries for which it had long-term data (1993–2005), concluded that aid disbursements fell short of projections in 60 per cent of the fiscal years in question. In terms of magnitude, this amounted to an average shortfall in funds of 30 per cent across the thirteen countries (Celasun and Walliser 2008, pp. 34–37). A 2008 OECD report arrived at similar figures for discrepancies between commitments by OECD donors and scheduled disbursements, concluding that in 2008 only 46 per cent of ODA was disbursed within the year for which it was scheduled (OECD 2008, p. 24).
3. The project-based approach takes the form of externally funded interventions focused on a limited set of usually sector-specific outcomes and is

characterised by high levels of external expertise in project design, execution, monitoring and evaluation and the management of resources, including budgeting, procurement, recruitment of personnel and financial reporting.

4. US foreign aid is reported to Congress in the annual publication of "U.S. Overseas Loans and Grants", commonly known as the Green Book. It comprises all economic assistance defined as aid for programmes with a development or humanitarian objective and military assistance which is primarily for the benefit of a recipient government's armed forces.
5. See Morten Jervens (2013) in his book *Poor Numbers: How We Are Misled by African Development Statistics and What to Do About It* for a pioneering effort to analyse the parlous state of SSA's development statistics.
6. For a notable contribution to the literature on this theme, see Luis R. Martínez (2022) who analyses the distinction between reported GDP growth in autocracies and democracies by regressing reported GDP growth on the increase in night lighting (as recorded by satellites and an alternative measure of growth that cannot be manipulated) and measures of autocracy. He was able to show that there is higher night lighting elasticity of reported GDP in autocracies than democracies and that autocracies overstate annual GDP growth by approximately 35 per cent.
7. Shortly after the Paris Declaration, Kigali developed a document which set out how it planned to manage both aid flows and its development partners. The concept of national ownership occupied centre stage, and the government clearly stated its preference for budget support modalities of disbursement. Those donors who then agreed to this modality were treated as a privileged group in terms of the kinds of interactions they were able to have with government officials. In 2009 the government also produced an annual donor performance assessment framework, based on aid effectiveness indicators derived from the Paris Declaration and its subsequent iterations. The instrument enabled the Ministry of Finance and Economic Planning, through the donor reporting obligations it contained, to not only gain a better understanding of the amounts of aid flowing into the country, but also which sectors they were being applied to. Significantly, it also allowed central government to see which entities other than government bodies, such as NGOs, were benefitting from external assistance (Government of Rwanda 2010).
8. One of the most high-profile examples of the cover Beijing provided to repressive African regimes was its support of Zimbabwe. As relations between Robert Mugabe's regime and the West deteriorated, ties between Zimbabwe and the PRC strengthened. Harare adopted a 'Look East Policy' in its search for alternative sources of external assistance and successfully secured several deals with the PRC. Following the elections of

2008, during which the opposition had been bludgeoned into submission by the ruling party, Beijing blocked Western efforts to table a resolution in the UN Security Council calling for the imposition of mandatory sanctions against Zimbabwe.

9. The PRC's Belt and Road initiative is currently the world's largest infrastructure project and aims to enhance international trade through investments in maritime and overland routes.
10. For a uniquely insightful analysis of those factors driving Western donor officials to excuse the repressive behaviour of their African hosts, see Stephen Brown (2011).

References

African Union. 2012. "Remarks by H.E. Ato Meles Zenawi Prime Minister of the Federal Democratic Republic of Ethiopia at the Inauguration of the new African Union Commission Conference Centre and Office Complex". January 28, 2012.

Brown, Stephen. 2011. "'Well, what can you expect?': Donor Officials' Apologetics for Hybrid Regimes in Africa". *Democratization*, Vol 18 No 2, April 2011.

Celasun, Oya and Jan Walliser. 2008. *Managing Aid Surprises, Finance and Development*, Washington D.C.: International Monetary Fund, September, 2008

China Africa Research Initiative, School of Advanced International Studies, Johns Hopkins University, SAIS-CARI database. http://www.sais-cari.org/chinese-investment-in-africa (Accessed 2 May 2024).

Deaton, Angus. 2015. *The Great Escape*. Princeton University Press, 2015.

Deutsche Welle. 2018. "China's Xi Jinping strikes deals with Rwanda during four-nation African tour", Germany, July 23, 2018.

Embassy of Ethiopia Washington D.C. "On the U.S. Decision to Impose Visa Restrictions on Ethiopian Officials", Press Statement, May 24, 2021. https://ethiopianembassy.org/press-statement-on-the-u-s-decision-to-impose-visa-restrictions-on-ethiopian-officials-may-24-2021/ (Accessed April 1 2024).

Federal Democratic Republic of Ethiopia. 2002. "Sustainable Development and Poverty Reduction Program", Addis Ababa: Ministry of Finance and Economic Development, July 2002.

Government of Rwanda. 2002. "Poverty Reduction Strategy Paper", Kigali: Ministry of Finance and Economic Planning, June 2002.

Government of Rwanda. 2010. "Donor Performance Assessment Framework (DPAF) FY 2009–2010". Kigali: Ministry of Finance and Economic Planning, 2010.

Government of Uganda. 2000. "Uganda's Poverty Eradication Action Plan: Summary and Main Objectives", Kampala: Ministry of Finance, Planning and Economic Development, March 24, 2000.

House of Commons Hansard. 1998. "Oral Answers to Questions – International Development" Column 484, March 25, 1998. https://publications.parliament.uk/pa/cm199798/cmhansrd/vo980325/debtext/80325-17.htm#80325-17_sbhd2 (Accessed 13 March 2018).

IDD and Associates. 2006. "*Evaluation of General Budget Support: Synthesis Report*", University of Birmingham: International Development Department, School of Public Policy, May 2006.

International Development Association (IDA) and International Monetary Fund (IMF). 2002. *Rwanda* Poverty Reduction Strategy Paper – Joint Staff Assessment, IDA and IM, July 18, 2002.

International Monetary Fund (IMF). 2000. "Press Release: IMF and World Bank Support Debt Relief for Uganda", Press Release No.00/34, May 2, 2000. https://www.imf.org/en/News/Articles/2015/09/14/01/49/pr0034 (Accessed May 2, 2024).

International Monetary Fund (IMF). 2011. "The Federal Democratic Republic of Ethiopia: Poverty Reduction Strategy Paper– Joint Staff Advisory Note on the Growth and Transformation Plan 2010/11-2014/15". IMF Country Report No.11/303, October 2011.

International Monetary Fund (IMF). 2015. "The Federal Democratic Republic of Ethiopia: Staff Report for the 2015 Article IV Consultations". September 4, 2015.

International Monetary Fund (IMF). 2018. The Federal Democratic Republic of Ethiopia IMF Staff Country Reports 2018(18). https://doi.org/10.5089/9781484338506.002

International Monetary Fund (IMF). 2019. "Heavily Indebted Poor Countries (HIPC) and Multilateral Debt Relief Initiative (MDRI) – Statistical Update". Washington D.C., August 2019.

Jervens, Morten. 2013. *Poor Numbers: How we are misled by African Development Statistics and What to Do about it.* Cornell Studies in Political Economy, Ithaca, NY: Cornell University Press, 2013.

Kagame, Paul. 2010. Inauguration Day Speech. September 6, 2010. (https://www.paulkagame.com/speech-by-president-kagame-on-inauguration-day/).

Kagame, Paul. 2018. "Remarks by President Paul Kagame at the State Banquet in honour of President Xi Jinping of the People's Republic of China", July 23, 2018. https://www.paulkagame.com/remarks-by-president-paul-kagame-at-the-state-banquet-in-honour-of-president-xi-jinping-of-the-peoples-republic-of-china/.

Martínez, Luis R. 2022. "How Much Should We Trust the Dictators GDP Growth Estimates". *Journal of Political Economy*, Vol 130, No 10, University of Chicago Press, October 2022.

Ministry of Foreign Affairs of the People's Republic of China. 2021. "Ugandan President Yoweri Museveni meets with Yang Jiechi", Beijing, 09.17, February 22, 2001. (https://www.fmprc.gov.cn/mfa_eng/zxxx_662805/t1855639.shtml).

Ministry of Foreign Affairs, Office of the Minister. 2021. "Response to EU Resolution" Letter to the European Parliament. Kampala, February 15, 2021. https://washington.mofa.go.ug/sites/default/files/Respose%20to%20EU%20Resolution%20Official.pdf .

Mission of the People's Republic of China to the European Union. 2018. "Full text of Chinese President Xi's signed article On Rwandan media", July 21, 2018. http://www.chinamission.be/eng/mhs/t1579380.htm (Accessed 6 May 2024)

National Institute of Statistics of Rwanda. 2015. *Rwanda Poverty Profile Report 2013/2014.* Kigali, August 2015.

OECD. 2005. *Paris Declaration on Aid Effectiveness*, Paris: OECD Publishing, 2005. https://doi.org/10.1787/9789264098084-en.

OECD. 2008. "Survey on Monitoring the Paris Declaration – Making Aid More Effective by 2010'. p. 24. Paris.

Organisation for Economic Co-operation and Development (OECD). 2023 "Aid (ODA) disbursements to countries and regions [DAC 2a]" OECD.Stat https://stats.oecd.org/index.aspx?r=723463#. Accessed October 10 2023.

Politico. 2021. "EU considers aid cut to Ethiopia amid violence", August 19, 2021. (https://www.politico.eu/article/eu-considers-aid-cut-to-ethiopia-amid-conflict-violence/)

Reuters. 2014. "US cuts aid to Uganda, cancels military exercise over anti-gay law", June 19, 2014. (https://www.reuters.com/article/us-usa-uganda-gay-announcement-idUSKBN0EU26N20140619)

Reyntjens, Filip. 2015. "Lies, damned lies and statistics: Poverty reduction Rwanda style and how the aid community loves it". African Arguments, November 3, 2015. https://africanarguments.org/2015/11/lies-damned-lies-and-statistics-poverty-reduction-rwandan-style-and-how-the-aid-community-loves-it/ (Accessed 2 May 2024).

Uganda Media Centre. 2021. H.E. Yoweri Yaguta Museveni Swearing in Speech, Ministry of ICT and National Guidance, May 12, 2021. (https://www.media-centre.go.ug/media/he-yoweri-kaguta-museveni-swearing-speech)

US Government Foreign Assistance Tracker. 2024. Accessed August 2 2024. https://www.foreignassistance.gov

Uwimana, Eugene. 2019. "Rwanda Accused of Manipulating Poverty Statistics", *Voice of America*, August 27, 2019. (https://www.voanews.com/a/africa_rwanda-accused-manipulating-poverty-statistics/6174662.html).

Wilson, Tom and David Blood. 2019. "Rwanda: where even poverty data must toe Kagame's line", *Financial Times* August 13 2019.

CHAPTER 13

The New Cold War: Competing for African Allies and the Place of Democracy Promotion

A Short-Lived Zeal for Democracy Promotion

As highlighted in Chap. 2, the early days of the Biden administration had seen a reinvigorated discourse on the need to promote liberal democracy in the face of global democratic backsliding, while its willingness to use its resources to encourage the necessary reforms in those countries benefitting from American assistance was on display at a White House Summit on Democracy in December 2021. At that event Washington had undertaken to spearhead a campaign of 'democratic renewal' and to confront authoritarian regimes, with USAID planning to strengthen its work in the areas of democracy promotion, anti-corruption and support to human rights defenders and those engaged in the struggle for media freedoms.

These themes found their way into the Biden administration's new "U.S. Strategy Toward Sub-Saharan Africa" of August 2022. In it, Washington committed to work with African partners to enshrine "laws, reforms and practices that promote shared democratic norms" and to respond to democratic backsliding and human rights abuses through "a targeted mix of positive inducements and punitive measures such as sanctions" (White House 2022, p. 7).

The absence of Museveni, Kagame and Abiy Ahmed at the December 2021 Summit was taken as a sign these leaders were no longer viewed as paragons of enlightened reformist leadership in Africa, and they in turn had expressed their displeasure at their exclusion. Nevertheless, all three

M. Simpson, *Donors, Democracy and Development in Africa*,
https://doi.org/10.1007/978-3-031-74917-9_13

leaders did attend a US-Africa Leaders Summit in Washington in December 2022, an event to which all heads of state and governments of AU member countries were invited (with the exception of those countries suspended from the AU following military coups, such as Sudan, Burkina Faso, Mali and Guinea, and President Mnangagwa of Zimbabwe who was under US sanctions). After the low point in US-Africa relations reached during the previous Trump administration, the Biden White House hoped to rebuild ties with the continent. However, it was also already evident that Russia's earlier invasion of Ukraine in February 2022 had fundamentally altered Washington's calculus and that a renewed competition with Moscow for allies in Africa was underway.

New Old Western Strategic Priorities

As Russia and the PRC sought to challenge the US' role as the dominant superpower, what some analysts saw as a 'New Cold War' took shape. Characterised by increasingly tense relations between the Western military alliance and both Beijing and Moscow, the rivalries between Washington, Moscow and Beijing have played out in the competition for influence in Africa.

Answers to what happened to the earlier American undertakings at the December 2021 Washington summit to confront authoritarian regimes in Africa for violations of the political and civil rights of their citizens, and to support democratisation efforts, can be found in the US' August 2022 Africa Strategy, drafted only a few months after the Russian invasion of Ukraine in February 2022. In the Strategy, the importance Washington attached to the continent as an arena in which to pursue its geo-political goals, and compete with its adversaries, was clearly on show. What was also evident was how this contest was once again likely to take precedence over concerns regarding the political governance trajectory of its African partners.

Under Putin, Moscow has sought to re-establish itself as a global player, and such ambitions extended to Africa. There, and like Beijing, the Kremlin has attempted to project Russia as both a great power (though with significantly fewer development resources and enticing trade deals it is able to offer than Beijing) and a counterweight to Western influence. Where it has gained an advantage over Western powers, this has been done through its supply of armed personnel, equipment and training (both unofficially through the private security firm, the Wagner Group, and its successor, the Africa Corps established by the Russian Ministry of Defence), to support military regimes in regions such as the Sahel, such as those in Mali, Burkina Faso and Niger facing armed insurrections by Islamist groups. Such interventions have served to displace both UN peacekeeping operations—such as the UN mission in Mali, which at Bamako's request began its withdrawal in July 2023—and French contingents following a rapid deterioration, after their military coups, in relations between these African countries and Paris.

One component of its diplomatic offensives has been to emphasise the historic ties between Moscow and those governments and rebel movements it had supported during the Cold War and to capitalise on its history of assistance to anti-colonial struggles in Africa. In addition, and again like Beijing, one of its major selling points is its stated policy of non-interference in the internal affairs of other states and a willingness to overlook any repression of political, civil and human rights by those it was courting. It has also been able to take advantage of situations of state fragility and protracted conflicts, striking deals with African governments sanctioned by the West, the AU and the Economic Community of West African States (ECOWAS), such as those in Niger, Mali and Burkina Faso. Such assistance has enabled the Kremlin to cultivate a network of African friends to counter Western efforts to build an international coalition against Russia. According to Washington's Africa Strategy:

> Russia views the region as a permissive environment for parastatals and private military companies, often fomenting instability for strategic and financial benefit. Russia uses its security ties, as well as disinformation, to undercut Africans' principled opposition to Russia's further invasion of Ukraine and related human rights abuses. (White House 2022, p. 5)

Washington's efforts to check growing Chinese and Russian influence on the continent, and to secure African support for motions of censure against Moscow in bodies such as the UNGA following Russia's invasion of Ukraine, had to be reconciled with the fact that many African states it wooed ranked poorly on international political governance indices. The circle had somehow to be squared given American commitments in its Africa Strategy to support democracy and human rights activists, and the Strategy's recognition that in Sub-Saharan Africa "democracy remains in short supply...[and that] autocratic leaders retain a tight hold on power" (White House 2022, p. 6).

Wooing, Selective Censuring and Continuity

Following Moscow's vetoing of a draft resolution in the Security Council which called for the withdrawal of Russian troops from Ukraine, an emergency session of the UNGA was convened on March 2, 2022. UNGA Resolution ES-11/1 condemned the Russian invasion and demanded the withdrawal of Russian forces and reversal of Moscow's decision to recognise the self-declared People's Republic of Donetsk and Luhansk, territories which Moscow had already occupied in 2014 and then annexed in September 2022 (United Nations General Assembly 2022a, 2022b).

While the UNGA resolution was overwhelmingly approved, the voting pattern was a source of concern to Washington and other Western powers. Seventeen of the thirty-five abstentions were by African states, and of the twelve countries absent from the vote, eight were from Africa. Amongst those African states that had been beneficiaries of Western development assistance over decades, Rwanda voted in favour of the resolution, Uganda abstained, and Ethiopia was absent from the UNGA session.

Following the vote, both the US Secretary of State and Russian Foreign Minister Sergey Lavrov embarked on tours of Africa, each seeking support for the respective positions of their governments. Sergey Lavrov included visits to Ethiopia and Uganda in his four-nation tour of Africa in July 2022, during which he referenced an upcoming Russia-Africa summit to be held in 2023, an initiative clearly intended at countering Washington's recent summitry efforts. In Addis Ababa, he met with officials of a government which had been severely criticised by Western countries for its conduct of the war in Tigray and accused of war crimes and crimes against humanity. Capitalising on a Russian track record of blocking draft Security Council resolutions condemning Ethiopia for the conflict in Tigray, Lavrov declared that Russia supported the central government's efforts to subdue the rebels, that it respected Ethiopia's sovereignty, and contrasted Moscow's position with the interference of Western powers in Ethiopia's internal affairs (Al Jazeera 2022a).

The benefits of reminding its African interlocutors of Moscow's role in the continent's anti-colonial struggles were clearly on show during Lavrov's visit to Uganda, a country which had abstained from the March 2022 UNGA resolution vote. Museveni praised Moscow's historic support for African liberation movements, and this was reciprocated by Lavrov, who characterised Kampala's stance in the UNGA as a "responsible and balanced position" and indicative of a refusal by Africans to be influenced by Western pressure to adopt an anti-Russian stance (Al Jazeera 2022b).

Blinken embarked on his own tour of African states in August 2022, with trips to South Africa, the DRC and Rwanda. He took the opportunity to promote the Biden White House's new Africa strategy and to persuade certain African states to adopt a more critical position towards Russia. He repeatedly stated that the growing economic problems faced at the time by many African countries (rising oil and food prices) were the results of Russia's war in Ukraine, and he also made it clear that Washington stood ready to help them overcome these challenges. At an event in Pretoria, and using language redolent of American Afro-optimism of the early post-Cold War years, Blinken informed his audience that Washington was seeking to place US-Africa relations, once again, on a new footing. Highlighting the geo-political importance of the continent, he called for (yet another) 'new partnership' between the US and Africa:

> Put simply, the United States and African nations can't achieve any of our shared priorities, whether that is recovering from the pandemic, creating broad-based economic opportunity, addressing the climate crisis, expanding energy access, revitalising democracies, strengthening the free and open international order -we can't do any of that if we don't work together as equal partners. (U.S. Department of State 2022a)

As to the place of democracy promotion in those relations, in the same remarks Blinken re-emphasised the historic importance Washington attached to democratic practices worldwide, noting that the "overwhelming majority of Africans prefer democracy to any other form of government". And in line with the importance Washington attached to equality in its partnerships with its African friends, he added, "We won't treat democracy as an area where Africa has problems and the United States has solutions. We recognize that our democracies face common challenges, which we need to tackle together, as equals, alongside other governments, civil society and citizens" (U.S. Department of State 2022a).

His visits to the DRC and Rwanda reflected Washington's interest in resolving the long-standing conflict in the eastern DRC between the two countries, as well as to express gratitude to both Kinshasa and Kigali for having voted in favour of the March 2022 UNGA resolution. Rwanda's yes vote can be seen as an attempt to dial down the condemnations from Washington following continued reports of Rwandan support, despite

Kigali's repeated denials, to the M23 rebels in the DRC and to counter continued outrage in Washington over the abduction, trial and imprisonment of Rusesabagina during the pandemic.

Kigali would have been aware that in the run-up to Blinken's visit there were moves on Capitol Hill to further censure the Rwandan government and threats to cut American economic and military assistance. In July 2022, Senator Robert Menendez, the Democrat Chairman of the Senate Foreign Relations Committee, wrote a forceful letter to Blinken regarding US assistance to Rwanda, in which he listed a series of concerns regarding Rwanda, on the basis of which he called for a "more effective U.S. policy". He accused the Rwandan government of "continuing disregard for democratic and human rights" and specifically referenced Kagame's "efforts to silence journalists, human rights activists, and opposition voices" and of "targeting dissidents living outside Rwanda". He touched upon the hybrid authoritarian nature of the political system developed under RPF rule, and noted, "After changing the Rwandan constitution in 2015 to eliminate presidential term limits so as to remain in office in perpetuity, Kagame won re-election in 2017 with an implausible 99% of the vote" (U.S. Senate Committee on Foreign Relations 2022).

In addition to the continued detention of Rusesabagina, a US permanent resident whom Menendez pointed out in the same letter had been classified by the US government as "wrongfully detained", he also detailed the Rwandan government's role in destabilising the region. He reminded Blinken that in the late 1990s Rwanda had invaded the DRC, and thereby triggered a regional war with catastrophic humanitarian consequences, that in 2012 it had supported the M23 rebels in another military operation leading to more loss of life and massive displacements of civilians, and that in 2022 it had again sent troops into the DRC and "reactivated M23 as a proxy militia now responsible for killing Congolese civilians, Congolese troops and UN peacekeepers" (U.S. Senate Committee on Foreign Relations 2022).

His criticisms went to the heart of the tensions between, on the one hand, the promotion of democracy and human rights in American foreign policy, specifically their place in Washington's relations with Africa's 'new leaders', and on the other its pursuit of geo-strategic goals in the context of the New Cold War with Russia and China, its search for African allies and its interest in supporting African countries such as Rwanda in international peacekeeping operations that were important to America's own national security. Given the US had become Rwanda's largest bilateral donor, and Rwanda's security forces were a major beneficiary of US capacity-building assistance and training programmes, Menendez homed in on the problem of aid fungibility and the misuse of external assistance by recipients, arguing that the "United States cannot support Rwandan contributions to peacekeeping in some parts of Africa while looking the other way as Rwanda foments rebellion and violence in other parts of the country". He ended his letter by informing Blinken that he planned to:

> carefully review all assistance notified to Congress for Rwanda and will place a hold on all security assistance....as I am concerned that any U.S. support for the Rwandan military while it is deployed to the DRC...sends a troubling signal that the U.S. tacitly approves of such actions. (U.S. Senate Committee on Foreign Relations 2022)

In a joint press conference with the Rwandan foreign minister on August 11, 2022, Blinken stated he had held frank discussions with his counterparts on Rwanda's support for M23 in the DRC conflict and Rusesabagina's continued detention. Yet he also highlighted the fact that in his view Rwanda was a leader "internationally on priorities that we share", amongst which making "critical contributions to the United Nations and regional peacekeeping missions; speaking up for Ukraine's right to sovereignty and territorial integrity in the face of Russia's unprovoked and brutal invasion" (U.S. Department of State 2022b). It was easy to conclude that such geostrategic objectives, the need to keep Kigali onside in terms of votes in the UN and involved in peacekeeping operations, were the focus of Blinken's efforts. While there may have been a frank exchange of views on Rwanda's political governance and human rights record, as well as its involvement in the DRC, it was nevertheless clear these would not be treated as stumbling blocks and that the Biden administration would not be exerting any significant pressure on Kigali to address the political governance issues raised by Senator Menendez.

Kigali understood well the dynamics at work in Washington. American foreign assistance to Rwanda had already dropped in terms of obligations from a high of close to US$270 million in 2016 to US$168 million in 2022 (US Government Foreign Aid Tracker 2024). In an effort to head off any further reduction in US aid, and the threat of sanctions, in March 2023 Kagame commuted Rusesabagina's twenty-five-year sentence, and he was released and allowed to return to the US to his family. Kagame's decision was welcomed by President Biden, who later thanked "the

Rwandan government for making this reunion possible" (White House 2023b).

At the time, Kigali was likely to have had fewer concerns about possible cuts to American assistance given its recent success in diversifying funding sources. As previously noted, it had already reset relations with Paris during the pandemic, with Rwandan troops containing the Islamic insurgents in northern Mozambique and thereby protecting the investment of the French energy giant Total, and as a result of which Kigali had then benefitted from a major boost in French development assistance. It would also gain the financial support of the EU in December 2022 to help pay for the continued deployment of Rwandan forces in Mozambique. Amounting to twenty million euros, this represented another useful source of revenue for Kigali, allowing it to further boost the capabilities of its defence forces. Thanking the EU for the funds, the Rwandan Minister of Foreign Affairs took the opportunity to remind the Europeans that "Rwanda remains a reliable partner in the fight against terrorism on the continent" (Ministry of Foreign Affairs and International Cooperation 2022).

Kagame had even less reason to be concerned about London's reactions to the continued flow of reports on levels of political repression in Rwanda and its destabilising role in the region. As a long-established cheerleader amongst Western European donors of the RPF regime—a role dating back to the days of Clare Short as Secretary of State for International Development—the Kagame regime continued to receive transfers of British ODA throughout, and since, the pandemic. These transfers took place notwithstanding the fact that as a permanent member of the UN Security Council, the UK was one of the intended primary recipients of UN reports on Rwanda's involvement in the bloody conflict in the DRC and despite yet another UN Panel of Experts report in June 2023 on the situation in the DRC. This again exhaustively detailed the continued violations of the DRC territorial integrity by the RDF and its support to the sanctioned M23 Congolese rebel movement which "had engendered a catastrophic humanitarian crisis, causing the displacement of more than 1 million civilians in North Kivu Province" (United Nations Security Council 2023). While ODA transfers to Rwanda were down compared to previous levels, this was partly a reflection of the UK government's decision in 2020 to temporarily reduce its ODA/GNI target from 0.7 per cent to 0.5 per cent given its fiscal challenges during COVID, its prioritisation of the humanitarian crises in Afghanistan in the run-up to and aftermath of the fall of Kabul to the Taliban, and in Ethiopia in the context of the Tigray war, and its contributions to multilateral responses to COVID-19.

In addition to the concern London shared with Washington to not put excessive pressure on Rwanda at a time when its vote in the UN on resolutions condemning Moscow for its invasion of Ukraine was being sought, other considerations loomed large in London's calculus. Firstly, there was a need to operationalise the refugee deportation arrangement with Rwanda referenced in Chap. 1, a programme upon which the Conservative government had placed great store. The UK Home Secretary, Suella Braverman, visited Rwanda in March 2023 to view the installations built to house the deportees, even though the plan was then still facing numerous legal challenges in the UK (the Appeals Court in June 2023 and then the Supreme Court in November 2023 would both rule it 'unlawful'), though an amended Bill was eventually passed by the UK Parliament on April 22, 2024. Ducking questions during an interview about a deadly incident in 2018 in which Congolese refugees had been killed by the Rwandan police,[1] Braverman had declared Rwanda to be a "safe country" for refugees (Morton and Kuenssberg 2023). The endorsement was welcomed by Kigali as an indication of the British government's determination to proceed with the initiative despite repeated delays, as it had become an important source of foreign exchange for Rwanda which had already benefitted from transfers to the tune of hundreds of millions of pounds, with further flows planned to pay for the programme.

Secondly, there was the fact that Rwanda was scheduled to host the 2022 Commonwealth Heads of Government Meeting (CHOGM) in June 2022. The Conservative government placed great store in boosting both the Commonwealth and its own position within it to compensate for its loss of global influence following Brexit. The imposition of targeted sanctions against RPF leaders, and cuts in ODA to Rwanda whose President as host of the CHOGM was about to take on the role of Commonwealth Chair-in-Office, was therefore always highly unlikely.

The willingness shown by London and Washington to set aside any concerns over the RPF regime's repressive behaviour internally, and the resetting of the latter's relations with Paris, paid off in terms of ensuring that Rwanda remained aligned with Western positions on the war in Ukraine. In another Special Session of the UNGA on October 12, 2022, Rwanda voted in favour of a resolution condemning Russia for its annexation of four regions of Eastern Ukraine under the occupation of its military after Moscow held "illegal so-called referendums", actions which had "no validity under international law" (United Nations General Assembly 2022a, pp. 2–3). On the anniversary of the invasion, another Special Session of the UNGA was convened in February 2023, and Rwanda again voted in favour of a resolution condemning Russia and calling for its immediate withdrawal of Russian forces from Ukrainian territory (United Nations General Assembly 2023).

Washington's efforts to normalise relations with Ethiopia following friction between the two countries during the Tigray war, which ended with the signing of a peace agreement in November 2022, led to Blinken's visit to Ethiopia in March 2023. Abiy Ahmed attended the December 2022 US-Africa leaders summit in Washington and met Blinken, with the discussions reported to have revolved around the implementation of the peace agreement.

Ethiopia had abstained from voting on the March 2022 UNGA resolution on Ukraine. It did so again on the October 2022 resolution condemning Russia's annexation of Ukrainian territory, as well as the February 2023 resolution calling for the withdrawal of Russian troops. Prior to his March 2023 visit to Addis Ababa, Blinken had been pressured by American human rights organisations to place the issue of human rights violations during the Tigray war at the centre of discussions with his Ethiopian counterparts. HRW argued that, despite the peace agreement, human rights abuses were still perpetrated and that in terms of the broader picture "Ethiopia has been backsliding on democracy and freedoms across the country" (Solomon and Saine 2023). Addis Ababa had placed obstructions in the way of human rights organisations seeking to carry out investigations into war crimes and crimes against humanity committed during the conflict, and Blinken was aware that Addis Ababa had sought to close down the operations of the International Commission on Human Rights Experts on Ethiopia (ICHRE), established by the UN Human Rights Council in December 2021 to investigate human rights violations during the Tigray war.

Therefore, at the same time as Blinken sought to prevent Ethiopia from succumbing to Moscow's blandishments and placing itself in the pro-Russian camp by voting against the UNGA resolutions, this objective had to be reconciled with the need to demonstrate that democracy and human rights considerations remained central to the Biden administration's Africa strategy. For Abiy Ahmed on the other hand, the objectives were to secure American support for urgently needed debt restructuring and new loans from the BWIs for recovery purposes and the restoration of Ethiopia's access to AGOA's trade benefits which had been suspended in January 2022.

Blinken walked a careful line to repair relations. In his meeting with the Ethiopian Prime Minister on March 15, 2023, the issues discussed ranged from American support to implementation of the peace agreement, American commitments to provide humanitarian assistance in the context of an ongoing drought, as well as accountability for human rights violations during the Tigray war, with the State Department characterising the meeting as "a reaffirmation of the important partnership between the United States and Ethiopia" (U.S. Department of State 2023). In a press conference following his meeting with the Ethiopian Prime Minister, Blinken stated that in terms of the AGOA programme, the Biden administration would "continue to work closely with the government to achieve that objective, which we share" (U.S. Embassy in Ethiopia 2023).

Blinken's press conference in Addis Ababa shed light on Washington's efforts to build another set of 'new partnerships' with African governments, specifically to repair ties with an important African state in the context of the new Cold War. In a remarkable statement—one that strongly resembled Clinton's admission in 1994 that Cold War American policy towards Africa had allowed interests other than political and civil freedoms and human rights to determine its support to regimes—Blinken stated that in terms of Ethiopia and the years of repressive TPLF/EPRDF rule, "the United States acknowledges the human rights violation and repression committed during the past three decades...We and others were insufficiently vocal about these abuses in the past" (U.S. Embassy in Ethiopia 2023).

Shortly after Blinken's visit to Ethiopia, the consequences of longstanding Western support to the TPLF/EPRDF—and specifically tacit acceptance of its Ethnic Federalist divide and rule tactics, and resulting entrenchment of ethnic identity in national politics, coupled with past tepid Western responses to the central government's regular use of violent repression to deal with dissent—again came to the fore. In early 2023 conflict erupted in the Amhara National Regional State, pitting armed Amhara militia groups against Federal forces. Proximate causes included Amhara resentment of the central government of Abiy Ahmed's PP, based on perceptions it was dominated by Oromo, and that Amhara demands on a range of issues were being ignored (such as re-drawing the State of Amhara's boundaries to include pockets of its ethnic kin in Tigray). In a crackdown on the independent media, in April 2023 Abiy Ahmed's government resorted to the playbook regularly used by the TPLF/EPRDF, with security forces detaining at least eight journalists (Committee to Protect Journalists 2023). And on August 4, 2023, a state of emergency was declared in the Amhara region, which granted the police sweeping powers of arrest without warrant.

US-Ugandan relations were already under pressure as a result of American sanctions against Ugandan officials following the 2021 elections. Though Museveni attended the US-Africa Leaders Summit in December 2022, tensions between Washington and Kampala increased after he resuscitated the anti-homosexuality bill of 2014 which had previously been ruled invalid by the country's Supreme Court. A new bill, with provisions for even more draconian sentences than the earlier 2014 bill, including the death penalty, was approved by the Ugandan parliament in early May 2023 and later that month signed into law by Museveni.

Western condemnation was swift, with the EU and UK Parliaments strongly denouncing the law. President Biden called the legislation a "shameful Act" and was "the latest development in an alarming trend of human rights abuses" (White House 2023a). Washington then introduced a new set of visa restrictions on Ugandan officials. In May 2023, the Chair of the US Senate Finance Committee moved to have Uganda suspended from the AGOA arrangement, and Biden later removed Uganda from the list of AGOA beneficiaries. Yet whether this turbulence would also impact on American security assistance to its longstanding East African ally was unclear. In the midst of growing Islamist insurgencies on the continent, as well as a new Cold War, it was unlikely that Washington would risk jeopardising relations with a country that as late as March 2022 the State Department saw as "a reliable partner in promoting stability in the Horn and East/Central Africa and in combatting terror" (U.S. Department of State 2022c), and in particular put at risk the US$300 million in security assistance in the form of equipment and training to Uganda which had been provided by the Pentagon between 2011 and 2019 (Congressional Research Service 2019, p. 2). The continued importance attached to supporting Uganda's role in peacekeeping operations, and in particular its anti-terrorism activities in Somalia against Al-Shabaab, was clear. While access to AGOA was withheld, significant American military assistance continued to be provided in the course of 2023 (US Government Foreign Assistance Tracker 2024), even as the anti-homosexuality bill was being drafted and then tabled in February 2023, and notwithstanding Uganda's abstention from the March 2022 UNGA resolution vote condemning Russia's invasion of Ukraine.

Returning to Business as Usual

Given the new international situation following Russia's invasion of Ukraine, the Western focus on the situation in the Middle East following the Hamas attacks on Israel on October 7, 2023, and increasing Western efforts to secure African support for its positions in the New Cold War, all three regimes clearly felt reduced Western pressure to introduce political reforms, especially when compared to the pandemic years. Given Western distraction, they also believed they could resume their regime preservation efforts without fear of Western opprobrium and any serious and long-lasting punitive measures.

In March 2024, the RPF Congress selected Kagame as its candidate for the country's Presidential elections scheduled for July 2024, with the RPF's allied parties confirming their support for Kagame. Given he had won the previous elections of 2017 with more than 98 per cent of the vote, there was little doubt he would win the next contest. This would mean he would enjoy a fourth term in office and remain at the helm of Rwanda's fortunes until 2029, after which, as a result of the constitutional amendment of 2015, he would be entitled to run for another five-year term.

The need to show unanimous national support for the President and the RPF meant measures were again taken to eliminate the threat of any serious challengers to the President. The main opposition figure, Victoire Ingabire Umuhoza, who as noted had been prevented from running in the 2010 elections and gone on to spend eight years in prison after being convicted of terrorism and genocide denial, was released in 2018. However, in March 2024, her request to be 'rehabilitated', and have her political rights restored so she could run in the 2024 elections, was refused by the High Court (*Guardian* 2024). With the country's main opposition figures disqualified, Kagame went on to win a landslide victory in the July 2024 Presidential elections, receiving over 99 percent of the valid votes cast.

In Uganda, it was also clear Museveni saw a business-as-usual approach to regime preservation as feasible given the West's focus on more pressing geopolitical matters. He also made clear his intention to run in the presidential elections scheduled for 2026, and in February 2024 the NRM confirmed him as their candidate. And to ensure the necessary regime props remained in place and under his control, in March 2024 he appointed his son Muhoozi Kainerugaba, a general in the UPDF, as Chief of the Defence Forces (Al Jazeera 2024). This meant Museveni could continue, through his son, to exercise a firm grip on the security apparatus to guarantee continued NRM rule (and given the broader situation prevailing in Africa, and Uganda's own history, cut off at the pass any possibility of a military coup). In addition, and given Kainerugaba's widely known political ambitions to succeed his father, once he eventually left office Museveni's own personal safety, and immunity from prosecution for past violations of the political, civil and human rights of Ugandan citizens, would be secured through such a dynastic succession.

Following the November 2022 peace agreement with Tigrayan forces, Abiy Ahmed's government took the opportunity of Western distraction, and Western concerns not to ostracise African states in the context of efforts to build an anti-Russian alliance, to carry out military operations to deal with unrest around the country. It had apparently learned little from its earlier instinctive recourse to the use of military force against the TPLF, rather than negotiations, which had plunged Ethiopia into its most recent bloody civil war. The limited capacity of Ethnic Federalism to contain inter-ethnic rivalries—largely attributable to the entrenchment under the EPRDF of ethnicity as the basis of the country's political arrangements and a means to perpetuate EPRDF control—remained in place under Abiy Ahmed and facilitated the eruption of conflict in other parts of the country.

Following the Tigray agreement, alliances struck during the war between various ethnic militia and central government forces rapidly unravelled. As noted above, by 2023 Amhara militia were battling Federal forces—driven in part by grievances that the interests of the Amhara in regaining territory previously granted to Tigray under earlier regional state boundary demarcation exercises, and on the basis of which they had participated in the conflict, had been ignored in the peace agreement. Unrest also continued amongst the Oromo. In early April 2024 Bate Urgessa, a prominent critic of the government in Addis Ababa and member of the OLF known for his advocacy of non-violent political opposition, was found murdered. On April 10, 2024, the Chair of the US Senate Foreign Relations Committee issued a statement urging the Ethiopian authorities to allow a thorough investigation to be carried out while at the same time asserting that:

> the Abiy regime has clamped down on political opposition, the media, and dissidents not only in Oromia, but throughout Ethiopia, contributing to the country's widespread insecurity and overall instability. It is past time for those responsible for the policy of repression and abuse to be exposed and held accountable for their actions. (U.S. Senate Foreign Relations Committee 2024)

African Democracy Activists and Western Aid

Democracy and civil and human rights activists in Ethiopia would not have been the only ones to share the American Senator's concerns. Confronting similarly authoritarian hybrid regimes in Uganda and Rwanda, opposition politicians and their supporters, anti-corruption activists, and those campaigning for media freedom and human rights in those countries would have all concurred with the Senator's diagnosis that it was in fact the repressive behaviour of these regimes driving the instability and insecurity those governments then claimed to be containing (and on the basis of which they continued to need Western assistance) and that accountability for their repression was long overdue.

In the case of the three African countries, some came to see a direct link between Western aid and the entrenchment of the repressive regimes they lived under. Less concerned with evaluating the effectiveness of foreign aid on economic growth rates, structural transformation, poverty rates or improvements in health and education indicators (the focus of primarily Western and Western-based African development experts), Ugandan, Rwandan and Ethiopian democracy activists and opposition politicians instead drew the attention of Western public opinion, and decision-makers, to the negative effects on the political, civil and human rights in their countries of the Western development assistance provided and the respectability such relationships conferred on these aid-recipient regimes, which in turn led to their sense of immunity from Western criticism.

For example, Victoire Ingabire Umuhoza took issue with the UK's scheme to send illegal migrants and failed asylum seekers to Rwanda. This was a highly lucrative one for the RPF regime, which it is worth recalling had been labelled the 'Migration and Economic Development Partnership', thus reviving the language of the Paris Declaration of previous decades and reaffirming the close relations between Kigali and London, built up over decades.

In December 2023 she expressed her dismay at London's continued support of Rwanda through the scheme. She highlighted the fact that London's decision to persevere with the arrangement had been taken even though in January 2021 (in the context of the UN Human Rights Council's thirty-seventh Universal Periodic Review on Rwanda), the UK government's own representative had highlighted concerns about the "continued restrictions to political and civil rights and media freedoms". This was in addition to the UK Supreme Court's ruling that the scheme was unlawful while it also expressed concerns regarding the human rights situation in Rwanda. Listing shortcomings in terms of the rule of law, and political and civil freedoms in Rwanda, she argued the best use of the UK's resources, as "one of Rwanda's most important development partners", would instead be to "reorient its efforts towards supporting Rwanda to improve its human rights situation" (Umuhoza 2024). In the event, one of the first measures taken by the new Labour government in the UK, following its election victory in July 2024, was to scrap the deportation scheme. The new British Home Secretary described the arrangement, which had occupied a prominent position in the UK-Rwanda relationship under the previous Conservative government, as "the most shocking waste of taxpayers' money I have ever seen" (BBC News 2024). And given the large amounts of money transferred to Rwanda, it would also have been of concern to Kigali that the new government in London also announced that it intended to recoup some of the funds it had already disbursed.

Bobi Wine, the main opposition leader in Uganda, and who on numerous occasions had suffered at the hands of Uganda's security forces, was more forthright in his condemnation of the role Western aid played in strengthening the repressive capacity of Museveni's government. In the run-up to what turned out to be the bloody 2021 elections, he wrote a piece directly connecting the provision of Western aid to the denial of political freedoms and violation of human rights in Uganda. Referencing Museveni's positioning of Uganda as a trusted ally of the West in the fight against terrorism, and Western support given to the country's security apparatus, Wine argued one consequence was that "just as often as Ugandan forces have trained their sights on terrorists abroad, they have trained them on Ugandan citizens at home" (Foreign Affairs 2021). Furthermore, he also referenced the consequences of aid fungibility, namely the likely 'displacement' of a World Bank loan to the tune of US$300 million, ostensibly for COVID relief, and disbursed through budget support, that is, direct transfers to the Ugandan authorities. The amount of these funds closely matched the total requested by the government prior to the elections in an earlier supplementary budget for 'classified expenditures' (and therefore not subject to parliamentary scrutiny), which in terms of the country's budget classifications represented allocations for the armed forces and police.[2]

When, following the January 2021 elections during which massive state violence was applied to repress opposition protests of the conduct of the poll, Wine himself found his house surrounded by security forces and prevented from leaving it, he gave an interview to a British magazine. He again highlighted the role Western donors had played in “propping up the Museveni dictatorship”. He nevertheless expressed hope that given Uganda was “a nation that depends largely on foreign aid”, they could exercise their leverage to make the President accountable for the repression, and that “we want to know that our partners in development are our partners in human rights, partners in democracy, and partners in real freedom” (*The Critic* 2021).

As a result of the Western support provided to these regimes, they have been able to tighten their hold on power and resist both domestic and external pressures to reform their political and economic governance systems. They have set limits on the scope for Western interference in how they ruled by taking advantage of post-Cold War international development frameworks and the definitions of development and priorities they contain, the changes to aid disbursement modalities, the discourse around ‘new partnerships’ and importance attributed to ‘national ownership’, and the restrictive definitions of what constituted ‘good governance’ (assisted by the West’s self-imposed restrictions on what Clare Short had characterised as any ‘hectoring’ of aid-recipient governments). In addition, their regime survival objectives have been met through their benefactors’ interest in supporting the rise of developmental states in Africa, with authoritarianism considered an acceptable price to be paid for economic and social progress and further facilitated by the reluctance amongst most donor agencies to develop clear indicators to monitor the status of political freedoms and civil and human rights in aid recipient countries (and to use these as a firm basis for aid allocation decisions), in combination with their own skills in dressing up their hybrid illiberal systems and practices as meeting international standards of governance. To these factors contributing to the perpetuation of authoritarian practices should be added the enduring problem of aid fungibility and the scope for external funds to be used for regime preservation purposes, as well as regime awareness of the strong reluctance amongst donor agencies to review their support given their extensive prior investments. Finally, their leaders had a solid understanding of the gap between declarations on the primary importance attached by Western countries to the promotion of democracy in their aid programmes and their other foreign policy objectives. They were conscious that history demonstrated that Western intentions to promote democratisation in the beneficiaries of their aid always tended to be subordinated to changing Western national security and wider geo-strategic interests and therefore that any turbulence in relations with their donors due to violations of governance standards was always likely to be merely temporary.

On numerous occasions Western donor countries have chosen to completely ignore, downplay or excuse the increasingly disturbing reports on the status of civil and human rights in all three countries, and in terms of progress on democratisation donors have often even turned a blind eye to the successive negative reports produced by their own election monitoring teams. In general, and with few exceptions, the taps of Western development assistance have remained open, and resources have continued to flow. In this context it is worth recalling the thoughts of George Ayittey, the eminent Ghanaian economist referenced in Chap. 4 in the context of the 1998 US Senate Sub-Committee on Africa hearings on what were then considered to be the continent's promising 'New Leaders', and which retain their relevance today. On that occasion he had called for policy consistency and clarity and laid down some basic criteria on the basis of which aid might be provided or withheld, namely that while the West should not impose the specific type of democracy it judged suitable for Africa, it should "indicate what it will not accept: democratic malfeasance (manipulation or control of the transition process by one side) or unlevel playing fields (opposition parties denied access to the state media and stripped of state resources)" (U.S. Senate 1998, p. 21).

Notes

1. According to Human Rights Watch, this incident took place in February 2018. Rwandan police used live ammunition against DRC refugees protesting against their living conditions outside the offices of the UNHCR, resulting in the death of twelve refugees (Human Rights Watch 2019).
2. On December 22, 2020, members of the New York City Bar Association sent a letter to Senator Chris Coons, a member of the Senate Foreign Relations Subcommittee on Africa and Global Health Policy, in which they brought to his attention the World Bank loan, and which they had reason to believe "may be financing ongoing human rights abuses committed by the security forces against political opposition candidates and their supporters ahead of the January 2021 presidential and parliamentary elections" (Center for International Justice 2020).

References

Al Jazeera. 2022a. "Lavrov denigrates West's stance towards Africa on Ethiopia visit", July 27, 2022. https://www.aljazeera.com/news/2022/7/27/lavrov-denigrates-wests-stance-towards-africa-on-ethiopia-visit (Accessed May 1, 2024).

Al Jazeera. 2022b. "Uganda's Museveni extols Africa-Russia ties during Lavrov visit". July 26, 2022. https://www.aljazeera.com/news/2022/7/26/ugandan-leader-extols-africa-russia-friendship-during-visit-by-lavrov. (Accessed May 1, 2024).

Al Jazeera. 2024. "Uganda's President Museveni promotes son to army chief". March 22, 2024. https://www.aljazeera.com/news/2024/3/22/ugandas-president-museveni-promotes-son-to-army-chief (Accessed May 8, 2024).

Center for International Justice. 2020. "Letter to Chris Coons, U.S. Senator" New York: New York City Bar, December 22, 2020. https://www.nycbar.org/reports/letter-raising-concerns-as-to-whether-a-recent-world-bank-loan-made-to-the-ugandan-government-may-be-financing-ongoing-human-rights-abuses/ (Accessed May 4, 2024).

Committee to Protect Journalists. 2023. "At least 8 journalists detained amid renewed unrest in Ethiopia" Webpage published April 14, 2023, at 1:27 PM EDT. https://cpj.org/2023/04/at-least-8-journalists-detained-amid-renewed-unrest-in-ethiopia/#:~:text=Six%20of%20the%20journalists–Amara,as%20of%20Friday%2C%20April%2014%2C (Accessed May 1, 2024).

Congressional Research Service. 2019. "Uganda", Version 7, updated. Washington D.C. August 2019. https://crsreports.congress.gov/product/pdf/IF/IF10325/7 (Accessed May 4, 2024).

Guardian. 2024. "Rwanda court upholds election ban on opposition leader". March 13, 2024.

Human Rights Watch. 2019. "Rwanda: A Year On, No Justice for Refugee Killings". February 23, 2019. https://www.hrw.org/news/2019/02/23/rwanda-year-no-justice-refugee-killings.

Komireddi, Kapil. 2021. "Exclusive Interview: Uganda's Bobi Wine on the country's 'fraudulent' election" *Critic*, January 26, 2021. https://thecritic.co.uk/ugandas-bobi-wine-remains-under-house-arrest-for-refusing-to-concede-after-fraudulent-election/.

Ministry of Foreign Affairs and International Cooperation. 2022. "Rwanda Welcomes Support of European Peace Facility to Joint Operations in Cabo Delgado". Kigali, December 1, 2022. https://www.minaffet.gov.rw/updates/news-details/rwanda-welcomes-support-of-european-peace-facility-to-joint-operations-in-cabo-delgado (Accessed May 4, 2024).

Morton, Becky and Laura Kuenssberg. 2023. "Suella Braverman says Rwanda is safe for migrants despite evidence of 2018 killings", *BBC News*, April 2, 2023. https://www.bbc.co.uk/news/uk-politics-65153807. (Accessed 2 May 2024)

Solomon, Salem and Cindy Saine. 2023. "Advocates Call on Blinken to Demand Accountability for Atrocities in Ethiopia". *Voice of America*. March 14, 2023. https://www.voanews.com/a/advocates-call-on-blinken-to-demand-accountability-for-atrocities-in-ethiopia/7005879.html (Accessed May 1, 2024).

U.S. Department of State. 2022a. "Vital Partners, Shared Priorities: The Biden Administration's Sub-Saharan Africa Strategy", Washington D.C.: Office of the Spokesperson, August 8, 2022.

U.S. Department of State. 2022b. "Secretary Antony J. Blinken and Rwandan Foreign Minister Vincent Biruta at a Joint Press Availability", Kigali, Rwanda, Office of the Spokesperson, August 11, 2022. https://www.state.gov/secretary-antony-j-blinken-and-rwandan-foreign-minister-vincent-biruta-at-a-joint-press-availability/. (Accessed May 2, 2024).

U.S. Department of State. 2022c. "U.S. relations with Uganda", Bilateral Relations Factsheet. Washington D.C., Bureau of African Affairs, March 18, 2022. https://www.state.gov/u-s-relations-with-uganda/ Accessed May 4 2024.

U.S. Department of State. 2023. "Secretary Blinken's Meeting with Ethiopian Prime Minister Ahmed". Office of the Spokesperson, Washington, D.C., March 15, 2023. https://www.state.gov/secretary-blinkens-meeting-with-ethiopian-prime-minister-ahmed-2/ (Accessed May 4, 2024).

U.S. Senate Committee on Foreign Relations. 2022. "Update: Increased Violence by Rwandan Supported M23 Rebels In the DRC/Congo—Chairman Menendez Speaks Out" Communication received into the National Security Division, Foreign Agents Registration Act (FARA) Unit, Department of Justice (NSD/FARA Unit) on July 25, 2022, at 10:10 am. Published by the U.S. Department of Justice. 2022. https://efile.fara.gov/docs/6305-Informational-Materials-20220725-13.pdf. (Accessed 2 May 2024).

U.S. Senate Committee on Foreign Relations. 2024. "Chair Cardin Statement on the Killing of Bate Urgessa in Ethiopia". Chairman's Press, April 10, 2024. https://www.foreign.senate.gov/press/dem/release/chair-cardin-statement-on-the-killing-of-bate-urgessa-in-ethiopia.

Umuhoza, Victoire Ingabire. *2023*. "The new 'Rwanda Deal' was a shock to Rwandans. We know this is no place for asylum seekers". *Guardian*. December 12, 2023. https://www.theguardian.com/commentisfree/2023/dec/12/rwanda-deal-rwandans-asylum-seekers-human-rights (Accessed May 4, 2024).

United Nations General Assembly. 2022a. "Territorial Integrity of Ukraine; Defending the Principles of the Charter of the United Nations", A/RES/ES-11/4 Adopted 12 October 2022.

United Nations General Assembly. 2022b. United Nations General Assembly Resolution A/RES/ES-11/1: "Aggression against Ukraine", Adopted in New York on March 2, 2022.

United Nations General Assembly. 2023. "Principles of the United Nations Charter underlying a comprehensive, just and lasting peace in Ukraine". A/RES/ES-11/6. New York, Adopted February 23, 2023.
United Nations Security Council. 2023. "Final report of the Group of Experts on the Democratic Republic of the Congo, (S/2023/431)". New York, 2023.
United States Senate Committee on Foreign Relations. 1998. "Democracy in Africa: The New Generation of African Leaders". Hearing before the Subcommittee on African Affairs of the Committee on Foreign Relations, U.S. Government Printing Office, Washington D.C., March 12, 1998.
US Embassy in Ethiopia. 2023. "Secretary Antony J. Blinken at a Press Availability", March 15, 2023. https://et.usembassy.gov/secretary-antony-j-blinken-at-a-press-availability/ (Accessed May 2, 2024).
US Government Foreign Assistance Tracker 2024, Accessed August 2 2024. https://www.foreignassistance.gov
White House. 2022. "U.S. Strategy Toward Sub-Saharan Africa". Washington D.C. August 2022.
White House. 2023a. "Statement from President Joe Biden on the Enactment of Uganda's Anti-Homosexuality Act". Washington D.C., May 29, 2023.
White House. 2023b. "Statement from President Joe Biden on the Release of Paul Rusesabagina". Washington D.C., March 24, 2023.
Wine, Bobi. 2021. "The West Helped Cripple Uganda's Democracy". *Foreign Affairs*, January 13, 2021. https://www.foreignaffairs.com/articles/africa/2021-01-13/west-helped-cripple-ugandas-democracy.

Index[1]

[1] Note: Page numbers followed by 'n' refer to notes.

M. Simpson, *Donors, Democracy and Development in Africa*, https://doi.org/10.1007/978-3-031-74917-9

R

SPRINGER NATURE

GPSR Compliance

The European Union's (EU) General Product Safety Regulation (GPSR) is a set of rules that requires consumer products to be safe and our obligations to ensure this.

If you have any concerns about our products, you can contact us on ProductSafety@springernature.com

In case Publisher is established outside the EU, the EU authorized representative is:

Springer Nature Customer Service Center GmbH
Europaplatz 3
69115 Heidelberg, Germany

The manufacturer's authorised representative in the EU is Springer Nature Customer Service Centre GmbH, Europaplatz 3, 69115 Heidelberg, Germany. If you have any concerns regarding our products, please contact ProductSafety@springernature.com

Printed and bound by CPI Group (UK) Ltd, Croydon, CR0 4YY

30/09/2026

02225565-0016